ETHICS FOR THE LEGAL PROFESSIONAL

ETHICS FOR THE LEGAL PROFESSIONAL

6TH EDITION

Deborah Orlik

PEARSON

Prentice
Hall

Upper Saddle River, New Jersey 07458

Library of Congress Cataloging-in-Publication Data

Orlik, Deborah K.
   Ethics for the legal professional / Deborah K. Orlik—6th ed.
      p. cm.
   Includes index.
   Rev. ed. of: Ethics for the legal assistant, c1986.
   ISBN 0-13-243647-7
   1. Legal assistant—United States. 2. Legal ethics—United States. 3. Paralegal I. Orlik, Deborah K.
Ethics for the legal assistants. II. Title.
   KF320. L4075 2007
   174′ .3—dc22

                                                    2006100377

Editor-in-Chief: Vernon R. Anthony
Senior Acquisitions Editor: Gary Bauer
Associate Editor: Linda Cupp
Development Editor: Deborah Hoffman
Marketing Manager: Leigh Ann Sims
Marketing Coordinator: Alicia Dysert
Managing Editor—Production: Mary Carnis
Manufacturing Buyer: Ilene Sanford
Production Liaison: Denise Brown
Full-Service Production and Composition: Heather Willison/Carlisle Publishing Services
Media Production Project Manager: Lisa Rinaldi
Senior Design Coordinator: Christopher Weigand
Cover Design: Rob Aleman
Printer/Binder: Edwards Brothers, Inc.
Cover Printer: Phoenix Color

ABA *Model Code of Professional Responsibility*, 1980 Edition. © 1980 by the American Bar Association. Reprinted with permission.

Copyright © 2008 by Pearson Education, Inc., Upper Saddle River, New Jersey 07458. Pearson Prentice Hall. All rights reserved. Printed in the United States of America. This publication is protected by Copyright and permission should be obtained from the publisher prior to any prohibited reproduction, storage in a retrieval system, or transmission in any form or by any means, electronic, mechanical, photocopying, recording, or likewise. For information regarding permission(s), write to: Rights and Permissions Department.

Pearson Prentice Hall™ is a trademark of Pearson Education, Inc.
Pearson® is a registered trademark of Pearson plc
Prentice Hall® is a registered trademark of Pearson Education, Inc.

Pearson Education Ltd.   Pearson Education North Asia Ltd.
Pearson Education Singapore, Pte. Ltd.   Pearson Educación de Mexico, S.A. de C.V.
Pearson Education Canada, Ltd.   Pearson Education Malaysia, Pte. Ltd.
Pearson Education—Japan   Pearson Education, Upper Saddle River, New Jersey
Pearson Education Australia PTY, Limited

10 9 8 7 6 5 4 3
ISBN 13: 978-0-13-243647-2
ISBN 10:   0-13-243647-7

CONTENTS

PREFACE

Ethics for the Legal Professional has set the standard for professional responsibility textbooks for over two decades. Now in its sixth edition, the text has been reorganized to reflect changes in the paralegal profession and to improve the flow of material to enhance student understanding. The sixth edition now begins with a discussion defining the fundamental characteristics of first lawyers and then paralegals and the ethics rules that apply to them. This is followed by a discussion of concrete concepts that have been given some clear direction in the courts and state legislatures (UPL, confidentiality, and conflicts) before moving on to the more technical, rule-driven concepts (advertising, billing, and fees), and then to the most abstract rules (competence, zealous representation, and integrity). Written from the viewpoint of the paralegal, this book uses plain English and an upbeat tone to keep readers engaged.

Each chapter's learning objectives are reinforced and applied in enhanced end-of-chapter exercises. There are several different types of end-of-chapter exercises to meet the learning styles of all students. There are multiple choice, fill in the blank, and true/false questions for in-class or take home. There are critical thinking hypotheticals for class discussion or essay writing. These hypotheticals include the citation to the case on which each is based so students can discover how a court resolved the issues. There are collaborative assignments for small groups of students and assignments that include exercises such as discovering state law or local resources or watching a movie looking for ethical issues. Last, each chapter includes cases for consideration, followed by short essay questions.

Still the most popular book in its genre, the sixth edition continues to tackle the most important ethical issues facing paralegals today in a frank, conversational style. It is specifically written from the point of view of the paralegal. The lesson is "*we* should do this" and "*we* should avoid doing that" as opposed to "the paralegal should . . . or should not . . . ." The object is to draw the paralegal into the profession like a friendly embrace, not from a place above the station of a paralegal but from the same level. Ethics can be scary. The sixth edition makes every attempt to use humor, where appropriate, and to keep the tone warm and the language user-friendly.

Specific Changes in the Sixth Edition

The fifth edition (and previous editions) was organized in the order of the nine ABA Model Code Canons with an additional chapter on regulation of the paralegal profession tacked on the end. The sixth edition now begins with a discussion contrasting the roles and responsibilities of lawyers and paralegals and the rules of ethics that apply to them (previously covered in Chapter 10). Chapter 2 is now the "Unauthorized Practice of Law" (previously Chapter 3). Chapter 3 is now "Confidentiality" including the attorney/client and work-product privileges (previously Chapter 4). This chapter includes a much-expanded section on technology and how it has affected the duty of confidentiality and the attorney/client privilege, including a section on the use of metadata and a section on storing/destroying client files.

Chapter 4 is "Conflicts of Interest" (previously Chapter 5), including intimate relationships with clients (previously in Chapter 1 under "Integrity"). Chapter 5 is "Advertising and Solicitation," both of which used to be in Chapter 2 under "Making Legal Services Available" with fees and billing structures. We've taken fees and billing and given them a separate chapter—Chapter 6: "Fair Fees and Client Trust Acounts"—where you will also find a more complete discussion of client trust accounts than in the previous editions. Chapter 7 is "Competence and Negligence" (previously in Chapter 6). In the discussion of competence, we include becoming "incompetent" via drug or alcohol addiction (previously in Chapter 1 and Chapter 8). Chapter 8 is now "The Duty of Zealous Representation" (previously Chapter 7) and includes a section on how technology has made it more tempting to use unethical resources such as "pretexting." And Chapter 9 is "The Umbrella Duty of Integrity" (previously Chapter 1) and includes the duty (if there is one) to report the misconduct of others. We conclude with the concept of "protecting the public trust," the largest and perhaps the most difficult rule to get our arms around.

It is still important for students to read the Introduction to the book, because that continues to be the place where we define the important concepts of "ethics" versus "morals" and where we discuss how to find the rules of ethics and other resources the student will need to study the law: statutory law, case law, opinions, and Rules of Professional Conduct.

Chapter Structure

Each chapter still begins with a hypothetical situation. However, instead of providing the answer only in the Teacher's Manual, each chapter now concludes with a question that draws the student back to the "Hypothetical" at the beginning of the chapter and gives the student real-world case law to apply to answer the "Hypothetical."

The sixth edition is all about questions and answers. Each section of every chapter begins with a question that a person who is new to the law would typically ask such as: "What does it mean to be competent?" or "Why should the practice of law be limited to lawyers?" The section then answers that question.

Clear definitions and explanations are a hallmark of this text. One of the most difficult concepts for students is the difference between the attorney/client privilege and the duty of confidentiality. Here, at last, is a clear, step-by-step explanation of the differences and similarities and an easy-to-apply rule for when each concept should be applied.

Key terms that student may not know are defined in the margin.

Relevant laws are provided in boxes accompanying the text. As the student is reading along, the law that is referenced in the text is right there. This cuts down on shuffling back and forth between text and appendix or outside resources. These boxes may also include references to specific state law, Web sites with information, or other places where the student can find additional information.

To provide a more fluid reading experience, all of the case citations have been taken out of the text and placed in the End Notes at the end of the book. Yes, it's cool to have all of those volume numbers, abbreviations, and dates to read out loud, but the truth is that students don't need to actually utilize those citations enough to warrant having them take up room (and disrupt the flow of the thought) in the text. If you need them, they are still there, but in the back of the book where they are out of the way and take up less room.

Our goal was to have students find this edition to be a much more pleasant reading experience than a typical textbook. This is due in large part to the conversational writing style and in no small measure due to those missing string citations. Textbooks should be about allowing the student to learn in a friendly, supportive atmosphere, not about impressing them with legal jargon. Statistics show that textbooks that are above a student's reading level give the student only a 10 percent chance of success in the classroom. Our goal is a 100 percent success rate.

Expanded End-of-Chapter Material

Previous editions provided several hypotheticals at the conclusion of every chapter. The sixth edition provides much more! Each chapter concludes with multiple choice, true/false, and short answer questions, as well as essay starters to help students with their review of the chapter material. Hypotheticals are still provided (now called Critical Thinking) as a way of getting students talking about what they have just learned and putting new concepts into action.

Additionally, each chapter end includes real cases (Cases for Consideration—typically edited to include only that part of the case that relates to the chapter subject) and follow-up questions about the case to help the student relate the case law to the chapter.

Each chapter also provides several Collaborative Assignments. Classrooms aren't about just lecturing anymore, so we provide interactive learning activities for students that relate to every chapter. Some of these activities include watching a movie; doing some outside research before class; and creating, writing, and working in groups.

End-of-Book Material

Appendix materials are as complete as we could make them in the sixth edition. We have provided the NALA, NFPA, and NALS codes so the student doesn't have to look to too many outside resources. Much of the ABA Model Rules is in Appendix E.

The index and case index have been completely and professionally rewritten to make finding things easier.

Resources for Teaching

New! Paralegal Professional Ethics Classroom Video Series on DVD

This series contains twenty-four scenarios written by the author that present common ethical situations paralegals will encounter on the job. These scenarios provide a terrific platform for bringing the real world into the classroom. Teaching notes are provided for each video in the Instructor's Manual. These videos are provided free of charge to adopters of the sixth edition.

- UPL Issue: Giving Advice
- UPL Issue: When Friends Ask for Legal Advice
- UPL Issue: Helping the Client without Practicing Law
- UPL Issue: Traditional Exceptions
- UPL Issue: Disclosure of Status
- UPL Issue: Interviewing a Client
- UPL Issue: Working with a Witness
- UPL Issue: Working with Experts
- UPL Issue: Improper Supervision
- UPL Issue: Helping Client Fill Out Forms
- Attorney/Privilege Issue: Misdirected E-Mail
- Confidentiality Issue: Need-to-Know Circle
- Confidentiality Issue: Public Information
- Confidentiality Issue: Disclosure of Damaging Information
- Confidentiality Issue: Family Exception?
- Confidentiality Issue: Attorney/Client Privilege
- Conflict of Interest Issue: Relationships with Clients
- Conflict of Interest Issue: Independent Paralegal
- Conflict of Interest Issue: Gift to Judge
- Fees and Billing Issue: Contemporaneous Timekeeping
- Fees and Billing Issue: Using Time Effectively
- Zealous Representation Issue: When You Are Asked to Lie
- Zealous Representation Issue: Handling Evidence
- Zealous Representation Issue: Candor to the Court
- Zealous Representation Issue: Signing Documents

Instructor's Manual with Test Item File

PowerPoint Lecture Presentation Package

All instructor resources are available by downloading them from the Instructor Resource Center at http://www.prenhall.com. Register once and gain access to instructor materials for all of your Prentice Hall textbooks.

Ethics for the Legal Professional, Sixth Edition, Web Site

To accommodate those students who do not have access to case law via the Internet, important cases are available from the book Web site along with case and statutory change updates. Go to http://www.prenhall.com/orlik.

Acknowledgments

Special thanks to the reviewers of this text: Jean Volk, Middlesex County College, Edison, New Jersey; Kathleen Mercer Reed, University of Toledo, Toledo, Ohio; Roberta Lahr, Mt. San Antonio College, Walnut, California; Julia Tryk, Cuyahoga Community College, Cleveland, Ohio; George William Jenkins, III, University of Memphis, Memphis, Tennessee; Ronald A. Feinberg, Suffolk Community College, Suffolk County, New York; Bruce M. Rands, Pikes Peak Community College, Colorado Springs, Colorado; Lawrence A. Joel, Bergen Community College, Paramus, New Jersey.

INTRODUCTION

Welcome to our study of legal ethics! Let's start with some definitions of words we'll be using so we can be sure we're all talking about the same thing.

First, we need to differentiate the concepts of *ethics* and *morals*.

The word *ethics* is derived from the Greek word *ethos*, which originally meant "customs, usages," and, later, "character." *Morals* is derived from the Latin *mores*, which also means "customs or habits." *Webster's Dictionary* defines *ethics* as "the discipline dealing with what is good and bad." We think of *morality* as those norms that we acquire throughout our childhood from our parents, our teachers, our peers, and places of worship. By the time we are adults, our morals are pretty much in place.

The study of legal ethics does not include the study of morals. That is to say that you are bound to abide by the rules of ethics, but no one has written a standard of morality for the legal profession. We assume that you come to the legal profession with your own morality. We like to talk about morality. It's fun and is ripe for debate. Classroom discussion always gets carried away with concepts of "right and wrong" and why we act as we do. Here's a dichotomy to start your classroom discussion on the first day of class: Who is correct: Hobbes, Locke, or Shaftesbury?

Thomas Hobbes, one of the world's greatest moralists, wrote that man is, by nature, a selfish animal constantly in conflict with his fellow man and the only thing that keeps us in line is our fear of social retribution. If Hobbes's theory that social order and cooperation are a result of man's fear, could it be said that we do what we do within the bounds of the law because we fear the law's punishment? How can that possibly be true? What about all of the gratuitous good deeds of man? Do people risk their lives trying to save others because of fear of punishment? Surely not.

John Locke, another great philosopher, believed that right and wrong are products of God's fiat. "Moral good and evil, then, is only the conformity or disagreement of our voluntary actions to some law, whereby good or evil is drawn on us, from the will and power of the law-maker; which good and evil, pleasure or pain, attending our observance or breach of the law by the decree of the lawmaker, is that we call reward and punishment."[1] That is to say that moral good gives pleasure because God ultimately rewards it and moral evil gives pain because God ultimately punishes it. Do we do what we do because we crave reward and shun punishment? If that is true, does that mean that atheists always behave badly because they do not fear God? That can't be true.

A student of Locke, Shaftesbury, would later write that man is born with an instinctual moral sense that must be educated and developed, just as man's sense of what is beautiful is instinctive but can be trained. "To love the public, to study universal good, and to promote the interest of the whole world, as far as lies within our power, is surely the height of goodness. . . ."[2] We can't disagree with loving the public, and promoting the public good is a great thing; but can we say that we are truly born with a sense of right and wrong and thereafter some of us are trained and others are not? The trained people go on to be good and the untrained do not?

These are theories of human morals (the theories of good and bad). They are also theories of human ethics (customs and usages of society). They are not, however, theories about legal ethics (or professional responsibility). While it will always be true that the choices we make about professional responsibility are colored by our personal sense of morals, it is equally true that our responsibilities as legal professionals are governed by written rules, statutes, and case law. While the study of philosophy is interesting, it sheds little light on the study of legal ethics that follows. What we will be studying, then, are rules of law. Just as all rules of law, ethics rules are subject to different interpretations.

Moral dilemmas will overlap your study and practice of legal ethics. You may be asked to participate in the representation of a person who is loathsome to you or a cause you cannot abide, causing you to question your values. You may question the morals of others in your workplace when you see them cheating on time sheets. You may have to make a choice between your moral makeup and your job. But these questions cannot be answered here. These questions, the questions of the threshold of each person's morality, can only be answered by each person. The study of legal ethics, then, is not an attempt to change your morality. You may make some changes yourself upon reflection on your studies here, but that is solely up to you. The study of legal ethics is the study of law.

The rules we are about to study should be viewed as general principles of conduct, not a handbook for knowing what the "right thing" to do is in every circumstance. Some rules may look like they set forth only the minimally acceptable conduct, but many of them are lofty goals to which we should all aspire, such as the rule that compels us to make the legal system better. Some of the principles we will study are by their nature in conflict with each other in their various applications, such as the prosecutor's duty to represent the people zealously but to "seek justice," not victory. You will see that many of these rules are qualified imperatives that must give way to competing considerations. And you will find that they are principles of law that are colored by personal deliberation. One of the most important parts of the study of legal ethics is reflection. It may be interesting to keep a reflection journal as you study legal ethics. How do you feel about what you have learned? Are there places in the law that should be changed in your opinion? Are there applications of the law in cases that are erroneous?

If nothing else, it is our goal to give you a starting point for your research when professional responsibility issues arise. We have provided statutory authority, the ABA *Rules of Professional Responsibility,* the ABA Model Codes of Professional Conduct and case law. You will have to provide your own personal deliberation. The decisions are ultimately yours.

If you are reading this book, that means you are interested in the legal profession. Here's your number 1 rule: the primary goal of the law of legal ethics is to protect the public.

The goal of your study of legal ethics is this: At the end of your study, you should be able to recognize a potential ethical problem, categorize it, and research the possible answers. After you have completed each chapter, you will be able to recognize the ethics issues in that subject and give them a name. (This is a conflict of interest issue. This is a confidentiality issue. This is an issue in the unauthorized practice of law.) There are nine primary issues, each of which has subissues that fall into categories you will be able to name. Then you will have to research the law that applies to you in your own state.

To research the law, you can typically start in an encyclopedia (such as *American Jurisprudence*) under the categorization you have already given your issue. The encyclopedia should explain the basics and give you both statutory authority and case authority.

In Chapter 1, we learn that lawyers, those who are licensed to practice law, have their own codes of ethics. For the most part, the genesis of these codes is the American Bar Association (ABA). The ABA has written some "model" codes, samples if you will, and they have been adopted by the states in various forms. Almost all of the states have patterned their rules of ethics after the ABA *Model Rules of Professional Conduct* (*Model Rules*). The precursor, *Model Code of Professional Responsibility* (*Model Code*), is the format still used by a state or two although they are transitioning from a Model Code format to the Model Roles format. If you are reading this book in California, please go to the publisher's Web site and look for the California supplement. California has never adopted any form of the ABA models, so the law there has a completely different format.

When you go looking for your state's set of ethics rules or codes in your state law, you should note that all of the rules pertaining to professional conduct are not likely to be found in one place. Many states have codified at least some of the rules that pertain to the legal professional in their state law on "business and professions." For example, in Montana's *Professions and Occupations Code* (Title 37), Chapter 61, you can find an additional twenty or thirty rules pertaining to admission to the bar and other provisions regulating the practice of law. In California, in addition to the *Rules of Professional Conduct* that are not found in the state code, you will find many rules of ethics in the *Business & Professions Code*. It is also likely that at least some of the rules pertaining to attorney/client privilege will be found in each state's *Evidence Code,* and rules about the public's right to hire and fire counsel will be found in yet a different code.

West's "Rules of Court," which is published for many states, often contains the unannotated rules or codes of professional conduct for each state, as well as state bar rules (on discipline) and rules pertaining to admission to the bar. For the states that use Michie's publications, there is a similar compilation of professional conduct rules. These are good research tools to keep on your desk.

No matter where you find them, you need to use the professional responsibility laws that have been enacted in your state.

After you have found the rules of law, you will need to know how your state courts, federal courts, and the U.S. Supreme Court have interpreted that law. That's what case law does: it tells us how the words of the statute or rule have been interpreted by the courts. The interpretation of the highest court of your state will be considered binding on all of the lower courts. When a court interprets a rule of law, this is called *precedent*. That means that the lower courts are bound to follow it unless they can differentiate the precedential case from the one in front of them on the facts. If the facts are different, perhaps the rule of law should be interpreted differently, as well. The rule that tells the courts to interpret the law consistently is called *stare decisis*. This is Latin for "let the decision stand." If you think about it, it is only fair that people know how a court will rule. If courts are allowed to rule on the same issue helter-skelter, we would never know what we are supposed to do. *Stare decisis* gives us at least some clue as to how this court will rule, because it is supposed to rule the same way another court before it ruled. We study the case law of the highest court of the land (the U.S. Supreme Court) because it is binding on all of the other courts (unless, of course, something in the facts is different). *Stare decisis* and the rule of precedent don't always work, as you will see. One example of this is a Supreme Court case that said that the time that paralegals bill working on a case (doing legal, not clerical, work) is billable and can be charged to the client. Even though the highest court in the country made this a part of a larger ruling—and logic would dictate that the issue is settled—some states are still discussing the billable nature of paralegal work and some courts are still ruling against paralegal billable time. Go figure.

There are other sources of law on legal ethics that you will see used in this text include opinions of bar associations and paralegal codes of ethics.

But the most important sources of law for you are in your own state law. Get a copy of your state's rules of professional conduct for lawyers, including any evidence code sections that apply, and get all of that itty-bitty print enlarged. Create a notebook where you can divide your state's codes into categories corresponding to the chapters of this book. Leave room for annotation to cases you will find along the way as we move through the chapters. Gather up your common sense and your own sense of right and wrong. Now you're ready. Good luck.

REGULATION OF THE LEGAL PROFESSION

HYPOTHETICAL

Paralegal Mary Rose acts as both paralegal and calendar clerk in the law firm of Attorney Smith. Smith asks Mary to calendar the date an answer to a complaint is due. Mary makes a mistake and calendars the date sixty days from the day the complaint was served instead of thirty days. As a result, Smith does not answer the complaint on time and his client's default is taken.

Why Are We Here?

A discussion of the regulation of the legal profession would be brief and simple if all members of the legal profession subscribed to the same rules and were responsible to the same authorities. Like most things, it's just not that simple. So, we're going to start our discussion of the regulation of paralegals with a discussion of the regulation of lawyers. After we understand how lawyers are regulated (including where their rules of ethics come from) we'll take a look at what paralegals are, how they are regulated and what rules of ethics apply to them. What we will find is that the

CHAPTER OBJECTIVES

By the end of this chapter, you will know the answers to these questions:

Why Are We Here?
What Are Lawyers?
Where Do Lawyer Ethics
 Rules Come From?
What Is the Authority of the
 ABA Models?
How Are Lawyers
 Disciplined?
What Are Paralegals?
How Are Paralegals
 Regulated?
What Choices Are Available
 for Regulating Paralegals?
What Does It Mean to Be
 "Regulated by the Courts"?
Have Paralegals Considered
 Self-Regulation?

rules of ethics for lawyers make them responsible for "regulating" the ethical obligations of the paralegals they employ and paralegals are responsible for the same ethical obligations to which lawyers subscribe. And we'll find that paralegal organizations have written codes of ethics that reiterate these same ethical obligations. What about paralegals who don't work for lawyers? That question has a more complex answer. Not all of the questions about paralegal regulation have answers here. Some of them will be up to you to answer. The future of the paralegal profession is yours. That's why we're here.

We start, then, with an understanding of what lawyers are.

What Are Lawyers?

A lawyer (also called an attorney) is also sometimes referred to as "a member of the bar." Membership in the bar (short for "bar association") is a privilege that is given to people who have certain credentials. These credentials include education, a bar examination, and fitness of character. Each jurisdiction also has its own additional requirements such as minimum age restrictions and/or mandatory fees.

What Kind of Education Is Required?

Typically, people who want to be lawyers attend a four-year college and then a three-year law school. About half of all states require some undergraduate education, ranging from two years of college to a four-year degree. Most jurisdictions require a Juris Doctor (JD) degree. A few states allow applicants to the bar who have been educated by means of law office study (something like an apprenticeship) or correspondence courses. (See http://www.abanet.org/legaled for all of the states' requirements and rules regarding law degrees from other countries.)

What Is the Bar Examination?

After that, in most states, these people must take a "bar examination." Also called "the bar exam," this test is long, comprehensive, and grueling. (In California, the exam is three days long and fewer than 50 percent pass.) Bar exams across the nation are made up of essay questions and multiple choice questions. Most but not all states have made the Multistate Bar Examination a part of their general bar exam. The Multistate Bar Exam is a six-hour, two hundred multiple choice question exam. It is given on the same day in all of the states so that the questions and answers cannot be shared between a test taker in New York and one in California, for example. Most states also use the Multistate Professional Responsibility Exam (MPRE) as part of their general bar exam.

Each states' bar exams are different. Some exams have a "practical" component in which the examinee is, for example, given a file and asked to produce a memorandum of law, just as would happen on the job. These "practical" components were phased in to state bar exams in response to complaints that the bar doesn't test a person's lawyering skills but, rather, determines how well the person can take a test. Some states test many subjects of law on their state bar. Some test just a few subjects but expect the examinee to have greater depth of knowledge. Yet another group of states allow any graduate of that state's law schools to become a member of that state bar without taking a test. (Wisconsin is an example.) This is presumably due to the state's belief that anyone who can graduate from their law schools must have enough skill and knowledge to practice law. On the other hand, California, a state that has many law schools that are unaccredited by the American Bar Association (ABA) and the state, is of the opinion that everyone is entitled to an education in the law but if you want to actually practice law on behalf of other people, you have to show that you've learned enough to pass the test—thus, the low passing rate on the California bar as compared to other states.

Is There a Moral Character Requirement?

The requirement of good moral character seems obvious for bar membership. The question is, how do we measure it? It is certainly an ambiguous term but not so ambiguous that the courts have disallowed its application. Each applicant has to prove his or her own good moral character on the bar membership application. For the most part, good moral character is shown by letters of reference from people who have known the bar candidate for some time. If there are no complaints in your file and your references are good (one would think you would only get references from people who will say good things about you), you have proven good moral character.

Some states publish standards of "bad" moral character. For example, a prior criminal conviction will prevent you from being a member of the Florida, Indiana, Mississippi, Missouri, or Pennsylvania bars. The famous case on moral character is *Konigsberg v. California State Bar*.[1] This case comes from the cold war era, when many Americans were afraid of "the Communist influence." Mr. Konigsberg's record showed that he may have attended Communist Party hearings and criticized U.S. participation in the Korean War. The U.S. Supreme Court did not believe that these things were enough to prevent him from being a member of the California Bar. However, in the next *Konigsberg v. California State Bar*,[2] (also known as *Konigsberg II*), the Supreme Court affirmed the California State Bar's rejection of Konigsberg because of his refusal to answer certain questions concerning membership in the Communist Party. Refusing to answer the questions, while not grounds for supporting an inference that he lacked good moral character, was a sufficient impediment to the investigation of his application.

There is a large body of case law on the issue of moral character requirements for bar membership. Cheating in law school probably will not disqualify you from becoming a member of the bar,[3] but cheating on the bar exam probably will.[4] Traditionally, it is telling the truth about prior misdeeds that is more important than the actual misdeeds themselves.[5]

What Else Is Required?

Some states require U.S. citizenship to be a member of their state bar.[6] States are permitted to levy an "occupational tax" on the practice of law.[7]

An Oath

After satisfying the requirements to become a lawyer, in many states the lawyer is "sworn in." That means that the applicant must show up at a swearing-in ceremony or appear in front of a judge and take an oath to perform his or her knowledge skillfully and ethically in addition to support the constitution of his or her state and the Constitution of the United States. The applicant does not have to swear an oath that invokes the name of God, however, as invoking the name of God cannot be made a prerequisite to entering the practice of law.[8] The next step is becoming a member of the bar association, and that typically involves paying dues and adhering to state regulations regarding continuing education. (Later, we will see that paralegal associations require continuing legal education, too.)

Proper Titles

When you graduate from law school, technically you are "a JD," meaning that you have a Juris Doctor degree. Only after you become a licensed lawyer can you call yourself "Esq." (short for Esquire) or Attorney at Law or attorney or lawyer. To call yourself any of those things and not be a member of the bar fits under the general category of the unauthorized practice of law, or UPL, which we cover in Chapter 2. Lawyers who are partners in law firms are called "partners." The lawyers who work for the partners are called "associates."

Many states require membership in the state bar association in order to have the right to practice law in the state.[9] These states are said to have "integrated" or "unified" bars. Becoming a member of the state bar association makes each lawyer subject to the rules of ethics enacted by the state and requires the lawyer to pay annual dues. Every state has rules of ethics, also called rules of professional responsibility or rules of professional conduct. These are the rules that govern lawyers.

Where Do Lawyer Ethics Rules Come From?

In addition to membership in a state bar association, many lawyers choose to join local bar associations. These local bars may be county bars, city bars, or regional bars. Many lawyers also choose membership in the American Bar Association (ABA). Contrary to urban legend, membership in the ABA is voluntary. ABA membership offers lawyers many benefits such as continuing education courses and eligibility to be involved in ABA committees, commissions, and other activities. The ABA is a private organization. It has no authority to discipline anyone. That is why the *Rules of*

Professional Conduct and the *Codes of Professional Responsibility* we look at in this text are preceded by the word *Model*. The ABA has over the years created committees and commissions to study the regulation of lawyers and to create these models.

Early Canons

The first set of rules offered by the ABA was the 1908 Canons of Professional Ethics. They were written by the ABA Committee on Professional Ethics and adopted by the ABA at its thirty-first Annual Meeting in 1908. There were - thirty-two original canons that were used and adopted by many states for the next sixty-plus years. They were based on the *Code of Ethics* adopted by the Alabama State Bar Association in 1887, which was borrowed largely from the lectures of Judge George Sharswood, published in 1854 under the title of *Professional Ethics*, and from the fifty resolutions included in David Hoffman's *A Course of Legal Study*.[10] Piecemeal amendments to the Canons were occasionally made by the ABA. Some of those early canons look rather like rules we have today such as the original Canon 9:

> A lawyer should not in any way communicate upon the subject of controversy with a party represented by counsel; much less should he undertake to negotiate or compromise the matter with him, but should deal only with his counsel.

That's the same rule we have today! Another follows.

> It is the duty of a lawyer to preserve his client's confidences. This duty outlast(s) the lawyer's employment and extends as well to his employees; and neither of them should accept employment which involves or may involve the disclosure or use of these confidences, either for the private advantage of the lawyer or his employees or to the disadvantage to the client, without his knowledge and consent, and even though there are other available sources of such information. A lawyer should not continue employment when he discovers that this obligation prevents the performance of his full duty to his former or to his new client.[11]

In other rules from the early ABA Canons, we see that the law has changed. An example is *Canon 34*[12] that appears to permit **referral fees,** unlike the ABA's position on them now. *Canon 34* states:

> No division of fees for legal services is proper, except with other lawyers upon a division of service or responsibility, or with a forwarding attorney.

A referral fee is any amount of money paid for no reason other than sending a case to a lawyer. Also called a **forwarding fee.**

1960s Model Code of Professional Responsibility

The second ABA model was the Model Code of Professional Responsibility. This model was released in the late 1960s and adopted in some form or another by

Some examples of state adoptions of the ABA Models:

If you are in Nevada, your rules differ dramatically from the ABA Model even though the Nevada Supreme Court recently updated the format and numbering system to resume the ABA Model.

Nebraska changed from a Model Code based set of rules to a Model Rules format in 2005 and adopted an interesting new rule concerning "support person" and conflicts of interest. We study conflicts in Chapter 4.

Iowa dropped its Model Code based standards in 2005 and patterned its new rules largely on the new ABA Rules except for some very different provisions on attorney advertising. We study advertising in Chapter 5.

forty-nine states. (California was the only holdout.) The Model Code had only nine canons, each of which was followed by *Ethical Considerations* and *Disciplinary Rules*. The Canons of the Model Code of Professional Responsibility state in general terms the standards of professional conduct expected of lawyers in their relationships with the public, with the legal system, and with other legal professionals. The *Ethical Considerations* (EC) include reasons for the Canons and guidelines that lawyers may consider while making ethical assessments. Also provided are the *Disciplinary Rules* (DR), a violation of which is unethical as a matter of law. If lawyers should fall below the standards set forth, they will be subject to disciplinary action by the state supreme court or state bar association, depending upon the state. As changes were made in the law, the Model Code was also amended.

When you are researching in the area of professional responsibility, you will come across cases that refer to, for example, EC 4-3 so you should know what they are. Because all of the states that once used the Model Code now use or are transitionary to the Model Rules, however, you need to be able to translate from the Model Code to the Model Rules.

Model Rules of Professional Conduct

Only a brief seven years passed before the Model Code's shortcomings inspired the creation of a new ABA commission. It would be called the Kutak Commission after its chair Robert Kutak, an inspired ethicist/lawyer from Nebraska. With Watergate in the news and the public's awareness of lawyer ethics on the rise, the Kutak Commission released the Model Rules of Professional Conduct in the mid-1980s. As of this writing, almost all states have adopted some form of the Model Rules. Again, California is a holdout. The remaining states are in the process of or have completed amending their rules of professional responsibility to look more like the Model Rules and less like the Model Codes. The ABA released new changes to the Model Rules in 2002. Now would be a good time to look at your state's rules.

ABA Model Code examples:

Canon 1: A lawyer should assist in maintaining the integrity and competence of the legal profession.

EC 1-1 A basic tenet of the professional responsibility of lawyers is that every person in our society should have ready access to the independent professional services of the lawyer of integrity and

DR 1-101(B) A lawyer shall not further the application for admission to the bar of another person known by him to be unqualified in respect to character, education, or other relevant attribute.

* The Model Codes of Professional Responsibility are presented here as a historical reference and are not currently used.

Compare your state rules to the ABA Model. How closely aligned are your rules to the Model? One of the places to look is Rule 8.3 on the lawyer's duty to report the misconduct of other lawyers. Also look at the exceptions to Rule 1.6 on confidentiality. These are two places where the states differ in their viewpoint.

Since the ABA released 2002 Model Rules changes, many states have updated their state codes to reflect the changes suggested by the ABA. You can always find a full copy of the updated ABA Model Rules on the ABA's Web site: http://www.abanet.org.

What Is the Authority of the ABA Models?

Committees and commissions of professional organizations sometimes produce "uniform codes" such as the *Uniform Commercial Code*. A "uniform" code is meant to create the same law in all of the states. Model codes, on the other hand, are meant to be just that: models. The Models themselves have no authority. The Model is only given authority when it becomes a state's enactment within its own state codes. Some parts of the Model may be omitted by a state. And some states may rely on the ABA Model for something that they have intentionally omitted.

Again, using Nevada as an example, Nevada did not adopt the Preamble or Scope sections of the Model Rules, nor did it adopt the "Comments" to the Model Rules. (The Comments take each rule and put it into the context of a hypothetical so we can see how the rule may work in action.) Instead, Nevada adopted its own *Guidelines for Interpreting the Nevada Rules of Professional Conduct*, which states that the ABA Model Rules may be "consulted for guidance" in understanding and using the Nevada Rules.

Most states agree that the rules of ethics are the basis for lawyer discipline, not for the purpose of civil liability. (We discuss civil liability later when we talk about professional negligence in Chapter 7.) In other words, the rules of ethics are evidence of a lawyer's duty to the client but the violation of a rule of ethics does not by itself create a cause of action for professional negligence.[13] Many courts, especially federal courts, use the Models to fill in where the state law of ethics may have a gap. So, a way of looking at it is this: if the court can't find a direct rule of state law on the issue, it will typically fill in that gap with part of the ABA Model.

So, you don't want to quote or cite the ABA Model Rules in your work (unless specifically instructed to do so). What you want to do is find your own state's enactment of its version of the ABA Model Rules and cite that.

So, What Would a Complaint against a Lawyer Look Like?

> This fact pattern is taken from *In re Lane's Case*, 153 N.H. 10, 889 A2d 3 (2005).

Here's an ethics complaint start to finish: Attorney Jameson represented the estate of Robert Bennett, who had died in a car accident. Bennett was survived by his wife (Jane), a son (Dick), and a daughter (Sarah). Dick served as executor of his father's estate. In preparation for her own death, Jane set up a trust with herself and Dick as cotrustees. The trust was to benefit both Dick and Sarah after Jane's death. As Jane's mental health began to fail, Sarah became convinced that Dick was taking money out of the trust account and using it for himself. Sarah called Attorney Jameson and told him about missing assets and money. Jameson retrieved his firm's file from storage and discovered certain evidence that tended to show that Dick was not handling the trust properly. Jameson gave a copy of that evidence to Sarah who gave it to her own lawyer who used it to file a motion to have Dick Bennett removed as trustee of his mother's trust. Dick hired another lawyer, and that litigation was later settled.

Dick Bennett's new lawyer contacted his State Supreme Court Committee on Professional Conduct and made a complaint against Jameson. When Jameson represented the estate of Robert Bennett, Dick was his client. As a result, Jameson owed Dick a duty of loyalty and confidentiality. By using evidence in the file against Dick (when he gave it to Sarah), he violated both of those duties.

The committee filed a petition recommending that James receive a six-month suspension from the practice of law for violating the state's professional conduct rules that restrict use of a former client's confidences. The state's supreme court reviewed the petition and held a hearing. The committee hired a lawyer to argue its position. Attorney Jameson was represented by his own lawyer. The supreme court ruled in Jameson's favor after finding that the disclosure of confidential information by Jameson was necessary to prevent a crime that would result in substantial injury to someone's financial interests. The court relied on its state's Professional Conduct Rule 1.6(e) that allows a lawyer to violate the duty of confidentiality to prevent an ongoing crime.

How Are Lawyers Disciplined?

> When a state makes bar membership mandatory, it is said to have an *integrated bar*.

After becoming a member of the bar association, lawyers are regulated by the disciplinary authority of their state. In some states, such as California, where bar membership is mandatory, it is the bar that regulates. In other states, it is a committee of the supreme court. The structure of each state's disciplinary system is different, but they all generally include the following:

- An office of disciplinary counsel that evaluates the complaint to see if it is something that is within the jurisdiction of this lawyer-discipline system.

It investigates the complaint and either dismisses the complaint or files a formal charge against the lawyer. This body will ultimately present its case in front of whatever adjudicative body this state uses.

- A hearing officer or a panel that hears the disciplinary counsel and the lawyer present their versions of the facts. This officer or panel issues a report on the proceedings.

- A statewide disciplinary board that reviews the report of the hearing officer or panel and either dismisses the case or recommends sanctions.

- The state's highest court. This is the ultimate decision maker in discipline cases. It imposes the more severe sanctions such as suspension or disbarment.

Reproval is another word for *reprimand*.

Disciplinary actions may result in disbarment, suspension from practice, public reproval, or private reproval. A lawyer who has been *disbarred* may no longer practice law. Some states have provisions for disbarred lawyers to show that they have been rehabilitated and allow them to apply for the right to practice law again. A lawyer who has been *suspended* may not practice law for the period of time specified in the suspension. A *public reproval* is in the form of an order that says this lawyer has done something wrong. These orders are published; therefore, the public knows about them. A *private reproval* is usually published but without the lawyer's name. This way, other lawyers can see what the error was, but the public does not know which lawyer was involved. Punishment can also include an order that the lawyer must make *restitution* to any people who have been harmed by the lawyer's misconduct, or that the lawyer pay the cost of prosecution, or that the lawyer take and pass the professional responsibility exam, or any combination of those punishments.

And!—A lawyer who is disciplined in one state may be disciplined again (and even more harshly) for the same acts in any other state where that lawyer is licensed to practice law. Florida, for example, disbarred a lawyer for bribery even though Massachusetts, where the bad acts occurred, only suspended the lawyer.[14] Lawyers have been disciplined for committing the unauthorized practice of law (UPL) by practicing law in a state where they are not licensed. (We discuss UPL and non-lawyers in depth in Chapter 2.)

Lawyers can be disciplined for wrongful behavior outside of the practice of law. For example, a lawyer who commits a homicide, even one that has nothing to do with his law practice, will probably be disbarred. Lawyers have been disciplined by the state bar for driving-while-intoxicated convictions and for criminal prosecution for the use or sale of drugs, as well as for filing fraudulent federal income tax returns, carrying a concealed weapon, and child molestation. (See *People v. Myers* at the end of this chapter.) These are all crimes of *moral turpitude* and proof of lack of fitness to be a member of the bar.

Entire law firms have been disciplined for a pattern of discourteous, neglectful, and demeaning conduct toward clients.[15] And senior lawyers have been disciplined not for doing anything wrong themselves but for failing to supervise junior lawyers so that they don't do something wrong.[16]

The choices are limited for the disbarred lawyers. Many states have laws that prevent these people from acting as paralegals.[17] This makes sense, doesn't it? If you have committed acts that were so bad that you've been disbarred, the public will likely be harmed again if you are allowed to work in the law office as a paralegal. The lawyer who hires a disbarred or suspended lawyer as a paralegal also takes a tremendous risk. Take the case of Comish, a Louisiana lawyer, who represented Attorney Michael Matthews in some criminal proceedings and hired Matthews as a paralegal after Matthews was disbarred. Matthews couldn't stop telling clients that he was a lawyer, however. He told clients, opposing counsel, and an insurance adjustor. He wrote letters on Comish's law firm stationery without clarifying that he was a paralegal, and he received letters from them addressed to "Michael Matthews, Attorney." The Supreme Court of Louisiana found that Comish failed to properly supervise Matthews and suspended him (Comish) from the practice of law for three years.[18] In 2002, Louisiana amended its Rules of Professional Conduct to forbid lawyers from employing disbarred lawyers in any legal capacity.

What Are Paralegals?

Over the years, the paralegal profession has grown and changed. Twenty years ago, the preferred term was *legal assistant*. Since that time, the term *paralegal* has become the preferred term and other meanings for the word *paralegal* have emerged, including one that includes people who do not work under a lawyer's supervision.

The ABA's definition of a paralegal is

> . . . a person, qualified by education, training or work experience who is employed or retained by a lawyer, law office, corporation, governmental agency or other entity and who performs specifically delegated substantive legal work for which a lawyer is responsible.

Following are some of the other widely used definitions for *paralegal*.

National Association of Legal Assistants

The National Association of Legal Assistants (NALA) was incorporated in 1975 and represents over 100,000 legal assistants through its individual membership and eighty-five state and local affiliated associations. NALA's definition of a legal assistant or paralegal is

http://www.nala.org

> . . . persons who assist attorneys in the delivery of legal services. Through formal education training and experience, legal assistants have knowledge and expertise regarding the legal system and substantive and procedural law which qualify them to do work of a legal nature under the supervision of an attorney.

NALA also adopted the ABA definition of a paralegal in 2001.

NALA has a code of ethics that you will find in Appendix A. It was written in 1984 and last amended in 1997. Its emphasis is on not practicing law without a license and working under the close supervision of a lawyer. NALA does not, as you can see from its definition of a paralegal, recognize paralegals who work independently.

National Federation of Paralegal Associations

The National Federation of Paralegal Associations (NFPA) was first organized in 1974 and represents over fifteen thousand paralegals through its fifty-two local affiliated associations. NFPA's definition of a paralegal is

> ... a person qualified through education, training or work experience to perform substantive legal work that requires knowledge of legal concepts and is customarily, but not exclusively, performed by a lawyer. This person may be retained or employed by a lawyer, law office, governmental agency, or other entity or may be authorized by administrative, statutory, or court authority to perform this work.

http://www.
paralegals.org

NFPA has a code of professional conduct that you can find in Appendix B. NFPA also has a disciplinary code to give teeth to its code of conduct. The strongest disciplinary measure it can take against a paralegal, however, is revocation of membership. This will be true of any voluntary organization that seeks to regulate. In May 2002, NFPA paralegals voted to officially drop the *legal assistant* name (not the concept) as synonymous with the term *paralegal* in order to avoid increasing confusion with other members of the legal team who do not perform substantive (and in most cases billable) legal work. Most educational institutions, hiring corporations, and law firms, however, still use the expressions interchangeably.

NALS

The National Association of Legal Secretaries began with a small group of secretaries that met in Long Beach, California in 1929. Keeping up with the times, the organization changed its name to "NALS . . . the association for legal professionals" in 1999. NALS members are paralegals, secretaries, legal administrators, and office managers. In July 2002, NALS adopted the following definition:

> A legal assistant/paralegal is a person, qualified by education, training or work experience who is employed or retained by a lawyer, law office, corporation, governmental agency or other entity and who performs specifically delegated substantive legal work for which a lawyer is responsible.

http://www.nals.org

American Association for Paralegal Education

The American Association for Paralegal Education (AAfPE) Web site provides this definition:

> Paralegals perform substantive and procedural legal work as authorized by law, which work, in the absence of the paralegal, would be performed

by an attorney. Paralegals have knowledge of the law gained through education, or education and work experience, which qualifies them to perform legal work. Paralegals adhere to recognized ethical standards and rules of professional responsibility.

Department of Labor

Some states (including California and Arizona) now have statutes that define who can use the term *paralegal* and who cannot. Those statutes are provided for you on the publisher's Web site.

Is a paralegal a "professional"? Absolutely! But not necessarily in every sense of the word in every state. One of the ongoing debates has to do with "overtime pay." Traditionally, professionals are called "exempt" personnel. That means that they are exempt from overtime regulations and overtime pay. In *Reich v. Paige & Addison*, at the end of this chapter, you will see that a U.S. District Court in Texas told the Department of Labor (DOL) in 1994 that the employee's title (paralegal, clerk, secretary) was not as much of a determining factor as what the employee actually does at work. In 2004, however, the DOL modified its law[19] with Section 541.301(e)(7), which states:

> Paralegals and legal assistants generally do not qualify as exempt learned professionals because an advanced specialized academic degree is not a standard prerequisite for entry into the field. Although many paralegals possess general four-year advanced degrees, most specialized paralegal programs are two-year associate degree programs from a community college or equivalent institution. However, the learned professional exemption is available for paralegals who possess advanced specialized degrees in other professional fields and apply advanced knowledge in that field in the performance of their duties. For example, if a law firm hires an engineer as a paralegal to provide expert advice on product liability cases or to assist on patent matters, that engineer would qualify for exemption.

So, as of 2004, the DOL considers paralegals as nonexempt employees (people who are paid overtime). What is the effect of this? Many have argued that it takes the paralegal profession out of the "professional" category. Others say that the paralegal profession is a profession nonetheless.

The Future

So, what is a paralegal? For many, a paralegal is a person who performs preparatory legal work. For others, a paralegal is a person who does investigation of legal matters. For yet another group, a paralegal is a person who completes legal forms. What will a paralegal be in ten years? Ten years from now, there will be traditional paralegals even more widely used than they are today. The future will also undoubtedly bring us more specialization in law and more people who cannot afford a lawyer; so, hopefully, the future will also bring a solution to that problem in the form of the future of the paralegal profession. Who will regulate paralegals? There's another question we can't answer just yet.

Paralegals, contrary to lawyers, are not regulated by state law. (There are a few exceptions we discuss later.) That is to say that even though a lot of time and effort has gone into writing, redrafting, discussing, enacting, and enforcing the rules of ethics for lawyers, there isn't much in the way of enforceable, distinct law for the paralegal profession. Most paralegals are regulated, instead, by the state's regulation of the employing lawyer. We discuss this type of removed regulation in two parts:

1. The laws that regulate lawyers say that the lawyer is responsible for nonlawyers under his/her supervision, and

2. Case law says that nonlawyers and lawyers are bound by the same ethical duties.[20]

Rule 5.3 aside, there are many cases that say, without equivocation, that paralegals are obligated to adhere to the same rules of ethics that lawyers use. So, in the case of *Richards v. Jain*,[21] a federal court in Washington looked at the culpability of the lawyer whose paralegal reviewed almost one thousand pages of the opposition's attorney/client privileged documents. Even if the paralegal didn't know that he should not have been looking at privileged documents that belonged to the opponent (which is hard to believe), his supervising lawyers should have known that the computer files contained privileged information and should have instructed the paralegal not to look at them. And even if the paralegal did not actually transmit any of the privileged information to the lawyers he worked for (which is also hard to believe), the legal presumption is that the information was shared. The court logically concluded that it was the lawyers' duty under that state's version of ABA Model Rule 5.3 to ensure that the paralegal complied with professional ethical obligations.

ABA Model Rule 5.3

With respect to a nonlawyer employed or retained by or associated with a lawyer:

(a) a partner, and a lawyer who individually or together with other lawyers possesses comparable managerial authority in a law firm shall make reasonable efforts to ensure that the firm has in effect measures giving reasonable assurance that the person's conduct is compatible with the professional obligations of the lawyer;

(b) a lawyer having direct supervisory authority over the nonlawyer shall make reasonable efforts to ensure that the person's conduct is compatible with the professional obligations of the lawyer; and

(c) a lawyer shall be responsible for conduct of such a person that would be a violation of the Rules of Professional Conduct if engaged in by a lawyer if:

(1) the lawyer orders or, with the knowledge of the specific conduct, ratifies the conduct involved; or

(2) the lawyer is a partner or has comparable managerial authority in the law firm in which the person is employed, or has direct supervisory authority over the person, and knows of the conduct at a time when its consequences can be avoided or mitigated but fails to take reasonable remedial action.

* Full Model Rule and commentary can be found in Appendix E.

Here's the logic leap you have to make. The U.S. Supreme Court and courts all over the United States have consistently protected paralegals with the same protections given to lawyers. For example, the attorney/client privilege and the work product privilege (Chapter 3) extend to paralegals (and other nonlawyers in the law office). In exchange for the protections, the paralegal (and other nonlawyers who work in the law office) are expected to abide by the same rules of ethics as the lawyers, with the possible exception of 5.3. (Paralegals can't very well be expected to be responsible for the lawyer supervising them, can they?)

That's how we arrive at this simple truth with which we started this chapter: the rules of ethics that apply to lawyers also apply to paralegals. Look at this list of ethical obligations that lawyers have and, if you think there are any on the list that don't apply to paralegals, give me a call and let me know.

- Duty of integrity
- Duty to not practice law without a license
- Duty of zealous representation within the bounds of the law
- Duty to be competent
- Duty of confidentiality
- Duty of loyalty
- Duty to protect the public
- Duty to make legal services available at an affordable price

A paralegal cannot be disciplined by the state bar or state disciplinary committee for a violation of any of those duties because the paralegal isn't a member of the bar. So who will discipline the paralegal? At the present time, only the employing lawyer. In rare instances, the court can discipline the paralegal. In some states, regulatory bodies are being created or changed to take on this responsibility.

Here's a case you should look at:

Disqualification is justified under three alternate theories. First, *nonlawyers and lawyers are bound by the same ethical duties.* Mr. Haegele's review of privileged material was an ethical violation regardless of his status as a paralegal. Secondly, Hagens Berman failed to fulfill its duties under RPC 5.3(b) when it did not take reasonable measures to ensure the ethical conduct of a nonlawyer. Lastly, Mr. Haegele's conduct in reviewing the privileged material and the knowledge gained by that review are imputed to the Hagens Berman firm under RPC 5.3(c). *Richards v. Jain*, 168 F.Supp.2d 1195 (W.D. Wash 2001)

What Choices Are Available for Regulating Paralegals?

Most paralegals and other nonlawyers are not regulated and are not subject to minimum educational requirements. (The exceptions to this are discussed subsequently.) Even the definition of *paralegal* or *legal assistant* is different from state to state.

Until twenty years ago, few people recognized the paralegal as a professional. Since the 1989 case of *Missouri v. Jenkins,*[22] most of the legal profession has agreed that paralegals perform nonclerical (and therefore billable) work. *Missouri v. Jenkins* was a case stemming from the desegregation cases of the 1950s. The issue of the value of paralegal work arose when the U.S. Supreme Court discussed awarding "attorney's fees" for work performed by paralegals. The following is an often quoted portion of that case:

> Clearly, a "reasonable attorney's fee" under [42 U.S.C. 1988] cannot have meant to compensate only work performed personally by members of the bar. Rather, the term must refer to a reasonable fee for the work product of an attorney . . . [including] . . . secretaries, . . . and others whose labor contributes to the work product for which an attorney bills her client . . .

In an accompanying footnote, the Court wrote:

> Of course, purely clerical or secretarial tasks should not be billed at a paralegal rate regardless of who performs them.

When it comes to assessing the value of paralegals in the world of law, then, there can't be a much better authority than the U.S. Supreme Court. Paralegals are professionals in the eyes of the Court.

Nevertheless, few states have created regulatory statutes for paralegals aside from the unauthorized practice of law provisions.

Regulation is used here as an umbrella term. Among the different types of regulatory schemes for paralegals are licensing, certification, registration, and title schemes. Each of the regulatory schemes is different and has different goals. Regulations also fall into three other general categories: (1) those directed at professionals delivering legal services directly to the public (legal technicians); (2) those directed at professionals (both traditional paralegals and independent or project paralegals) who are working under the supervision of lawyers; and (3) those directed at lawyers to give them guidance in the use of paralegals.

Licensing

The theory of licensing runs like this: Just as lawyers are licensed to practice law and dentists are licensed to practice dentistry, paralegals could be licensed to practice law, or law in limited subject areas. Licensing would probably involve a certain amount of education and passing an exam, just as the other professions that require a license.

Various states over the last ten years have looked at licensing schemes for paralegals; but, as of this writing, no state has adopted licensing as a regulation method. This is an evolutionary process, however, so don't be surprised if you see licensing schemes in the near future.

Certification

Certification is the process by which the government or other organization grants recognition to those who have met certain qualifications. Certification schemes usually require successful completion of a course of study and passing an exam. The recognition granted is typically in the form of a title you are allowed to use that others cannot.

NALA Certification

NALA has developed a voluntary "certification exam." The exam takes two days and is given three times annually. It includes sections covering basic skills common to all paralegals: verbal and written communication, which covers English grammar and writing proficiency; judgment and analytical ability; ethics; human relations; legal terminology; and legal research. It also includes sections testing knowledge of the American legal system and substantive law in the areas of litigation, real estate, criminal law, bankruptcy, corporations, contracts, administrative law, family law, and estate planning and probate. The candidate must complete four of nine sections. The test includes both subjective and objective test questions. It is graded by the certifying board, which is made up of certified legal assistant specialists, attorneys, and paralegal educators working with a professional testing consultant.

Passing NALA's certified legal assistant (CLA) exam entitles paralegals to use the designation "CLA" as a part of their title or description on business cards, when signing letters, and the like. NALA has registered "CLA" as a certification mark; therefore, unless you have taken and passed the NALA exam, you cannot designate yourself as a "certified legal assistant." If you have a certificate from a paralegal program, you are a "certificated" legal assistant or paralegal.

As a second phase of the certification process, specialty certification is available to those who pass the general CLA exam and a four-hour advanced-level examination. Specialties are available in the areas of civil litigation, criminal law and procedure, bankruptcy, corporations and business, estates and trusts, intellectual property, and real estate. A specialty entitles you to use the designation "CLA Specialist." No state laws are tested on the exam, only federal and general common law. California, Louisiana, and Florida offer state specialties to those who already have a CLA designation. The certification program plays an important role in encouraging and exemplifying an attitude of professionalism and professional development. Studies show that CLA designation brings with it higher salaries and a higher billing rate. Some state courts are recognizing the CLA designation in their guidelines for fee applications. The CLA exam has many years of recognition. Passing the exam does not certify the paralegal to perform any tasks other than the duties permitted for any other paralegal, however, because the exam has not been adopted by any state bar nor has any legislature or other governmental branch endorsed NALA's certification as a license to practice law even in a limited capacity.

The CLA must be renewed every five years by taking approved continuing education classes (fifty hours in a five-year period) and supplying an affidavit of continuing good moral and professional character. There are over 13,000 legal assistants who have the CLA designation with over 25,000 legal assistants participating since the beginning of the program.

NFPA Certification

NFPA's Paralegal Advanced Competency Exam (PACE) is a certification type of exam. The successful candidate may use the certification "Registered Paralegal" (RP). Technically, because it involves an exam, NFPA's PACE is classified as a certification process, not a registration scheme.

The PACE is a two-tier exam. Tier I addresses general legal issues and ethics. Tier II addresses specialty areas of the law. The PACE is exclusively multiple choice and can be taken in computerized testing centers at any time that is convenient for the applicant. If you are interested in seeing exactly what the PACE is all about, from NFPA's Web site you can link to a PACE practice exam. To maintain the PACE RP credential, paralegals are required to obtain twelve hours of continuing legal education, including at least one hour in ethics, every two years. There is a list of PACE Registered Paralegals by state on NFPA's Web site if you are interested in seeing how popular the test is in your state.

North Carolina Voluntary Paralegal Certification

The Supreme Court of North Carolina approved the voluntary certification of paralegals in 2004. The North Carolina State Bar Board of Paralegal Certification began accepting applications in 2005. The law currently provides for certification on the basis of the following requirements:

> http://www.
> nccertifiedparalegal.org

A—Possess at least a high-school diploma *and* have five thousand hours of experience working as a North Carolina paralegal during the five (5) years prior to application *and* have taken a three- (3) hour ethics course.

B—Possess a current CLA, RP, or other national paralegal credential approved by the board *and* have two thousand hours of experience working as a North Carolina paralegal during the two (2) years prior to application.

C—Possess a degree in paralegal studies from a qualified paralegal studies program or possess an undergraduate degree in any field plus the equivalent of eighteen hours of paralegal coursework from a qualified paralegal studies program *and* have two thousand hours of experience working as a North Carolina paralegal during the two (2) years prior to application.

After June 30, 2007, certification will require the educational requirements and an examination.

What does certification give you? The right to use titles that will identify you as a paralegal who has been certified by the North Carolina State Bar. The Web site includes information for lawyers about why they should support this certification effort.

Ohio State Bar Certified Paralegal

In 2006, the Ohio State Bar Association established a "credential" program for paralegals. Satisfying the requirements (including a written exam) entities paralegals to call themselves an OSBA Certified Paralegal. We've put the law on the Web site for you.

Arizona Certification of Legal Document Preparers

Arizona has a Legal Document Preparer statute (a certification program), that includes a *Code of Conduct*, a written exam on ethics, legal terminology, client communication, data gathering, document preparation, and administrative responsibilities. This is part of the *Arizona Code of Judicial Administration* and administered by its Certification and Licensing Division. This law became effective July 1, 2003. From the Web site: "[The] Legal Document Preparer Program certifies nonattorney legal document preparers in Arizona who provide document preparation assistance and services to individuals and entities not represented by an attorney. Legal Document Preparers may provide general legal information but may not give legal advice." *Arizona Code of Judicial Administration*, Section 7-208G(4), requires all certified legal document preparers to attend a minimum of ten hours of board-approved continuing education each year. One of those ten hours must be ethics based, and no more than three hours can be in the areas of business management and tax preparation.

Paralegals can receive a legal document preparer's certification if they have a paralegal certificate from an ABA-approved program or a non-ABA-approved, accredited program with a minimum of twenty-four semester units in legal specialization courses.

These are just some examples of certification schemes being used by different states across the United States. In the years to come, we'll see if certification is the path the majority of the states take.

Registration

Registration is primarily the identification of members of a specific profession. Registration traditionally does not require minimum educational or training requirements, although bonding is sometimes necessary. Much like registration of a motor vehicle simply allows the state to find the owner, registration of paralegals may merely provide the state with a list of names, addresses, and telephone numbers of paralegals pursuing their profession within the state.

California's Registration Statutes

In 1994, California began requiring nonlawyers assisting people facing eviction to register with the state when it passed the Unlawful Detainer Assistant's Act. The registration requirement includes posting a $25,000 bond. The law was enacted in response to complaints that these nonlawyers were taking money from people and promising to help them stay in their homes, but their services consisted only of bad faith delaying tactics, such as frivolous bankruptcy filings or advising the tenant not to appear at eviction hearings.

California also has a Legal Document Assistant Act (like document preparers) that is a registration act.

http://www.calda.org

California's proposal aligned Unlawful Detainer Assistants and Legal Document Assistants under the supervision of the Department of Consumer Affairs. Most states seem to prefer regulation by the same organization that regulates lawyers in the state.

Title Schemes

Some states are looking at regulation from the point of view of restricting the use of terms *paralegal* and *legal assistant* to those people with certain qualifications. *Business and Professions Code,* Section 6450 *et seq.*, enacted in California and effective January 2001, includes a definition of paralegal, minimum qualifications for who can be called a paralegal, and mandatory continuing legal education and imposes a penalty for the inappropriate use of the term *paralegal*. The statute states:

> "Paralegal" means a person who holds himself or herself out to be a paralegal, who is qualified by education, training, or work experience, and who either contracts with or is employed by an attorney, law firm, corporation, governmental agency, or other entity, and who performs substantial legal work under the direction and supervision of an active member of the State Bar of California, as defined in Section 6060, or an attorney practicing law in the federal courts of this state, that has been specifically delegated by the attorney to him or her.

Business and Professional Code, Section 6450, also details the minimum qualifications necessary to enter the profession and use the title of paralegal as:

1. A certificate of completion of a paralegal program approved by the American Bar Association.

2. A certificate of completion of a paralegal program at, or a degree from, a postsecondary institution that requires the successful completion of a minimum of 24 semester, or equivalent, units in law-related courses and that has been accredited by a national or regional accrediting organization or approved by the Bureau for Private Postsecondary and Vocational Education.

> A "grandfather clause" is an exception that allows an old rule to continue to apply to some existing situations when a new rule will apply to future situations.

3. A baccalaureate degree or an advanced degree in any subject, a minimum of one year of law-related experience under the supervision of an attorney who has been an active member of the State Bar of California for at least the preceding three years or who has practiced in the federal courts of this state for at least the preceding three years, and a written declaration from this attorney stating that the person is qualified to perform paralegal tasks.

The original statute included a "grandfather clause" for people in the profession who did not satisfy the formal educational requirements but had been working in the profession. That part of the statute sunsetted at the end of 2003.

> A "sunset" provision in a statute is a part of the law that ends at a certain time.

4. A high-school diploma or general equivalency diploma, a minimum of three years of law-related experience under the supervision of an attorney who has been an active member of the State Bar of California for at least the preceding three years or who has practiced in the federal courts of this state for at least the preceding three years, and a written declaration from this attorney stating that the person is qualified to perform paralegal tasks. This experience and training shall be completed no later than December 31, 2003.

The statute also says that in order to maintain the proper use of the title, paralegals must complete continuing legal education: four hours of mandatory continuing legal education in legal ethics every three years. Every two years, all California paralegals are required to certify completion of four hours of mandatory continuing education in either general law or in a specialized area of law.

Although Business and Professional Code Section 6450, does not create a regulatory body or a licensing requirement, certification of these continuing education requirements "shall be made with the paralegal's supervising attorney. The paralegal shall be responsible for keeping a record of the paralegal's certifications." This is a perfect example of what we were talking about (on page 1) of paralegals being regulated by lawyers.

Other states have opted for simply defining "paralegal," as opposed to regulating them. See, for example, Maine Section 1.4 MRSA, Chapter 18 (1999) provided for you on our Web site. The Oklahoma Bar Association set forth minimum qualifications for paralegals in 2000, specifically disallowing disbarred attorneys from being paralegals or legal assistants.

What Does It Mean to Be "Regulated by the Courts"?

There are states that see regulation of paralegals as just the line between who can practice law and who cannot. When we talk about regulation by the court, then, we are really talking about regulation of the unauthorized practice of law. We cover UPL in depth in Chapter 2. With respect to regulation, however, you should know that this is the most prevalent method of regulation for nonlawyers. There's an example from California in the early 1990s before California developed any of its current regulatory methods. The San Diego city attorney's office prosecuted an "independent paralegal" who was working out of a storefront in San Diego. The paralegal was convicted by a jury in San Diego Municipal Court. (UPL is a misdemeanor in California.) The judge sentenced him to forty-nine days in jail.[23]

Then there is the story of Rosemary Furman, a Florida independent paralegal we discuss in Chapter 2. A vocal advocate for the right for independent paralegals to directly aid members of the public with their legal problems, Ms. Furman also spent some time in jail for her cause. You will see her cases at the end of Chapter 2.

These types of case are often argued as "right-to-work" issues rather than regulation cases because they don't deal with ethics issues in the paralegal profession. They have the effect, however, of "regulating" the paralegal profession insofar as these cases keep people away from the independent paralegal profession.

Have Paralegals Considered Self-Regulation?

Thus far, discussions of regulating paralegals focus on outside regulation, that is, regulation by the state or bar associations. In the states that have integrated bars, such as California, it is the bar (the lawyers) who regulates itself. Although the state supreme court is ultimately in charge of lawyer discipline, the judicial branch and not the executive or legislative branches is regulating itself. Generating self-regulation is a daunting task but perhaps a direction for the future of the paralegal profession.

SUMMARY

So, what do we know about regulation? We know that the regulation of lawyers has been going on for a long time and that the different states have similar methods of regulating lawyers. We also know that the American Bar Association is a voluntary organization that has provided model rules of professional responsibility since the early 1900s and that almost all of the states have adopted some form of those models for the regulation of lawyers. That means that even though different states have different rules, because they come from that same "root" of the ABA model, most lawyer regulation is the same across the United States. But we have also learned that the regulation of paralegals is not clear-cut and there is no "model" that the states have adopted. We have learned that there are national paralegal associations that have written codes of professional conduct for paralegals and that membership in these associations is voluntary. We have also learned that there are many different paths the paralegal profession could take and many different forms of regulation that could be applied to it. Hopefully, we've learned that the future of the paralegal profession is in your hands.

CHAPTER REVIEW AND ASSIGNMENTS

CRITICAL THINKING

1. Let's go back to the "Hypothetical" at the beginning of this chapter. Who is at fault? Should the client have to forfeit his right to defend the action because the paralegal made a calendaring error? What should the penalty be against the lawyer? Against the paralegal? To aid you in your answer, read *Hu v. Fang* at the end of this chapter.
2. Compare the NFPA Model Code to the NALA Model Standards. Which organization's philosophy most closely resembles your own regarding the profession? Do you intend to perform legal services only under the supervision of a lawyer, or do you see yourself working directly with the public?
3. Do you think that self-regulation will enhance the paralegal profession? What are some of the problems of self-regulation? What steps should be taken toward self-regulation?
4. Do you think that paralegals should be regulated by the same authorities that regulate lawyers in your state? Why or why not? What are some of the problems of regulation by the organized bar? How would you approach the solutions?

ASSIGNMENTS

1. What kinds of tasks will you be doing in the law office? Make a list. Compare your list of tasks to the criteria discussed in the *Page & Addison* case (Case 1 at the end of this chapter). Are the clerical tasks incidental to your primary duties? Does your anticipated salary compare to other professionals who are exempt from overtime pay? Should your job title enter into your formula regarding professionalism? What other factors do you believe make you a professional?

2. For a terrific movie about the legal system, watch *Twelve Angry Men* with Henry Fonda and a host of other famous actors. There are many interesting legal issues in this classic movie.

COLLABORATIVE ASSIGNMENTS

1. Gather into teams of no more than five students. Each team takes a different form of regulation (certification, licensing, registration) and creates a list of what that regulation form would look like in your state.

2. Both NFPA and NALA have drafted codes of ethics for paralegals. Divide into two teams. Each team should review one of the two codes and be able to explain the Code to the other team. Use the following questions as guidelines.

   a. What place does this code intend for the paralegal to have in delivering legal services to the public?

   b. What term does this code use to refer to paralegals? Why do you think they chose that term?

   c. What does this code have to say about future regulation of the paralegal profession?

   d. Review each of the other eight chapters of this book and compare them to the issues raised in the Code. Are all of the issues addressed in the Code?

   e. On a scale of 1 to 10, 10 being the most liberal viewpoint and 1 being the most conservative, where does this code belong on the scale?

3. Using the "Rule of 4" questionnaire on the publisher's Web site, create a bill for your state legislature's consideration setting forth a regulatory scheme for your state in teams of no more than five students.

REVIEW QUESTIONS

Multiple Choice

Select the best answer for each of the following questions.

1. Methods by which paralegals may be regulated include
   a. licensing, certification, and registration.
   b. civil penalties for the unauthorized practice of law.
   c. criminal penalties for the unauthorized practice of law.
   d. all of the above.
   e. none of the above.

2. The American Bar Association
   a. is a voluntary organization for lawyers.
   b. has no disciplinary authority.
   c. has drafted sample or model rules of ethics for lawyers.
   d. all of the above.
   e. none of the above.

3. The American Bar Association's *Model Rules of Professional Conduct*
   a. are the nationally recognized rules of professional responsibility in all fifty states.
   b. are rules that have been adopted in almost all of the states.
   c. are very old and not used any more.
   d. are the rules that govern pharmacists.
   e. none of the above.

4. Local bar association ethics opinions
   a. are binding on all lawyers in the territorial jurisdiction of the bar association.
   b. are binding on all lawyers and paralegals in the states.
   c. are never published and have no legal effect.
   d. are advisory and persuasive.
   e. are simply learning exercises for local bar association members.

5. If a lawyer violates the rules of professional conduct, the lawyer is subject to
   a. disbarment.
   b. suspension.
   c. reprimand or reproval.
   d. criminal penalties.
   e. any of the above depending upon the severity of the offense.

6. Paralegals may be regulated by
   a. licensing.
   b. certification.
   c. registration.
   d. restricting the use of the term *paralegal*.
   e. all of the above.

7. A "grandfather clause" is
   a. a rule of law that only applies to grandfathers.
   b. an exception that allows an old rule to continue to apply to some existing situations, when a new rule will apply instead in all future situations.
   c. a clause in a contract that will apply to situations that have passed but not to future situations.
   d. the federal rule of law that allows larger companies to employ older Americans without enforcing retirement regulations.
   e. none of the above.

8. A "sunset provision" is
   a. a rule of law pertaining to air quality.
   b. a federal rule of law that allows states to choose whether or not to elect daylight savings time.
   c. part of a law that ends at a certain time.
   d. a provision in a contract that specifies when the contract will end.
   e. none of the above.

9. A "title scheme" is
   a. a type of regulatory act that restricts the use of certain titles.
   b. a law that prevents improper use of subtitles in movies and television production.
   c. the format used by the federal government to give titles to different statutes.
   d. the informal but widely used convention for naming new scientific discoveries.
   e. none of the above.

10. A legal document preparer is
   a. any paralegal.
   b. any person who helps another person create a document.
   c. another name for a legal secretary.
   d. a law clerk.
   e. people certified in Arizona to assist members of the public prepare their own legal documents.

Fill in the Blank

Complete each of the following sentences with the best word(s) or phrase(s).

1. Paralegals who work outside the supervision of lawyers are called _____.
2. The largest, voluntary association for lawyers and the one that drafts model codes of professional responsibility is called _____.
3. The two largest and oldest paralegal associations are called _____ and _____.
4. Your state paralegal association is called _____.
5. The local paralegal association in your community is called _____.
6. Registration as a form of regulation of the paralegal field is _____.
7. Certification is _____.
8. Licensing is _____.
9. The CLA exam is _____.
10. The PACE exam is _____.

True/False

Decide whether each of the following statements is true or false and write your answer on the line provided.

____ 1. Paralegals are bound by the same rules of ethics as lawyers.
____ 2. The majority of paralegals work under the supervision of lawyers.
____ 3. Membership in the American Bar Association is mandatory for lawyers.
____ 4. The bar exam is a national exam given once a year.
____ 5. A person's moral character is of no relevance in bar membership.
____ 6. The ABA's Model Code of Professional Responsibility is the highest authority in ethical conduct in the United States.
____ 7. Lawyers can be disciplined by suspension and disbarment.
____ 8. Model Rule 5.3 makes lawyers responsible for the conduct of the paralegals they employ.
____ 9. The U.S. Supreme Court has said that charging attorneys' fees for work performed by paralegals is unconstitutional.
____ 10. National paralegal associations have written codes of professional conduct for paralegals.

CASES FOR CONSIDERATION

CASE 1

REICH v. PAGE & ADDISON
1994 WL 143208
(N.D. Tex. 1994)

[The Judge's charge to the jury regarding use of the jury instructions, bias, judicial notice, veracity of witnesses, weight to be given evidence, burden of proof (preponderance of the evidence), the proper measure of damages, completing the jury questionnaire and communicating with the court during deliberations are omitted.]

PLAINTIFF'S CONTENTIONS

Plaintiff, the Secretary of Labor, claims that during the period since January 1989, Defendant, Page & Addison, has willfully violated the overtime provisions of Section 7 of the Act, ("the Act" or "The FLSA"), 29 U.S.C. § 207, by failing to compensate some of its employees for all employment in excess of 40 hours per workweek, at rates of at least one and one-half times the regular rates at which said employees were employed. Further, Plaintiff claims that during the period since January 1989, Defendant has willfully violated the provisions of Section 11(c) of the Act, 29 U.S.C. § 211(c), in that it has failed to make, keep and preserve adequate and accurate records of its employees and of the wages, hours and other conditions and practices of employment maintained by defendant as prescribed by regulations issued by the Administrator of the Employment Standards Administration, U.S. Department of Labor, 29 C.F.R. Part 516. Further, Plaintiff claims that back wages are due to Defendant's employees and former employees for unpaid overtime compensation which have become due to such employees under Section 7 of the Act, during the period from January 1989 to the date of entry of judgment plus liquidated damages.

DEFENDANT'S CONTENTIONS

1. Defendant claims it has not violated the overtime and record keeping requirements of the FLSA, 29 U.S.C. §§ 207, 211(c) (West. 1965 & Supp. 1992), regarding the legal assistant employees at issue in this litigation.

2. Further, Defendant claims it has not willfully violated overtime and record keeping requirements of the FLSA with respect to the legal assistant employees at issue in this litigation. 29 U.S.C. § 255 (West. 1985 & Supp. 1992).

3. Further, Defendant claims its non-supervisory legal assistant employees at issue in this litigation are exempt from the overtime requirements of the FLSA because they are employed in a bona fide administrative capacity. 29 U.S.C. § 213(a)(1) (West Supp. 1992).

4. Further, Defendant claims that Plaintiff is not entitled to any relief he seeks, including back wages or liquidated damages.

STIPULATED FACTS

1. Defendant has been since January 1989 a professional corporation with a place of business and doing business at 14651 Dallas Parkway, Suite 700, Dallas, TX 75240, within the jurisdiction of this Court.

2. Defendant, since January 1989, has been an enterprise within the meaning of Section 3(r) of the Act, 29 U.S.C. § 203(r).

3. Defendant, since January 1989, has been an enterprise engaged in commerce or in the production of goods for commerce within the meaning of Section 3(s)(1) of the Act, 29 U.S.C. § 203(s)(1).

4. From January 1989 until January 1991, the pay and employment practices of Defendant were investigated by the Wage and Hour Division of the United States Department of Labor.

5. The only employees at issue in this litigation are certain of Defendant's current and former legal assistant employees.

6. All of the legal assistant employees at issue in this litigation are or were compensated on a salary basis of more than $250 per week, exclusive of board, lodging or other facilities.

INSTRUCTION FOR QUESTION NO. 1

There is an administrative exemption to the law requiring employers to pay overtime compensation. Exemptions from the FLSA are to be construed narrowly. The employer has the burden of proof on the applicability of this exemption on an employee-by-employee and week-by-week basis. To prove this exemption is applicable, Defendant must prove plainly and unmistakably that:

1. the employee's primary duty
2. requires the exercise of discretion and independent judgment
3. in the performance of office or non-manual field work
4. directly relating to the management policies or general business operations of their employers or their employer's customers.

A determination of what an employee's primary duty is must be based on all the facts in a particular case. The amount of time spent in the performance of the primary duties is one factor to consider in making this determination. Some other pertinent factors are the relative importance of the primary duties as compared with other types of duties, the frequency with which the employee exercises discretionary powers, her relative freedom from supervision, and the relationship between her salary and the wages paid other employees for the kind of nonexempt work performed by the supervisor.

The employee's primary duty will usually be what she does that is of principal value to the employer, not the collateral tasks that she may also perform, even if they consume more than half her time.

"Discretion and independent judgment" involve the comparison and evaluation of possible courses of conduct and acting or making a decision after the various possibilities have been considered. An employee exercises discretion and independent judgment if that employee has the authority or power to make an independent choice, free from immediate direction or supervision and with respect to matters of significance. An employee who merely applies his knowledge in following prescribed procedures or determining which procedures to follow is not exercising discretion and independent judgment.

The discretion and independent judgment exercised must be real and substantial, that is, they must be exercised with respect to matters of consequence. The fact that an employee's work is subject to approval and possible rejection by a supervisory employee does not mean that the employee does not exercise discretion and independent judgment.

"Directly relating to management policies or general business operations" describes those types of activities relating to the general business operations of a business. To satisfy this requirement, an employee must be performing work of substantial importance to the operation of the business of his employer or his employer's customers. The employee's job title alone is of little or no assistance in determining the employee's exempt or non-exempt status.

QUESTION NO. 1

During the period from January 1989 through the present, do you find that any of the following paralegal employees are exempt on a week-by-week basis from the overtime requirements of the Fair Labor Standards Act?

Answer:

(In this section, the jury checked the "yes" box for all 23 of the paralegals named on the questionnaire.)

INSTRUCTION FOR QUESTION NO. 2

An employer is required to make, keep, and preserve for each of their employees records of the following items unless the employee is exempt from both the minimum wage and overtime provisions of the Act:

1. Daily and weekly hours actually worked by an employee;

2. Regular hourly rate of pay for all weeks when more than forty (40) hours are worked;

3. Basis on which wages are paid (i.e., $3.50 per hour, $200 per week, etc.);

4. Total weekly straight-time earnings, that is, compensation due exclusive of premium pay for overtime hours;

5. Total weekly premium compensation paid over and above all straight-time earnings paid. Responsibility for complying with this requirement may not be evaded by delegation of the record keeping function to others, including employees.

QUESTION NO. 2

Plaintiff has the burden of proof on this question by a preponderance of the evidence. Did Defendant fail to make, keep, and preserve records of the daily and weekly hours actually worked by any of those persons whose names are listed on Plaintiff's Summary of Unpaid Wages (Plaintiff's Exhibit No. 1)?

Yes_____ No _____X_____

INSTRUCTION FOR QUESTION NO. 3

Plaintiff may recover from Defendant unpaid overtime compensation due since January 1989 if the Defendant is found to have willfully violated the law. Otherwise, Plaintiff may recover only for the employees' unpaid overtime compensation due since January 1990. A person has willfully violated the law if either he knew or showed reckless disregard that his conduct was prohibited by law. If Defendant acted reasonably in determining its legal obligations under the Act, its actions were not willful even if you find that some or all of the legal assistants are non-exempt. Even if Defendant acted unreasonably, but not with reckless disregard for the law, its actions were not willful.

QUESTION NO. 3

Plaintiff has the burden of proof on this question by a preponderance of the evidence. Was the Defendant's failure to pay overtime to their paralegal employees a willful violation of the Fair Labor Standards Act?

Yes_____ No _____X_____

CERTIFICATE

We, the jury, have answered the above and foregoing questions as herein indicated, and herewith return same into court as our verdict. We, the jury, have answered the above and foregoing questions as herein indicated, and herewith return same into court as our verdict.

CASE QUESTIONS

1. Why do you think the people on this jury accepted legal assisting as a *profession*, not merely an occupation?
2. Overtime pay is thought of inside out. What does "exempt" mean? What is "nonexempt"?
3. What could some "primary duties" of the paralegal be?
4. What are some collateral tasks?
5. What is "discretion and independent judgment"? How might those things be demonstrated in the law office?
6. How would you determine if you should be paid overtime?
7. Are there sacrifices you can think of that come with being paid overtime?

CASE 2

HU v. FANG
104 Cal.App.4th 61, 127 Cal.Rptr.2d 756
(2002)

The trial court denied relief under Code of Civil Procedure Section 473, subdivision (b) from a default judgment because it found that the error resulting in the default was made by a paralegal, not an attorney. We hold that, in the context of a motion under Section 473, a paralegal's mistake is attributable to the attorney responsible for supervising the paralegal. We reverse the default judgment.

FACTUAL AND PROCEDURAL BACKGROUND

Sylvia Wei-Ting Hu sued Amy Fang for breach of contract and common counts. Fang, represented by J. Flores Valdez, answered the complaint. On February 16, 2001, Valdez failed to appear at a status conference. The trial court issued an order to show cause (OSC) for failure to appear and for striking Fang's answer. Valdez was mailed a copy of the trial court's minute order.

The hearing on the OSC was set for March 15, 2001, but Valdez again failed to appear. At the March 15, 2001, hearing, the case was transferred from West Covina to Pomona and the hearing on the OSC was continued to April 5, 2001. Valdez was given notice, but again failed to appear. The trial court ordered Fang's answer stricken and ordered counsel for Hu to file a request for entry of default.

On April 25, 2001, Valdez filed a motion, under Section 473, to set aside the order of default (Motion). The Motion was based, inter alia, on the declaration of Valdez and the declaration of his paralegal, Ben Lui. Valdez stated that "[t]here was a mistake on the part of my paralegal in the calendaring of my appearances" and consequently Valdez understood that the appearance was on April 6th before the Citrus Court instead of April 5th in Pomona. Lui stated "I am the paralegal/calendar clerk for J. Flores Valdez" and "I made a mistake in calendaring the matter in that I set it for April 6th in Citrus Court instead of the noticed time and date of April 5th at the Pomona Court." At the hearing on the Motion, Valdez argued that his employee's mistake should be imputed to him. The trial court denied the Motion, finding "473 only grants relief for mistake, inadvertence, surprise, or excusable neglect of an attorney, not a paralegal." The court further concluded: "It's a tough call, but if you choose to use paralegals and have them do your work, then I don't think it's your mistake that they make a mistake." Subsequently, the trial court entered a default judgment. Fang timely appealed.

DISCUSSION

Section 473, subdivision (b) contains a mandatory provision. (*Lorenz v. Commercial Acceptance Ins. Co* (1995) 40 Cal.App.4th 981, 989.) "[T]he court *shall*, whenever an application for relief is made no more than six months after entry of judgment, is in proper form, and is accompanied by an attorney's sworn affidavit attesting to his or her mistake, inadvertence, surprise, or neglect, vacate any . . . resulting default judgment or dismissal entered against his or her client, unless the court finds that the default or dismissal was not in fact caused by the attorney's mistake inadvertence, surprise, or neglect." (§ 473, subd. (b), emphasis added.) The purpose of the attorney affidavit provision "is to relieve the innocent client of the burden of the attorney's fault, to impose the burden on the erring attorney, and to avoid precipitating more litigation in the form of malpractice suits." (*Metropolitan Service Corp. v. Casa de Palms, Ltd.* (1995) 31 Cal.App.4th 1481, 1487.)

We review an order denying relief under Section 473 under the abuse of discretion standard. (*In re Marriage of Connolly* (1979) 23 Cal.3d 590, 597–598.) We conclude the trial court abused its discretion in finding that Valdez was not the cause of the default judgment because the mistake was made by his paralegal.

The attorney is the professional responsible for supervising the work of his legal assistants. (*Vaughn v. State Bar* (1972) 6 Cal.3d 847, 857.) "[E]ven though an attorney cannot be held responsible for every detail of office procedure, he must accept responsibility to supervise the work of his staff." (*Ibid.*; see also *Spindell v. State Bar* (1975) 13 Cal.3d 253, 260 ["An attorney has an obligation to adequately supervise his employees. . . . "]; ABA Model Rules Prof. Conduct, rule 5.3, com. ["A lawyer should give such assistants appropriate instruction and supervision concerning the ethical aspects of their employment, particularly regarding the obligation not to disclose information relating to representation of the client, and should be responsible for their work product"].) Thus, Valdez was responsible for supervising Lui's work and is responsible for Lui's work product, including his mistake in calendaring the OSC hearing. (Cf. *Zamora v. Clayborn Contracting*

Group Inc. (2002) 28 Cal.4th 249, 259 [assuming error of legal assistant attributable to counsel]; *Alderman v. Jacobs* (1954) 128 Cal.App.2d 273, 276 [assuming error of secretary attributable to counsel].)

Valdez, as required, acknowledged that Liu's error was attributable to the attorney and requested relief from default. The trial court should have granted the Motion and considered whether sanctions were appropriate. Granting relief from default does not condone Valdez's failure to appear, but serves the purpose of relieving "the innocent client of the burden of the attorney's fault. . . ." (*Metropolitan Service Corp. v. Casa de Palms, Ltd., supra,* 31 Cal.App.4th 1481, 1487.)

Hu's remaining arguments lack merit. First, Hu contends that Liu did not make a mistake and that the motion for relief from default should have included copies of Mr. Valdez's calendar. Hu's contention is inconsistent with the trial court's statement that "apparently your paralegal [Liu] isn't a licensed lawyer and didn't know what they were doing." Her contention is also inconsistent with Section 473, which requires only the "attorney's sworn affidavit attesting to his or her mistake . . . ," not additional evidence demonstrating the mistake. (§ 473, subd. (b).)

Second, Hu argues that Fang was required to file a copy of her answer with her Motion. Section 473, subdivision (b) does state that a request for relief "shall be accompanied by a copy of the answer or other pleading proposed to be filed therein. . . ." (§ 473, subd. (b).) However, "[t]he objectives of the 'accompanied by' requirement, i.e., a screening determination that the relief is not sought simply to delay the proceedings, is satisfied by the filing of a proposed answer at any time before the hearing." (*County of Stanislaus v. Johnson* (1996) 43 Cal.App.4th 832, 838.) Here, the answer, which previously had been filed "g[a]ve adequate notice that the [order was] under attack and the basis for the attack" even though a copy of the answer was not attached to the Motion. (*Ibid.*) In addition, the answer was filed prior to the grant of default, and therefore was obviously "no more than six months after entry of judgment. . . ." (§ 473, subd. (b).)

The judgment of default is reversed. Appellant is entitled to costs on appeal. Rubin, J., and Boland, J., concurred.

CASE QUESTIONS

1. How does your reading of this case answer the "Hypothetical" at the beginning of this chapter?
2. What does this case tell you about Mary Rose's calendaring error?
3. What do you think an appropriate penalty for the lawyer should be?
4. What should an appropriate penalty for the paralegal be?
5. Why did the appellate court say the trial court was obligated to set aside the default?
6. What does it mean that the paralegal's calendaring error was "imputed" to the lawyer?

PEOPLE v. MYERS
969 P.2d 701
(Colo. 1998)

The lawyer in this discipline case, Nancy L. Myers, defaulted before the hearing board and has not appeared in this court. Myers failed to appear at her own trial for driving under the influence of alcohol. A hearing panel of the grievance committee approved the findings and recommendation of the hearing board that Myers be suspended for one year and one day. We accept the recommendations and suspend the respondent for a year and a day.

I.

Nancy L. Myers was admitted to practice law in Colorado in 1990. She did not answer the formal complaint filed in this case and a default was entered against her. The allegations of fact contained in the complaint were therefore admitted. C.R.C.P. 241.13(b); *People v. Pierson*, 917 P.2d 275, 275 (Colo. 1996). Based on the default and the evidence presented, the hearing board found that the following had been established by clear and convincing evidence.

On August 14, 1996, the vehicle that Myers was driving was stopped in Chaffee County because of her failure to use a turn signal. The officer who stopped Myers smelled the odor of an alcoholic beverage on her breath and, after asking her to perform a roadside sobriety test, arrested her for driving under the influence of alcohol. A breath test indicated that Myers had a blood alcohol content of 0.117%. She was charged with Driving Under the Influence. After a change of venue to Lake County on the respondent's motion, Myers's first court appearance was set for November 7, 1996. In early November 1996, however, Myers left the United States to teach in South Korea.

When Myers did not appear on November 7, the county court issued a bench warrant for her arrest. Although the county court judge denied her request to enter a plea by mail, he granted her motion to stay the bench warrant until November 4, 1997, at which time Myers was to appear and proceed with the case. Myers did not appear in the county court at any time in November 1997.

Since Myers defaulted, we find an admission of the substance of the charges for purposes of this proceeding. When she drove under the influence of alcohol, Myers violated the criminal law of this state, contrary to C.R.C.P. 241.6(5), and she engaged in conduct adversely reflecting on her fitness to practice law, in violation of Colo. RPC 8.4(h). Her failure to appear in the county court constituted conduct prejudicial to the administration of justice, *see* Colo. RPC 8.4(d), and again adversely reflected on her fitness to practice, *see* Colo. RPC 8.4(h).

II.

The hearing panel approved the board's recommendation that the respondent be suspended for a year and a day. Myers has not filed exceptions to the panel's action or otherwise appeared in this court.

If the respondent's misconduct involved only driving under the influence, a public censure might be appropriate. *See People v. Rotenberg*, 807 P.2d 642, 643 (Colo. 1996). Her failure to appear in the county court exacerbates the misconduct, however.

Under the ABA *Standards for Imposing Lawyer Sanctions* (1991 & Supp. 1992) (ABA *Standards*), in the absence of aggravating or mitigating factors, suspension is an appropriate sanction "when a lawyer knowingly violates a court order or rule, and there is injury or potential injury to a client or a party, or interference or potential interference with a legal proceeding." ABA *Standards* 6.22. A period of suspension is therefore appropriate in this case.

We suspended the lawyer in *People v. Hughes*, No. 97SA369, slip op. at 7 (Colo. Oct. 19, 1998), for three years. Hughes drove on at least four occasions after his driver's license was revoked, and failed to appear in two cases involving his illegal driving. *See id.* at 2–3. Hughes had a history of discipline, which is an aggravating factor for disciplinary purposes. *See* ABA *Standards* 9.22(a).

Like Hughes, Myers has previous discipline. She was suspended for thirty days in 1995 for neglecting a client's criminal case and for filing a misleading witness and exhibit list. *See People v. Myers*, 908 P.2d 101, 102 (Colo. 1995). Because she did not appear before the hearing board, no mitigating factors were found. Considering the seriousness of Myers's conduct together with her total non-participation in these proceedings, we conclude that a long period of suspension with the requirement of reinstatement proceedings is warranted. Accordingly, we accept the recommendations of the hearing board and hearing panel.

III.

It is hereby ordered that Nancy L. Myers be suspended from the practice of law for one year and one day, effective thirty days after the issuance of this opinion. It is further ordered that Myers pay the costs of this proceeding in the amount of $124.11 within thirty days after this opinion is announced to the Supreme Court Grievance Committee (or the successor entity), 600 Seventeenth Street, Suite 300 South, Denver, Colorado 80202-5435. Myers shall not be reinstated until after she has complied with C.R.C.P. 251.29.

CASE QUESTIONS

1. Do you think Attorney Myers received the appropriate penalty?
2. Do you think the penalty would have been more or less harsh if she was not an experienced lawyer?

3. Should the penalty have been more harsh because she never answered the complaint or made an appearance in court to defend herself?
4. Even after a bench warrant was issued for Myers, she still did not make an appearance. Should her punishment have been more harsh because of that?
5. Should the court have made it a part of its order that Myers seek counseling for alcohol addiction?

CHAPTER

2

UNAUTHORIZED PRACTICE OF LAW

HYPOTHETICAL

Hamed has just entered a paralegal program and is taking several classes dealing with law. His friend Antonio asks Hamed to help him with a software package Antonio just bought. The software purports to construct living wills and trusts. It came with a workbook and a step-by-step guide, but Antonio says he doesn't understand some of the terminology the program and books are using.

Why Should the Practice of Law Be Limited to Lawyers?

The general rule is that the practice of law is limited to those who are licensed after satisfying certain state requirements of education, moral character, and understanding of the law, as we learned in Chapter 1. This is the rule because licensed lawyers are subject to the profession's disciplinary regulations as set out by each state and have been educated in the law and disciplinary rules. Those people who have not been qualified as

CHAPTER OBJECTIVES

By the end of this chapter, you will know the answers to these questions:

Should the Practice of Law Be Limited to Lawyers?

What Is UPL?

What Does History Say about UPL?

What Do the Modern Rules Say about UPL?

What Is It, Exactly, That Nonlawyers Cannot Do?

What Activities Look Like the Unauthorized Practice of Law But Aren't?

What's So Bad about UPL?

How Do Lawyers Help Others Commit UPL?

How Is Misrepresentation UPL?

How Are UPL Laws Enforced?

lawyers but who, nevertheless, practice law are subject to civil penalties or, in some states, criminal penalties. Just as we don't want people who are not really doctors to practice medicine, we don't want people who are not really lawyers to practice law. You may counter that argument by saying that doctors deal with life and death situations so they should be regulated more carefully because people's lives are at risk. If you think about it, that's true of lawyers, too. The defendant facing the death penalty or life in prison wants (and is entitled to) a lawyer who is educated and trained, has good moral character, and understands the rules of professional conduct.

OK (here comes your next argument), but if I'm the client, shouldn't I have the right to be represented by someone who isn't a lawyer and isn't so expensive? It's true that prohibitions on the practice of law by nonlawyers have been criticized for exactly that reason by both lawyers and lay people. These prohibitions have been challenged on First Amendment, due process, and antitrust theories. They have been called paternalistic and self-serving.[1] People argue that very few of the unauthorized practice of law (UPL) prosecutions and civil cases involve actual injury to a member of the public and that, in many instances, lawyer intervention is much more costly for the public and the service provided is substantially slower. In other words, there is a big part of society (about 85 percent) that needs legal assistance but cannot afford a lawyer.[2] When a member of the public gets good assistance from a nonlawyer who is practicing law in violation of the UPL laws, usually nothing happens. Nothing happens until either someone is harmed or a lawyer finds out and reports the "UPL-er" to the authorities. At the end of this chapter are some cases that address a nonlawyer who repeatedly harmed his "clients," a nonlawyer who didn't seem to be hurting anyone, and an old case about secretarial services (just to illustrate how fervently some states have protected the public from UPL and how long the issue has been around). After reading these cases, you can reach your own conclusion. It is our duty, as legal professionals, to "protect the public." Is the public protected best by restricting the practice of law to lawyers, or would the public be better served another way?

Primary across the boards in UPL regulation are two suppositions: (1) that the public is best served by maintaining the high standards of quality achieved by self-regulation of the legal profession and (2) that only licensed lawyers are subject to regulation under the ethical considerations. Maybe we can poke some holes in those suppositions. Maybe they are old and outdated suppositions that are standing in the way of cost-effective legal representation for everyone who needs it. Maybe, however, they are as correct today as they were when they were created.

> ABA Model Codes Canon 2: A lawyer should assist in preventing the unauthorized practice of law.
>
> * The Model Codes of Professional Responsibility are presented here as a historical reference and are not currently used.

> ABA Model Codes EC 3-1: The prohibition against the practice of law by a layman is grounded in the need of the public for integrity and competence of those who undertake to render legal services. . . .
>
> * The Model Codes of Professional Responsibility are presented here as a historical reference and are not currently used.

What Is UPL?

It seems as though it ought to be a fairly clear concept: lawyers can practice law and others cannot. However, there are differences in opinion on what, exactly, constitutes the practice of law. There are also time-honored exceptions to what ought to be a

A Google search
of the term
*unauthorized
practice of law*
will turn up
thousands of
resources!

ABA Model Code
EC 3-5: It is
neither necessary
nor desirable to
attempt the
formulation of a
single specific
definition of what
constitutes the
practice of law. . . .

* The Model Codes
of Professional
Responsibility are
presented here as
a historical
reference and are
not currently used.

simple and clear-cut rule. There are states that are extending the right to undertake tasks that we used to call "practicing law" to nonlawyers in limited circumstances. It is clear that lawyers themselves cannot meet the ever-expanding need for legal services and solutions need to be created that may involve nonlawyers practicing law. And, here's the fun part, there are conservative and liberal views on what is "good" nonlawyer practice and what is "bad" nonlawyer practice. We talk about each of those concepts, one at a time, in this chapter. After studying this chapter, you'll be able to recognize UPL and have some strategies for spotting and avoiding the bad kind.

If you go back and research UPL in the 1980s and 1990s, you'll find many "experts" loosely using the quote from Justice Potter Stewart's opinion on obscenity: "I don't know what it is but I'll recognize it when I see it."[3] It was popular way back when to say "no one really knows what UPL is" or "we can't define it clearly." But we can define it clearly. We just need to look at it from two different angles: the giving side and the receiving side.

To start with, UPL does have a definition. It is the application of a rule of law to a particular person's fact pattern and giving a response or answer. Here's how that works from the giving side. Sam has been in a car accident. He knows that you have some knowledge of the law so he asks you what his legal rights are. He tells you his facts; you recognize it as a negligence fact pattern; and you tell him your "conclusion": you have a cause of action for negligence against the driver of the other car. If you are a lawyer, you have given legal advice and everything is fine. If you are a bartender, probably everything is still fine, but if you are a paralegal, you've committed UPL. That doesn't seem fair, does it? How come a bartender can give legal advice and get away with it but a paralegal, who presumably knows more about the law (and therefore can give better advice), cannot? The answer lies in the second angle from which we must review the problem: the receiving side. When Sam asks a lawyer about his car accident, he is clearly looking for legal advice. When he asks the bartender, he is not looking for a legal opinion. But when he asks the paralegal, what is he asking for? There's the second angle for our UPL definition: the receiving side asks what is the person (or is it a "client"?) asking for?

UPL occurs when the person is seeking legal advice from a person who he knows has legal knowledge but who is not a lawyer. Here's our rule again: The practice of law is the application of a rule of law to a particular person's fact pattern and giving a response or answer. Notice that it has three parts: (1) application of law (2) to a person's fact pattern and (3) giving an answer.

Let's take another example: Antonio entered the United States on a student visa. His education has come to a conclusion, but he would like to stay and gain his U.S. citizenship. When he asks his priest for advice, he is told that his J visa can be swapped for a permanent visa and then changed into citizenship by filing a CS56 form. Alternatively, the priest says, the fastest way to gain citizenship is to marry a U.S. citizen. Has the priest committed UPL? The liberal side of the fence would say no. Antonio didn't go to the good father for legal advice but more likely for spiritual advice and support and perhaps because the priest is wise and well respected. The district attorney isn't going to arrest the priest for UPL. But if Antonio goes to the ABC Immigration Clinic where everyone who works there is a nonlawyer, he goes there for the express purpose of getting legal advice. When one of the employees (Claudia) applies her knowledge of the law to Antonio's facts and tells him that he should file a CS56 form, Claudia has committed UPL. The fact that the priest's advice was free and Claudia's advice cost $1,000 may or may not have anything to do with the criminal prosecution of the case, but it definitely doesn't have anything to do with the advice being UPL. (There is an exception to this we discuss later specifically to do with immigration law.) Antonio goes to Claudia for legal advice. Claudia takes Antonio's facts, applies her knowledge of the law to those facts, and gives Antonio a conclusion. Claudia is not a lawyer. Voila! UPL.

What Does History Say about UPL?

The activities that constitute the unauthorized practice of law are subject to the interpretation of each state. Unfortunately, therefore, there is no universal standard and as our society needs more legal advice and more people can't afford it, the line we thought would be clear keeps getting fuzzier. Most states provide no clear definition; others, on a case-by-case basis, have laid the foundation for some common themes. Historically, among the circumstances considered by the courts in determining if there has been unauthorized practice are whether an unlicensed person is engaged in an activity that

- is one traditionally practiced by lawyers;[4]
- is one "commonly understood" to involve the practice of law;[5]
- requires legal skill or knowledge beyond that of a layperson;[6]
- is characterized by the personal relationship between lawyer and client;[7] or
- is such that the public interest is best served by limiting performance to those who are lawyers.[8]

When you read the cases, then, these are the themes you will see. Now you know why people typically said they didn't know what UPL was. The rules used by the courts don't look very bright-line.

What Do the Modern Rules Say about UPL?

The rules of professional conduct of most states don't brighten the line.

Rule 5.5
A lawyer shall not: (a) practice in a jurisdiction where doing so violates the regulation of the legal profession in that jurisdiction; or (b) assist a person who is not a member of the bar in the performance of activity that constitutes the unauthorized practice of law.

* Full Model Rule and commentary can be found in Appendix E.

Note that this rule has two parts: it is improper to practice law without a license, and it is improper to assist another in doing so. Remember that the Model Rules are rules for lawyers. The rule is telling them not to practice law in any jurisdiction where they can't practice law. When would that happen? Typically, it happens when the lawyer licensed in State A practices law in State B. Unless the lawyer gets permission from a State B court to practice before it, the lawyer is committing UPL. This rule also addresses another problem: the suspended or disbarred lawyer. If the lawyer was licensed in State A but has been suspended or disbarred, the lawyer cannot practice law in State A and to do so constitutes UPL.

The (b) section of Rule 5.5 is an admonition to lawyers to not help others practice law if they are not licensed. Lawyers do that in all sorts of interesting ways, which we cover in this chapter. But section (b) tells us not to do an activity that is UPL, but doesn't tell us what that is.

> NFPA Model Code EC 1.8(a) A paralegal shall comply with the applicable legal authority governing the unauthorized practice of law in the jurisdiction in which the paralegal practices.

Recognizing that the law on the unauthorized practice of law is changing continually and is different in every jurisdiction, the NFPA Model Code admonishes only that each paralegal is responsible for complying with legal authority governing the unauthorized practice of law in his or her jurisdiction. NALA's Model Standards has a very complete discussion of that association's stance on UPL. NALA's position on UPL is more strict than that of NFPA because of the difference in their definitions of what a paralegal is. NALA's view is that paralegals or legal assistants are "a distinguishable group of persons who *assist attorneys in the delivery of legal services*." Under the NALA definition, then, you are only a paralegal if you are assisting a lawyer. This is in contrast to NFPA's definition of a paralegal:

> . . . a person qualified through education, training, or work experience to perform substantive legal work that requires knowledge of legal concepts and is customarily, but not exclusively performed by a lawyer. *This person may be retained or employed by a lawyer, law office, governmental agency or other entity or may be authorized by administrative, statutory or court authority to perform this work.*

The NFPA definition leaves room for what was once called a "legal technician" (i.e., a nonlawyer who delivers legal services directly to the public) because it does not require that the legal work be performed at the behest of a lawyer. If it were legal for a nonlawyer to represent, for example, a landlord in uncontested evictions, then performing such representative acts would not be the "unauthorized" practice of law. Under the NALA definition, a nonlawyer could not perform such a task unless supervised by a lawyer; but under the NFPA definition, a nonlawyer could. Consider that one of the reasons that a nonlawyer might be permitted to "practice law" in limited areas is to minimize the cost of the representation. (We see an example of this in the cases at the end of this chapter.) If the nonlawyer must be supervised by a lawyer, the cost necessarily increases.[9] Later in this chapter, we see that several states have authorized nonlawyers to do certain sorts of tasks that were traditionally restricted to lawyers. These people are no longer called "legal technicians," but the concept is the same.

NFPA rule 1.8(a) is intentionally broad to accommodate the changing state laws on who can do what legal tasks directly with the public. We'll see that states have their conservative or liberal views on this issue, too.

What Is It, Exactly, That Nonlawyers Cannot Do?

The unauthorized practice of law is one of the greatest concerns to those in the paralegal field. They don't have to concern us, however, when we understand what UPL is and how we can avoid it. Nonlawyers potentially practice law when they:

1. give legal advice
2. create legal documents for others
3. represent others in court

Giving legal advice, as we discussed above, is the application of a rule of law to a specific person's fact pattern and giving an opinion or conclusion. If you do that and you are not a lawyer, you commit UPL. The same application can be made to the creation of legal documents. If we are not lawyers, we cannot apply our knowledge of the law to a person's facts and create a document for another person. And representing others in court seems pretty self-explanatory. So, that's what we can't do.

Now we'll discuss some exceptions and the other three areas of concern in UPL: (1) lawyers aiding the unauthorized practice of law, (2) the responsibility of lawyers for their nonlawyer personnel, and (3) misrepresentations by nonlawyers as to their status. The ABA Model Rules, state and federal laws, a tradition of case-by-case determination, and the various state bar associations' opinions all contribute to the diverse points of view on all three areas.

What Activities Look Like the Unauthorized Practice of Law But Aren't?

There are, of course, exceptions to the prohibition on the practice of law by nonlawyers; and, because determinations in this area have been made on an *ad hoc,* case-by-case basis, the exceptions vary greatly among the jurisdictions. There are, however, common themes and exceptions established as a matter of constitutional right that are universally recognized by the states. These exceptions permit self-representation; law student practice, especially in the area of indigent representation; lay participation in certain administrative proceedings; and lay participation in the exercise of federally protected rights.

- *Self-representation.* The right of self-representation in federal courts is codified in 28 U.S.C. Section 1654:

  In all courts of the United States the parties may plead and conduct their own cases personally or by counsel as, by the rules of such courts, respectively, are permitted to manage and conduct causes therein.

  Faretta v. California[10] brought the right of self-representation to the states when it was upheld by the Supreme Court as a constitutional right in criminal cases.

- *Law students.* The California Supreme Court held in 1979 that valuable practical training and increasing the availability of legal services for indigent people were strong enough reasons to permit "limited practice of law" by law students, providing they are properly supervised.[11] Of course, the states vary immensely as to in what area and under what circumstances law students may practice law. All states that allow law students to represent others, however, include adequate supervision caveats, permit appearances at special administrative hearings and preparation of legal documents, set specifications as to the educational background of the student, and provide for the student's proper introduction to the court.

- *Administrative agencies.* An overwhelming majority of federal agencies permit lay representation.[12] The National Labor Relations Board and other administrative bodies allow any layperson to represent others before them, while other agencies, such as the Patent Office and the ICC, require specific educational qualifications and the passing of an examination. With regard to state administrative agencies, however, there is a great deal of inconsistency. Some state courts have even ruled that the state legislature has no power to authorize practice before agencies created by the legislature. Others have followed the Florida ruling in *Florida Bar v. Moses*[13] that held that the legislature and the judiciary have concurrent authority in this area and either may make such rules to assist the public in attaining adequate representation.

But the states have no authority to say who can represent others before federal agencies. In *Sperry v. Florida,*[14] the U.S. Supreme Court held that the Supremacy Clause of the Constitution answers that question clearly.[15] Likewise, the U.S. Supreme Court held in *Johnson v. Avery* that the states could not interfere if the lay representation was the only alternative to protect federally guaranteed rights. As previously discussed, the Supreme Court held that in the preparation of various petitions for post-conviction relief, inmates were allowed to furnish assistance to other inmates who were poorly educated and unable to retain counsel.

Some examples of federal law allowing nonlawyer representation are:

Small Business Administration (13 C.F.R. 121.11, 134.16)

National Credit Union Administration (12 C.F.R. 747)

Federal Energy Regulatory Commission (18 C.F.R. 385.2101)

Drug Enforcement Administration (21 C.F.R. 1316.50)

Aid to Families with Dependent Children (45 C.F.R. 205)

Food and Drug Administration (32 C.F.R. 12.40, 12.45)

Comptroller of the Currency (12 C.F.R. 19.3)

Immigration and Naturalization Service (8 C.F.R. 292.1–3)

Environmental Protection Agency (40 C.F.R. 124, 164.30, 22.10)

—just to name a few.

The "Incidental To" Rule

There are those activities that are *incidental to activities* typically conducted by nonlawyers that are not considered the unauthorized practice of law.[16] Here's our rule: activities performed by lay people in the course of business that would ordinarily be considered the practice of law but are *incidental to* functions properly performed by them are exempt from UPL prohibitions. Examples of these "incidental to activities" are:

1. preparation of instruments by title companies and real estate brokers,[17]
2. estate planning by banks and insurance agencies,[18]
3. debt collection by commercial agencies,[19] and
4. tax practice by accountancy agencies.[20]

Let's think about calling your accountant about that $20,000 check your Aunt Minnie left you. The accountant says to you, "You should put that in a ten-year CD because then it would be double tax free." You don't have a clue what "double tax free" means so you ask. The accountant goes on to explain that while your money is invested in the certificate of deposit you don't have to pay federal or state taxes on it. Sounds like tax advice, right? And tax advice sounds like the practice of law, right? So why isn't that UPL? Because your accountant is in the business of accounting. Giving you that little tiny bit of tax advice is *incidental to* the business of accounting. Therefore, we're not going to call it UPL. The same is true in some states of the legal documents real estate and escrow companies prepare for the purchase and sale of a house. Yes, they prepare legal documents, but the law usually lets them do that as incidental to the real estate business. (The operative word here is *usually*. Some states do not allow this practice.) And you should not think that these categories are otherwise cast in stone. Like all of UPL, there is an ebb and flow of law. Cases and statutory changes can amend the legality of these *incidental to* activities at any time. Try thinking of UPL as a pendulum.

What Is Definitely Not UPL Because There Is No "Giving Legal Advice"?

For a Kentucky Bar Association opinion on the "conduit" theory, see KBA U-47, which you can find through the University of Kentucky College of Law's Web site: http://www.uky.edu.

Working in the field of law requires common sense. A common sense approach to UPL will prevent you from becoming paralyzed by the fear of violating one of what seems to be an infinite list of rules. In the traditional law office setting, you will often hear a lawyer say to a paralegal: "Call Client X and tell her. . . ." Even if the paralegal is instructed to give Client X what would technically be called "legal advice," that the advice is relayed by the paralegal does not mean that it is UPL. The paralegal is simply acting as a conduit of the legal advice from the lawyer to the client, just as if the lawyer had written the advice in a letter and sent it to the client. The *conduit theory,* then, covers most instances of the paralegal giving legal advice to the client. Ordinarily, the paralegal has been instructed in what to say.

Here's where it gets more interesting. What if the paralegal has been instructed in what to say to one client in one circumstance and would now like to give that same advice to a different client in a similar circumstance? Here the line begins to blur. In certain circumstances, it may be perfectly all right to give the advice to the client and in others it may not. In yet other circumstances, it may be acceptable to say, "This is what I think the answer is, but I'm going to check with a lawyer and if the answer isn't right, I'll call you back." In that way, the client has gotten a more immediate answer, you have been helpful, and you are going to discuss the question with that conduit lawyer so that you can verify your answer. This is a situation in which it would be nice to know if you are in a UPL-conservative state or a UPL-liberal state.

What about Secretarial or Typing Services?

The secretarial/typing services debate starts with *Florida Bar v. Brumbaugh*,[21] but the more famous story is the case of Rosemary Furman, which you will find at the end of this chapter. In the 1970s, not everyone had a way to type forms. At that time, many laypeople had to go to a typing service where a nominal fee could be paid to have a professional typist or secretary type the form and get all of the information you provide into the correct spaces. That all seems like very long ago and a little quaint right now when anyone who doesn't have a computer can find one in a public library.

So, it has long been the case that secretarial services can sell printed materials, forms, and samples and type the forms for people from written information provided by clients. They may not, however, advise how best to fill out the forms or assist in filling them out. They may not "correct" what they believe to be errors by the customer. They also may not use the word "paralegal" in their advertising material, as that may mislead reasonable laypeople into believing that they are permitted to provide legal assistance.[22] Rosemary Furman went to jail in the 1980s standing up for her right to assist people with their legal forms.[23]

In Florida recently, the court issued an injunction against a We The People outpost after finding that its members provided customers with legal assistance in the selection, preparation, and completion of legal forms; they corrected customers' errors in those forms; they corresponded with opposing parties as the representative of the customer in some instances; and they hired a lawyer to provide legal advice to some customers.[24] We the People then hired a lawyer to give its customers legal advice. The question that comes to mind is, if the lawyer was paid a salary by We The People, how did he supervise its members' work?

The State of Connecticut shut down an organization called Doc-U-Prep.[25] The defendant in that case gave customers a form to fill out. He typed up the completed form and sent it to the Doc-U-Prep headquarters in Massachusetts. That organization completed the forms with the information provided, made them look

The American Pro Se Association (http://www.legalhelp.org) provides detailed instructions on how to file and answer complaints and counterclaims, serve a summons, and make legal motions.

A site called FreeAdvice.com (http://www.freeadvice.com) provides answers to thousands of commonly asked questions on legal topics ranging from accidents to bankruptcy, business, employment, estate planning, family law, immigration, insurance, intellectual property, litigation, real estate, and tax.

The Pro Se Law Center (http://www.pro-selaw.org) provides lists and links to legal software, legal information, and training sites, as well as legal aid programs.

official, and returned the completed documents to the defendant who delivered them to the customers. All of the legal forms were for uncontested matters such as a will, corporation, or name change but included Chapter 7 bankruptcy, a subject in which many legal technicians practice as Bankruptcy Petition Preparers (BPPs). The court shut down this newfangled typing service holding that "prohibiting unsupervised paralegals from work with legal consequences is rationally related to public protection."

Are Kits and Books UPL?

Most courts apply the "personal relationship between attorney and client" test to books such as *How to Avoid Probate* and kits like the "Divorce Yourself Kit." The consensus of the courts is that such kits are not the unauthorized practice of law so long as they are sold to the general public and the seller does not answer questions relating to specific individuals. In New York, in the case of *State v. Winder*,[26] it was held that the so-called "Divorce Yourself Kit" did not represent the unauthorized practice of law in spite of the fact that the inventor and distributor of the kit was not a lawyer. The court specifically held that the essential element of legal practice was the representing and advising of a particular person in a particular situation—a concept that looks strikingly similar to the definition we started with at the beginning of this chapter! Since kits, at most, offer only general advice on common problems for simple divorces, they cannot constitute the unauthorized practice of law. But, as the court pointed out, selling a kit doesn't mean there isn't UPL involved. If the defendant was giving legal advice to specific individuals in conjunction with the sale of the kit, he was committing UPL. And, in fact, companies selling a kit and personal legal services have been shut down by law enforcement agencies, such as the Doc-U-Prep company discussed earlier. Another example is a "trust mill" in California that was closed in 1997 after a state bar investigation revealed that nonlawyers were selling living trust "packages" on behalf of a lawyer. The sales agents used a sample living trust that they promised to customize for each purchaser.[27]

The State of Texas unsuccessfully tried to shut down the sale of Nolo Press books under the UPL regulations of that state.[28] The Texas UPL Committee started by writing a letter to NOLO Press (based in California) asking it to stop selling the book *How to Do Your Own Divorce* in Texas. The problem was only exacerbated by the Internet. Could the State of Texas prohibit a state resident from buying the book through Amazon.com? Apparently not. And in *Unauthorized Practice of Law Committee v. Parsons Technology Inc.*,[29] the State Bar of Texas convinced a federal court to enjoin the sale of Quicken Family Lawyer '99. The software manufacturer, which also produces other financial self-help programs such as Turbo Tax, appealed the decision. Quicken Family Lawyer contains more than one hundred legal forms, from real estate leases to employment contracts to prenuptial agreements, with instructions on how to fill out and execute these legal documents. The program is interactive as it "interviews" the user to determine which state's laws apply and proceeds with a series of questions needed to select the "right" form and complete the blank spaces. The federal court vacated its decision six months later after Texas amended its UPL regulations so that selling software is not illegal.[30]

NOLO Press has a motto on its Internet site: Legal Information Is Not Legal Advice. What do you think?

What Is the Deal with Corporations?

Corporations present a special problem because they are not "persons" as we traditionally think of them. Therefore, corporations cannot utilize the right of self-representation. Most states agree that a corporation must be represented by a lawyer in a court of law but that nonlawyers can represent them in administrative proceedings.[31] Some states permit nonlawyer employees to represent a corporation in small claims court because small claims court is a place where nonlawyers should be litigating, not lawyers.[32]

In a Florida Bar Advisory Opinion,[33] Florida, traditionally very hard on UPL offenders, opined that a nonlawyer property manager could represent the individual or corporate landlord in uncontested residential evictions, so long as the authority was given to the property manager in writing and the action did not involve a judgment for past rent. And then there's the *Pearlman* case at the end of this chapter for more on this issue.

Paralegals working in corporations face interesting UPL problems when they are not working under the supervision of lawyers. It is commonplace to see a corporate legal department staffed solely with paralegals. When the corporate paralegal is asked for legal advice by someone in the corporation, does she commit UPL when she responds? The answer is, maybe, depending upon the nature of the question. An employee of a corporation doesn't really have a "client" in the typical sense of the word—just other employees. If we liken this paralegal's position to that of the typical personnel manager, who is often called upon to answer legal questions regarding personnel issues, then it is not UPL; the answer to the legal question is *incidental to* the person's primary job. If the corporate paralegal's primary job is coordinating outside legal counsel, when the paralegal is asked, "What do you advise we do in the Brown case?" by a corporate officer, the paralegal's response, "Take Mr. Brown's deposition," is not necessarily UPL. To commit UPL, the offender has to have a client. In the case of the corporation that employs this paralegal, who's the client? The other concern regarding corporate employees practicing law without a license is that this sort of in-house advice is not made public. If it's not public, how would the UPL authorities find out about it?

Is Just Asking the Court for a Continuance UPL?

In *People v. Alexander*,[34] a law clerk appeared in court on two occasions to advise the court that the lawyer who employed him was engaged in another trial, that this lawyer could not get away, and that the case at bar had not yet been settled. The Illinois trial court held that the clerk's actions in court constituted the unauthorized practice of law even though he had done nothing other than report fact. The appellate court reversed the decision of the trial court, saying:

> We agree with the trial judge that clerks should not be permitted to make motions—or participate in other proceedings which can be considered as "managing" the litigation. However, if apprising the court of an employer's engagement or inability to be present constitutes the making of a motion, we must hold that clerks may make such motions for continuances without being guilty of the unauthorized practice of law. Certainly with the large volume of cases appearing on the trial calls these days, it is imperative that this practice be allowed.

This topic—the "Is asking the court for a continuance UPL?" topic—is a great one for class debate and has been for many years. In this day of technology, however, the practical application of your answer to this tough question seems remote. Now, even the busiest of us can e-mail the court clerk on our Blackberry or call on our cell phone. There will likely never be a need for a paralegal to ask the court for a continuance in a personal appearance; so if you can't decide if it's UPL or not, not to worry.

What's So Bad about UPL, Anyway?

The plain, unadulterated fact is that the public is often harmed by UPL. *In re McCarthy*[35] is a good illustration of the consequences of the potential harm UPL causes to the public in a bankruptcy setting. In that case, a nonlawyer calling himself a paralegal and typing service incorrectly listed a secured loan as unsecured. The company that made the loan to the debtor made a motion to set aside her bankruptcy filing and foreclose on its collateral (household furnishings). The paralegal filed responsive pleadings to the company's motion to dismiss. When he later made the argument that he was just a service that helped people fill out forms, the court didn't agree. He had filed responsive papers that contained statutory and case authority. In addition to making a mistake on the bankruptcy filing, he dug himself in deeper when he tried to defend his client from the loan company. That "fresh start" the debtor was looking for with her bankruptcy filing turned into a nightmare. As *McCarthy* illustrates, nonlawyer representation can and does result in a great financial loss to the customer. Obviously, both lawyers and nonlawyers can make mistakes that ultimately harm the client. The differences are: (1) lawyers have the authority to correct the error; (2) lawyers can be sued for professional negligence whereas most nonlawyers cannot; and (3) where there is a pattern of below-standard legal work, lawyers may be subject to discipline but nonlawyers are exempt from state bar disciplinary actions.

In an effort to get assistance to people who need it but cannot afford a lawyer, California enacted two sets of regulations in the 1990s, one addressing unlawful detainers (eviction) defense and the other for other types of self-help matters such as simple wills, living trusts, and so on. Both of these allow non-lawyers to be registered with the state and help people fill out forms so they can represent themselves. Both require the posting of a substantial bond. The purpose of the bond here is twofold: to only register the serious people, the bond being a method for winnowing out the fly-by-nights, and to provide a source for recompense in the event a customer was harmed. The statute tries to cover the UPL problem in two ways: the registration of both the Unlawful Detainer Assistants and the Legal Document Assistants can be revoked if they are found to be incompetent to perform the services they are hired to perform, and the bond can be taken to recompense anyone who is harmed by their services. A copy of the statutory authority is provided for you on the publisher's Web site. California's regulatory choice was registration under the auspices of the Department of Consumer Affairs.

So, if in fact the rationale for the prohibition against nonlawyer practice of law is, as it says in the ABA Model Code, "grounded in the need of the public for integrity and competence of those who undertake to render legal services" then if we can address those two issues for nonlawyers, we won't need to have a license to practice law.

But, all states have their viewpoints on what nonlawyers can do without crossing the UPL line. One that is fairly easy to research is in the area of residential real estate closings. Can a nonlawyer supervise a residential real estate closing in your state, or is a lawyer needed to oversee the execution of documents and disbursement of any proceeds?

How Do Lawyers Help Others Commit UPL?

Lawyers can violate the regulations that prohibit their aiding the unauthorized practice of law

1. by improperly supervising their employees and associates (including improper delegation),
2. by entering into an improper business relationship with a nonlawyer (including splitting fees), or
3. by allowing (or helping) a nonlawyer to misrepresent the nonlawyer status.

ABA Model Rule 5.3 says that the lawyer must make reasonable efforts to ensure that nonlawyer staff members obey the rules of ethics. We don't know exactly what "reasonable efforts" are because it is one of those standards that evolves over time through case law, like so many of our professional responsibility standards.

How Is Improper Supervision UPL?

A lawyer can unknowingly "aid" a paralegal in committing UPL by not properly supervising the paralegal. For example, if you are asked to write responses to interrogatories and your draft is never reviewed by a lawyer, the lawyer who failed to review your work just helped you commit UPL. For a story of failure to supervise taken to an extreme, read *In re Schelly*.[36] Granted, this case is not about a paralegal. It's about a lawyer employing a disbarred lawyer as a law clerk. Even so, it is illustrative. Schelly, even after having been repeatedly disciplined by the bar and the court for allowing this disbarred-lawyer-now-law-clerk to practice law, continued to employ the clerk; and the clerk continued to try cases when Schelly instructed him to only ask the court for continuances. Finally, Schelly was charged with aiding his employee in the unauthorized practice of law and failure to supervise and convicted him of not restricting or supervising his law clerk.

It's not just supervising legal work that can cause improper supervision type of UPL. In a case from Ohio,[37] the supreme court suspended a lawyer for improper supervision of his paralegal when it was discovered that she had stolen in excess of $200,000 from estate and guardianship accounts during a ten-year period. If the lawyer had been properly supervising the paralegal, it is logical to assume that he would have noticed her thievery more immediately.

Here's one more, from New Mexico, where the lawyer was disciplined for failure to supervise his paralegal. In that case, the court found that the paralegal's failure to identify himself as a nonlawyer, quoting legal fees, and cashing a settlement check payable to the client with no supporting documentation were all improper conduct but the court had no jurisdiction to discipline the paralegal. Instead, the court imputed all of the paralegal's bad acts to the lawyer. The lawyer's failure to identify his assistant as a nonlawyer was the lawyer's improper conduct, and all of the other improper conduct of the paralegal was imputed to the lawyer by virtue of the lawyer's duty to ensure that the conduct of his assistant comported with the lawyer's own professional obligations.[38]

And Improper Delegation Is UPL, Too?

NALS Code of Ethics Canon 8: Members of this association, unless permitted by law, shall not perform any of the duties restricted to lawyers or do things which lawyers themselves may not do and shall assist in preventing the unauthorized practice of law.

We all know that a lawyer may delegate work that does not require the exercise of lawyerly judgment to paralegals. Tasks that require giving legal advice (other than conveying information received from the lawyer), representing clients in courts, or signing legal documents may not be delegated because these tasks are reserved to lawyers.

What this means from a practical standpoint is that it is often the nonlawyer's responsibility to say "no" to a lawyer who tries to delegate an improper task. For example, while it may be acceptable for a lawyer to instruct his paralegal to sign the lawyer's name to an enclosure letter, it is not acceptable for him to ask the paralegal to sign his name to a pleading. As another example, it is an accepted practice to send a paralegal to a deposition to take notes and observe in place of a lawyer, but it would be UPL for the lawyer to send the paralegal to ask questions of the deponent. Proper delegation enables the legal profession to bring legal services to the public more economically and efficiently. Improper delegation can be UPL.

ABA Model Rule 5.4(b)
A lawyer shall not form a partnership with a nonlawyer if any of the activities of the partnership consist of the practice of law.
* Full Model Rule and commentary can be found in Appendix E.

How Is an Improper Business Relationship UPL?

ABA Model Rule 5.4 prohibits lawyers and nonlawyers from being in business together if any part of that business will be the practice of law. Historically, this was to prevent a nonlawyer from having any say about the outcome of a legal matter. Give this a thought. If a nonlawyer was funding a venture that was the practice of law, wouldn't that nonlawyer want some authority over decisions affecting the financial well-being of the company? And couldn't those decisions have to do with how long a case is litigated?

This rule and the rules on lawyers and nonlawyers not sharing fees are subject to criticism by those organizations that are trying to make access to the judicial system more affordable. To that end, in 1990, the District of Columbia modified the ABA version of Rule 5.4 to allow partnerships between lawyers and nonlawyers.

District of Columbia Rule 5.4 states that a lawyer may practice law in a partnership or other form of organization in which a financial interest is held or managerial authority is exercised by an individual nonlawyer who performs professional services that assist the organization in providing legal services to clients but only if

Model Rule 5.4(c)
A lawyer shall not permit a person who recommends, employs, or pays the lawyer to render legal services for another to direct or regulate the lawyer's professional judgment in rendering such legal services.
* Full Model Rule and commentary can be found in Appendix E.

1. the partnership or organization has as its sole purpose providing legal services to clients;
2. all persons having such managerial authority or holding a financial interest undertake to abide by these Rules of Professional Conduct;
3. the lawyers who have a financial interest or managerial authority in the partnership or organization undertake to be responsible for the nonlawyer participants to the same extent as if nonlawyer participants were lawyers under Rule 5.1; and
4. the foregoing conditions are set forth in writing.

This arrangement allows the lawyer and paralegal to pool their resources to start a law firm. It also allows the paralegal to work with, not for, the lawyer. This relationship will benefit the public by making the judicial system more attainable.

What Is an Improper Division of Fees and How Is It UPL?

Repeat after me: Fee splitting is evil and I'll never do it. Here's the reason: Legal decisions are supposed to be made by lawyers. This is traditionally said to be true because lawyers are "trained in the law and bound by the rules of professional responsibility." If a nonlawyer has the opportunity to be paid part of the fee from a case, he might be tempted to solicit clients or engage in UPL. Paying a paralegal a percentage of legal fees is "fee splitting." Think about it. If you knew you were going to get a third of all of the fees generated by a new client, wouldn't you be tempted to solicit clients?

ABA Model Code DR

3-102: A lawyer shall not share legal fees with a non-lawyer.

* The Model Code of Professional Responsibility are presented here as a historical reference and are not currently used.

ABA Model Rules 5.4(a)(3): A lawyer or law firm shall not share legal fees with a nonlawyer, except that a lawyer or law firm may include nonlawyer employees in a compensation or retirement plan, even though the plan is based in whole or in part on a profit-sharing arrangement.

* Full Model Rule and commentary can be found in Appendix E.

Now would be a good time to look at your state's Rule 5.4 on fee splitting. The subtitle of that rule is about the professional independence of a lawyer. Lawyers should be making decisions about clients for clients. Nonlawyers should not be making those decisions. Again, this is said to be because lawyers are "educated in the law and governed by the rules of professional conduct of the state." Again, give this a little thought. If you knew that you were entitled to a third of whatever fees were generated by some case, wouldn't you be tempted to run those fees up or advise against settling so that more litigation fees could be generated? Well, you probably wouldn't, but some unscrupulous person would. That's the one we make these laws for.

The law that says fee splitting is bad doesn't say that the paralegal is not allowed to receive a bonus. A bonus, whether annual or not, doesn't constitute "sharing fees" so long as it is not based on a percentage of law firm profits or on a percentage of particular legal fees. It also doesn't include those "profit-sharing" plans such as 401Ks or other compensation or retirement plans so long as the amount of money doesn't appear to be tied to one case. So splitting annual profit is okay, but splitting the profit from one case is not.

The good news for the paralegal is that some courts have found that fee-splitting agreements are illegal for the lawyer only. In the 1993 Texas case of *Atkins v. Tinning*,[39] the court awarded the nonlawyer his share under the fee-splitting agreement and disciplined the lawyer. An interesting contrast is that illegal referral fees are ordinarily held to be illegal for both parties and will therefore not be enforced by the court.[40] We discuss referral fees in Chapter 6.

So, the bottom line is this: Many law firms reward employees who bring cases into the office with a percentage of the legal fees eventually paid to the firm on those cases. Such arrangements are illegal fee-splitting agreements. They are evil. We all pledged never to split a fee at the beginning of this section.

What about Multidisciplinary Practices? Don't They Split Fees?

A *multidisciplinary practice* is a partnership, professional corporation, or other association that includes lawyers and nonlawyers and that provides both legal and nonlegal services. At present, the ethics and unauthorized practice of law rules in every state except the District of Columbia forbid lawyers from sharing fees or entering partnerships with nonlawyers. But doesn't it make a lot of sense to have a company that has accountants and lawyers? Wouldn't that save time and money for the client who could tell his story once and get all of the legal and accountancy help he needs? The estate-planning lawyer who wants to accept a job with a financial-planning company and render legal advice to the clients of the financial-planning company will find himself at odds with the state bar with every state in the union but perhaps not in the District of Columbia. At this writing, however, many states are taking a look at this time-honored but perhaps outdated prohibition against multidisciplinary practices.

Those states that have taken steps to regulate the activities of paralegals have taken great interest in ensuring that nonlawyers will not be mistaken for lawyers. In order to protect the public from innocent mistakes regarding the identity of paralegals and those tasks they may perform, several states have made regulations pertaining to the image projected by nonlawyers. States differ in listing lay personnel on letterhead, business cards, telephone directories, and the like. The supervising lawyer will ultimately be responsible for errors, but here are some general guidelines. Again, it is always important to check your state law on these rules.

- Paralegals have responsibility for identifying themselves as nonlawyers. Lawyers do not have any obligation to tell people they are lawyers. Nonlawyers, on the other hand, have an absolute duty to identify themselves appropriately and to correct any misunderstandings about their title, their authority, and what questions they can or cannot answer. Whenever you meet with someone from outside of your firm or company, introduce yourself as a paralegal to ensure that the person knows you are not a lawyer.[41]

- Paralegals can have business cards identifying them as being employed by a law firm or other entity but, again, the card must identify them as a paralegal or legal assistant. Make sure that your business card does not imply that you are an "associate" with the firm.

- Most states allow paralegals to sign correspondence to clients on firm stationery when the letter contains no legal advice and when the letter is a standard one. Your designation or title should always follow your name. One proper method for signing a letter is:

    Very truly yours,

    R.P. Jones
    Paralegal

- Paralegals can be listed on letterhead stationery in some jurisdictions when accompanied by the paralegal designation.

- Paralegal names cannot be listed on the door of the office or in advertisements for the firm in most states. Most jurisdictions agree that this would tend to mislead the public. Just as the designation "Paralegal" should follow your name on a business card, it should follow your name on the sign outside your door. Think about walking down the hallway of a law firm. If some signs have names and "Attorney" and other signs just have names, would the average person be confused about who is a lawyer and who is not? What if all of the signs just had names and no titles?

How Are UPL Laws Enforced?

> *Quo warranto* is Latin for "by what authority." The writ asks "by what authority are you practicing law" and asks for the "cease and desist" remedy.

Injunction, criminal prosecution, citation for contempt of court, and writs of *quo warranto* are the most widely used methods of enforcement of the unauthorized practice regulations. Nearly all jurisdictions have misdemeanor statutes, although most people think that injunctive relief is the most effective method for stopping the offender. Some states have increased the level of UPL to felony to show how serious they are about clamping down on illegal practices. For example, in 1999, Nevada enacted law increasing the penalty for UPL and restricting the work paralegals and legal assistants can perform that is not "under the supervision of an attorney."

Who is in charge of initiating the proceeding for an injunction? Many states allow suits by the integrated bar. Those states that allow class actions by lawyers require a showing of irreparable injury or some proof that the lawyers represent the public interest. Lawsuits that have been attempted to prevent the unauthorized practice of law on the theory that lawyers have the exclusive right to practice law and, therefore, the right to be protected from competition from unlicensed people are steeped in antitrust problems. This theory, furthermore, does not consider that the prohibition on the unauthorized practice of law is to *protect the public* from incompetent representation, not to protect lawyers from competition.

Criminal contempt citations have been called an overreaction to a trivial problem, but they are, nevertheless, common. Where the alleged UPL is closely connected to the court or a pending case, a direct citation can be issued by the court on its own motion. For those activities that occur without the court's knowledge, an indirect citation may be sought by the state attorney general, a bar association, or an individual lawyer by a petition to the court.

Quo warranto writs are used to restrain corporations from exceeding their chartered purposes. This action is brought by the attorney general on behalf of the public to prevent corporations from practicing law incident to their primary purpose or business. An example of this is a situation in which the attorney general seeks to prevent real estate brokers from giving legal advice or filling out certain real estate documents for their customers as part of their ordinary business.

There are other ways to prevent or stop the unauthorized practice of law found in negligence, *Biakanja v. Irving*,[42] and in contract, *Divine v. Watauga Hospital*.[43] In *Estate of Drischler*,[44] a Pennsylvania court held that lawyers who were inactive bar members (because of their failure to pay dues) committed a misdemeanor by holding themselves out as entitled to practice law and the court denied Drischler recovery for the legal services he performed. More recently is the case of *Birbower*,[45] a law firm not licensed in California but that provided legal services in California for a California company. When the company refused to pay the legal fees, the law firm sued. It was denied fees on the grounds that its lawyers were not licensed to practice in California and therefore committed UPL.

SUMMARY

In Chapter 1, we talked about the "what" of lawyers and paralegals. In this chapter, we have explored the "why" and "how" of limiting the practice of law to licensed lawyers. We have also looked at the various forms of unauthorized practice of law. To figure out what UPL is, the first step is to define as closely as possible "practice of law." It is the application of a rule of law to a particular person's fact pattern and giving a response or opinion, whether orally or in the form of a document. We learned that we need to look at those elements from both the point of view of the person asking for legal advice and the point of view of the person giving the advice. We took a short walk down UPL memory lane with Rosemary Furman, and we looked at what the rules of professional conduct say about UPL. We discussed typing services, people who are not lawyers but are authorized to help people with their legal problems, and how books and computer software don't commit UPL. We learned that lawyers can help others commit UPL by improperly delegating and supervising work and by splitting fees or having an improper business relationship with someone who is not. We also know now that if we misrepresent ourselves or our status to others, it is just like committing UPL.

As paralegals, we are not going to be paralyzed by UPL regulations. Now that we know what UPL is and how to avoid it, we will be able to service clients, get the job done, and stay within the bounds of the law.

CHAPTER REVIEW AND ASSIGNMENTS

CRITICAL THINKING

1. Let's go back to Hamed, the paralegal in the Hypothetical at the beginning of this chapter. Can he explain legal terminology to his friend without committing UPL? Can he help his friend answer the questions posed in the workbook and by the software? To aid you in your answer, take a look at *In re Gaftick*, 333 B.R. 177 (Bankr. E.D.N.Y. 2005).

2. Lawyers typically take at least 33 percent of a personal injury judgment. You think that's outrageous, so you want to start a business whereby you act as a go-between for people who have been in car accidents. You get a power of attorney from each client that authorizes you to negotiate on his or her behalf with the insurance company. Together, you and your client agree on a reasonable amount of damages. You write letters and speak on the telephone with employees of insurance companies. Settlement checks are made out to you. You take only 10 percent and give the rest to the client. If the insurer and client cannot agree, you refer the client to a lawyer. This seems so reasonable and fair to the client. What could possibly be wrong? To help you with your work, find *Green v. Unauthorized Practice of Law Committee*, 883 S.W.2d 293 (Texas 1994).

ASSIGNMENTS

1. Locate legal service (pro bono) organizations in your community and create a list of names, contact information, and specialties (if any). Brainstorm places in your community where such a list would be accessible by people in your community.
2. Watch the movie *Erin Brockovich*. Keep track of each time you think she crosses the UPL line and compare lists at the end of the movie.
3. What is the process by which an out-of-state lawyer can practice law in your state? Create an interoffice memorandum answering that question in response to a request from a lawyer.

COLLABORATIVE ASSIGNMENTS

1. Divide into groups of three. Two students create a fact pattern in which they are the clients and they are having a meeting with a paralegal (the third student). The object of this exercise is to ask the paralegal questions relating to your "case." Some of your questions should be those the paralegal can answer. Some should require the paralegal to "practice law." Keep track of which questions each student believes require UPL.
2. Divide into working teams of not more than five students. Each team should create an informative pamphlet on an issue of interest to the public (trusts, living wills, no asset divorce, bankruptcy) that provides information for the people of your community.

REVIEW QUESTIONS

Muliple Choice

Select the best answer for each of the following questions.

1. If you prepare a letter that contains information that might be construed as legal advice, you should
   a. Ask another more experienced paralegal who should sign the letter.
   b. Sign the lawyer's name.
   c. Give it to the lawyer for his or her review and signature.
   d. Sign the lawyer's name and put your initials after the signature.
   e. Sign the letter.
2. If immediate family members (spouse, mother, father, sibling, or child) ask you for legal advice, you should

   a. Advise them that you cannot give legal advice and do not give the answer.
   b. Give the advice, cautioning them that your answer is just your opinion, not advice.
   c. Give them the answer, but refer them to a lawyer for confirmation of the answer.
   d. Offer to call a lawyer to get the answer to their question.
   e. Give the advice because you know that they will never tell anyone that you did.
3. If your supervising lawyer is not available and a client calls and describes a life-threatening situation and asks for advice about what to do, you should

a. Refer him or her to another lawyer outside the firm.

b. Refer him or her to the police.

c. Give him or her the answer because it is a life-threatening situation.

d. Take his or her name and phone number; advise him or her that you will contact the lawyer and return the call within twenty-four hours; and then do as you advised the client.

e. Give him or her the answer but preface it with an explanation that you are a paralegal.

4. If you disagree with the decision made by your supervising lawyer and the client asks for your opinion, you should

a. Wink and tell the client your opinion when the lawyer leaves the room.

b. Disagree with the lawyer when the client leaves the office.

c. Agree with the lawyer while the client is there and call the client afterward.

d. Discuss your disagreement with the lawyer privately.

e. None of the above.

5. If the lawyer is on vacation and there are no other lawyers in the firm from whom you can obtain an answer to a client's question seeking legal advice, you should

a. Advise the client that you will obtain an answer from the lawyer and return the client's call as soon as possible.

b. Give the answer you know the lawyer would give anyway.

c. Give the client the answer, but caution him or her that you must confirm the answer with the lawyer.

d. Look up the answer provided by the lawyer in another case with similar circumstances and give the client that answer.

e. None of the above.

6. If a client asks you how his or her case or matter is progressing, you should

a. Respond with your opinion about the chance of winning, stating it is only an opinion based on your years of experience as a paralegal.

b. Tell him or her that you do not know because you are only a paralegal.

c. Tell him or her that you cannot respond because that would be considered the unauthorized practice of law.

d. Tell him or her that you cannot guess because juries are unpredictable.

e. Tell the client the procedural steps that have been taken in the case.

7. If a client asks you whether he or she will prevail (win, be successful) in a legal matter, you should

a. Tell him or her that you are not allowed to answer or you will be fired.

b. Tell him or her to call you at home and you will give your opinion since it differs from the lawyer's opinion.

c. Tell the lawyer that the client wants to know whether he or she will prevail.

d. Ask the lawyer to make a prediction about the matter so that you can give it to the client.

e. None of the above.

8. A paralegal may provide legal advice if

a. It is statutorily or administratively permitted.

b. The advice is received from the lawyer and the paralegal is repeating what the lawyer advised him or her to say.

c. The work is performed as a pro bono legal service for someone who cannot afford access to the legal system from a lawyer.

d. All of the above.

e. None of the above.

9. A paralegal may appear in court on behalf of the client if

a. That client consents to the appearance.

b. The paralegal's representation is on the paralegal's own behalf.

c. The paralegal's representation is permitted administratively or statutorily.

d. The paralegal identifies himself or herself as the lawyer.

e. None of the above.

10. The unauthorized practice of law may be
    a. prohibited by statute.
    b. prohibited by court rule.
    c. prohibited by ethical obligations.
    d. all of the above.
    e. none of the above.

Fill in the Blank

Complete each of the following sentences with the best word(s) or phrase(s).

1. All states have statutes that limit the _____ to licensed lawyers.
2. The unauthorized practice of law statutes exist to protect the _____.
3. A paralegal is not engaged in the unauthorized practice of law if his or her work is delegated by a lawyer and _____ by a lawyer.
4. Agencies such as the National Labor Relations Board, the Social Security Administration, and the Department of Defense permit _____.
5. A/An _____ who aids a paralegal in the unauthorized practice of law is violating his or her regulations and ethical obligations.
6. Rule of Professional Conduct number _____ applies to the unauthorized practice of law.

7. Three possible penalties for the unauthorized practice of law are:
    a. _____
    b. _____
    c. _____
8. The enforcement of UPL regulations in your state is vested in _____.
9. A practice (partnership, corporation, or other) that provides both legal and nonlegal services is called _____.
10. Putting the designation "Lawyer's Assistant" on your business card is an example of _____.

True/False

Decide whether each of the following statements is true or false and write your answer on the line provided.

____ 1. It is improper for a lawyer to form a partnership with a nonlawyer if any of the activities of the partnership constitute the practice of law.
____ 2. Engaging in the unauthorized practice of law is a matter of ethics and a matter of the law.
____ 3. A lawyer may share legal fees with a paralegal so long as the client consents to the arrangement.
____ 4. Some states have case law in which the court has attempted to define acts that constitute the practice of law.

____ 5. If the supervising lawyer approves releasing certain documents that contain information about the client, then the paralegal does not engage in the unauthorized practice of law by complying with those instructions.
____ 6. A disbarred or suspended lawyer who engages in the practice of law during his or her disbarment or suspension may be guilty of violating unauthorized practice of law statutes.

_____ 7. It would not be considered the unauthorized practice of law to discuss the facts of a case being handled by you and your supervising lawyer with other lawyers at the law firm by which you are employed.

_____ 8. To interpret the judge's decisions for a news reporter during a trial is considered the unauthorized practice of law.

_____ 9. Giving legal advice to your spouse is exempted from unauthorized practice of law violations by the spousal privilege.

_____ 10. Giving legal advice on a pro bono basis is acceptable and does not violate the unauthorized practice of law statutes because the client is indigent.

CASES FOR CONSIDERATION

CASE 1

SOUTH CAROLINA v. DESPAIN
319 S.C. 317, 460 S.E.2d 576
(1995)

The State brought this declaratory judgment action in the Court's original jurisdiction seeking to enjoin defendant from engaging in the unauthorized practice of law. See *In re Unauthorized Practice of Law Rules*, 309 S.C. 304, 422 S.E.2d 123 (1992). We grant the injunction.

FACTS

In its complaint, the State alleges that defendant, who is not licensed to practice law in South Carolina or in any other state, is engaged in the unauthorized practice of law by performing services which only a licensed lawyer is authorized to perform.

Defendant argues that she merely operates a business which allows customers, who pay a fee, to access a computer program for the preparation of documents to be used in legal proceedings. Defendant expressly denies that she is engaged in the unauthorized practice of law or that operation of her business amounts to the unauthorized practice of law.

By Order of this Court, the Honorable Walter J. Bristow, Jr., was appointed as a Special Master in this matter for the purpose of conducting an evidentiary hearing and issuing a report. A hearing was held on October 10, 1994, and a report issued on May 10, 1995. The Master's factual findings, which neither party has challenged, are summarized as follows:

In the course of operating a business known as Professional Document Services, defendant gives legal advice to individuals, for a fee, about divorce, custody, separation, and child support. By utilizing a computer software program she purchased, defendant also prepares legal documents for others to present in family court.

In at least one case, defendant undertook representation of an individual by mailing to the individual's estranged wife certain documents including a Complaint, Acceptance of Service, and Marital Settlement Agreement, and requesting that those documents be completed and returned for processing in order to obtain a divorce. In at least one other case, defendant represented, and received payment from, both parties in a divorce action. Further, defendant requires her customers to sign an agreement which purports to absolve her of any liability for damages which may result from her preparation of any legal document.

DISCUSSION

The generally understood definition of the practice of law "embraces the preparation of pleadings, and other papers incident to actions and special proceedings, and the management of such actions and proceedings on behalf of clients before judges and courts." *In re Duncan,* 83 S.C. 186, 189, 65 S.E. 210, 211 (1909). Applying this definition, we have held that the preparation of a deed for another individual, having the deed executed, and filing the deed, without the approval of a licensed lawyer, constitutes the unauthorized practice of law. *In re Easler,* 275 S.C. 400, 272 S.E.2d 32 (1980). We have also held that the preparation of deeds, mortgages, notes, and other legal instruments related to mortgage loans and transfers of real property by a commercial title company constitutes the unauthorized practice of law. *State v. Buyers Service Co., Inc.,* 292 S.C. 426, 357 S.E.2d 15 (1987).

Consistent with these cases, we now hold that the preparation of legal documents for others to present in family court constitutes the practice of law when such preparation involves the giving of advice, consultation, explanation, or recommendations on matters of law. Further, instructing other individuals in the manner in which to prepare and execute such documents is also the practice of law. *Accord State Bar v. Cramer,* 399 Mich. 116, 249 N.W.2d 1 (Mich 1976); *Oregon State Bar v. Gilchrist,* 272 Ore. 552, 538 P.2d 913 (1975). The reason such activity must be held to constitute the practice of law is not for the economic protection of legal profession. Rather, it is for the protection of the public from the potentially severe economic and emotional consequences which may flow from the erroneous preparation of legal documents or the inaccurate legal advice given by persons untrained in the law. See *State v. Buyers Service Co., Inc.,* supra.

By giving legal advice to individuals about divorce, custody, separation, and child support, and by preparing and processing legal documents for others, defendant has engaged in the unauthorized practice of law. Therefore, we enjoin defendant from engaging in any further conduct of this nature.

Injunction granted.

CASE QUESTIONS

1. What is a declaratory action? What does it mean to *enjoin*? What is an injunction?
2. What is the court's definition of the unauthorized practice of law?
3. What activities did the defendant engage in that were arguably UPL?
4. What is the court's reason for not allowing the defendant to have her computer generated legal forms business?
5. After reading this case, can you answer the "Hypothetical" posed at the beginning of this chapter?

CASE 2

CLEVELAND BAR ASSN. v. PEARLMAN
106 Ohio St.3d 136, 832 N.E.2d 1193
(2005)

I.

This matter arises from the amended complaint and certificate filed September 23, 2002, by the Cleveland Bar Association ("CBA") against respondent, Alan G. Pearlman. Pearlman manages apartment buildings owned by Roosevelt Investments, Ltd. ("Roosevelt") and Boulevard Investments, Ltd. ("Boulevard"), limited liability companies formed August 14, 1995. Pearlman owns a 99 percent interest in both companies; his wife owns one percent. Previously, the Pearlmans' general partnerships owned the apartment buildings.

Pearlman is not, and has never been, admitted to the practice of law. He has, however, filed at least 13 complaints in the Small Claims Division of Cleveland Heights Municipal Court on behalf of Roosevelt or Boulevard seeking money damages from tenants or former tenants. These filings were consistent with practices approved by the small claims division. The clerk of courts supplied the rent complaint forms, notarized Pearlman's signature, and accepted the complaints for filing.

> 1. The portion of the complaint concerning filing in the small claims division or the general division of Cleveland Heights Municipal Court on behalf of no-longer-existing partnerships has been dismissed without prejudice.

Magistrates of the small claims division have not allowed Pearlman to cross-examine witnesses, but have permitted him to testify on behalf of Roosevelt and Boulevard as their agent. Pearlman has never held himself out as an attorney nor filed complaints on behalf of any person or entity other than Roosevelt and Boulevard. He maintains that his activities in the small claims division are authorized by R.C. 1925.17.

Based upon the parties' stipulations, the Board on the Unauthorized Practice of Law found that Pearlman had engaged in the unauthorized practice of law by preparing and signing pleadings for Roosevelt and Boulevard and by appearing for them in the Cleveland Heights Municipal Court. The board recommended that Pearlman be enjoined from his activities, but did not recommend additional sanctions.

After the board's final report was filed, we issued an order for the parties to show cause why the report should not be confirmed with an appropriate order. Gov.Bar R. VII(19)(A). Pearlman filed objections, and the case is now before us for the determination specified in Gov.Bar R. VII(19)(D).

II.

Section 2(B)(1)(g), Article IV of the Ohio Constitution gives the Supreme Court of Ohio original jurisdiction over the "[a]dmission to the practice of law, the discipline of persons so admitted, and all other matters relating to the practice of law." Section 5(B), Article IV of the Ohio Constitution states that the Supreme Court "shall make rules governing the admission to the practice of law and discipline of persons so admitted."

The rule pertinent to this case, Gov.Bar R. VII(2)(A), states, "The unauthorized practice of law is the rendering of legal services for another by any person not admitted to practice in Ohio * * *." The term "rendering of legal services" has been defined further: "The practice of law is not limited to the conduct of cases in court. It embraces the preparation of pleadings and other papers incident to actions and special proceedings and the management of such actions and proceedings on behalf of clients before judges and courts, and in addition conveyancing, the preparation of legal instruments of all kinds, and in general all advice to clients and all action taken for them in matters connected with the law." *Land Title Abstract & Trust Co. v. Dworken* (1934) 129 Ohio St. 23, 1 O.O. 313, 193 N.E. 650, at paragraph one of the syllabus.

Relying upon this broad definition, the CBA asserts that Pearlman, a nonlawyer, provided legal services by appearing for Roosevelt and Boulevard in small claims court at least 13 times. As limited liability companies, Roosevelt and Boulevard are separate legal entities. R.C. 1705.01(D)(2)(e). It is the ordinary rule that a corporation may not litigate or appear in court represented by nonlawyer corporate officers or agents. *Union Sav. Assn. v. Home Owners Aid, Inc.* (1970), 23 Ohio St.2d 60, 64, 52 O.O.2d 329, 262 N.E.2d 558. This same rule also generally governs appearances before administrative agencies. *Cleveland Bar Assn. v. Woodman,* 98 Ohio St.3d 436, 2003-Ohio-1634, 786 N.E.2d 865 (nonattorney trustees of a nonprofit corporation may not file actions before the PUCO, representing their corporation and others). Thus, by representing Roosevelt and Boulevard and by filing complaints on their behalf in small claims court, the CBA maintains, Pearlman was involved in the unauthorized practice of law.

The CBA used this same analysis in *Cleveland Bar Assn. v. CompManagement, Inc.*, 104 Ohio St.3d 168, 2004-Ohio-6506, 818 N.E.2d 1181. There, the board adopted CBA's argument, concluding that nonlawyers had improperly rendered legal services in Industrial Commission and Bureau of Workers' Compensation cases. The board declined to consider whether lay representation was a hazard to the public or whether proceedings in these cases called for a measure of flexibility. Id. at ¶ 7.

When the *CompManagement* case reached us, we explained that an uncompromising approach to unauthorized-practice-of-law cases may not always be appropriate. After analyzing the purpose of Ohio's workers' compensation system, the functions performed by lay representatives, and the potential impact of enjoining the nonlawyers, we commented:

> "[W]hile this court unquestionably has the power to prohibit lay representation before an administrative agency, it is not always necessary or desirable for the court to exercise that power to its full extent. The power to regulate includes the authority to grant as well as the authority to deny, and in certain limited settings, the public interest is better served by authorizing laypersons to engage in conduct that might be viewed as the practice of law.
>
> "* * * Of course, Gov.Bar R. VII is built on the premise that limiting the practice of law to licensed attorneys is generally necessary to protect the public against incompetence, divided loyalties, and other attendant evils that are often associated with unskilled representation. But not all representation requires the level of training and experience that only attorneys can provide, and in certain situations, the protective interest is outweighed by other important considerations." Id. at ¶ 39–40.

In conclusion, we held that nonlawyers who appeared and practiced in a representative capacity before the Industrial Commission and Bureau of Workers' Compensation in conformance with administrative limitations were not engaged in the unauthorized practice of law. Id. at syllabus.

Similarly, lay representation has been authorized at unemployment-compensation hearings. *Henize v. Giles* (1986) 22 Ohio St.3d 213, 22 OBR 364, 490 N.E.2d 585, syllabus. In *Henize* we examined the Unemployment Compensation Board of Review's longstanding policy of permitting parties to be assisted by nonlawyers in presenting their claims. We concluded that the proceedings were designed to function as "alternatives to judicial dispute resolution so that the services of a lawyer are not a requisite to receiving a fair hearing and just decision." Id. at 216, 22 OBR 364, 490 N.E.2d 585.

III.

Although *CompManagement* and *Henize* involved administrative proceedings, the goal of small claims court is similar—to provide fast and fair adjudication as an alternative to the traditional judicial proceedings. For example, attorneys may appear, but are not required to appear, on behalf of any party in small claims matters. R.C. 1925.01(D). Jurisdiction of the small claims division is limited to $3,000, and there is no subject-matter jurisdiction over claims for libel, slander, replevin, malicious prosecution, or abuse of process. R.C. 1925.02(A)(1) and (2)(a)(i). Claims for punitive damages, exemplary damages, and prejudgment attachment are not permitted. R.C. 1925.02(A)(2)(iii) and 1925.07. There is no jury in small claims court. R.C. 1925.04(A). Since claims must be set for hearing within 15 to 40 days after the complaint is filed, cases move quickly. R.C. 1925.04(B). The hearings are simplified, as neither the Ohio Rules of Evidence nor the Ohio Rules of Civil Procedure apply. See Evid.R. 101(C)(8); Civ.R. 1(C)(4). Thus, by design, proceedings in small claims courts are informal and geared to allowing individuals to resolve uncomplicated disputes quickly and inexpensively. Pro se activity is assumed and encouraged. The process is an alternative to full-blown judicial dispute resolution.

The guide posted by the Cleveland Heights Municipal Court on its website highlights how the small claims division is a different type of forum for claim resolution. It states that lawyers are not needed to file claims:

> "Small Claims Court is designed to handle small matters in the simplest manner possible. You do not need a lawyer to file a small claims action * * *.
>
> "An individual, company or corporation may file a claim against another individual, company or corporation." (Emphasis added). See http://www. clevelandheights court.com/main.html.

Pearlman argues that the above statement in the Cleveland Heights Municipal Court guide and R.C. 1925.17 permit him to appear on behalf of Roosevelt and Boulevard in the small claims division. Unchanged since its enactment in 1969, R.C. 1925.17 reads:

> "A corporation which is a real party in interest in any action in a small claims division may commence such an action and appear therein through an attorney at law. *Such a corporation may, through any bona fide officer or salaried employee, file and present its claim or defense* in any action in a small claims division arising from a claim based on a contract to which the corporation is an original party or any other claim to which the corporation is an original claimant, *provided such corporation does not*, in the absence of representation by an attorney at law, *engage in cross-examination, argument, or other acts of advocacy.*" (Emphasis added.) In other words, a corporation may use the small claims court through an authorized lay representative, as long as its activities are confined appropriately.

The CBA, however, contends that R.C. 1925.17 is unconstitutional as a violation of the separation of powers. It claims that the statute interferes with this court's authority to regulate the practice of law by permitting a nonattorney to represent another in small claims court. The constitutionality of R.C. 1925.17 has been addressed at the appellate level. Compare *Alliance Group, Inc. v. Rosenfield* (1996), 115 Ohio App.3d 380, 387, 685 N.E.2d 570 (holding that R.C. 1925.17 is unconstitutional), with *George Shima Buick, Inc. v. Ferencak* (Dec. 17, 1999), Lake App. No. 98-L-202, 1999 WL 1313675 (holding R.C. 1925.17 constitutional), vacated on jurisdictional grounds (2001), 91 Ohio St.3d 1211, 741 N.E.2d 138. In both cases, the question was whether R.C. 1925.17 infringed on our power to regulate the practice of law.

We note that the legislature has acknowledged our authority in regulating the practice of law. R.C. 4705.01 states:

> "No person shall be permitted to practice as an attorney and counselor at law, or to commence, conduct, or defend any action or proceeding in which the person is not a party concerned, either by using or subscribing the person's own name, or the name of another person, unless the person has been admitted to the bar by order of the supreme court in compliance with its prescribed and published rules."

This enactment shows the deference the General Assembly gives to the court on this issue. Furthermore, by its own terms, R.C. 1925.17 recognizes the need for attorney representation by circumscribing what an authorized corporate representative may do. In the absence of an attorney at law, a corporate representative may not "engage in cross-examination, argument, or other acts of advocacy."

Rather than view R.C. 1925.17 as intruding on our authority to regulate the practice of law or our rule-making power, we see it as a mere clarification, stating that corporations may use small claims courts as individuals may, i.e., without attorneys, so long as their representatives do not otherwise act as advocates. Pearlman's activities fall squarely within the limits of R.C. 1925.17. As the majority shareholder in his family-owned limited liability company, he was a "bona fide officer" of Roosevelt and Boulevard, filing the type of action that small claims courts allow. He merely filled out preprinted complaint forms that required the name, address, and phone number of the plaintiff and defendant, a statement of the claim, and the amount of the judgment requested. He did not cross-examine witnesses, argue, or otherwise act as an advocate.

The CBA, however, finally suggests that because the Pearlmans chose to create separate legal entities, they should be required to retain an attorney to represent those separate legal entities. According to the CBA, Pearlman could act pro se if he gave up the corporate form. The argument is interesting, but unpersuasive as it applies to small claims actions.

In refusing to enjoin Pearlman's activities in the small claims division of municipal court, we recognize an exception, albeit a narrow one, to the general rule that corporations may be represented only by licensed attorneys. R.C. 1925.17 limits what a corporate representative may do. Pearlman observed these limitations. The public is not harmed by Pearlman's actions. In small claims cases, where no special legal skill is needed, and where proceedings are factual, nonadversarial, and expected to move quickly, attorneys are not necessary. We decline to require corporations to hire attorneys to represent them in small claims courts.

IV.

In summary, we hold that a layperson who presents a claim or defense and appears in small claims court on behalf of a limited liability company as a company officer does not engage in the unauthorized practice of law, provided that the layperson does not engage in cross-examination, argument, or other acts of advocacy.

Because we conclude that Pearlman's activities in the small claims division do not constitute the unauthorized practice of law, we reject the final report and recommendation of the Board on the Unauthorized Practice of Law and dismiss the case.

Judgment accordingly.

CASE QUESTIONS

1. According to the court, what is the unauthorized practice of law?
2. What are Roosevelt and Boulevard and what was Pearlman's association with them?
3. What was Pearlman doing that the Cleveland Bar Association argued constituted the unauthorized practice of law?
4. This court has held that there are some exceptions to the UPL law. What are they?
5. Corporations can't practice law by themselves. They need to have a person represent them. What things can a layperson do on behalf of a corporation according to this Ohio court?
6. Ultimately, what does this court decide?

CASE 3

THE FLORIDA BAR v. FURMAN (FURMAN I)
355 So.2d 1186
(Fla. 1978)

The Florida Bar has petitioned this Court to enjoin Rosemary W. Furman, d/b/a Northside Secretarial Service, from unauthorized practice of law in the State of Florida. Our jurisdiction to rule in this matter is provided by article V, section 15 of the Florida Constitution and by The Florida Bar Integration Rule, article XVI. We find the activities of the respondent to constitute the practice of law and permanently enjoin her from the further unauthorized practice of law.

The Florida Bar alleged, through an amended petition dated September 23, 1977, that Furman, a non-lawyer, engaged in the unauthorized practice of law by giving legal advice and by rendering legal services in connection with marriage dissolutions and adoptions in the years 1976 and 1977. The bar specifically alleges that Furman performed legal services for at least seven customers by soliciting information from them and preparing pleadings in violation of Florida law. The bar further contends that through advertising in the *Jacksonville Journal*, a newspaper of general circulation, Furman held herself out to the public as having legal expertise in Florida family law and sold "do-it-yourself divorce kits." The bar does not contend that Furman held herself out to be a lawyer, that her customers suffered any harm as a result of the services rendered, or that she has failed to perform the services for which she was paid.

In describing her activities, Furman states that she does not give legal advice, that she does prepare pleadings that meet the desires of her clients, that she charges no more than $50 for her services, and that her assistance to customers is in aid of their obtaining self-representative relief from the courts. In general, the respondent alleges as a defense that the ruling of this court in *Florida Bar v. Brumbaugh*, 355 So.2d 1186 (Fla. 1978), violates the First Amendment to the United States Constitution by restricting her right to disseminate and the right of her customers to receive information which would allow indigent litigants access to the state's domestic relations courts. She alleges that our holding in *Brumbaugh* is so narrow that it deprives citizens who are indigent of equal protection of the laws as provided by the Florida and United States constitutions. When this case was at issue, we referred it to retired Circuit Judge P. B. Revels of the Seventh Judicial Circuit, one of Florida's most experienced trial judges, to serve as referee. The referee has filed his report which, in pertinent part, indicates:

A. That the Respondent, Rosemary W. Furman, d/b/a Northside Secretarial Service, is the sole proprietor and owner of said secretarial service. The Northside Secretarial Service has never registered under the fictitious name law.

B. Respondent has never received any legal training or education; is not now nor ever been a licensed attorney of law of the State of Florida or elsewhere; that she is not now and never has been a member of The Florida Bar.

C. That the Respondent under the guise of secretarial services for a fee prepares all papers considered by her to be necessary for the filing and securing a dissolution of marriage, as well as detailed instructions as to how the papers should be filed, service secured, hearings set and a briefing session as to the questions and answers to be offered at the trial of the case before the Court and for entry of Final Judgment of Dissolution.

D. The Respondent admitted, when a person comes to her place of business, they state they want to get a divorce or they want her to help them get a divorce, although many of the people deposed insisted that they only asked that she type papers to enable them to obtain the divorce. So after some discussion, the customer is provided with the appropriate intake sheet for the facts listed at the first visit either Respondent's Exhibit 11 or 12. In addition to the intake sheet the Respondent furnishes papers outlining the legal steps, the law and the procedures, as shown by Respondent's Exhibits 13, 14 and 15, advising them to read the matter and it will help them in filling out the intake sheet.

E. The Respondent admits that the customer returns with the intake sheet not completed, because the people are unfamiliar with the legal terms and some are illiterate and, of course, she then proceeds to ask questions to complete the intake sheet for preparing the Petition for Dissolution of Marriage. Then after she types the Petition for Dissolution of Marriage, she advises the customer to take the papers for filing to the Office of the Clerk of Circuit Court, and Respondent follows the progress of the case every step of the way until it is at issue. She then notifies the customer to come in for a briefing session preferably the day before the date set for trial. In the course of briefing Respondent furnishes the customer with a diagram of the Court chambers and where to find the Judge to which that particular case has been assigned. A copy of the diagram of chambers that she furnishes to the customer is shown by Respondent's Exhibit 10.

F. She also explains the full procedure that will take place before the Judge, including the questions the customer should ask the customer and the resident witness. A copy of same is shown by Respondent's Exhibit 20. The facts in the record of this case establish very clearly that the Respondent performs every essential step in the legal proceedings to obtain a dissolution of marriage, except taking the papers and filing them in the Clerk's office and going with the customer to the final hearing and interrogating the witness.

G. Respondent admitted that she could not follow the guidelines as set forth in the *Florida Bar v. Brumbaugh*, Supreme Court Opinion, for the reason that the customers who come to obtain her services are not capable for various and sundry reasons, mainly not being familiar with legal terminology or illiterate, and were unable to write out the necessary information. Therefore, she was compelled to ask questions and hold conferences with her customers.

H. Pre-trial Stipulation, Joint Evidentiary Exhibit 1, briefly enumerates the factual situation in each of the cases which I believe I can state the substance of the Stipulation, even though there are some varying circumstances in each case, for the purpose of my findings without quoting the Stipulation in full. The cases involved were Green v. Gr*een, Ammons v. Ammons, Kirkby-Petition for Adoption, Howland v. Howland, Mayden v. Mayden, Holmes v. Holmes, and Touchton v. Touchton.* The substance of this Stipulation is as follows:

The factual information contained in the pleadings was obtained by Respondent from the customer as a result of oral questions asked by Respondent and answered by the customer, which information was written upon Respondent's standardized intake sheet. Respondent by both oral and written instructions informed the customer as to the procedures to be followed in filing the pleadings and in processing the same to final hearing. Respondent specifically informed customers that she was not an attorney nor licensed to practice law in the State of Florida and at no time did the customers believe that the Respondent was an attorney or licensed to practice law. In paragraphs 16 and 17 of said stipulation the parties agreed that the customers did not think or know that they had suffered any damage as a result of

Respondent's services; that they did not think that the Respondent gave them legal advice or engaged in legal counseling.

The referee made the following findings:

1. The foregoing facts show by a great weight of the evidence, Rosemary W. Furman, shielded behind the cloak of Northside Secretarial Service, has been engaged in the unauthorized practice of law for approximately three years.

2. That the Opinion in *Florida Bar v. Brumbaugh* is being interpreted by many as a license to individuals, who are trained and experienced in secretarial work, to practice law. This creates a grave danger to the citizens of Florida.

Rosemary W. Furman should be adjudged guilty of contempt of the Supreme Court of Florida, and permanently enjoined from engaging or pursuing any course of action personally or in her secretarial service that touches or resembles in any way the practice of law. She should be prohibited from typing legal papers of any kind, filling blanks on any legal forms, or giving oral or written advice or directions. The fact she is an expert stenographer does not give her any legal right to engage in divorce and adoption practice anymore than a nurse has the right to set up an office for performing tonsillectomy or appendectomy operations or a dental assistant to do extractions or fill teeth.

The referee's findings must be approved unless they are erroneous or wholly lacking in evidentiary support. *Florida Bar v. Wagner*, 212 So.2d 770 (Fla. 1968).

We do not write on a clean slate in this case. Last year we took the opportunity to clearly define to non-lawyers the proper realm in which they could operate without engaging in the unauthorized practice of law. In *Brumbaugh*, we clearly stated what services a similar secretarial business could lawfully perform. We said:

We hold that Ms. Brumbaugh, and others in similar situations, may sell printed material purporting to explain legal practice and procedure to the public in general and she may sell sample legal forms. To this extent we limit our prior holdings in Stupica and American Legal and Business Forms, Inc. Further, we hold that it is not improper for Marilyn Brumbaugh to engage in a secretarial service, typing such forms for her clients, provided that she only copy the information given to her in writing by her clients. In addition, Ms. Brumbaugh may advertise her business activities of providing secretarial and notary services and selling legal forms and general printed information. However, Marilyn Brumbaugh must not, in conjunction with her business, engage in advising clients as to the various remedies available to them, or otherwise assist them in preparing those forms necessary for a dissolution proceeding. More specifically, Marilyn Brumbaugh may not make inquiries nor answer questions from her clients as to the particular forms which might be necessary, how best to fill out such forms, where to properly file such forms, and how to present necessary evidence at the court hearings. Our specific holding with regard to the dissolution of marriage also applies to other unauthorized legal assistance such as the preparation of wills or real estate transaction documents. While Marilyn Brumbaugh may legally sell forms in these areas, and type up instruments which have been completed by clients, she must not engage in personal legal assistance in conjunction with her business activities, including the correction of errors and omissions. 355 So.2d at 1194.

Our directions could not have been clearer.

Before the referee and before this court, Furman admitted that she did not abide by the dictates of *Brumbaugh*. She says that it is impossible for her to operate her "do-it-yourself divorce kit" business in compliance with this court's ruling in that case. The bar alleges that Furman has engaged in the unauthorized practice of law as previously defined by this court. The referee so found. She so admits. We believe the referee's findings are supported by the evidence.

In other portions of the referee's report, he urges that as part of our disposition in this case we require the bar to conduct a study to determine how to provide effective legal services to the indigent. Without question, it is our responsibility to promote the full availability of legal services. We deem it more appropriate, however, to address this issue in a separate proceeding. By doing so under our supervisory power, we insure a thorough consideration of the overall problem without delaying the present adjudication. Devising means for providing effective legal services to the indigent and poor is a continuing problem. The Florida Bar has addressed this subject with some success. In spite of the laudable efforts by the bar, however, this record suggests that even more attention needs to be given to this subject.

Therefore, we direct The Florida Bar to begin immediately a study to determine better ways and means of providing legal services to the indigent. We further direct that a report on the findings and conclusions from this study be prepared and filed with this court on or before January 1, 1980, at which time we will examine the problem and consider solutions.

Accordingly, we find that Rosemary Furman, d/b/a Northside Secretarial Service, has been guilty of the unauthorized practice of law by virtue of the activities recited herein and she is hereby permanently enjoined and restrained from further engaging in the unauthorized practice of law in the State of Florida.

It is so ordered.

CASE 4

THE FLORIDA BAR v. FURMAN (FURMAN II)
451 So.2d 808
(Fla. 1984)

The Florida Bar filed petitions charging Rosemary W. Furman, d/b/a Northside Secretarial Service, with engaging in the unauthorized practice of law in the State of Florida, in contempt of this Court's order of November 1, 1979, as reported in *The Florida Bar v. Furman*, 376 So.2d 378 (Fla. 1979), appeal dismissed, 444 U.S. 1061, 62 L.Ed. 2d 744, 100 S. Ct.1001 (1980). The charges were assigned to a referee and a report returned for our consideration. We have jurisdiction under article V, section 15 of the Florida Constitution and The Florida Bar Integration Rule, article XVI.

A brief recitation of the prior history of this case is necessary. Respondent Furman is not and never has been a member of The Florida Bar (Bar) and is not licensed to practice law within this state. In 1977, the Bar filed petitions with this Court alleging that respondent had engaged in the unauthorized practice of law by giving legal advice and by rendering legal services in connection with marriage dissolutions and adoptions in the years 1976 and 1977. More specifically, the Bar alleged that respondent performed legal services by soliciting information from customers and by preparing legal pleadings for them in violation of Florida law and that, through advertising, respondent held herself out to the public as having legal expertise in Florida family law. We appointed a referee to receive evidence and to make findings of fact, conclusions of law, and recommendations as to the disposition of the case. In due course the referee submitted findings that respondent had engaged in the unauthorized practice of law and recommended that she be adjudged guilty of contempt of this Court. We found respondent guilty and permanently enjoined and restrained her from further engaging in the unauthorized practice of law, as specified, but did not find her guilty of contempt.

On September 28, 1982, and March 9, 1983, the Bar filed petitions alleging six and ten instances, respectively, wherein respondent had continued her unauthorized practice of law in contempt of this Court's order. We issued rules to show cause on November 30, 1982, and March 21, 1983, respectively, and appointed a referee to receive evidence and to make findings of fact, conclusions of law, and recommendations. The referee conducted pretrial hearings, consolidated the rules, and set evidentiary hearings for June 20 and 21, 1983. On June 20, 1983, we denied respondent's motions for a stay of the proceedings and for trial by jury. Respondent chose not to testify at the evidentiary hearings. The uncontradicted testimony of former customers of respondent was that she advised them to falsify information in marriage dissolution papers and to conceal relevant information from the courts acting on the dissolution petitions. Her purported reasons were various: it's none of their damn business, they don't pay any attention to the information, or you'll (either) get less or give more money in the dissolution judgment. In one instance, respondent advised a wife who had been married, divorced, and remarried to the same husband but could not remember the date of the remarriage to insert the date of the dissolved first marriage as the date of the second marriage in the petition for dissolution. Another couple who disagreed on whether their stipulation on child custody provided for $35 per week or $35 per child was advised that it didn't matter because the judge awarded whatever he wanted to anyway. In a particularly egregious instance, respondent assisted a husband seeking a marriage dissolution in preparing a stipulation in which he agreed to child custody by the wife. While the dissolution petition and child custody stipulation were pending before the court, the husband became aware that the wife was abusing the children, took actual custody of the children, and consulted respondent about withdrawing his stipulated agreement on child custody. Respondent advised him not to do so because this would require "starting over" on the dissolution petition and he should let the social agency (HRS) handle the child abuse and custody problem.

At the conclusion of the evidentiary hearings, the referee scheduled briefing and the case was orally argued on August 15, 1983. Both parties were given an opportunity thereafter to submit proposed orders for the referee's consideration. On September 28, 1983, the referee set a hearing for October 10, 1983, to announce his findings and recommendations and to hear arguments in aggravation or mitigation, if appropriate. At the beginning of the hearing, the referee distributed draft copies of his prospective order and announced the highlights of the order from the bench. The draft recommended that respondent be held in indirect criminal contempt and that she be sentenced to unspecified terms of imprisonment. The referee then offered respondent an opportunity to present evidence and argument in mitigation and recessed the hearing for a short time to permit respondent to consider her options. Respondent chose not to testify or present evidence, but joined the Bar in presenting arguments, after which the referee entered the order under consideration. The order recommended concurrent four-month sentences in state prison.

Respondent raises five objections to the referee's report.

The discussion regarding right to a jury trial is omitted.

Respondent's second objection is that the referee upheld an erroneous legal standard in determining whether respondent violated this Court's injunction. The gist of respondent's argument is that our order enjoining respondent, which incorporated *The Florida Bar v. Brumbaugh*, 355 So.2d 1186 (Fla. 1978), is unclear as to what activities are enjoined and that the referee adopted an unreasonably expansive reading of the injunction in making his findings. In considering respondent's argument, we follow the rule that the referee's findings must be approved unless they are erroneous or wholly lacking in evidentiary support. *Furman*, 376 So.2d at 381; *Florida Bar v. Wagner*, 212 So.2d 770 (Fla. 1968). In *Furman*, we relied on and quoted at length from *Brumbaugh*, a case involving a similar secretarial business, in order to determine whether respondent's activities warranted an injunction restraining her from the unauthorized practice of law, as the referee had recommended. Drawing from that extended quote, we extract only that portion dealing with enjoined activities:

> [Respondent] must not, in conjunction with her business, engage in advising clients as to the various remedies available to them, or otherwise assist them in preparing those forms necessary for a dissolution proceeding. More specifically, [respondent] may not make inquiries nor answer questions from her clients as to the particular forms which might be necessary, how best to fill out such forms, where to properly file such forms, and how to present necessary evidence at the court hearings. Our specific holding with regard to the dissolution of marriage also applies to other unauthorized legal assistance such as the preparation of wills or real estate transaction documents. While [respondent] may legally sell forms in these areas, and type up instruments which have been completed by clients, she must not engage in personal legal assistance in conjunction with her business activities, including the correction of errors and omissions.
>
> *Furman*, 376 So.2d at 381, quoting *Brumbaugh*, 355 So.2d at 1194.

We then noted:

> Before the referee and before this court, Furman admitted that she did not abide by the dictates of *Brumbaugh*. She says that it is impossible for her to operate her "do-it-yourself divorce kit" business in compliance with this court's ruling in that case. The bar alleges that Furman has engaged in the unauthorized

practice of law as previously defined by this court. The referee so found. She so admits. We believe the referee's findings are supported by the evidence. *Furman,* 376 So.2d at 381.

We repeat now what we said then: "Our directions could not have been clearer." *Id.* Respondent's contention that her activities were premised on a good-faith but erroneous interpretation of a vague and nonspecific order of this Court is totally meritless. Respondent's claimed uncertainty about the nature and contents of our injunction appears to arise from a deliberate and intentional mis-apprehension of the effect of an injunction and the nature and posture of this case. In their briefs, respondent and amicus curiae (Southern Legal Counsel, Inc., which formerly represented respondent), have favored us with dissertations on what should or should not constitute the unauthorized practice of law and what measures this Court should initiate in order to provide free legal services in civil proceedings. Respondent's brief, for example, asserts that "what has been at issue in both the prior proceedings and in this case is whether [respondent's] activities constitute the unauthorized practice of law." Not so. We are not here, in this instance, to consider the broad questions of what constitutes the unauthorized practice of law or what, if any, free legal services should be provided in civil actions. We are also not here to revisit *Brumbaugh* or *Furman* in order to determine whether the guidance and strictures therein should be amended. Had respondent initiated a motion before this Court requesting that we reexamine *Brumbaugh* and *Furman,* and perhaps modify the terms of our injunction, we would have considered such motion and the arguments presented on their merits. This is not the posture of the case. Respondent has been brought before this Court on charges of violating the terms of an earlier injunction and will not be permitted to reargue the merits of whether the injunction should have been issued. As we said long ago:

> An injunction or restraining order must be obeyed until vacated or modified by the court awarding it, or by superior authority, or until the order or decree which granted it has been reversed on appeal, no matter how unreasonable and unjust the injunction may be in its terms, and no matter how flagrantly the rules of equity practice have been violated by the court in ordering it to issue.

Seaboard Air Line Railroad v. Tampa Southern Railroad, 101 Fla. 468, 477, 134 So. 529, 533 (1931). See also *Walker v. City of Birmingham,* 388 U.S. 307, 18 L.Ed.2d 1210, 87 S.Ct. 1824 (1967); *Howat v. Kansas,* 258 U.S. 181, 66 L.Ed. 550, 42 S.Ct. 277 (1922).

We turn then to the referee's findings that respondent contemptuously continued the unauthorized practice of law in violation of our injunction. The referee found in pertinent part:

> J. Ms. Furman prepared pleadings that went beyond just transposing information from an intake sheet to a form. She articulated that information in a fashion which raised justiciable issues regarding child custody, child support, division of property.

K. Ms. Furman explained legal remedies and options to litigating parties which affected the procedural and substantive legal rights, duties, and privileges of those parties.

L. Ms. Furman construed and interpreted the legal effects of Section 61.13, Florida Statutes, pertaining to shared parental responsibility.

M. Ms. Furman gave advice on how to construct and prepare a financial picture that would result in increased monetary benefits or decreased monetary obligations as the case may be for the one seeking her advice, without regard for the truth, in some instances.

N. Ms. Furman, as part of her comprehensive legal assistance, gave advice and direction on how and where to file documents with instructions on how to technically prepare and litigate the case in Court.

O. Ms. Furman was available to her customers to correct erroneous or legally deficient pleadings that she had prepared, and to remedy problems experienced by her customers during the dissolution hearing which otherwise frustrated a conclusion thereto.

P. Ms. Furman professed to her customers to have knowledge of the weight and credibility that judges attach and give to legal documents and crucial legal information and evidence.

Q. Ms. Furman participated in oral dialogues with her customers regarding such issues as money for the support of children, safety of children from abusing parents, the placement of children with the most deserving parent, available remedies and options for litigating parties, her interpretation and understanding of legal documents and pertinent statutes, the financial status of husbands and wives as they bore on their need or ability to receive or pay, the ability of her customers to comply with financial Court-ordered obligations, the importance of Court orders and complications therewith, and corrective procedures for defective dissolution proceedings.

R. Ms. Furman, in each case, was paid a monetary fee ranging up to $100.00.

Of the sixteen alleged instances of unauthorized practices of law, four were *nolle prossed* by the Bar. The referee's findings were based on a case-by-case examination and analysis of the twelve instances where evidence of unauthorized practice of law was introduced. The evidence consisted of the testimony of the customers involved in the specific instance and relevant documents or forms that respondent had prepared for the customer.

This evidence was almost entirely uncontradicted except for cross examination. We have reviewed the findings on these twelve charges and find that they are supported by the evidence. We find no error and approve the findings of the referee.

(The discussion of laches and procedural irregularities is omitted.)

Turning to the referee's recommendations, we approve the findings that respondent has violated the terms of our order enjoining and restraining her from performing the specific acts therein prohibited. We hold her in contempt of court. We, however, do not accept the referee's recommendation that she be imprisoned in the state prison for two concurrent four-month terms. Under the facts of this case, we find it more appropriate to sentence respondent to the Duval County jail for a single term of 120 days. We suspend 90 days of the 120-day term of imprisonment. When this opinion becomes final, the sheriff of Duval County is authorized and directed to take respondent into custody and to imprison her for 30 days. If respondent does not violate the terms of our continuing injunction for a period of two years, the suspended term of 90 days shall be deemed satisfied.

The terms and provisions of our previous order permanently enjoining and restraining respondent remain in effect.

Costs of these proceedings are taxed against the respondent, Rosemary Furman. It is so ordered.

CASE QUESTIONS

1. Why was Rosemary Furman tried again?
2. Who is the "watch dog" in this case?
3. Furman argued that the court's earlier order was "vague." What do you see in the order that is vague?
4. Furman wants to re-argue whether her actions constitute the unauthorized practice of law. Why does the court say it will not allow that argument?
5. The court said: "Of the sixteen alleged instances of unauthorized practices of law, four were *nolle prossed* by the Bar." What does *nolle prossed* mean?
6. What were the consequences for Rosemary Furman?

CHAPTER

3

CONFIDENTIALITY

CHAPTER OBJECTIVES

By the end of this chapter, you will know the answers to these questions:

What's the Big Deal about Confidentiality?

What Does It Mean That Information Is "Confidential"?

How Long Does the Duty of Confidentiality Last?

What Is the Attorney/Client Privilege?

Where Do the Two Concepts Overlap?

How Can I Make Sure I Do My Duty?

What Confidential Information Can Be Divulged?

So, Then, What's the Work Product Privilege?

Are There Any Exceptions to the Work Product Privilege?

How Has Technology Changed Confidentiality?

What about Old Client Files?

HYPOTHETICAL

April works for a law firm that has been involved in the defense of an accused criminal for a number of years. The crime and the ensuing trial were given a substantial amount of attention by the news media. The client is now in prison serving a life sentence, but he still maintains that he is innocent. April has always been interested in writing and would like to write a series of magazine articles based on this client's story. April and the client have become "pen pals" over the years, and the client now writes letters to April at home. April thinks that the letters contain excellent material that she could use to show "what the convicted criminal thinks about." She thinks readers would be interested in the thoughts, feelings, and fantasies of the criminal.

What's the Big Deal about Confidentiality?

Most law firm employees are aware that it is improper to talk about the client's secrets to a third person. Most people have a vague idea that whatever they tell their lawyers will not be divulged improperly. The strange and interesting ways problems arise in this area, however, are not well publicized by the legal community or the media. In fact, most lawyers, even well-educated, experienced lawyers, do not understand the differences between *confidentiality* and the *attorney/client privilege*. This chapter is designed to provide some clear explanations of confidentiality and attorney/client privilege and how the two are different. Confidences naturally lead to conflicts of interest, so we discuss them later in the chapter.

ABA Model Code
EC 4-1: Both the
fiduciary
relationship
existing between
lawyer and client
and the proper
functioning of the
legal system
require the
preservation by
the lawyer of
confidences and
secrets of one
who has
employed or
sought to employ
him. . . .

* The Model Codes
of Responsibility
are presented here
as a historical
reference and are
not currently used.

According to Comment 2 to Model Rule 1.6, the *duty of confidentiality* consists of two separate but dependent concepts: (1) the clients' need to feel secure that the information they give their lawyers will remain confidential, based on (2) the legal professionals' need to have all relevant information from the clients and the clients' need to seek early legal assistance.

Think about this for a moment. If you are asked to defend a defendant in a criminal matter, to do your job competently, you need to know all of the facts. You need to know all of the facts, even the ones that seem insignificant and perhaps especially the incriminating ones. But your client is afraid to tell you the facts. Your client is afraid that you will use the facts against him, or that if you know all of the facts, you won't want to defend him, or that you will tell the authorities his secrets. So, you tell your client: It's all right. I'll keep your secrets confidential. But what does that mean exactly?

What Is "Confidential"?

It is commonly said that it is improper to divulge "confidential information." Without knowing what is "confidential," however, we do not know what it is we should not divulge.

Model Rule of Professional Conduct 1.6:

A [legal professional] shall not reveal information *relating to representation of a client* unless the client consents after consultation, except for disclosures that are impliedly authorized in order to carry out the representation, and except as stated in paragraph (b).[1]

Confidential information, then, is made up of three parts: (1) all information, (2) relating to the representation of a client, (3) regardless of the source.

1. *All information.* If it is "all information," it need not be personal secrets of the client or information learned from the client. It doesn't have to be "bad" information or "damaging" information. It doesn't have to be "secret" in that no one knows it. It doesn't have to be "confidential" as we normally use that word. It can be information that is publicly known. The very fact that this person *is* your client is "information." (Is there something about the word "all" that you don't understand?)

2. *Relating to the representation.* But it is obviously not "all" information about "everything." Confidential information, for our purposes as a paralegal, is only information relating to the representation of the client. The thing is, we rarely know what information will eventually relate to the representation of the client and what will not. For example, if your firm is hired to create a corporation for a client and during your conversations he tells you that he has an illegitimate child (clients are funny that way), it would seem at first blush that the child information is not related to the representation. The problem is that the client believes that everything he says to his lawyer (and you, his lawyer's agent) is confidential. Further, it is possible that the illegitimate child will become an issue sometime down the road in the representation. What is "related to the representation"? It's safe to say everything that you know is somehow related to the representation.

3. *Regardless of the source.* It doesn't matter where you got the information about the client or the representation. You could have read it in public files. You could have gotten it directly from the client. You could have heard it from a witness or somebody's mom. You could have read it in the newspaper or on the credit report. Are you getting the picture here? The information could come from anywhere. It's still confidential *as to you.*

What Does It Mean That Information Is "Confidential"?

The duty of confidentiality means one thing: you can't talk about all information related to the representation regardless of the source. That means you can't talk to your mom or your spouse about what you learned at work. You can't share war stories with your friends.

You can, of course, talk to other people working on the client's matter with you. These are the people in the "need-to-know" circle: your supervising lawyer, associates working on the case, other paralegals working on the case, and secretaries. Not all of the people in your law firm are in the need-to-know circle. Your best friend who works in accounting obviously works for your same law firm, but she is not in the need-to-know circle so you cannot share information about clients with her without violating your duty of confidentiality.

How Long Does the Duty of Confidentiality Last?

Here's how that would work in real life. Let's say you know all about this client's guilt. He did it. He confessed. So, that's information that you have as a member of the legal team representing this defendant. In this morning's paper is a big article about how the defendant confessed. It is, fact for fact, exactly as you know it. Can you go outside now and tell everyone you know (or those you don't know) that the defendant did it and he confessed? It's in the newspaper. Everyone has read it. Everyone knows. Is it fair game for you to talk about? If your instinct is telling you "no," you are correct. It's one thing for the paper to report something. It's entirely another for someone on the legal team to ratify it. The information is still confidential *as to you.* After the client is tried and found guilty or not, can you then tell anyone about the confession? No. The client's confidential information remains confidential after the case is completed. Can you tell anyone after the client dies? Releasing this information could still harm the client, so, no, the information is still confidential. In fact, confidential information remains confidential forever. Forever.

Attorney/Client Privilege Contrasted

The attorney/client privilege is a rule of evidence. (In some states, you'll find it in the Evidence Code—a sure giveaway.) It only applies to information that is received directly from the client or the client's agent. It only applies to information

The modern approach to attorney/client privilege was first adopted in the Model Code of Evidence drafted by the American Law Institute in 1942. Since that time, the model has been enacted in varying forms in twenty-six states. Find the ALI at http:// www.ali.org.

that is secret, that is, information that no one else knows about. That means it can't be public record, it can't be written down anywhere. It also means that no one else can be in the room when the client is telling you this secret. In other words, the client can't come into your office with his mom or his best friend and tell you this information. If the mom knows or the best friend knows, then it's not a secret. All the privilege does is protect the client from having his lawyer divulge client secrets while under oath. It only applies when the lawyer or his agent (that's you) is under oath. The holder of the privilege is the client, but the keeper is the lawyer (or you). That means that the client can always tell the lawyer to not release this secret. In the absence of a direct instruction from the client, it is the lawyer's duty to not release the secret.

Your state's rule on attorney/client privilege will say something like: the lawyer cannot be called upon to testify as to information the client has given to the lawyer. This is true of the lawyer and all nonlawyer personnel to whom the client may have divulged information. In *United States v. Kovel*,[2] one of the first cases that extended the attorney/client privilege to a nonlawyer employed by a law firm, the court used the analogy of the employment of an interpreter in order to extend the privilege to an accountant. The court said that, just as lawyers may have to employ an interpreter through which to speak to a foreign client, they may employ an accountant to interpret complex financial matters for them. The court reasoned that both the interpreter and the accountant should be protected by the privilege because they were conduits of information between the lawyer and client. Thus, the accountant in *Kovel* could not be made to testify as to information given to him in confidence by a client of the lawyer who employed him.

Kansas' attorney/client privilege statute (K.S.A 60-426): ". . . communications found by the judge to have been between lawyer and his or her client in the course of that relationship and in professional confidence, are privileged, and a client has a privilege (1) if he or she is the witness to refuse to disclose any such communication, and (2) to prevent his or her lawyer from disclosing it . . ."

Wisconsin's attorney/client privilege (Section 905.03(2)): "A client has a privilege to refuse to disclose and to prevent any other person from disclosing confidential communications made for the purpose of facilitating the rendition of professional legal services to the client. . . .

Arizona's attorney/client privilege (Evidence Code §12-2234):

In a civil action an attorney shall not, without the consent of his client, be examined as to any communication made by the client to him, or his advice given thereon in the course of professional employment. An attorney's paralegal, assistant, secretary, stenographer or clerk shall not, without the consent of his employer, be examined concerning any fact the knowledge of which was acquired in such capacity.

Wigmore, in his treatise on evidence, claims "it has never been questioned that the privilege protects communications to the attorney's clerks and other agents."[3] *Procunier v. Martinez*[4] extended the attorney/client privilege to the paralegal for the first time. The U.S. Supreme Court in that case held that the assistance of paralegals, secretaries, outside investigators, and the like is "indispensable" to the work of a lawyer and, because communications to the lawyer from the client must often be made through such assistants, the privilege must apply to them. Further, an unjustifiable restriction on the use of such assistants by lawyers representing prisoners was held to be an unconstitutional restriction on the right of access to the courts.

> In *People v. Mitchell* [448 N.E.2d 121 (N.Y. 1983)], the defendant, accused of murder, made disclosures to two legal secretaries and a paralegal at an attorney's law office. The court held that the attorney/client privilege did not apply but pointed out that this decision was based on the dubious existence of an employment contract between the defendant and the attorney and between the two secretaries and the attorney. Although this case appears to say that the attorney/client privilege is not extended to employees of the attorney, this case turned on the admissions of the defendant made to an attorney who was not retained by him and to persons who were not employed by the attorney. They could not, therefore, be considered "conduits" of information between attorney and client.

How long does the attorney/client privilege last? Forever. However there is some authority for loss of the privilege after the death of the client in certain circumstances. It can be lost during the client's life, however, if the lawyer or the client (or you) release the information to third parties. It can also be waived by the client.

An example of the use of the attorney/client privilege is that the grand jury cannot subpoena the lawyer to testify as to what the client said. Similarly, the lawyer cannot be called upon to testify in court about privileged information. In a civil court, the opposing side that serves an interrogatory requesting all information that the client told the lawyer will receive only "Objection. Attorney/client privilege" as a response. All of the times when testimony is required are the times when the attorney/client privilege would come into play: grand jury, deposition testimony, in-court testimony, answers to interrogatories, requests for admission, answers to document requests.

Let's review the many differences between what is *confidential* and what is protected by the *attorney/client privilege*. The attorney/client privilege does not protect information that is available to the public. However, the obligation to keep information confidential does encompass information that is public. Consider this scenario: The district attorney announces to the news media that your client was found in the possession of the murder weapon. The press reports that information, and it appears in the newspaper. Your client has told you that he was found with the murder weapon. Can the district attorney call upon you to testify that your client was found with the murder weapon? No. Because if your client told this information to you, it is protected by the attorney/client privilege. Can you go home and tell your roommate that your client was found with the murder weapon? No. Because you

In *Swidler & Berlin v. United States*, the U.S. Supreme Court considered a request by Independent Counsel Kenneth Starr to recognize a limited exception to the attorney/client privilege in the context of a pending criminal investigation. At issue were notes made by James Hamilton, an attorney for Vincent Foster, who was then Deputy White House Counsel. Foster met with Hamilton for about two hours. Nine days later, Foster committed suicide. Starr was investigating a White House scandal. It was reasonable to assume that Foster said something to Hamilton about that scandal during their two hours together. How did the Supreme Court rule? See 524 U.S. 399 (1998).

have a duty to keep it confidential. It may seem illogical that you have to keep information confidential that is already reported in the press, but the duty of confidentiality is a duty that is *personal to you*. It does not matter what others are doing or saying. By accepting the representation of the client, you have given your word that you will not disclose the client's confidences. Confidentiality is a duty you have promised to your client.

The attorney/client privilege encompasses information that the lawyer (or lawyer's agent) obtains from the client only. Confidentiality encompasses all information "relating to representation of a client," regardless of its source.

The attorney/client privilege only prevents disclosure inside the judicial process. Confidentiality prevents disclosure anywhere at any time to anyone.[5]

The fact that a person is a client of your firm is confidential but is ordinarily not covered by the attorney/client privilege. The exception to this general rule is those few cases in which the identity of a client may lead to criminal prosecution. In those cases, some courts have extended the attorney/client privilege to the identity of the client.[6]

Disclosure of confidential information doesn't penalize the client, but disclosure of attorney/client privileged information blows the privilege. To maintain the privilege, the information has to remain secret.

Attorney/client privileged information should be labeled "Attorney/client privileged." That designation may not protect you if the information falls into the wrong hands, but it certainly gives you a better argument for protecting the privilege.

In brief, the duty of confidentiality is a duty—a responsibility. The attorney/client privilege is an evidentiary privilege—a protection against disclosure.

Where Do the Two Concepts Overlap?

The client who discloses to you that he killed his wife and buried her in the backyard has given you two things: confidential information and information that is protected by the attorney/client privilege. The first means that you cannot tell anyone (aside from your need-to-know circle) what that client has said to you (even if you change the names, dates, places, or other identifying information),

The NALA Model Standards state that "Legal Assistants should preserve the confidences and secrets of all clients."

and the second means that you cannot be called upon to testify about what the client said to you. If you were asked to testify, you should refuse to answer the question on the ground of attorney/client privilege. When your friends ask you about the client who killed his wife and buried her in the backyard, your proper response is "What client?"

How Can I Make Sure I Do My Duty?

The NFPA Model Code: Canon 5

A paralegal shall preserve all confidential information provided by the client or acquired from other sources before, during, and after the course of the professional relations.

NALS Code of Ethics Canon 4.

Members of this association shall preserve and protect the confidences and privileged communications of a client.

The duty of confidentiality is always of concern to people in the legal profession, especially because of the increasing number of freelancers and contract employees who come into contact with so much different confidential information from all sorts of sources. It must also be of prime concern when changing jobs (discussed in depth later in this chapter). The most difficult aspect of this concept, however, may be the vigilance required in ordinary conversation. Here's an example: Balana, a law firm employee, is asked to do some research on a prospective corporate takeover attempt for a client of her law firm, John Smith. She is instructed that Smith is secretly buying ABC Corporation stock in order to gain a majority of shares for voting purposes. That evening, Balana tells her husband Mark about her research project. Balana does not divulge the name of the corporation or the name of the client. Mark does not work for a law firm. The next day, Mark is playing racquetball with his friend Jordan, who is a lawyer. Mark doesn't see any harm in telling Jordan about Balana's new research project, because the names are not divulged and because Jordan does primarily probate work. Later that day, Jordan is at a partnership strategy meeting at his firm. Something is mentioned about their major client, ABC Corporation, and the seemingly large blocks of shares being traded. Jordan puts two and two together and suggests that someone has been buying ABC stock using the names of various businesses or subsidiaries. Jordan's firm is able to thwart the takeover attempt because of the advance warning given very innocently by Mark. Balana has breached her duty to preserve the confidences of the client.

This example illustrates how adversely even a small or partial disclosure of a client confidence can affect the client. Law firm employees, as well as corporate employees, should not discuss confidential information regarding clients with their spouses, with other relatives, with friends, or with strangers. An exception to this rule *may* be when a legal professional is undergoing psychiatric care and feels the need to discuss a case with regard to his or her feelings about it. In this instance, although the duty of confidentiality has technically been violated, the mental health professional is also bound to keep the confidences from being revealed.

Just as states enacted versions of the Model Rules in different forms, the confidentiality rules differ slightly from state to state. As with all of the rules of ethics, it is important to read and understand the authority on confidentiality in your

NFPA's EC 1.5(a) says that the paralegal should familiarize himself with the legal authority in his jurisdiction as to confidential information and abide by that authority. EC 1.5(b) says that the confidential information shall not be used to the disadvantage of the client.

jurisdiction. The thrust of every state's rule is that information about the client or the representation, regardless of the source, should not be discussed with anyone.

Federal Rules of Evidence Rule 501 is the general rule that deals with the subject of privileges.

> Except as otherwise required by the Constitution of the United States or provided by Act of Congress or in rules prescribed by the Supreme Court pursuant to statutory authority, the privilege of a witness, person, government, State, or political subdivision thereof shall be governed by the principles of the common law as they may be interpreted by the courts of the United States in the light of reason and experience. However, in civil actions and proceedings, with respect to an element of a claim or defense as to which State law supplies the rule of decision, the privilege of a witness, person, government, State, or political subdivision thereof shall be determined in accordance with State law.

What Confidential Information Can Be Divulged?

Exception 1: Doing Your Job

Quite obviously, some confidential information must be disclosed. For example, Model Rule 1.6 specifically exempts from the nondisclosure rules "disclosures that are impliedly authorized in order to carry out the representation." This allows the disclosure of information as necessary to do your job: draft the complaint, answer the interrogatories, or respond to other discovery. And, as discussed earlier, you can discuss client confidences with the people in the need-to-know circle in your law firm.

Exception 2: Express Waiver

Sometimes your client will waive the duty of confidentiality regarding some information. That waiver can be very formal or casual. If you are going to rely on a waiver from the client, it would be best to have it in writing.

Exception 3: Defending against Client Actions

Even though all of the information relating to the representation of the client is confidential, the law firm may use it to defend itself against a negligence (malpractice) claim by the client or to collect its fees from the client. Care should be taken not to reveal more than is necessary to accomplish the task. Using the release of confidential information as a weapon against the client is prohibited.

Exception 4: Commission of a Crime

According to ABA Model Rule 3.3, information that the lawyer gains relating to the representation of the client while ordinarily confidential loses its confidential nature when it becomes part of the commission of a crime. So too does the criminal or fraudulent activity of the employees of the law firm.

Exception 5: Preventing a Crime

The most interesting part of this rule is the part that exempts from confidentiality information that the legal professional may have to reveal "to prevent the client from committing a [serious] criminal act." Various states adopted this part of ABA Model Rule 1.6 in different forms. Some states made revealing the crime mandatory while others leave it to the discretion of the legal professional. Some states limited "the crime" to a crime of death or serious bodily harm, and others enlarged it to include fraud.

> This is worth looking up so that you are aware of the standard in your state. When the emergency arises, you may not have time to conduct in-depth legal research. To start your research, see *Rocca v. Southern Hills Counseling Center* [671 N.E.2d 913 (Ind.App. 1996)].

Exception 6: Not "Client Information"

The facts surrounding the smoking gun brought in by the firm's criminal defendant is confidential and therefore must not be disclosed by law firm personnel. The client's false income tax reports are also protected. The documents that show that your client breached the contract willfully and maliciously are confidences, as well. However, the lawyer standing over the paper shredder destroying those documents is not covered by the confidentiality duty because: (1) the shredding is not "information gained in the representation of the client," although you may be engaged in the representation of your client while you are standing in the doorway watching the destruction of the client's documents; (2) the shredding is criminal activity constituting the lawyer's intent to commit a fraud upon the court; (3) so, therefore, that the papers are being shredded is not confidential.

Just as we saw with unauthorized practice of law, we don't want to become paralyzed by the rules of ethics. We want to understand them and use them and protect the public with them.

So, Then, What's the Work Product Privilege?

Work product is simply the work produced by a lawyer or his agent. Some examples are research memoranda, witness interviews, and notes resulting from other investigation. Work product is accorded almost absolute protection from discovery. Historically, this is because any slight factual content that such items may have is generally outweighed by the legal system's interest in maintaining privacy of the legal professional's thought processes and in ensuring that each side relies on its own wit in preparing its respective cases. This is true of lawyers, paralegals, investigators, and others who work for lawyers.

Federal Rules of Civil Procedure 26(b)(3) sets out the work product privilege. It applies to documents and things prepared in anticipation of litigation or trial by or for a party or his representatives. It says that generally a party may not obtain discovery of documents and tangible things prepared in anticipation of litigation.

> "Attorneys often must rely on the assistance of investigators and other agents in the compilation of materials in preparation for trial. It is therefore necessary that the [work product] doctrine protect materials prepared by agents of the attorney as well as those prepared by the attorney himself."
> *U.S. v. Nobles*, 422 U.S. 225 (1975)

The work product doctrine is distinct from and broader than the attorney/client privilege. The attorney/client privilege applies only to information from the client. The work product doctrine encompasses all work prepared in anticipation of litigation regardless of the source of the information. The work product privilege extends to both tangible and intangible work product, and the protection extends to materials prepared by the lawyer's agents and consultants.[7]

E-mail is protected by both the attorney/client privilege (assuming the e-mail is between lawyer and client) and the work product doctrine (assuming that the e-mail discusses or transmits information relating to or prepared in anticipation of trial).[8]

Both clients and lawyers can assert the work product privilege.[9] But the privilege typically does not belong to nonparties to the litigation.[10] And, the work product privilege probably is only good until the end of the litigation for which it was created, or perhaps it extends to later litigation that is related.[11]

Opinion work product will ordinarily be entitled to absolute protection.[12] This goes back to the idea that everyone should have to litigate their own case without help from the other side.

The holder of this privilege is the lawyer, but the client also has the right to assert it.

> If the judge needs to see the material to determine if it is protected by the privilege, the judge may take the documents and review them "*in camera*." That means privately, outside of the view of the parties or attorney in the action.

Are There Any Exceptions to the Work Product Privilege?

Unlike the attorney/client privilege (absolute if properly created and not waived), the work product privilege provides only limited protection from disclosure. Federal Rule 26(b)(3), for example, allows a party to overcome the privilege's protection if the party can prove "substantial need" for the information and cannot obtain the material any other way "without undue hardship." So, for example, if a witness cannot be located or has died, a court might order the disclosure of the notes of a witness interview.

Disclosure to an adversary waives the privilege.[13] But disclosure to cocounsel probably doesn't. And the lawyer may need to set aside the privilege to defend against a malpractice action brought by the client.

Inadvertent disclosure to the other side may or may not waive the privilege. See our discussion about *Rico v. Mitsubishi Motors Corp.*, 116 Cal.App.4th 51 (2004), in the next section.

How Has Technology Changed Confidentiality?

Oh No!!! I just faxed that crucial letter to opposing counsel instead of our client!!!!!

What did the invention of the fax machine do to the concepts we have just studied? Nothing, really. The fax machine delivers the lawyer's letter to the client faster than the postal system. If the letter is accidentally faxed to the wrong person, confidential information has been released. Before the invention of the fax machine (and after), the same thing would happen if the letter was accidentally addressed and mailed to the wrong person.

If the envelope is inadvertently addressed to opposing counsel instead of the client, what is opposing counsel's duty regarding receipt of privileged and confidential information? The answer depends on the jurisdiction, not on how fast the information reached the wrong person.

In the 2004 revisions to the Model Rules of Professional Conduct, the ABA added a new Rule 4.4(b) that states:

> A lawyer who receives a document relating to the representation of the lawyer's client and knows or reasonably should know that the document was inadvertently sent shall promptly notify the sender.

Take a look at your state rules. Did your state adopt this change? Is there any reason to believe that this rule does not apply equally to every person in the law office?

* Full Model Rule and commentary can be found in Appendix E.

Those jurisdictions that say the receiving party has a duty to return the correspondence without reading it say the same thing whether the correspondence went by mail carrier, messenger, e-mail, or fax. Cases about inadvertent receipt of confidential or privileged information are all over the boards. Some jurisdictions require the inadvertent recipient to return the information unread to the sender. In practical terms, this would mean that you're standing at the fax machine and see a new fax coming in. You read just enough of it to see that it's addressed to someone's client, not to you or your law firm. You wait for the fax to be fully transmitted and, with your eyes closed, you put it in an envelope, address the envelope to the sender, and stick it in the mail.

Formal Opinion 2004-F-150: The receiving lawyer should either refrain from reviewing the materials or should limit the review to determining how to proceed.	Maine Op 146 (1994) said that counsel could use the privileged information but withdrew that opinion for Opinion 172 (2000) in light of *Corey v. Norman, Hanson & DeTroy* (1999 ME 196).

New York Country Law Association formal Op 730 (2002) . . . the lawyer shall without further review or other use thereof, notify the sender and . . . abide by sender's instruction regarding return or destruction of the information.

Some courts say this flies in the face of your duty to represent your client zealously. It was zeal for his client that induced Attorney Johnson to pick up, read, photocopy, and distribute obviously confidential work product he found in a conference room in *Rico v. Mitsubishi Motors*. A California appellate court ruled that the attorney violated his ethical duties by reading the information.[14] The California Supreme Court has agreed to hear the case.

ABA Formal Ethics Opinion 99-413 says that we "may transmit information relating to the representation of a client by unencrypted e-mail sent over the Internet without violating the Model Rules of Professional Conduct because the mode of transmission affords a reasonable expectation of privacy from a technological and legal standpoint. The same privacy accorded U.S. and commercial mail, landline telephonic transmissions, and facsimiles applies to Internet e-mail. A lawyer should consult with the client and follow her instructions, however, as to the mode of transmitting highly sensitive information relating to the client's representation."

E-Mail

Because we live in the information age, we need to be more vigilant about maintaining client confidences. We need to be careful to whom we send e-mail. It is all too easy to click on the wrong "to" address and send sensitive information to the wrong person. What has e-mail done to confidentiality? It hasn't changed the standard. It has just made it easier to make a mistake. Although there was a great deal of discussion about sending only encrypted e-mails when e-mail was new, most jurisdictions have found that breaking into your computer isn't much different from breaking into your mailbox. Stolen information is the same today as it was yesterday, only faster.

Quite naturally, if the client is sharing an e-mail address, the risk of the release of confidential information goes up. This should be discussed with the client. It's not safe to assume that every client is technology knowledgeable.

Cell Phones

Likewise, the ubiquitous cell phone. Again, there was a great deal of discussion about cell communications not being "secure" and conversations being "stolen" out of the air. There could well be people who will use high-tech equipment to eavesdrop on your cell communication. But these are no doubt the same people who used high-tech equipment to bug your landline or otherwise listen in on your telephone conversations. Should we be vigilant? Absolutely. Has the standard changed? No.

Even though your cell phone is your best friend, you should not use it for client matters when out in public. Even your side of the conversation could inadvertently release confidential information ultimately to the detriment of your client.

It is worthwhile to take a look at the progress of the ongoing conversation in your state. Some states went conservative on the issue from the start: Illinois Formal Opinion 94-11 (". . . use of such a mode of communication may result in a loss of the attorney/client privilege with respect to such communications . . ."); Massachusetts Opinion 94-5 (". . . lawyers should not discuss confidential information on a cellular telephone if there is any nontrivial risk that such information could be overheard by a third party . . ."). Others have warned that cell phones may have harmful consequences for clients but have stopped short of declaring the use of a cell phone as an ethical breach. *See, e.g.*, Arizona Ethics Opinion 95-11.

Computers

We need to be careful if we are working on client matters in public places. If you're sitting at the Starbucks with your laptop working on a client matter, you need protection for your computer screen so that others can't read what's showing on your screen.

Your laptop should be passworded so that curious people cannot access confidential information. Your computer should be protected from spyware and other intrusions. We are constantly being reminded of operating system "holes" and worms, viruses, trojan horses, or other "techno-evils" that can ferret out information from our computers. Just as you would not leave a box of confidential client documents sitting around in a public place, you don't want to leave your computer open to others. We are obligated to do what a reasonable person would do to protect our clients' confidences.

Documents

There are *metadata* stored deep in the electronic storage part of every document created on a computer. These metadata show when the document was created and by whom and for which client (if that is part of your firm's computer filing system). Metadata show each edited version and what changes were made all along the way. There is a veritable treasure trove of information stored in computer-created documents, and all of this information can be "mined." That is, with the right software, all of this information can be discovered if the electronic version of the document is transmitted. That's a whole bunch of confidential information! There are ways to protect your documents from being "mined" for this information. The most obvious way is to only transmit hard copies of documents. There are also software programs that you can use that strip the metadata out of documents.

Client Files and Confidentiality?

Just think of all of the confidential information you are storing in the file room! And what do we do with all of that stuff after the case has concluded?

We know we have a responsibility to take care of things that belong to the client that we have in our possession. The *Restatement (Third) of Law Governing Lawyers* requires that a lawyer "take reasonable steps to safeguard documents in the lawyer's possession relating to the representation of a client or former client."[15] This means that we can't just toss the client files in the trash or recycle bin when the case or matter has concluded. In general, we can give the files back to the client. If your fee agreement specifies that the client is responsible for the files at the conclusion of the representation, with a few exceptions, we can box up the files and ship them out to the now former client. Exceptions to this rule are certain documents that are subject to a confidentiality agreement that, by agreement, the client cannot see; certain original documents that are subject to probate or criminal code restrictions or might have to be filed with the court later; and documents that for some other reason the client should not see.

If you are going to return all of the files to the client, consider keeping a copy for your use. If you photocopy the files so you can have a copy, you shouldn't charge the client for the copying. The files belong to the client. Any copies you want to make for your records must be done at your own expense.

If you are thinking about destroying the files, most states have record-retention requirements that are somewhere between five and ten years so you should definitely find your state's requirement first. You also should check with your professional liability insurance carrier. It will probably tell you that you should keep the files at least for the time during which a malpractice action or breach of contract action could be filed—usually between five and ten years.

You can store the files in any secure place. Your basement probably isn't a very good idea. There are lots of inexpensive document-storage facilities, and you can store them electronically. No matter what you do, store or destroy, you should keep a comprehensive index of what the file contains. Naturally, you should never destroy any document that has some intrinsic value such as money orders, traveler's checks, stocks, bonds, wills, original deeds, original notes, judgments, and the like that may have value in and of themselves or documents that create or extinguish legal rights or obligations.

"A lawyer may comply with the mandatory record retention provision by storing certain records as computer-generated images. The lawyer must ensure that the electronic storage technique will safeguard the records from inadvertent destruction at least as effectively as the paper record, and that it will permit prompt reproduction of accurate, unaltered copies upon proper request. Before disposing any of the paper records, the lawyer must ensure that all required copies have in fact, been transferred. Certain records must be retained in their original form: check books, check stubs, bank statements, pre-numbered and canceled checks, duplicative deposit slips and other documents that are not referred to as 'copies.' New York State Bar Association Opinion 680 (January 10, 1996).

The ABA offered an Informal Opinion in 1997 that recognized the continuing economic burden of storing retired and inactive files. Sympathetically, the ABA opined that the issue of how to deal with this burden is primarily a question of business management and not primarily a question of ethics or professional responsibility.

The ABA concluded that a lawyer does not have a general duty to preserve all files permanently. It pointed out that the public interest is not served by unnecessary additions to the costs of legal services required by substantial storage costs. However, the ABA also concluded that clients (and former clients) reasonably expect that valuable and useful information in the lawyer's files will not be prematurely and carelessly destroyed. The committee declined to state a specific time at which a lawyer must preserve all files and when those files may be destroyed. Instead, it offered the opinion that "good common sense" should provide the answers to most questions that arise regarding file retention and destruction. The committee did offer some general considerations in Informal Opinion 1384 (Appendix D).

If you don't have a clause in your fee agreement about retention of client files, which you probably don't, and you want to destroy these old files, many states require that you at least attempt to notify the client about the destruction of the files and the client's right to claim them. There will be technical requirements about how and when to give notice and how long you have to wait after you have not gotten a response from the former client. If the client is dead by the time you think to return his files, there will be even more requirements designed to protect the client's confidentiality requirement (which continues beyond the client's death) and any value the estate might find in the file such as continuing legal rights.

You don't have to do this the old-fashioned way. There are a number of readily available software programs to help you organize open and closed files and put together a storage and destruction schedule.

As you have an obligation to protect the confidentiality of the client files, destruction of the files should be as complete as possible such as confetti shredding or burning. There is no obligation to hire a professional to destroy the documents, and destruction of the documents is not billable time. So long as the information cannot be retrieved, the confidentiality has been protected.

SUMMARY

You are now able to differentiate between the duty of confidentiality and the attorney/ client evidentiary privilege. The duty of confidentiality lasts for your lifetime and beyond. Information you learn about your clients can never be divulged for a purpose other than to assist your client through the representation and must never be discussed with anyone other than those in the "need-to-know" sphere. This is true even if you change the names, dates, places, or other identifying information. The world is smaller than you think. If you ever consider divulging confidential information, ask yourself, "Would I want someone telling other people my personal business?" All of the secret information that you gained directly from the client is covered by the attorney/ client privilege so you can rest assured that you cannot be called upon to testify about it. When you are ready to box up and store those old client files, keep confidentiality in mind. That confidential information that you have from working with clients will be with you always and may create a conflict of interest for you in the future.

CHAPTER REVIEW AND ASSIGNMENTS

CRITICAL THINKING

1. Let's go back to April who wants to write magazine articles using information she has obtained from a former client of her law firm. Now that you understand more about the duty of confidentiality, what do you think? If you want to research an answer to April's question, you can start here: *Doe v. Roe,* 93 Misc.2d 201, 400 N.Y.S.2d 668 (N.Y.Supp. 1977).
2. Janelle is with a law firm that specializes in criminal defense. She has been working on the criminal defense of Robert Smith, an inmate at Santa Ramos penitentiary. Janelle goes to see Mr. Smith at the prison quite often. Mr. Smith is being represented by Janelle's firm in a civil matter, as well. During a trial in that matter, Janelle is called to the witness stand to testify as to what Mr. Smith told her about a particular business transaction in which he was engaged before he was incarcerated. Mr. Smith's lawyer (Janelle's employer) objects to the question. How will the judge rule on the objection and why? Does it make any difference if Janelle is a lawyer or a paralegal?
3. Sam, a law office employee, often tells his wife about the estates with which he is involved at work. Sam believes that so long as he doesn't tell his wife the

names (he refers to the cases as "Mr. A's estate" or "Ms. B's will") he has not divulged any secrets. Is Sam correct? Does it change your answer if Sam's wife is not involved in the field of law in any way?

4. George is leaving his civil litigation position and has been interviewing with other firms that do the same sort of work. During his interviews, George has been discussing the cases he works on so that he will not get involved in a conflict-of-interest problem with his new employment. Should George tell prospective employers about the clients he has worked for who are contemplating civil litigation but who have not yet filed a complaint? How can George clear potential conflicts without violating the duty of confidentiality?

ASSIGNMENTS

1. If you haven't already, this is the time for you to know your state law on these three issues: duty of confidentiality, attorney/client privilege, and work product privilege. Where is the law located? Is the duty in your Rules of Professional Conduct? Are the two privileges in your evidence code? Find them. Make copies. Put them in your ethics notebook for future reference.

2. This would be a good time to watch the movie *Class Action* with Gene Hackman (Jedediah Tucker Ward) and Mary Elizabeth Mastrantonio (Maggie Ward, his daughter). This movie is reminiscent of the Ford Pinto explosion cases of the 1970s. It has several ethical quandaries and tells a terrific David versus Goliath tale. Eventually Maggie must decide what to do with confidential information in a difficult ethical situation.

COLLABORATIVE ASSIGNMENTS

1. Read *Leone v. Fisher*, 2006 WL 2982145 (D. Conn. 2006) using a Reading 1 2 3 graphic organizer. (You can find both on the publishers website.) Then get together in groups of three or four and discuss three things you learned from the case, the two most interesting parts of the case and the one question you have.

2. In teams, write an informative brochure that has as its purpose explaining the duty of confidentiality, the attorney/client privilege, and the work product privilege to members of the public. Use a template for a tri-fold brochure or write it by hand. Make it interesting and informative.

Multiple Choice Questions

Select the best answer for each of the following questions.

1. Clients need to be sure that their confidences will remain confidential because
   a. The attorney needs to have all relevant information from the client.
   b. The client deserves anonymity.
   c. It is an ethical obligation required by law and rules of ethics.
   d. All of the above.
   e. None of the above.

2. Information obtained on behalf of the firm's client must be kept confidential
   a. except if the client is a minor.
   b. except if the client advises you on the phone that his or her permission to release it is granted.
   c. except if the adversary requests the information in a formal legal notice.
   d. except if the attorney advises that you may release it.
   e. none of the above.

3. Information you acquire about the representation of a client of the firm by which you are employed but obtained through your personal activities outside the office
   a. is not confidential because it is available to the public.
   b. is confidential because it is about the representation of the client.
   c. is arguably confidential and should be discussed with the supervising attorney.
   d. is not confidential at all.
   e. none of the above.

4. If you overhear a conversation between a lawyer you don't know and that lawyer's client in a restaurant,
   a. You have no obligation to keep that information confidential.
   b. The client has waived the privilege of confidentiality.

   c. The issue of waiving confidentiality will need to be decided by the courts.
   d. None of the above.
   e. All of the above.

5. Once a client has retained a lawyer to represent him or her,
   a. All information obtained in the course of representing that client is confidential.
   b. Only information about this particular matter is confidential.
   c. Only information coming directly from the client is confidential.
   d. Only that information that the client requests be confidential is confidential.
   e. None of the above.

6. Abbey Paralegal and her boyfriend are attending a Dodger baseball game. During the game, in a hushed voice, Abbey tells her boyfriend, "Yesterday my firm took a new client, Mr. Vincent Snodgrass. He's never paid income taxes!" Abbey has
   a. not done anything wrong because she spoke softly.
   b. violated her duty of confidentiality.
   c. violated the attorney/client privilege.
   d. violated the work product doctrine.
   e. violated her ethical duties only if what she said was not true.

7. Abbey is attending an office conference about the Mr. Snodgrass matter. He is not present. Abbey's two supervising lawyers discuss how best to "get Snodgrass off" of any potential tax fraud charges, criminal or civil. Abbey should
   a. talk to a higher supervising lawyer about this conversation.
   b. tell her office manager that the lawyers are planning a cover-up.
   c. call the state bar and report the conduct anonymously.

d. not worry. The conversation was perfectly ethical.

e. worry about it, but do nothing.

8. In preparation for taking Mr. Snodgrass as a client, and understanding that he owes the federal government a lot of money, Abbey's firm conducts a detailed credit check on Snodgrass. The results show that he owes a lot of money to BigStore, a major local company, from a purchase of equipment and that the debt is five years old. This information

a. is protected by attorney/client privilege.

b. is protected by the work product doctrine.

c. is confidential.

d. is public information and over four years old so perfectly okay to discuss in public.

e. all of the above.

9. Abbey is working late one evening and hears a grinding noise coming from a room down the hall from her office. She creeps down the hall and peeks in the door. Inside, she sees one of her supervising lawyers standing over the paper shredder feeding in papers that look like Mr. Snodgrass's business receipts and invoices. Abbey should

a. not tell anyone because the documents are confidential.

b. not tell anyone because the lawyer's activities on the matter are confidential.

c. offer to help because it is in the best interests of the client.

d. talk to the appropriate authority in her firm about what she saw.

e. immediately write a memo to the file, keep a copy, and put a copy in the client's file.

10. In general, knowledge paralegals gain about clients from the client is

a. protected work product.

b. confidential information.

c. protected by the attorney/client privilege.

d. both *b* and *c*.

e. none of the above.

Fill in the Blank

Complete each of the following sentences with the best word(s) or phrase(s).

1. Many people, including lawyers, get confused between the duty of confidentiality and the _____.

2. The duty of confidentiality covers all information relating to the representation of the client, regardless _____.

3. The duty of confidentiality means _____.

4. The duty of confidentiality lasts until _____.

5. The attorney/client privilege can be found in _____. (I'm looking for where in your state codes this privilege is defined; or, if it is found in the case law, tell me the name of the case.)

6. The attorney/client privilege protects _____ and only applies _____.

7. The attorney/client privilege lasts until _____.

8. Some exceptions to the duty of confidentiality are _____.

9. Some "non-exceptions" to the duty of confidentiality are _____.

10. The work product privilege protects _____ from disclosure.

True/False

Decide whether each of the following statements is true or false and write your answer on the line provided.

_____ 1. Attorney/client privilege and the duty of confidentiality are basically the same.

_____ 2. The duty of confidentiality does not appear in the Model Rules. States must rely on case law.

_____ 3. Information about the client is confidential regardless of the source.

_____ 4. The duty of confidentiality ends when the case or client matter has ended.

_____ 5. The duty of confidentiality is one of those duties that applies to paralegals as well as to lawyers.

_____ 6. The National Federation of Paralegal Associations' ethical rules advise paralegals to learn the law of their jurisdiction with respect to confidential information.

_____ 7. If there is an express waiver from the client, confidential information may be released.

_____ 8. Illegal activity that takes place in the law office, for example, selling marijuana, is covered by the duty of confidentiality. As a result, if you see this illegal activity, you cannot report it to anyone outside of the "need-to-know" circle.

_____ 9. Work product privilege is an old-fashioned rule that we don't need to know about.

_____ 10. Because e-mail is a technological development that came into existence after the rule of confidentiality was created, e-mail communications are not covered by the rules of confidentiality.

CASES FOR CONSIDERATION

CASE 1

RODRIGUEZ v. MONTALVO
337 F.Supp. 2d 212
(D. Mass. 2004)

A. FACTUAL BACKGROUND

In December 1998, Rodriguez rented a first-floor apartment located at 47 Salem Street, Fitchburg, Massachusetts ("the premises") from Montalvo. Her son, Jose, had Duchenne's Muscular Dystrophy and was a quadriplegic. Jose therefore used a wheelchair to ambulate and (beginning in early 2001) needed a ventilator to breathe. Rodriguez requested permission to make modifications to the dwelling in order to accommodate Jose's disability. Specifically, Rodriguez requested permission to install a permanent ramp at her own expense and offered to have access to the dwelling restored to its original condition when she moved out. That request was made several times during the tenancy but was consistently refused by Montalvo.

Instead, Montalvo allowed Rodriguez to use temporary and easily removable boards over the stairs to access the apartment.

The makeshift ramp was, however, problematic according to Rodriguez. First, it was unsafe during the winter because the boards were not affixed to the outside steps and thus were not secure in icy or snowy conditions. Second, even when the ramp was secure, it was of little help because two people were still required to assist Jose into the house, one from behind and one from the front. Third, Jose began using a medically necessary ventilator in June 2001 which required a special wheelchair that carried Jose and his ventilator, allowing him to be connected to the ventilator at all times. The new wheelchair was too big for both the temporary ramp and the doorway to the premises. As a result, in order for Jose to gain access to the premises, he needed to be disconnected from the ventilator and carried into the home.

From that time forward, Jose was afraid to leave his home because he had to be disconnected from his ventilator in order to do so. As a result, he rarely left the apartment except for necessary medical appointments. He suffered various minor injuries from having to be carried in and out of the premises on those occasions. Jose died on June 11, 2002.

Rodriguez sued Montalvo and his girlfriend, Lori Oltman ("Oltman"), who was allegedly the broker of the premises. Rodriguez alleged statutory violations of the Fair Housing Act, 42 U.S.C. § 3601–31, and the Massachusetts Anti-Discrimination Statute, M.G.L. c. 151B, and common law counts of intentional and negligent infliction of emotional distress, negligent failure to train and supervise and negligent retention. Rodriguez now moves this Court to attach Defendants' real estate up to the amount of $125,000.

I.

(The Legal Analysis for the Motion to Attach Real Estate is omitted.)

II.

The Motion to Disqualify Defense Counsel

In July 2001 Rodriguez contacted the Massachusetts Justice Project ("MJP") seeking legal assistance in her dispute with Montalvo and various collateral matters related to her rental property. Upon contacting MJP, at which defense counsel David Florio and Anna Phillips were then employed, Rodriguez spoke to paralegals Flor Cintron ("Cintron") and Keyda Montalban ("Montalban"). In her initial conversation, Rodriguez gave Cintron basic information pertaining to her legal problems concerning accessibility to Rodriguez's apartment. Cintron told Rodriguez that MJP would send her written information regarding her legal rights and that she should call back after reviewing that information.

After Rodriguez had done as instructed, she called MJP and spoke to Montalban. Rodriguez conveyed relevant financial information to determine her eligibility for MJP's services and background information regarding the facts of her case. The parties dispute whether Rodriguez disclosed information material to her state and federal claims against Montalvo. Attorneys Florio and Phillips were employed as staff attorneys at MJP at the time of Rodriguez's initial contact, but left in 2002 to form their own law firm which now represents Montalvo. While employed at MJP, Attorney Phillips was responsible for reviewing Montalban's intake file but the parties dispute the extent of that review function.

With Rodriguez's consent, MJP subsequently referred her case to the Legal Assistance Corporation of Central Massachusetts ("LACCM") for legal assistance, which subsequently led to the filing of this action. Following the October 17 hearing, Plaintiff's counsel submitted for in camera review a copy of Rodriguez's entire MJP written file. That file includes MJP's intake sheet pertaining to Rodriguez, the initial follow-up letter and a computer printout of MJP's intake sheet and an eligibility checker with financial and other information. Pending before the Court is Rodriguez's motion to disqualify Florio as the Defendants' counsel on the grounds that MJP's earlier advice to Rodriguez constitutes a conflict of interest.

B. LEGAL ANALYSIS

In deciding whether to disqualify an attorney based on a prior representation, Massachusetts courts have attempted to reconcile an individual's right to counsel of his choice with the obligation of maintaining the highest standards of professional conduct and the scrupulous administration of justice. See *Mailer v. Mailer*, 390 Mass. 371, 373, 455 N.E.2d 1211, 1212 (1983). Massachusetts Rules of Professional Conduct 1.9 and 1.10 govern conflicts of interest in the representation of a former client. Rule 1.9 provides, in relevant part, that:

> A lawyer shall not knowingly represent a person in the same or a substantially related matter in which a firm with which the lawyer formerly was associated had previously represented a client (1) whose interests are materially adverse to that person; and (2) about whom the lawyer had acquired information . . . that is material to the matter, unless the client consents after writing. Mass. R. Prof. C. 1.9(b) (emphasis added).

Rule 1.10 extends Rule 1.9's prohibition to any lawyer associated in a firm with a potentially conflicted lawyer. Mass. R. Prof. C. 1.10(a).

The relevant inquiry in a motion to disqualify based on a former representation is into the degree of relevance between the two representations, i.e., "whether the subject matter of the two representations is substantially related." See *Borges v. Our Lady of the Sea Corp.*, 935 F.2d 436, 439–40 (1st Cir. 1991) (identifying the proper inquiry as, "[C]ould the attorney have obtained confidential information in the first suit that would have been relevant to the second[?]").

Massachusetts courts have elaborated on this premise, explaining that under the "substantial relationship" test, a subsequent representation is proscribed on the grounds that the later suit, by virtue of its relationship to the former suit, exposes the attorney to "an intolerably strong temptation to breach his duty of confidentiality to the former client." E.g., *Bays v. Theran,* 418 Mass. 685, 691, 639 N.E.2d 720, 724 (1994), citing Note, Developments in the Law: Conflicts of Interest in the

Legal Profession, 94 *Harv. L. Rev.* 1244, 1318 (1981). The former client is not required to prove that the attorney actually misused the information, but only need show that the tempting situation existed because of an attorney-client relationship that was established in the former representation, and that the "former and current representations are both adverse and substantially related." *Bays,* 418 Mass. at 691, 639 N.E.2d at 724 (internal citation omitted).

Moreover, if a non-lawyer paralegal established a confidential relationship with a client, that relationship may be imputed to the attorney supervisor and consequently to the firm as a whole. The comment to Mass R. Prof. C. 5.3 provides that non-lawyer assistants such as paralegals "act for the lawyer in the rendition of the lawyer's professional services." The Supreme Judicial Court has held, at least in the context of a legal malpractice action, that knowledge by the attorney's employees acquired in the scope of their employment is attributable to the attorney. See *Miller v. Mooney,* 431 Mass. 57, 60, 725 N.E.2d 545, 548 n. 2 (2000), citing *DeVaux v. American Home Assurance Co.,* 387 Mass. 814, 818, 444 N.E.2d 355, 358 (1983). Finally, courts examining whether the actions or representations of an attorney's agent may be imputed to the attorney principal typically focus on the reasonable belief of the third party to whom such representations have been made. See *Kansallis Finance Ltd. v. Fern,* 421 Mass. 659, 670, 659 N.E.2d 731, 737 (1996).

In the instant case, an in camera review of MJP's files demonstrates that Montalban provided legal advice to Rodriguez such that Rodriguez reasonably could have relied upon the proffered advice during her dispute with Montalvo. Without divulging the specific information submitted to the Court, the intake file and subsequent correspondence from MJP to Rodriguez contain material information of a confidential nature. Rodriguez would have been objectively reasonable in following the advice provided by MJP and therefore would have been reasonable in imputing to MJP, as a whole, the existence of an attorney-client relationship.

Relevant case law supports the conclusion that Rodriguez established an attorney-client relationship with MJP by virtue of her communications with Cintron and Montalban. Although Rodriguez did not communicate directly with Attorney Phillips, Montalban was in a position such that Rodriguez might reasonably believe that Montalban had authority to establish an attorney-client relationship. See *DeVaux,* 387 Mass. at 819, 444 N.E.2d at 358. Although the court in *DeVaux* left to the jury the question of whether the attorney "permitted his secretary to act as she did, thereby creating the appearance of authority[,]" id., it is undisputed in this case that MJP permitted Montalban to advise Rodriguez on the appropriate course of action in her dispute with Montalvo. Indeed, Defendants admit that the handling of this case was typical of MJP's ordinary course of business. If this Court acknowledges Rodriguez's reliance interest, as is appropriate, it becomes apparent that Montalban acted as Phillips's agent. See *Kansallis Finance Ltd.,* 421 Mass. at 670, 659 N.E.2d at 737; see also *Sheinkopf v. Stone*, 927 F.2d 1259, 1265 (1st Cir. 1991) (emphasizing reliance interest). Thus, as Phillips's agent, Montalvo possessed the authority to advise Rodriguez.

The final step in this chain of reasoning leads to the conclusion that the establishment by Rodriguez of an attorney-client relationship with MJP disqualifies Attorney Florio by virtue of his former association with that legal services organization. See Mass. R. Prof. C. 1.10(a). The substantial relationship between the subject matters (indeed their identity) raises the specter that information gleaned from Rodriguez's communications with MJP could be used against her by her adversary in the very same action. Cf. *Mailer v. Mailer,* 390 Mass. 371, 374–75, 455 N.E.2d 1211, 1213 (1983) (holding that the public nature of the information conveyed did not merit disqualification of later counsel in the same matter). Although this case presents a somewhat novel context for the application of the foregoing principles, the fact that Ms. Rodriguez sought and obtained advice from a low-income legal services provider fails to alter the fundamental conflict of interest analysis.

ORDER

In accordance with and for the reasons set forth in the foregoing memorandum, Plaintiff's Motion to Attach Real Estate (Docket No. 13) is ALLOWED to the amount of $75,000 and her Motion to Disqualify Defense Counsel (Docket No. 25) is also ALLOWED.
So ordered.

CASE QUESTIONS

1. How was a "confidential relationship" established between the Plaintiff and paralegals at the Massachusetts Justice Project?
2. Can you explain "the substantial relationship test"?
3. If the two attorneys who now represent the defendant never actually met with the Plaintiff, how could they have any of the Plaintiff's confidential information?
4. What part did the paralegals play in this disqualification?

CASE 2

INSURANCE CO. OF NORTH AMERICA v. SUPERIOR COURT
108 Cal.App.3d 758, 166 Cal.Rptr. 880
(1980)

Insurance Company of North America (INA), a casualty insurer, seeks a writ of prohibition against the superior court to preserve the confidentiality of its attorney-client communications against discovery by GAF Corporation (GAF). INA is a defendant in a superior court action brought by GAF against INA, INA Corporation, INA Financial Corporation, and others, seeking declaratory and other relief with respect to liability insurance coverage for asbestos-related claims.

In the INA group of affiliated companies, INA Corporation is the parent holding company, and INA Financial Corporation, Life Insurance Company of North America, and INA are, directly or indirectly, wholly owned subsidiaries. The issue of attorney-client privilege arose under the following circumstances: Some 3,000 actions, 800 of them in Los Angeles County alone, are and have been pending against GAF and other manufacturers and commercial users of asbestos for damages for personal injuries assertedly the result of exposure of workers over substantial periods of time to asbestos fibers. From 1950 to 1975 INA was GAF's products liability insurer, and as a consequence of this and similar coverage for others INA found itself facing substantial liability for asbestos-related claims, whose potential amount, it is suggested, could reach $20 billion. As a consequence of this exposure INA employed the firm of Michael Gallagher in Cleveland, Ohio, as outside counsel to advise it on asbestos-related matters, and it solicited Gallagher's opinion on the extent of coverage of INA's products liability insurance policies with respect to asbestos-related claims against its insureds. On March 11, 1977, Gallagher undertook to report to his client on this and related legal matters at a meeting at INA's home office in Philadelphia, Pennsylvania, attended by eight full-time officers and employees of INA, five outside counsel, and two other persons. At this meeting Gallagher briefed senior management of INA on the nature and dimension of the asbestos litigation, the extent of INA coverage under its policies, its potential liability for asbestos-related claims, and possible initiation of an action for declaratory judgment. It is the events, memorandums, notes, and conversations of this meeting which GAF seeks to discover.

GAF, while recognizing that communications between attorney and client are ordinarily privileged (*Evid. Code,* § 954), asserts the privilege does not apply here, because two outsiders were present at the meeting and attorney-client communications in the presence of third persons are not privileged. (*Marshall v. Marshall* (1956) 140 Cal.App.2d 475, 480 [295 P.2d 131].) Two issues are presented. The narrow issue is whether the two persons present at the meeting were in truth and in fact outsiders to INA. The broad issue is whether, even if the two were legally unrelated to INA, disclosure to them furthered the interest of the client or was reasonably necessary to accomplish the purpose for which counsel had been consulted.

The two persons present at the conference were Earl McHugh, vice president–law of INA Corporation, attending in his capacity as a legal officer of the parent company; and Donald Heth, president of Life Insurance Company of North America, a wholly owned subsidiary of INA Corporation, attending in his capacity as a member of the reserve committee created by INA Corporation to supervise the reserve policies of its operating subsidiaries. The trial court rejected INA's claim that McHugh and Heth were present at the briefing to further the interest of the client INA in the consultation, and it concluded that their attendance destroyed confidentiality of communication between attorney and client and made Gallagher's legal opinions and advice discoverable. The court took the view that because Gallagher was retained only by INA and not by INA Corporation and Life Insurance Company of North America the presence at the conference with INA's consent of officers of the latter two companies resulted in a waiver by INA of its attorney-client privilege.

For reasons set out below we disagree with the trial court's conclusions, both on the narrow issue and on the broad issue, and we order a writ of prohibition to issue.

I.

The Evidence Code sets out a statutory privilege for attorney-client communication (§ 954) and declares all such communication presumptively confidential (§ 917). A confidential communication is defined in section 952: "As used in this article, 'confidential communication between client and lawyer' means information transmitted between a client and his lawyer in the course of that relationship and in confidence by a means which, so far as the client is aware, discloses the information to no third persons other than those who are present to further the interest of the client in the consultation or those to whom disclosure is reasonably necessary for the transmission of the information or the accomplishment of the purpose for which the lawyer is consulted, and includes a legal opinion formed and the advice given by the lawyer in the course of that relationship." It may be seen that under section 952 communication of information by an attorney to a client in the presence of a third person does not destroy the confidentiality of the communication if the third person is "present to further the interest of the client in the consultation." When the third person is present for that purpose, confidentiality of communication is maintained.

A corporate client, like other artificial entities, can only receive communications from its attorney by means of human agency—officers, agents, and employees of the corporation selected by the corporation's directors and officers to act on its behalf. [2] A corporation, like a natural person, is entitled to the full benefit of the attorney-client privilege (*D. I. Chadbourne, Inc. v. Superior Court* (1964) 60 Cal.2d 723, 736 [36 Cal.Rptr. 468, 388 P.2d 700]). And a corporation, again like a natural person, is not limited to employment of full-time officers, agents, and employees, but it may avail itself of the services of part-time employees, ad hoc consultants, temporary advisers, and other servants it selects for specific purposes. (*Corp. Code*, § 207; *Lab. Code*, §§ 3351, 3357.)

With these general principles in mind we consider the relationship of McHugh and Heth to INA. McHugh, according to papers submitted in support of the petition, was vice president–law of INA Corporation, the parent holding company of which INA was a wholly owned operating subsidiary. His duties included general supervision of legal affairs for INA Corporation's entire group operation, and general supervision of all major litigation involving INA Corporation and its subsidiaries. His responsibilities covered rendition of legal advice and assistance to the management, executives, and legal departments of various subsidiaries; selection of outside counsel in some cases; assistance and guidance to outside counsel during the course of major litigation; and advice to senior management on the status of particular litigated matters. Patently, McHugh was a chief legal officer of the INA Corporation enterprise charged with informing himself about important legal problems of the operating subsidiaries and with giving them the benefit of his advice, an attorney who not only advised INA Corporation but its principal subsidiaries as well. . . .

We turn to Heth, the other person at the conference, identified as president of Life Insurance Company of North America, another wholly owned subsidiary of INA Corporation, and as a member of the reserve committee created by INA Corporation to advise, coordinate, and review reserve policies for its principal operating subsidiaries. Review of reserve policies by the reserve committee served the dual purpose of insuring the financial health of the entire INA group and assuring the officers of the parent holding company that its operating subsidiaries were following sound actuarial practices. But like McHugh, because of the separate corporate existence of INA, neither the reserve committee nor Heth could directly order INA to adopt a particular reserve policy. Technically, all they could do is give advice, and although in overwhelming probability their advice, unless criminal or fraudulent, would be followed, it would remain no more than advice. . . .

We conclude that, factually, there were no outsiders at the meeting of March 11, 1977, that the confidentiality of the proceedings was never breached, that the legal communications remain privileged in that all those in attendance were functioning in the capacity of counsel, officers, agents, or consultants to INA to further the interest of the client INA in the consultation.

II.

We are told that other discovery matters of similar tenor are or may be pending in the underlying cause. For that reason we do not limit our opinion to a factual analysis of the status of McHugh and Heth in relation to INA, but consider the general question whether under California law an officer or employee of a holding or affiliated company can receive legal advice from counsel employed by a wholly owned subsidiary or affiliate without destroying the confidentiality of the attorney-client communication.

Our starting premise is that the attorney-client privilege exists to promote the attorney-client relationship by safeguarding the client's confidential disclosures and the attorney's advice. (*San Francisco v. Superior Court* (1951) 37 Cal.2d 227, 234–235 [231 P.2d 26, 25 A.L.R.2d 1418].) The privilege is that of the client and not the attorney, and the client must intend that communications be confidential. If the client discloses attorney-client communications to unnecessary third parties, he manifests an intent to waive confidentiality. (Witkin, Cal. Evidence (2d ed. 1966) § 783, p. 729.) The key concept here is need to know. While involvement of an unnecessary third person in attorney-client communications destroys confidentiality, involvement of third persons to whom disclosure is reasonably necessary to further the purpose of the legal consultation preserves confidentiality of communication. . . .

This concept of necessity is incorporated in that part of Evidence Code section 952 which provides that attorney-client communications remain confidential when disclosed to third persons present at the consultation to further the interest of the client or when disclosed to persons "to whom disclosure is reasonably necessary for the transmission of the information or the accomplishment of the purpose for which the lawyer is consulted." Of significance is the fact that disclosure may be made to persons not present at the attorney-client consultation, i.e., the third persons need not necessarily participate in the legal consultation.

It is apparent the authors of section 952 intended a comprehensive construction of the attorney-client privilege when they specified that neither (1) disclosures to third persons present to further the interest of the client, nor (2) disclosures to third persons which are reasonably necessary to transmit information or accomplish the purpose for which the attorney has been consulted, destroys confidentiality of communication. Such a comprehensive construction was forthcoming in *Cooke v. Superior Court* (1978) 83 Cal.App.3d 582 [147 Cal.Rptr. 915], a proceeding in which a husband sought to retrieve attorney-client communications that had been surreptitiously removed by a household servant and delivered to his wife's attorneys. Counsel for the wife contended the purloined documents were not privileged, because they had been circulated to persons other than the husband and his counsel in the divorce action, including business associates and attorneys for the husband in other matters. The court held such disclosures did not defeat the privilege. "[A]ll of the alleged recipients were either attorneys who represented Mr. Cooke in some capacity, or were members of his family or business associates who were legitimately kept informed of the progress of a lawsuit that directly involved the business with which they were associated . . . [The] privilege extends to communications which are intended to be confidential, if they are made to attorneys, to family members, business associates, or agents of the party or his attorneys on matters of joint concern, when disclosure of the communication is reasonably necessary to further the interest of the litigant." . . .

What we have said so far assumes the physical presence of the holding company president or his business associates at the attorney-client conference in which legal advice was given. But the specific language of Evidence Code, section 952 protects confidentiality of attorney-client communication, even when the communication is transmitted through intermediaries. Personal attendance at the legal briefing may not be necessary to preserve confidentiality of communication. The president could stay in his office, commission a deputy to report back to him on the legal advice given at the conference, and obtain the benefit of Gallagher's confidential advice and opinions through written communications or through the oral report of his deputy. Such relayed communications are likewise protected by section 952, which preserves the confidentiality of disclosures which are reasonably necessary to transmit the information. The same is true of dissemination of legal advice and opinion to those persons to whom such information is reasonably necessary to accomplish the purpose of the legal consultation. Disclosures to such persons remain confidential, even though the recipients have not been briefed by counsel in person. In our view such persons would include all officers and employees of the INA group for whom knowledge of the legal advice sought and given was reasonably necessary for the proper performance of their duties. Consequently, all written or oral communications of legal opinions and advice given to such persons as a consequence of legal consultation of counsel remain confidential.

To sum up, we construe section 952 to mean that attorney-client communications in the presence of, or disclosed to, clerks, secretaries, interpreters, physicians, spouses, parents, business associates, or joint clients, when made to further the interest of the client or when reasonably necessary for transmission or accomplishment of the purpose of the consultation, remain privileged. . . . As part of this general rule, we conclude that an officer or employee of a holding or affiliated company can receive legal advice from counsel employed by a wholly owned subsidiary or affiliate without destroying the confidentiality of the communication and, as applied to this cause, that the transmission of legal opinions and advice given by counsel for INA to representatives of INA Corporation and its affiliates was a disclosure reasonably necessary to accomplish the corporate client's purpose in consulting counsel and was protected from discovery by the attorney-client privilege.

III.

It appears the trial court inadvertently required production of memorandums and notes of a paralegal in Gallagher's law firm present at the briefing of March 11, 1977. Such materials, the work product of Gallagher's law firm, are not discoverable. (*Code Civ. Proc.* § 2016, subds. (b) and (g).)

Let a writ of prohibition issue prohibiting the superior court from enforcing its order of April 28, 1980, and directing that court to vacate and set aside its order requiring discovery of documents and testimony relating to the proceedings of March 11, 1977.

CASE QUESTIONS

1. What is a writ of prohibition? It's mentioned in the first and last sentences of the case.
2. What is the purpose of the attorney/client privilege?
3. What is the effect of having an outsider present when an attorney and client are speaking to each other?
4. In the case of a corporation, who is an outsider?
5. What is the work product privilege and why is it relevant in this case?

CONFLICTS OF INTEREST—THE DUTY OF LOYALTY

HYPOTHETICAL

Denny's law firm represents several large corporations. As senior corporate assistant, Denny always has access to information regarding the price of stock of those corporations, as well as the business deals those corporations are considering. Denny owns stock in one of the corporations that is represented by his firm. Because of his financial interest in that corporation, Denny spends most of his time doing work for that corporation while neglecting the others.

How Are Conflicts Created?

The simple answer to that question has two parts:

1. Our continuing obligation to preserve the confidences of our clients creates conflicts of interest.

2. Our duty of absolute loyalty to each and every client creates conflicts.

CHAPTER OBJECTIVES

By the end of this chapter, you will know the answers to these questions:

How Are Conflicts Created?
How Can My Personal Life Create Conflicts?
How Can Intimate Relations with a Client Create Conflicts?
What Conflicts Arise because of Outside Forces?
What Conflicts Are Created by Representing Multiple Clients?
If I Have a Conflict, What's Going to Happen?
How Can I Prevent Disqualification?
If I Want to Get a Waiver, Who Has to Waive What?
If a Conflict Walks in the Door, What Should I Do?

Sometimes those two duties conflict (pun intended) and that causes conflicts. Remember that we are obliged to preserve the confidences and secrets of a client *indefinitely,* even after the client's death, and that means that our duty of loyalty never ends.

A case that is still considered the legal authority for this principle is the 1975 case *Silver Chrysler Plymouth v. Chrysler Motor Corp.*[1] In that case, a man was employed by defendant's counsel as a law clerk and later as an associate for three years. Thereafter, he became a partner in the firm that represented the plaintiff. His former law firm (defendant's counsel) brought a motion to disqualify him from the case on the basis of conflict of interest. In the opinion on the disqualification motion, the court discussed the problems of young associates who are employed by large law firms. It acknowledged that it is common practice for young associates to change jobs and that in the course of employment they have access to confidential information about the firm's clients. The court called it "absurd," however, to assume that *every* lawyer in a large firm would have access to *every* client file and confidential information. The court held that if the lawyer's prior representation was *"substantially related"* to the present representation, the lawyer should be disqualified. A "peripheral" prior representation, on the other hand, would not be a sufficient basis for disqualification. The lawyer who had nothing (or very little) to do with the case while working at defendant's counsel should not be the cause of disqualifying plaintiff's counsel when that lawyer changes jobs—but there is reason to differentiate for disqualification purposes between lawyers who become heavily involved in the facts of a particular matter and those who enter briefly on the periphery for a limited and specific purpose related solely to legal questions.

> "Substantially related" test invented.

ABA Model Code EC 5-1: The professional judgment of a lawyer should be exercised, within the bounds of the law, solely for the benefit of his client and free of compromising influences and loyalties. Neither his personal interests, the interests of other clients, nor the desires of third persons should be permitted to dilute his loyalty to his client.

* The Model Codes of Professional Responsibility are presented here as a historical reference and are not currently used.

> "Substantially related" test enumerated.

The "substantially related" test invented in *Silver Chrysler Plymouth* is described more completely in *LaSalle National Bank v. County of Lake,*[2] in which the defendant's law firm moved to disqualify plaintiff's law firm because of defendant's former relationship with an associate of plaintiff's firm. On plaintiff's appeal, the court applied the "substantially related" test from *Silver Chrysler Plymouth* as the basis for determining disqualification. The court held that it consisted of a three-level inquiry:

1. the trial judge must reconstruct the scope of the lawyer's prior legal representation;

2. it must be determined whether the confidential information allegedly given over would have been given to a lawyer representing a client in those matters; and

3. it must be determined whether that information is relevant in the pending litigation against the former client. If, after this evaluation, it is found that a "substantial relationship" existed, *it will be presumed* that the lawyer *did* receive confidential information during the prior representation.[3]

In most jurisdictions, the court will not require that the two representations be identical, nor that the legal professional *actually receive* confidential information. The court will use the presumption from *LaSalle National Bank*. In *Trone v. Smith*,[4] the court said:

> . . . it matters not whether confidences were in fact imparted to the lawyer by the client. . . . The test does not require the former client to show that actual confidences were disclosed. That inquiry would be improper as requiring the very disclosure the rule is intended to protect. . . . It is the possibility of the breach of confidences, not the fact of the breach, that triggers disqualification. (at 999)

If you think about it logically, the client cannot very well say "I told my former lawyer this confidential information. . . ." because then the information will be released to the court and everyone else. Putting the burden on the former client to prove confidences were given to an earlier lawyer, then, doesn't work. It makes more sense to simply presume that if this lawyer worked on this case (in any depth), the lawyer has confidential information belonging to the client. (And, of course, the same is true of the paralegal.) Further, and perhaps this is the most odd part of this rule, the court will presume not only that the lawyer or paralegal walked away with client confidences but that upon getting hired at a new law firm gave all of the information to the people there! The court is presuming, then, that the lawyer or paralegal will not respect the duty of confidentiality.

When considering accepting a new job, take a look at your state equivalent of Model Rule 1.9. It uses the "substantial relationship" test in setting standards for accepting new employment:

A lawyer who has formerly represented a client in a matter shall not thereafter:

a. represent another person in the same or a *substantially related* matter in which that person's interests *are materially adverse* to the interests of the former client unless the former client consents after consultation; or

b. use information relating to the representation to the disadvantage of the former client except as Rule 1.6 would permit with respect to a client or when the information has become generally known.

So, new representation can't be the same or substantially related matter if the former client's interests and the new client's interests are "materially adverse." However, it's all okay if we can get the former client's consent. The consent can simply be an agreement where we agree never to release confidential information about the former client or use that information against him. And, of course, the agreement must be in writing.

This rule (obviously) will be applied to paralegals when they change jobs.

The most obvious problem in this area arises when legal professionals involve themselves in purchases from their clients.

Courts will carefully scrutinize purchases of property from clients and other business relationships with a client. Historically, courts have found that the "opportunity for overreaching" in attorney/client business relationships is cause for severe disciplinary action. Showing an overabundance of concern for even the appearance of a lawyer taking advantage of a client, courts have held that even in instances in which the lawyer has "acted in good faith and with an honest intent," the possibility that other members of the public would see these transactions as involving a fraudulent intent is sufficient grounds for reprimanding the lawyer.

The NFPA *Model Code* provides:

EC 1.6(a) A paralegal shall act within the bounds of the law, solely for the benefit of the client, and shall be free of compromising influences and loyalties. Neither the paralegal's personal or business interest, nor those of other clients or third persons, should compromise the paralegal's professional judgment and loyalty to the client.

South Dakota Rule 1.8
(a) A lawyer shall not enter into a business transaction with a client or knowingly acquire an ownership, possessory, security or other pecuniary interest adverse to a client unless:
(1) the transaction and terms on which the lawyer acquires the interest are fair and reasonable to the client and are fully disclosed and transmitted in writing in a manner that can be reasonably understood by the client;
(2) the client is advised in writing of the desirability of seeking and is given a reasonable opportunity to seek the advice of independent legal counsel on the transaction; and
(3) the client gives informed consent, in a writing signed by the client, to the essential terms of the transaction and the lawyer's role in the transaction, including whether the lawyer is representing the client in the transaction.

Overreaching or Fraud

This is what overreaching or fraud would look like: A lawyer buys a bar/restaurant from his client. He later sells it for a tidy profit that his client could have made. In this 1990 case, the court ordered a six-month suspension for the lawyer.[5] If suspension of license is the proper penalty for a lawyer who violates his fiduciary duties in this manner, what would the penalty be if a paralegal had committed the same offenses? Is there any difference in the fiduciary duty owed by the paralegal to the client?

Or, here's a case in which a lawyer bought the most valuable asset of an estate while he represented the executor of the will.[6] The court held that the lawyer who represents the representative of an estate is under an affirmative duty to seek the highest possible price on the sale of an estate asset. As a purchaser, the court continued, the lawyer would naturally be inclined to seek the lowest price. Because the conflict of interest is inherent in this situation, it must be scrutinized carefully. In its investigation, the court found that the attorney had purchased the asset from an aged and helpless client and misled the probate court in order to prevent disclosure

ABA Model Code
EC 5-3: The self-
interest of a
lawyer resulting
from his
ownership of
property in which
his client also has
an interest or
which may affect
property of his
client may
interfere with the
exercise of free
judgment on
behalf of his
client. . . .

* The Model Codes
of Professional
Responsibility are
presented here as a
historical reference
and are not
currently used.

of the transaction. In view of the moral turpitude involved, disbarment was warranted.[7] Would this transaction have been any better if the sale of the asset had been to a member of the lawyer's staff?

Transaction in Good Faith

There are a few cases in which courts have found that the transaction between lawyer and client was "in good faith." This means that the transaction had inherently fair terms and the lawyer advised the client to get his own lawyer to represent him. There are even fewer cases in which courts have found that what looked like an unfair transaction was really in the client's best interests. However, when we take into consideration the time, effort, money, and emotional turmoil involved in a lawsuit or state bar prosecution, the transaction with the client probably wasn't worth it.

> If you're looking for some language about what makes a lawyer-client transaction "in good faith," here are a few cases you can look at:
>
> *People ex rel. Kent v. Denious,* 196 P.2d 257 (Colo. 1948)
> *In re May,* 538 P.2d 787 (Ida. 1975)
> *Connor v. State Bar,* 791 P.2d 312 (Cal. 1990)

NALS Code of
Ethics: Canon 3.
Members of this
association shall
avoid a conflict of
interest pertaining
to a client matter.

> ABA Model Code EC 5-9 . . . An advocate who becomes a witness is in the unseemly and ineffective position of arguing his own credibility. . . .
>
> * The Model Codes of Professional Responsibility are presented here as a historical reference and are not currently used.

Witness

Where the lawyer or paralegal is likely to be a witness in the client's case, the lawyer or paralegal has a conflict of interest and should not participate in the representation of that client. Think about being both a witness *and* a person representing the client. If the jury did not like your testimony or thought that you were not truthful, that could have a disastrous effect on the client's case. Additionally, there is a real danger that your own personal interests would affect your professionalism in ways that would harm the client. That's why there is a Rule that prohibits representation where the lawyer will be a witness in the case. Check out Rule 3.7 and *Fernandez v. Jamron,* 780 N.Y.S.2d 164 (2004).

A Financial Interest in the Case

Champerty is a term that comes to us from the common law rule prohibiting the "assignment of a chose in action" (purchasing a cause of action). Before regulations preventing champerty, it was common practice for a solicitor to purchase

> **Rule 3.7**
>
> (a) A lawyer shall not act as advocate at a trial in which the lawyer is likely to be a necessary witness except where:
>
> (1) the testimony relates to an uncontested issue;
>
> (2) the testimony relates to the nature and value of legal services rendered in the case; or
>
> (3) disqualification of the lawyer would work substantial hardship on the client.

a cause of action from an injured party. This practice was ultimately decided to be an unlawful "upholding of quarrels leading to the disturbance of society and the hindrance of common right."[8] Eventually, all contracts for the sale of a claim at law were held to be invalid. Since that overreaction, however, the law of champerty has mellowed. The problems that arise in modern law ordinarily involve lawyers who (1) buy claims, (2) accept gifts from clients, or (3) otherwise become financially involved in the litigation of clients.

Buying a Claim Today

A modern expression for champerty involves runners and cappers, folks we discuss in the next chapter. In brief, a *runner* or *capper* is a person who is paid for bringing a case to a lawyer. We've all seen these people in television shows—the ambulance driver who gets paid $100 for giving a lawyer's business card to the injured person. This is quite literally "buying a client," and it is improper.

Another thing we see every day, however, is lawyers who advertise that if you don't win any money, you don't owe the law firm anything. These are typically personal injury lawyer advertisements. But by promising to pay for the costs of litigation at no obligation to the client, isn't the lawyer "buying" the client or claim? The answer can be found in Rule 1.8. Rule 1.8(e)[9] prohibits the lawyer or staff members from advancing money to a client, with two exceptions.

> A lawyer shall not provide financial assistance to a client in connection with pending or contemplated litigation except that: (1) a lawyer may advance court costs and expenses of litigation, the repayment of which may be contingent on the outcome of the matter (this is a typical contingency fee case); and (2) a lawyer representing an indigent client may pay court costs and expenses of litigation on behalf of the client.
>
> *Full Model Rule and commentary can be found in Appendix E.

Some investment companies are getting in on the act of "funding" lawsuits. Judgment Purchase Corp. (JPC) of San Francisco, for example, is called "a venture capital firm." It is not a law firm because it does not give legal advice or offer any legal services. All JPC does is provide "seed" money in cases in which a plaintiff has been awarded a verdict that the defendant is trying to overturn. A company in New Jersey doing the same thing is called Lions Group. A person who has been injured in a car accident would like to pursue a claim against the other driver but can't wait years for a case to go to trial. Lions Group gives the injured person money in exchange for part of the settlement or jury award. If the defendant's insurer refuses to settle and the plaintiff loses her case, Lions Group loses all the money it advanced to the injured party. On the other hand, if the plaintiff wins or gets a hefty settlement, Lions Group may have made a contract with the plaintiff whereby it gets twice the amount of its original investment.

These arrangements are not legal in all states because of the champerty laws. For a case explaining why, look at the *Rancman* case on the publisher's website.

And here's another twist on a similar theme. How about paying people to become plaintiffs? Truth is stranger than fiction. In California, lawyers were busted recently for paying people to become investors in different companies so that the lawyers would be able to use these people as plaintiffs to file a lawsuit against the companies. See the article on the publisher's website.

Gifts Create Conflicts

Lawyers and paralegals should not suggest that a "gift" be made to them, nor should they accept a gift from a client. Small tokens of appreciation, such as gifts costing a few dollars during the holiday season, are not in violation of this rule. The essence of this regulation is that lawyers should not suggest to the client that they become the executor of the client's estate for a fee, nor should lawyers or any of their employees receive anything other than a normal fee or salary for legal assistance. Of course, suggesting to the client that the lawyer or other paralegal should inherit property under the client's will should definitely be avoided. If a client will insist on such a gift, another law firm or disinterested lawyer must draft the will.

Publicity Rights Create Conflicts, Too

Another type of interest a paralegal or lawyer may try to acquire from a client is an interest in the publicity rights pertaining to the client's case. Rule 1.8 prohibits us from obtaining any media rights on the theory that this sort of interest may influence us to compound or prolong the litigation for publicity sake instead of ending the problem quickly, which is typically in the best interests of the client.

ABA Model Code EC 5-4: The lawyer who obtains publicity rights from his client. . . "may be tempted to subordinate the interests of his client to his own anticipated pecuniary gain." That would be bad.

* The Model Codes of Professional Responsibility are presented here as a historical reference and are not currently used.

Rule 1.8(d) says:

> This is Kansas Rule 1.8(d). It is identical to the ABA Model Rule.

Prior to the conclusion of representation of a client, a lawyer shall not make or negotiate an agreement giving the lawyer literary or media rights to a portrayal or account based in substantial part on information relating to the representation.

Protecting the Firm's Interest

Sometimes it will be necessary to secure your law firm's interests in getting paid by a client. This can be done by way of a "charging lien"—a lien on the proceeds of the case. If your client decides to hire a different law firm, you can see how the client's interests and your firm's interests have become conflicting. In a recent California case, the court said that because the lawyer's interest in a charging lien is detrimental and adverse to the client, the client's informed written consent is required.[10] The California rule requires the lawyer who wishes to obtain such a lien to explain the transaction fully, to offer fair and reasonable terms, to provide a copy of the agreement, to give the client an opportunity to seek independent legal advice, and to secure the client's written consent.

Your Other Interests Can Create Conflicts

If you think about it, any of your personal interests could create a conflict of interest. If you own ten thousand shares of IMEX stock, you probably shouldn't work on the team that is representing the shareholders against IMEX. Your strong personal feelings about the value of your stock would interfere with your ability to do your best for the client. If your law firm is hired to sue the church you belong to, you probably have a conflict. Although it is up to you to decide if your interest in the outside organization or company is strong enough to create a conflict, you should always bring a potential conflict to the attention of the lawyer you work for.

How Can Intimate Relations with a Client Create Conflicts?

Actually, it's all Arnie Becker's fault. If you don't remember Arnie Becker, he was the family law practitioner on the *LA Law* television program that aired from 1986 to 1994. Becker had an intimate relationship with every woman in the show: client, lawyer, secretary, everyone, or so it seemed. Suddenly, the idea of the lawyer taking advantage of clients leapt into the public's awareness. In the television program, it seemed benign, but people started to think about it—the lawyer in a position of apparent power; the client in a position of relative helplessness; the situation is ripe for abuse. As a result, many jurisdictions amended their professional responsibility rules to prohibit sexual or intimate relations between legal professional and client. These new laws were enacted to compensate for the difficulty in separating the sound judgment that a competent legal professional must use from emotion or bias that may result from an intimate involvement between lawyer and client.

> Some safe rules for dating within the legal profession were suggested in a law review article. 34 *Santa Clara Law Review* 1157 (1993), "Comments: Dating among the Profession: Ethical Guidance in the Area of Personal Dating Conflicts of Interest."

"Emotional detachment" is essential to the ability to render competent legal services according to the ABA Commission on Ethics and Professional Responsibility.[11] Some states have found that a sexual relationship with a client is *per se* unethical, even when the state has no specific rule prohibiting it, because of the general public perception that the legal professional's judgment will be impaired by such a relationship.[12] However rational that may be, it is little comfort to the legal professional whose primary contact with other people may be through the relationship that begins with legal representation. The bottom line here is that intimate relationships must wait until after the professional relationship has ended.[13]

What Conflict Problems Arise because of Outside Forces?

There is a legal duty to exercise independent professional judgment on behalf of each client. What does that mean? A legal professional must not compromise a client's needs and desires by allowing outside influences or other loyalties to interfere with his or her professional judgment. This is because the legal professional owes complete loyalty to each client. That loyalty should be demonstrated by professional judgment that is not influenced by outside forces.

> Review NFPA Model Code 1.6 and its ethical considerations on this topic. in Appendix C

Rule 5.4 covers *professional independence* and how that may be impacted by the payment of legal fees.[14] Where someone other than the client pays the legal fee, it is possible that the legal professional's loyalty will be turned from the client to the source of the fee. Nothing could be more logical, but it is improper. The legal professional owes complete loyalty to the client regardless of the source of the fee.

One of the longest and most complex of all of the Rules of Professional Conduct is 1.8 on *prohibited transactions*. The gist of these prohibitions is two rules we learned early on:

> A fiduciary relationship is one of trust and confidence, not necessarily one created by contract.

1. The legal professional's duty is to protect the public.
2. The legal professional stands in a *fiduciary position* to the client.

A perfect example of the conflict created by the paralegal's fiduciary duties is when she advertises her house for sale. The couple who make an offer on the house are former clients of her law firm. It is suggested that they can both save some money by drawing up the papers themselves. The problem arises because the paralegal neglected to advise the buyers to seek independent counsel. The couple, even though they no longer have a fiduciary relationship with the paralegal, still look on that person as one who is acting on their behalf. Like any other seller, the paralegal is acting only in her own best interests. Obviously, she wants the best price she can get for her house. The sale closes and the paralegal moves to another town and buys another home, but the former clients become disenchanted with their purchase and ask the court to set the sale aside. Who prevails? The former clients, of course! The paralegal had a higher duty to the purchasers even though the fiduciary relationship no longer existed.[15]

What Conflicts Are Created by Representing Multiple Clients?

ABA Model Code EC 5-14: Maintaining the independence of professional judgment required of a lawyer precludes his acceptance or continuation of employment that will adversely affect his judgment on behalf of or dilute his loyalty to a client. This problem arises whenever a lawyer is asked to represent two or more clients who may have differing interests. . .

* The Model Codes of Professional Responsibility are presented here as a historical reference and are not currently used.

This area is directly related to the rules that advise us to keep the confidences of a client. In certain situations, it is almost impossible. The areas to beware of are seller and purchaser; insured and insurer; husband and wife in matrimonial proceedings; debtor and creditor; adverse clients in unrelated actions; representing corporations and their officers, directors, and shareholders; and multiple accused in criminal actions.

Seller and Purchaser

It seems like it would be much cheaper and more efficient to have one lawyer draft papers for both parties to the transaction. They have already agreed to the price and the terms. They just need someone to write it down for them, so they go to one lawyer for this service. Unfortunately, it's never that easy any more. The contract will inevitably have conditions in it and necessary legal lingo that will be more advantageous to one party or the other. For that reason, it is good advice for each side of the transaction to be represented by its own law firm.

Legal professionals should be sure that they do not represent both sides of an issue, even inadvertently. The State Bar of New Jersey suspended a lawyer who represented both the borrower and the lender in a loan transaction. The court held that the lenders, who were sophisticated businessmen, hired the lawyer and gave him a bonus for negotiating a loan with unsophisticated borrowers. The borrowers also retained him and paid his fees without knowing that he had been hired by the lenders![16]

It is important to avoid not only obvious conflicts but also the possibility that a conflict will develop later. In *In re Camp*,[17] a lawyer drew up a contract between the purchaser and seller that specified that the purchaser was obligated to employ that lawyer for the title search and deed preparation. The court held that the lawyer was under a duty to communicate with the purchaser immediately, explain the nature of his relationship with the seller, and get the purchaser's consent. In *In re Lanza*,[18] the court ruled that it is not enough to advise clients that the lawyer foresees no conflict; the lawyer must withdraw from the employment at the first sign of conflict.

Insured and Insurer

When a law firm is retained by an insurance company to provide legal assistance to the insured under a liability policy, the law firm's client is the insured, not the insurance company.[19] It doesn't matter where the money is coming from. The law firm's duty is to the insured or injured party, not to the person or entity paying the bills. This can get tricky if there is a question of whether the allegations of the case fall within the confines of the insurance coverage. When an insurer receives a lawsuit against a policy holder, the first thing it does is compare the allegations of the complaint to the scope of coverage under the policy. If there are allegations of wrongdoing that fall outside of the coverage, the insurance company will send a "reservation of rights" letter to the insured—reserving the right to deny coverage for liability that is not covered. The insurance company then chooses a lawyer who, quite naturally, has an incentive to tilt the case in favor of the insurer to increase the likelihood of future work. The lawyer, then, represents the insured and has a legal duty of loyalty to that person that includes trying to have everything fall under the coverage but a logical obligation to the insurance company to have everything fall outside of the coverage. When there is a reservation of rights in California, the insured is entitled to "Cumis counsel," so called because it was first described in *San Diego Federal Credit Union v. Cumis Insurance Society*.[20] Not every reservation of rights creates a conflict and not all states handle conflicts the same way. The simple rule is that the duty is to the client, not necessarily the guy (or company) paying the bills.

Husband and Wife

Representation of husband and wife when they have the same interests doesn't seem like it should have a conflict of interest issue. Representation of a husband and wife in the sale of their store is going along swell until the husband and wife decide to get a divorce. Some courts have decided that it is unfair to make the lawyer drop both people as clients. Some courts have said that the conflict is inevitable and irreparable. The confidential information of both clients must be protected, so the lawyer must step out of the case completely.[21]

ABA Model Code EC 5-17: Typically recurring situations involving potentially differing interests are those in which a lawyer is asked to represent co-defendants in a criminal case, co-plaintiffs in a personal injury case, an insured and his insurer, and beneficiaries of the estate of a decedent.

* The Model Codes of Professional Responsibility are presented here as a historical reference and are not currently used.

Debtor and Creditor

Just as a lawyer should not represent both seller and purchaser, representation of debtor and creditor also creates a conflict of interest because the interests of the debtor naturally conflict with the interests of the creditor.

Adverse Clients in Unrelated Actions

No legal professional should accept employment that would be in conflict with any past or present client. We already covered that one on pages 108 through 109.

Representation of Corporations

When the client is a corporation, the general rule is that the legal professional's duty of loyalty is to the corporation, not to officers, directors, or any group of shareholders.

Rule 1.13 discusses the problem of representing the corporation against directors and officers at great length. You should review your state's law on this very complex issue. Here are the main points:

a. A lawyer employed or retained by an organization represents the organization acting through its duly authorized constituents.

b. If a lawyer for an organization knows that an officer, employee or other person . . . is engaged in action, intends to act or refuses to act in a matter related to the representation that is a violation of a legal obligation to the organization, or a violation of law which reasonably might be imputed to the organization, and is likely to result in substantial injury to the organization, the lawyer shall proceed as is reasonably necessary in the best interest of the organization. . . .

f. In dealing with an organization's directors, officers, employees, members, shareholders or other constituents, a lawyer shall explain the identity of the client when it is apparent that the organization's interests are adverse to those of the constituents with whom the lawyer is dealing.

g. A lawyer . . . may also represent any of its directors, officers, employees, members, shareholders or other constituents . . . [subject to the provisions of Rule 1.7 and] consent shall be given by an appropriate official of the organization other than the individual who is to be represented, or by the shareholders.

*Full Model Rule and commentary can be found in Appendix E.

A conflict of interest problem may arise when a law firm attempts to take sides in an intrafamily/corporation dispute. In *Brennan's Inc. v. Brennan's Restaurants, Inc.,*[22] a lawyer who had represented all the family members of a family-owned business was disqualified from representing one group of family members in an action against another. That makes sense. The lawyer held confidential information that belonged to each of the family members. The confidentiality rules prevent the lawyer from ever using that information against *any* of his former clients. In another case, two attorneys who were members of the same firm represented a family-owned corporation at the time the corporation entered into an agreement hiring a founding shareholder as president of the corporation. They had also acted as counsel for that shareholder during his years as president. The court held that it was improper for them to represent both sides in a later conflict between the corporation and the former president (after the president had lost control of the corporation), because of the confidential information they held about him.[23]

On the other hand, in *Universal Athletic Sales Co. v. American Gym, Recreational and Athletic Equipment Corp.*,[24] using the testimony of the lawyers in question that they had no confidential information that could be used by them or their client-corporation against the former president, the court held that the subsequent representation was not in conflict. In *Bobbitt v. Victorian House, Inc.*,[25] plaintiff, who was a director of the corporation, brought an action to dissolve the corporation. He moved to disqualify the corporation's lawyer and the entire firm on the ground that the director had given confidential information to that lawyer. The court found that the lawyer's prior individual representation of the director was not substantially related to the current cause of action and that the disclosures that were made to him were those revealed to other incorporators so they weren't really secrets.[26] You can see the court using the "substantially related" test from *Silver Chrysler Plymouth* here.

Joint Representation of Criminal Defendants

No one should work for one side of a criminal case and then for the other side because of the possibility of disclosing confidential information. Similarly, a legal professional who is part of the defense of a criminal defendant may have information that could be damaging to a codefendant. For this reason, dual representation of defendants may be unethical if there is a possibility of breach of confidentiality.

Rule 44(c) of the Federal Rules of Criminal Procedure says that when two or more defendants who are jointly charged are represented by the same retained or assigned counsel, the court *shall* investigate the representation and advise the defendants of their right to separate counsel. The Rule 44 inquiry does not differentiate between assigned and retained lawyers. And it doesn't matter if the lawyer thinks the case will go to trial or not.

In *Holloway v. Arkansas*,[27] the U.S. Supreme Court held that reversal by a higher court should be automatic if a trial judge has denied the timely objection to joint representation.

What about Pro Bono Law Providers and Lawyer Referral Services? Do They Create Conflicts?

> There is some very cool American history here, so just go with it for about 1½ pages.

If you think about it logically, a corporation cannot practice law. A corporation is a legal entity, not a person, and so it cannot be a licensed member of the bar. This issue was first discussed in a California case from 1922. In *People v. Merchants Protective Corporation*,[28] the California Supreme Court held that a lay organization existing for the purpose of bringing lawyers and clients together is engaging in the unauthorized practice of law because lawyers are retained and paid by the organization that controls the amount and kinds of legal services provided. Merchants Protective Corporation was representing its members in exchange for a yearly fee. The court held that the relationship of trust and confidence in an attorney/client relationship is essential. Those certain requirements of character, integrity, and learning, which lawyers possess, cannot be held by the corporate structure. For that reason, then, to allow a corporation to interject itself in the attorney/client relationship by paying for the representation or determining whether litigation should be pursued, is "a degradation of the bar."

Fast forward to the 1960s, the era of civil rights. The NAACP was very busy soliciting victims of discrimination for the purpose of filing litigation against people, governmental agencies, and companies who still denied Black Americans those basic rights guaranteed to them by the Constitution. *Brown v. Board of Education* was won in 1954, but it would be only the beginning of sweeping victories that the NAACP would achieve. The lawyers, most of whom were volunteers and not "employed" by the NAACP, were paid a small amount to cover their expenses. In an effort to fight the NAACP, a Virginia state court convicted the NAACP of solicitation and "accepting employment or compensation from a person or organization that is not a party to the action," a violation of state law. In other words, the NAACP, not a party to any action, was not permitted to compensate anyone (any lawyers) for participation in a lawsuit. Bottom line, the State of Virginia wanted the NAACP out of business and this seemed like a good approach. After being convicted by the Virginia state court, the NAACP took the matter to the U.S. Supreme Court in a case called *NAACP v. Button*.[29]

Basing its decision on freedom of political expression and association (protected by the First and Fourteenth Amendments), the Supreme Court held that the NAACP was using lawful means of vindicating legal rights by their representation of victims of discrimination. Further, the Court held that the Virginia statute "broadly curtailing group activity leading to litigation may easily become a weapon of oppression." The dissenting opinion of Justice Harlan maintained that there was substantial evidence that showed that the normal attorney/client relationship was not present in many instances. Forms were signed by prospective litigants that granted their permission to initiate the lawsuit, additional lawyers would be brought in, and the case would be concluded, all without the client ever having met the lawyer. In his opinion, the NAACP's activities were "stirring up" litigation. The opinion of Justice White noted, however: "[s]urely it is beyond the power of any State to prevent the exercise of constitutional rights in the name of preventing a lay entity from controlling litigation."

Basing its decision on *NAACP v. Button,* the Supreme Court would go on to hold in *Brotherhood of Railway Trainmen v. Virginia*[30] that the First and Fourteenth Amendments protect the rights of the members of the Brotherhood to maintain and carry out their plan for advising workers who are injured to obtain legal advice and for recommending specific lawyers because injured workers and their families were easily taken advantage of by persuasive claims adjusters. This case was one of many which granted the Brotherhood the ability to assist its members.[31]

Bar associations would get into the act of trying to put people who need lawyers and lawyers together via "referral services." Sometimes these are known as LRIS (Lawyer Referral and Information Service) or LRS. *Emmons, Williams, Mires & Leech v. State Bar*[32] cited *NAACP v. Button* to show that the bar association has a legitimate *nonprofit interest* in making legal services more readily available to the public. The activity of a state bar referral service does not have the inherent dangers applicable to solicitation of clients or interjecting the corporate structure between lawyer and client. Even where the bar association has accepted a percentage of the lawyer's fees, so long as the money is used to further the efforts of the association to make legal services available to the public and to increase public awareness with regard to legal rights, the activity of state bar referral services will be permitted.[33]

The duty of direct and personal contact with the client.

Ultimately, it is the lawyer's duty to remain in *direct and personal contact* with the client, even when the lawyer is working with paralegals and clerks. Effective use of paralegals to aid in providing quality legal services at a reduced cost, not to "practice law" or take the place of the lawyer, is essential. A planned, organized paralegal program within a law firm will allow paralegals to fulfill their roles and benefit the public while giving lawyers a way to remain in contact with clients and to exercise their professional judgment free from outside demands. The use of law students should also benefit the clients and the firm, as well as provide invaluable training for the students.

Paralegal ethical guidelines provided by various states and the ABA specifically state that lawyers may hire and train paralegals to perform services for them in their representation of clients. The proviso in each set of guidelines is that the lawyer maintain a *direct relationship* with the client, the lawyer accept *complete responsibility* for the paralegal's work, the lawyer *supervise* the paralegal, and the services performed by the paralegal are not those that require the professional legal judgment of a lawyer.

If I Have a Conflict of Interest, What's Going to Happen?

The first thing that is going to happen if you have confidential information that could be used adversely to the interests of a former client is that there will be a presumption that you will divulge your confidences and act adversely. Again, it doesn't seem logical that the presumption is that you would act unethically, but that's what the cases say.[34]

Certain courts have held that knowledge of an organization's internal workings will give rise to a presumption of conflict of interest.[35] If you have access to the intimate knowledge of the company's business methods, you could potentially use that information against the company later.

In *Prichec v. Tecon Corp.,*[36] the lawyers in question hired an investigator during their representation of the Cuban government. Because of the investigatory functions he performed, he knew who the Cuban government's agent for service of process was. In the *Prichec* case, in which the lawyers represented Tecon Corp., a pivotal issue had to do with proper service of process. Defendant Cuba maintained in its disqualification motion that the lawyers should be barred from representing Tecon against Cuba because they had, through their investigator, certain confidential information that was adverse to Cuba. The court agreed. The firm was disqualified.

The prior association need not be continuous or lengthy. In *In re Car Rental Antitrust Litigation,*[37] a lawyer who only briefly consulted with the principals of a car rental company was later disqualified from representing a competing car rental company on the basis of conflict of interest.

Will My Entire Firm Be Disqualified?

If confidential information has been given to a lawyer, the lawyer's entire firm would be disqualified on the presumption that every legal professional in the office had access to the confidential information, even if the firm is later dissolved.[38] There are cases holding that this rule applies to paralegals, as well, most notably in *In re Complex Asbestos Litigation* which you will read at the end of this chapter.[39]

In *Yaretsky v. Blum,* 525 F. Supp. 24 (S.D.N.Y. 1981), the entire law firm was disqualified because the tainted associate had worked for a small firm and for the same department that was handling the disputed case (although much of this opinion is based on the old ABA Model Code of Professional Conduct, Canon 9: An attorney must avoid even the appearance of impropriety).

The court in *Cook v. Cook,* 559 F. Supp. 213 (D.C. Penn. (1983) held that, generally, if a lawyer has been disqualified because of prior representation of an adverse party, the entire firm *should be disqualified* regardless of whether the other members of the firm had any involvement in the prior representation. The court opined that it might make an exception if the lawyer had been with a large law firm and, in that case, an examination of the lawyer's actual participation in the prior representation should be made. This court, like that of *Silver Chrysler,* acknowledged that to hold otherwise would severely restrict the mobility of legal professionals between law firms.

How Can I Prevent Disqualification?

One of the most important things to have from the beginning of your career as a paralegal is a complete personal conflict check system. The day will come when you will want to change jobs. You will need to know what cases you have worked on and what work you did. The best way to prevent disqualification is to know about and accommodate conflicts from the beginning of your association with a firm. (At the end of this chapter, you will begin to create your personal conflict check system.)

If you're reading this book in California, take a look at the Los Angeles County Bar Association's Formal Ethics Opinion #501 for a complete discussion of conflicts of interest and changing jobs. The LACBA's Web site is http://www.lacba.org/.

Before 1974, lawyers were prohibited from representing a client if any one lawyer in the law firm was required to decline the employment because of a conflict of interest. The problem with this rule was most obvious for those lawyers who had worked for the district attorney's office. These people had worked on thousands of cases, thus effectively eliminating the possibility of ever finding a private firm that could hire them without a conflict problem. As a result, it became almost impossible for government agencies to recruit bright young lawyers. In response to this problem, the ABA Ethics Committee issued Formal Opinion No. 342, opining that the prohibition should not apply to the firm of a disqualified lawyer who has been *screened* from participation in the work and has received no compensation stemming from the conflicting case. In other words, we're going to screen this lawyer off from the conflict case so that he or she has no contact with the case or others working on the case *and* we're going to make sure that this lawyer doesn't receive any money that may come from the case.

Ethical Wall Theory

A few years later, the court in *Kesselhaut v. United States*[40] ruled against the moving party in a disqualification motion because the lawyer with the conflict had been effectively isolated from his firm's handling of the case and that, in fact, the firm had erected a "wall" around him from the beginning of the representation of that client. Arguing in favor of what used to be called the "Chinese Wall" theory (now called the Ethical Wall theory), the court discussed the inherent unfairness of turning one lawyer who had worked for a governmental agency (in this case, the FHA) into a "Typhoid Mary." The purpose of the wall was to cut off communication from the "tainted" legal professional to members of the firm working on the case.

Ethical walls have not been accepted by all states in all circumstances. In Nebraska, the ethical wall does not exist at all; in other states it is reserved for former government employees. If you are considering changing jobs, you should research your state's law on ethical walls.

For information on how to build a successful wall, see the "How to" section on the publisher's Web site. To be of any use at all, the wall should be erected as soon as the conflict employee joins the firm or as soon as a potential client who creates a conflict becomes a client. If there is any delay, it may be presumed that the conflict employee has divulged all of the former client's secrets and the firm will probably be disqualified. If you (and everyone else in the firm) know about the matters that create conflicts, you will be able to head off a potential conflict before it becomes an issue.

> The "Chinese Wall" theory was named for the Great Wall of China. Originally built in the 3rd century B.C.E., the Great Wall of China's purpose was military defense—to keep people out.

If I Want to Get a Waiver, Who Has to Waive What?

Another way to remedy a potential conflict of interest is to get a waiver from the client. Remember: Rule 1.9's "substantial relationship" test sets the standards for accepting employment with a law firm:

A lawyer who has formerly represented a client in a matter shall not thereafter:

a. represent another person in the same or a substantially related matter in which that person's interests are materially adverse to the interests of the former client *unless the former client consents after consultation* . . .

There are some older cases that say that this consent is not enough. In *Westinghouse Electric Corp. v. Gulf Oil Corp.*,[41] the court held that the potential for abuse of confidential information outweighed the former client's express waiver. This case involved a continuing and increasingly complex antitrust suit in which the waiver was signed early in the case and before the former client realized the extent and complexity of the issues. The court struck down the express waiver and disqualified the lawyers with the conflict, saying that no one with ordinary business sense would permit his or her former counsel to use confidential information against him or her. The consent, though express, could not have been "informed and knowing," according to the court.

Kagel v. First Commonwealth Co., Inc.,[42] on the other hand, indicates that when the lawyer has obtained a written consent from all of the parties to a litigation and has fully disclosed all matters necessary for the parties to make a knowing and intelligent waiver, a conflict will be avoided.

In today's society, and depending upon the complexity of the case and the sophistication of the client, a written waiver is still a very good alternative to the ethical wall. Remember that the waiver must be obtained from the *former client* whose confidences and secrets you hold. The waiver is your further written promise not to disclose those confidences and secrets or to ever use them to the client's detriment, and the client's written acknowledgment of trust in your promise. Remember, also, as *In re Complex Asbestos Litigation* at the end of this chapter illustrates, the waiver must be in writing and signed by a person with the right to do so: either the former client or the former client's representative.

If a Conflict Walks in the Door, What Should I Do?

The first thing to do is resolve all doubts about a possible conflict of interest in favor of the client. We have a duty of loyalty and confidentiality that requires us to protect our past and current clients.

1. Bring the potential conflict to the attention of the lawyer in charge of this matter.
2. Explain the concerns to the potential client.
3. Inform all parties of the potential conflict.
4. If possible, get an informed, meaningful, express written waiver from the former client.
5. If you can't get a waiver, look at constructing an ethical wall if that is available in your state. The wall has to be in place before the firm receives confidential information from the new client.

6. If you are new to a firm and come in with a conflict, let the appropriate person in your firm know right away.

7. Never try to hide a conflict. It will be discovered eventually.

8. If the firm has a conflict and didn't know about it, firing the tainted employee won't help. Don't do that, either.

SUMMARY

In this chapter, we learned the various ways that conflicts of interest are created. Our personal life, our intimate relationships with clients, and outside forces are just three examples. Multiple clients create a multitude of conflicts, so we learned to be wary of representing husband and wife, seller and buyer, debtor and purchaser, and joint criminal defendants. We also learned that there are some special rules when it comes to representing insured parties, especially where there is a reservation of rights letter. Even though we didn't want to, we learned how the NAACP changed the course of history in America and defeated efforts to deny civil rights organizations the right to represent victims of discrimination by parties who tried to distort the rules that cover corporations representing clients. Lawyer referral services are okay, too, so long as there is direct and personal contact between the lawyer and client. Paralegals can facilitate that relationship and help lawyers fulfill that duty. We took a look at what will happen if a conflict of interest does occur, and we learned three ways we can prevent disqualification: having a thorough personal conflict check system will help to keep us out of harm's way. Some states allow for "ethical walls," and we can always try to get the consent of our former client on our promise not to use any confidential information we have against the former client (which we would never do anyway). This was a very intense chapter with many little rules.

CHAPTER REVIEW AND ASSIGNMENTS

CRITICAL THINKING

1. Let's go back to Denny's "Hypothetical" at the beginning of this chapter. What have you learned that will help you answer this question for Denny? What duty does he violate (if any) by spending most of his time working for the client in which he owns stock?

2. If a client of the firm asks you out on a date, what should you do? What would you say in response to the offer of a cup of coffee after work?

3. What are some "outside interests" you have that could potentially compromise your independent judgment?

ASSIGNMENT

1. Do you have a personal conflict check system? If you finished Collaborative Exercise # 2 above, you're well on your way to starting one. There are many conflict check computer programs available, some of which are free. Search the Internet and investigate some of these programs. Pick two and compare and contrast them. Some of the functions that are important are searches for names that look alike or sound alike, a place to keep information about clients as they move from one address to another, and the ability to search by firm names.

COLLABORATIVE ASSIGNMENTS

1. Be prepared to find a new job! This classroom activity is about conflicts of interest in real life. Your instructor has the components of this exercise.
2. Working alone, make a list of all of the things you are involved with, such as your church and civic groups, and a list of all of the things in which you have a financial stake. Now review your list with a classmate to see if anything should be added or clarified. In small groups, discuss this question: If the law firm you work for is involved in litigation against one of the entities or people or your list, what should you do? Make a list of steps you should take.

REVIEW QUESTIONS

Multiple Choice

Select the best answer for each of the following questions.

1. A paralegal's involvement in screening for potential conflicts of interest upon employment involves
   a. discussing with the supervising lawyer all former employers and names of parties from cases handled by those former employers.
   b. accepting the lawyer's decision that a conflict of interest exists in one or more matters.
   c. discussing with the supervising lawyer all outside personal interests and activities in which the paralegal is and has been involved.
   d. none of the above.
   e. all of the above.
2. Ethical obligations concerning conflicts of interest involve
   a. attorney/client confidentiality.
   b. the attorney/client relationship.
   c. the work product privilege.
   d. all of the above.
   e. none of the above.
3. Ethical obligations concerning conflicts of interest are designed to protect
   a. the lawyer and/or paralegal.
   b. the judge.
   c. a former or existing client.
   d. the adversary's client.
   e. none of the above.
4. A conflict of interest between a paralegal and a matter being handled by the firm at which he or she is employed may involve
   a. a paralegal's religious affiliation.
   b. a paralegal's hobbies, such as a bowling league or a swim team.

c. a paralegal's community interests, such as volunteer mediation in the court system or working on a political campaign for a neighbor.

d. none of the above.

e. all of the above.

5. One of the reasons that the courts and regulating bodies have permitted ethical walls to be created is

a. to ensure that firms may bill for paralegal work in attorney applications for fees.

b. to improve relations between China and the United States.

c. to avoid limitations on job mobility for members of the legal profession.

d. both *a* and *c*.

e. all of the above.

6. Isolating oneself from a matter in which a conflict of interest exists includes

a. red-flagging files to alert everyone that no communications about the matter are seen by the person with whom the conflict exists.

b. making sure that no discussions are held within hearing distance of the person with whom the conflict exists.

c. not participating in discussions about the matter on which a conflict exists.

d. all of the above.

e. both *a* and *b*.

7. NFPA Canon 8 says, "A paralegal shall avoid conflicts of interest. . . ." The rationale for this rule is

a. The paralegal should do whatever the employer instructs.

b. The paralegal should be free of any compromising influences and loyalties.

c. The employing lawyer could be disciplined for a violation of this rule.

d. Although changing jobs is all right, it should be discouraged.

e. Both *c* and *d*.

8. The conflict of interest rules apply to

a. conflicts arising from previous employment.

b. conflicts arising from personal relationships.

c. conflicts arising from outside business relationships.

d. all of the above.

e. none of the above.

9. John is a paralegal who works for Lawyer, a fellow who specializes in drafting wills and trusts and performing probate work. As a result of John's duties, many clients grow to love John like a son. Client One wants to leave John $100 in her will.

a. This is never proper.

b. This is always proper and a popular custom.

c. This is OK because it is a small amount.

d. This would be proper if it were under $100.

e. This is proper if Lawyer advises Client One that she should seek other counsel for advice about leaving John money in her will, if John has not asked for the money, and because it is a small amount.

10. Client Two has a 1994 Cadillac Seville that he no longer drives. He is ninety-two years old, so John is happy that Client Two has decided not to drive anymore. Client Two suggests that John find out how much the car is worth and sell it on Client Two's behalf. John tells Client Two that the car is only worth $3000 and he can get cash for the car from a reputable dealer. In reality, John is buying the car for himself. John

a. has violated his duty of loyalty to the client.

b. has created a conflict of interest.

c. is guilty of fraud.

d. all of the above.

e. none of the above.

Fill in the Blank

Complete each of the following sentences with the best word(s) or phrase(s).

1. Disqualification of a firm from handling a matter in which a conflict of interest exists means _____.

2. Screening for conflicts of interest, disclosing the conflict to the adversary and client, and barring communication from and to the person with whom the conflict exists are all steps taken to erect a/an _____.

3. It may not be a paralegal's own interests that cause conflict of interests to exist for the paralegal but may involve a member of his or her _____.

4. Rule of Professional Conduct number _____ applies to conflicts of interest.

5. One of the primary goals achieved through the ethical obligations concerning conflicts of interest is protection of the client's _____.

6. The judiciary may use its _____ when making decisions about conflicts of interest.

7. If prior representation was _____ _____ to the present representation, a conflict of interest will be presumed.

8. The presumption of a conflict of interest means _____.

9. One way to avoid raising a conflict of interest when moving from one job to another is _____.

10. If one legal professional in a law firm is disqualified from a case because of a conflict of interest, it is likely that _____.

True/False

Decide whether each of the following statements is true or false and write your answer on the line provided.

_____ 1. A paralegal is required to refrain from working on all matters that involve confidential information she or he possesses from personal activities where that information is adverse to the client.

_____ 2. A firm that has an employee with a conflict of interest in a matter is not automatically disqualified from handling the matter.

_____ 3. If a conflict of interest exists for a law clerk, once that individual has passed the bar exam and been admitted to practice, the conflict of interest no longer exists.

_____ 4. A paralegal may not have a conflict of interest with a matter being handled by the firm by which he or she is employed and his or her prior employer if he or she did not work on the case at the prior firm nor will he or she be working on the case at the current employing firm.

_____ 5. Provided a paralegal receives no compensation or fees from a case in which a conflict of interest exists, the paralegal may work pro bono on the matter.

_____ 6. Attending a meeting at which a matter for which a conflict of interest exists with one of the attendees is not in violation of the ethical wall so long as the person with whom the conflict exists does not say anything.

_____ 7. Obtaining the opposing counsel's permission to create an ethical wall is necessary for the continued representation of a client in a matter in which a conflict of interest exists.

_____ 8. A client's right to have counsel of choice may be a factor considered by the courts when considering motions to disqualify the attorney/law firm from handling a matter in which a conflict of interest exists.

9. A lawyer may not accept employment that is adverse to a client or former client if in the representation of the client or former client the lawyer has obtained confidential information material to the employment except with the informed written consent of the client or former client.

____10. The potential for abuse of confidential information is automatically waived when a former client signs a waiver concerning the conflict of interest.

CASES FOR CONSIDERATION

CASE 1

In re Complex Asbestos Litigation
232 Cal.App.3d 572, 283 Cal.Rptr. 732
(1991)

Attorney Jeffrey B. Harrison, his law firm, and their affected clients appeal from an order disqualifying the Harrison firm in nine asbestos-related personal injury actions.

The appeal presents the difficult issue of whether a law firm should be disqualified because an employee of the firm possessed attorney-client confidences from previous employment by opposing counsel in pending litigation. We hold that disqualification is appropriate unless there is written consent or the law firm has effectively screened the employee from involvement with the litigation to which the information relates. . . . Therefore, we affirm the order of the trial court.

FACTS

Michael Vogel worked as a paralegal for the law firm of Brobeck, Phleger & Harrison (Brobeck) from October 28, 1985, to November 30, 1988. Vogel came to Brobeck with experience working for a law firm that represented defendants in asbestos litigation. Brobeck also represented asbestos litigation defendants, including respondents. At Brobeck, Vogel worked exclusively on asbestos litigation.

During most of the period Brobeck employed Vogel, he worked on settlement evaluations. He extracted information from medical reports, discovery responses, and plaintiffs' depositions for entry on "Settlement Evaluation and Authority Request" (SEAR) forms. The SEAR forms were brief summaries of the information and issues used by the defense attorneys and their clients to evaluate each plaintiff's case. The SEAR forms were sent to the clients.

Vogel attended many defense attorney meetings where the attorneys discussed the strengths and weaknesses of cases to reach consensus settlement recommendations for each case. The SEAR forms were the primary informational materials the attorneys used at the meetings. Vogel's responsibility at these meetings was to record the amounts agreed on for settlement recommendations to the clients. Vogel sent the settlement authority requests and SEAR forms to the clients. He also attended meetings and telephone conferences where attorneys discussed the recommendations with clients and settlement authority was granted. Vogel recorded on the SEAR forms the amount of settlement authority granted and distributed the information to the defense attorneys.

The SEAR form information was included in Brobeck's computer record on each asbestos case. The SEAR forms contained the plaintiff's name and family information, capsule summaries of medical reports, the plaintiff's work history, asbestos products identified at the plaintiff's work sites, and any special considerations that might affect the jury's response to the plaintiff's case. The SEAR forms also contained information about any prior settlements and settlement authorizations. Information was added to the forms as it was developed during the course of a case. Vogel, like other Brobeck staff working on asbestos cases, had a computer password that allowed access to the information on any asbestos case in Brobeck's computer system.

Vogel also monitored trial events, received daily reports from the attorneys in trial, and relayed trial reports to the clients. Vogel reviewed plaintiffs' interrogatory answers to get SEAR form data and to assess whether the answers were adequate or further responses were needed.

In 1988, Vogel's duties changed when he was assigned to work for a trial team. With that change, Vogel no longer was involved with the settlement evaluation meetings and reports. Instead, he helped prepare specific cases assigned to the team. Vogel did not work on any cases in which the Harrison firm represented the plaintiffs.

During the time Vogel worked on asbestos cases for Brobeck, that firm and two others represented respondents in asbestos litigation filed in Northern California. Brobeck and the other firms were selected for this work by the Asbestos Claims Facility (ACF), a corporation organized by respondents and others to manage the defense of asbestos litigation on their behalf. The ACF dissolved in October 1988, though Brobeck continued to represent most of the respondents through at least the end of the year. Not long after the ACF's dissolution, Brobeck gave Vogel two weeks' notice of his termination, though his termination date was later extended to the end of November.

Vogel contacted a number of firms about employment, and learned that the Harrison firm was looking for paralegals. The Harrison firm recently had opened a Northern California office and filed a number of asbestos cases against respondents. Sometime in the second half of November 1988, Vogel called Harrison to ask him for a job with his firm.

In that first telephone conversation, Harrison learned that Vogel had worked for Brobeck on asbestos litigation settlements. Harrison testified that he did not then offer Vogel a job for two reasons. First, Harrison did not think he would need a new paralegal until February or March of 1989. Second, Harrison was concerned about the appearance of a conflict of interest in his firm's hiring a paralegal from Brobeck. Harrison discussed the conflict problem with other attorneys, and told

Vogel that he could be hired only if Vogel got a waiver from the senior asbestos litigation partner at Brobeck.

Vogel testified that he spoke with Stephen Snyder, the Brobeck partner in charge of managing the Northern California asbestos litigation. Vogel claimed he told Snyder of the possible job with the Harrison firm, and that Snyder later told him the clients had approved and that Snyder would provide a written waiver if Vogel wanted. In his testimony, Snyder firmly denied having any such conversations or giving Vogel any conflicts waiver to work for Harrison. The trial court resolved this credibility dispute in favor of Snyder.

While waiting for a job with the Harrison firm, Vogel went to work for Bjork, which represented two of the respondents in asbestos litigation in Northern California. Vogel worked for Bjork during December 1988, organizing boxes of materials transferred from Brobeck to Bjork. While there, Vogel again called Harrison to press him for a job. Vogel told Harrison that Brobeck had approved his working for Harrison, and Harrison offered Vogel a job starting after the holidays. During their conversations, Harrison told Vogel the job involved work on complex, non asbestos civil matters, and later would involve processing release documents and checks for asbestos litigation settlements. Harrison did not contact Brobeck to confirm Vogel's claim that he made a full disclosure and obtained Brobeck's consent. Nor did Harrison tell Vogel that he needed a waiver from Bjork.

Vogel informed Bjork he was quitting to work for the Harrison firm. Vogel told a partner at Bjork that he wanted experience in areas other than asbestos litigation, and that he would work on securities and real estate development litigation at the Harrison firm. Initially, Vogel's work for the Harrison firm was confined to those two areas.

However, at the end of February 1989, Vogel was asked to finish another paralegal's job of contacting asbestos plaintiffs to complete client questionnaires. The questionnaire answers provided information for discovery requests by the defendants. Vogel contacted Bjork and others to request copies of discovery materials for the Harrison firm. Vogel also assisted when the Harrison firm's asbestos trial teams needed extra help.

In March 1989, Snyder learned from a Brobeck trial attorney that Vogel was involved in asbestos litigation. In a March 31 letter, Snyder asked Harrison if Vogel's duties included asbestos litigation. Harrison responded to Snyder by letter on April 6. In the letter, Harrison stated Vogel told Snyder his work for the Harrison firm would include periodic work on asbestos cases, and that Harrison assumed there was no conflict of interest. Harrison also asked Snyder to provide details of the basis for any claimed conflict. There were no other communications between Brobeck and the Harrison firm concerning Vogel before the disqualification motion was filed.

In June, a Harrison firm attorney asked Vogel to call respondent Fibreboard Corporation to see if it would accept service of a subpoena for its corporate minutes. Vogel called the company and spoke to a person he knew from working for Brobeck. Vogel asked who should be served with the subpoena in place of the company's retired general counsel. Vogel's call prompted renewed concern among respondents' counsel over Vogel's involvement with asbestos litigation for a plaintiffs' firm.

On July 31, counsel for three respondents demanded that the Harrison firm disqualify itself from cases against those respondents. Three days later, the motion to disqualify the Harrison firm was filed; it was subsequently joined by all respondents.

* * *

Brobeck's computer system access log showed that on November 17, 1988, Vogel accessed the computer records for 20 cases filed by the Harrison firm. On the witness stand, Vogel at first flatly denied having looked at these case records, but when confronted with the access log, he admitted reviewing the records "to see what kind of cases [the Harrison firm] had filed." At the time, Vogel had no responsibilities for any Harrison firm cases at Brobeck. The date Vogel reviewed those computer records was very close to the time Vogel and Harrison first spoke. The access log documented that Vogel opened each record long enough to view and print copies of all the information on the case in the computer system.

The case information on the computer included the SEAR form data. Many of the 20 cases had been entered on the computer just over a week earlier, though others had been on the computer for weeks or months. The initial computer entries for a case consisted of information taken from the complaint by paralegals trained as part of Brobeck's case intake team. Vogel denied recalling what information for the Harrison firm's cases he saw on the computer, and Brobeck's witness could not tell what specific information was on the computer that day.

Vogel, Harrison, and the other two witnesses from the Harrison firm denied that Vogel ever disclosed any client confidences obtained while he worked for Brobeck. However, Harrison never instructed Vogel not to discuss any confidential information obtained at Brobeck. Vogel did discuss with Harrison firm attorneys his impressions of several Brobeck attorneys. After the disqualification motion was filed, Harrison and his office manager debriefed Vogel, not to obtain any confidences but to discuss his duties at Brobeck in detail and to assess respondents' factual allegations. During the course of the hearing, the Harrison firm terminated Vogel on August 25, 1989.

The trial court found that Vogel's work for Brobeck and the Harrison firm was substantially related, and that there was no express or implied waiver by Brobeck or its clients. The court believed there was a substantial likelihood that the Harrison firm's hiring of Vogel, without first building "an ethical wall" or having a waiver, would affect the outcome in asbestos cases. The court also found that Vogel obtained confidential information when he accessed Brobeck's computer records on the Harrison firm's cases, and that there was a reasonable probability Vogel used that information or disclosed it to other members of the Harrison firm's staff. The court refused to extend the disqualification beyond those cases where there was tangible evidence of interference by Vogel, stating that on the rest of the cases it would require the court to speculate.

The trial court initially disqualified the Harrison firm in all 20 cases Vogel accessed on November 17, 1988, which included 11 cases pending in Contra Costa County. However, on further consideration, the trial court restricted its disqualification order to the 9 cases pending in San Francisco. The Harrison firm timely noticed an appeal from the disqualification order, and respondents cross-appealed from the denial of disqualification in the Contra Costa County cases and all asbestos litigation.

DISCUSSION

The Standard of Review

A trial court's authority to disqualify an attorney derives from the power inherent in every court, "[t]o control in furtherance of justice, the conduct of its ministerial officers, and of all other persons in any manner connected with a judicial proceeding before it, in every matter pertaining thereto." (cites omitted)

On review of an order granting or denying a disqualification motion, we defer to the trial court's decision, absent an abuse of discretion. (cites omitted) The trial court's exercise of this discretion is limited by the applicable legal principles and is subject to reversal when there is no reasonable basis for the action. (cites omitted)

* * *

Concerns Raised by Disqualification Motions

Our courts recognize that a motion to disqualify a party's counsel implicates several important interests. These concerns are magnified when, as here, disqualification is sought not just for a single case but for many and, indeed, an entire class of litigation. When faced with disqualifying an attorney for an alleged conflict of interest, courts have considered such interests as the clients' right to counsel of their choice, an attorney's interest in representing a client, the financial burden on the client of replacing disqualified counsel, and any tactical abuse underlying the disqualification proceeding. (cites omitted)

An additional concern arises if disqualification rules based on exposure to confidential information are applied broadly and mechanically.

* * *

Accordingly, judicial scrutiny of disqualification orders is necessary to prevent literalism from possibly overcoming substantial justice to the parties. (cites omitted) However, . . . the issue ultimately involves a conflict between the clients' right to counsel of their choice and the need to maintain ethical standards of professional responsibility. The paramount concern, though, must be the preservation of public trust in the scrupulous administration of justice and the integrity of the bar. The recognized and important right to counsel of one's choosing must yield to considerations of ethics that run to the very integrity of our judicial process.

Confidentiality and the Attorney-Client Relationship

Preserving confidentiality of communications between attorney and client is fundamental to our legal system. The attorney-client privilege is a hallmark of Anglo-American jurisprudence that furthers the public policy of insuring "'the right of every person to freely and fully confer and confide in one having knowledge of the law, and skilled in its practice, in order that the former may have adequate advice and a proper defense.' [Citation.]" (cites omitted) One of the basic duties of an attorney is "[t]o maintain inviolate the confidence, and at every peril to himself or herself to preserve the secrets, of his or her client." (*Bus. & Prof. Code* Section 6068(e).) To protect the confidentiality of the attorney-client relationship, the California Rules of Professional Conduct bar an attorney from accepting "employment adverse to a client or former client where, by reason of the representation of the client or former client, the [attorney] has obtained confidential information material to the employment except with the informed written consent of the client or former client." (Rules Prof. Conduct, Rule 3-310(D); other cites omitted)

> Notice that in this section the court blurs the distinction between "confidential information" and "attorney/client privileged information." This will have an effect on the court's discussion of its determination later in the case.

For these reasons, an attorney will be disqualified from representing a client against a former client when there is a substantial relationship between the two representations. (cites omitted) When a substantial relationship exists, the courts presume the attorney possesses confidential information of the former client material to the present representation.

Confidentiality and the Nonlawyer Employee

The courts have discussed extensively the remedies for the ethical problems created by attorneys changing their employment from a law firm representing one party in litigation to a firm representing an adverse party. Considerably less attention has been given to the problems posed by nonlawyer employees of law firms who do the same. The issue this appeal presents is one of first impression for California courts. While several Courts of Appeal have considered factual situations raising many of the same concerns, as will be discussed below, the decisions in those cases hinged on factors not present here. In short, this case is yet another square peg that does not fit the round holes of attorney disqualification rules. (cites omitted)

Our statutes and public policy recognize the importance of protecting the confidentiality of the attorney-client relationship. (cites omitted) The obligation to maintain the client's confidences traditionally and properly has been placed on the attorney representing the client. But nonlawyer employees must handle confidential client information if legal services are to be efficient and cost-effective. Although a law firm has the ability to supervise its employees and assure that they protect client confidences, that ability and assurance are tenuous when the nonlawyer leaves the firm's employment. If the nonlawyer finds employment with opposing counsel, there is a heightened risk that confidences of the former employer's clients will be compromised, whether from base motives, an excess of zeal, or simple inadvertence.

Under such circumstances, the attorney who traditionally has been responsible for protecting the client's confidences—the former employer—has no effective means of doing so. The public policy of protecting the confidentiality of attorney-client communications must depend upon the attorney or law firm that hires an opposing counsel's employee. Certain requirements must be imposed on attorneys who hire their opposing counsel's employees to assure that attorney-client confidences are protected.

Limits on Protecting Confidentiality

We emphasize that our analysis does not mean that there is or should be any broad duty owed by an attorney to an opposing party to maintain that party's confidences in the absence of a prior attorney-client relationship. The imposition of such a duty would be antithetical to our adversary system and would interfere with the attorney's relationship with his or her own clients. The courts have recognized repeatedly that attorneys owe no duty of care to adversaries in litigation or to those with whom their clients deal at arm's length. (cites omitted) Instead, we deal here with a prophylactic rule necessary to protect the confidentiality of the attorney-client relationship and the integrity of the judicial system, and with the appropriate scope of the remedy supporting such a rule.

The Harrison firm argues that conflict of interest disqualification rules governing attorneys should not apply to the acts of nonlawyers. The courts in both cases [cited by Harrison] refused to disqualify attorneys who possessed an adverse party's confidences when no attorney-client relationship ever existed between the party and the attorney sought to be disqualified.

* * *

In *Maruman Integrated Circuits, Inc. v. Consortium Co.,* 166 Cal.App.3d at p. 451, 212 Cal.Rptr. 497, the adversary's confidences came to the attorney through an employee of the client, the former assistant to the adversary's corporate secretary. There can be no question that the information the assistant possessed was attorney-client privileged. (See *Evid. Code,* §§ 952, 954.) However, the information was disclosed to the attorney, in effect, by the attorney's own client. Since the purpose of confidentiality is to promote full and open discussions between attorney and client (*Mitchell v. Superior Court, supra,* 37 Cal.3d at p. 599, 208 Cal.Rptr. 886, 691 P.2d 642), it would be ironic to protect confidentiality by effectively barring from such discussions an adversaries confidences known to the client. A lay client should not be expected to make such distinctions in what can and cannot be told to the attorney at the risk of losing the attorney's services.

Similarly, in *Cooke,* the client in a dissolution proceeding gave her attorney copies of eight attorney-client privileged documents belonging to her husband. The source of the documents was the husband's butler, who eavesdropped on the husband's discussions with his attorneys and surreptitiously copied the documents and mailed them to the wife. The Court of Appeal upheld an order requiring the wife's attorneys to surrender the copies, but also affirmed that the attorneys need not be disqualified. (*Cooke v. Superior Court, supra,* 83 Cal.App.3d at pp. 589, 592, 147 Cal.Rptr. 915.) In summarizing the precedents, the court stated that "it is confidences acquired in the course of an attorney-client relationship which are protected by preventing the recipient of those confidences from representing an adverse party."

The court found no case imposing disqualification solely as a punitive or disciplinary measure, and there was no prior relationship between the complaining party and the attorneys sought to be disqualified. Significantly, though, the court concluded that "[o]ur function is to protect Mr. Cooke from improper use of any privileged data . . . ," and that was done by ordering the wife's attorneys to give up the documents.

The salient fact that distinguishes the present appeal from *Maruman* and *Cooke* is the person who disclosed the adverse party's attorney-client communications. If the disclosure is made by the attorney's own client, disqualification is neither justified nor an effective remedy. A party cannot "improperly" disclose information to its own counsel in the prosecution of its own lawsuit. Even if counsel were disqualified, the party would be free to give new counsel the information, leaving the opposing party with the same situation. (cite omitted) However, preservation of open communication between attorney and client is endangered when an attorney's employee discloses client confidences.

Confidentiality and the Gregori Rule

Gregori v. Bank of America presented circumstances more nearly analogous to this case. An attorney for the plaintiffs initiated a social relationship with a secretary administering the case for an opposing law firm. The attorney admitted discussing with the secretary certain aspects of the case, primarily the personalities of the lawyers involved. The Court of Appeal recognized that the Rules of Professional Conduct did not explicitly proscribe the attorney's conduct. The court also acknowledged that the rules and statutes governing attorneys and privileged information "cannot be applied to the facts of this case without procrustean effort." Nor was the court inclined to rely solely on the appearance of impropriety standard because that standard lacks precision. The *Gregori* court distilled the case law and legal literature to produce a new rule for such situations. "Since the purpose of a disqualification order must be prophylactic, not punitive, the significant question is whether there exists a genuine likelihood that the status or misconduct of the attorney in question will affect the outcome of the proceedings before the court. Thus, disqualification is proper where, as a result of a prior representation or through improper means, there is a reasonable probability counsel has obtained information the court believes would likely be used advantageously against an adverse party during the course of the litigation."

We cannot entirely agree with the rule formulated in *Gregori*. First, as Justice Benson noted in his separate opinion, the rule focuses attention on the end result of the challenged conduct without including the paramount concern of preserving public trust in the scrupulous administration of justice and the integrity of judicial proceedings. Second, the rule requires the trial judge to predict the effect on the proceedings of information likely to be unknown to the court. Although requiring some showing of the general nature of the information and its relationship to the proceeding can be proper (cite omitted), requiring disclosure of the information itself is not. (cite omitted) Third, the rule's emphasis on attorney "misconduct" and use of "improper means" distracts from the prophylactic purpose of disqualification.

Thus, the rule in *Gregori* does not address the situation in this case, where the integrity of judicial proceedings was threatened not by attorney misconduct, but by employee misconduct neither sanctioned nor sought by the attorney. The Harrison firm's disqualification is required not because of an attorney's affirmative misconduct, but because errors of omission and insensitivity to ethical dictates allowed the employee's misconduct to taint the firm with a violation of attorney-client confidentiality.

Protecting Confidentiality—The Cone of Silence

Hiring a former employee of an opposing counsel is not, in and of itself, sufficient to warrant disqualification of an attorney or law firm. However, when the former employee possesses confidential attorney-client information, materially related to pending litigation, the situation implicates " '. . . considerations of ethics which run to the very integrity of our judicial process.' [Citation.]" (cite omitted) Under such circumstances, the hiring attorney must obtain the informed written consent of the former employer, thereby dispelling any basis for disqualification. Failing that, the hiring attorney is subject to disqualification unless the attorney can rebut a presumption that the confidential attorney-client information has been used or disclosed in the new employment. We specifically mean the phrase, "confidential attorney-client information," to correspond to the definition of "confidential communication between client and lawyer" contained in *Evidence Code* section 952: "information transmitted between a client and his [or her] lawyer in the course of that relationship and in confidence by a means which, so far as the client is aware, discloses the information to no third persons other than those who are present to further the interest of the client in the consultation or those to whom disclosure is reasonably necessary for the transmission of the information or the accomplishment of the purpose for which the lawyer is consulted, and includes a legal opinion formed and the advice given by the lawyer in the course of that relationship." The definition encompasses an attorney's legal opinions, impressions, and conclusions, regardless of whether they have been communicated to the client. (cite omitted)

A law firm that hires a nonlawyer who possesses an adversary's confidences creates a situation, similar to hiring an adversary's attorney, which suggests that confidential information is at risk. We adapt our approach, then, from cases that discuss whether an entire firm is subject to vicarious disqualification because one attorney changed sides. (cites omitted) The courts disagree on whether vicarious disqualification should be automatic in attorney conflict of interest cases, or whether a presumption of shared confidences should be rebuttable. (cite omitted) An inflexible presumption of shared confidences would not be appropriate for nonlawyers, though, whatever its merits when applied to attorneys. There are obvious differences between lawyers and their nonlawyer employees in training, responsibilities, and acquisition and use of confidential information. These differences satisfy us that a rebuttable presumption of shared confidences provides a just balance between protecting confidentiality and the right to chosen counsel.

The court is talking about an ethical wall here. It was not typically called "the cone of silence," which is a reference to a television show from the 1960s, *Get Smart*. Perhaps the court was not aware that, in the show, the cone of silence never worked. See http://www.wouldyoubelieve.com.

The most likely means of rebutting the presumption is to implement a procedure, before the employee is hired, which effectively screens the employee from any involvement with the litigation, a procedure one court aptly described as a "cone of silence." (cite omitted) Whether a potential employee will require a cone of silence should be determined as a matter of routine during the hiring process. It is reasonable to ask potential employees about the nature of their prior legal work; prudence alone would dictate such inquiries. Here, Harrison's first conversation with Vogel revealed a potential problem—Vogel's work for Brobeck on asbestos litigation settlements.

The leading treatise on legal malpractice also discusses screening procedures and case law. (1 Mallen & Smith, *Legal Malpractice* (3d ed. 1989) §§ 13.18–13.19, pp. 792–797.) We find several points to be persuasive when adapted to the context of employee conflicts. "Screening is a prophylactic, affirmative measure to avoid both the reality and appearance of impropriety. It is a means, but not the means, of rebutting the presumption of shared confidences." Two objectives must be achieved. First, screening should be implemented before undertaking the challenged representation or hiring the tainted individual. Screening must take place at the outset to prevent any confidences from being disclosed. Second, the tainted individual should be precluded from any involvement in or communication about the challenged representation. To avoid inadvertent disclosures and to establish an evidentiary record, a memorandum should be circulated warning the legal staff to isolate the individual from communications on the matter and to prevent access to the relevant files.

The need for such a rule is manifest. We agree with the observations made by the *Williams* court: "[Nonlawyer] personnel are widely used by lawyers to assist in rendering legal services. Paralegals, investigators, and secretaries must have ready access to client confidences in order to assist their attorney employers. If information provided by a client in confidence to an attorney for the purpose of obtaining legal advice could be used against the client because a member of the attorney's [nonlawyer] support staff left the attorney's employment, it would have a devastating effect both on the free flow of information between client and attorney and on the cost and quality of the legal services rendered by an attorney." (*Williams v. Trans World Airlines, Inc., supra*, 588 F.Supp. at p. 1044.) Further, no regulatory or ethical rules, comparable to those governing attorneys, restrain all of the many types of nonlawyer employees of attorneys. The restraint on such employees' disclosing confidential attorney-client information must be the employing attorney's admonishment against revealing the information.

The Substantial Relationship Test and Nonlawyer Employees

We decline to adopt the broader rule urged by respondents and applied by other courts, which treats the nonlawyer employee as an attorney and requires disqualification upon the showing and standards applicable to individual attorneys. Respondents argue that disqualification must follow a showing of a "substantial relationship" between the matters worked on by the nonlawyer at the former and present employers' firms. However, the substantial relationship test is a tool devised for presuming an attorney possesses confidential information material to a representation adverse to a former client. (cite omitted) The presumption is a rule of necessity because the former client cannot know what confidential information the former attorney acquired and carried into the new adverse representation. The reasons for the presumption, and therefore the test, are not applicable though, when a nonlawyer employee leaves and the attorney remains available to the client. The client and the attorney are then in the best position to know what confidential attorney-client information was available to the former employee.

Respondents' alternative formulation, that a substantial relationship between the type of work done for the former and present employers requires disqualification, presents unnecessary barriers to employment mobility. Such a rule sweeps more widely than needed to protect client confidences. We share the concerns expressed by the American Bar Association's Standing Committee on Ethics and Professional Responsibility: "It is important that nonlawyer employees have as much mobility in employment opportunity as possible consistent with the protection of clients' interests. To so limit employment opportunities that some nonlawyers trained to work with law firms might be required to leave the careers for which they are trained would disserve clients as well as the legal profession. Accordingly, any restrictions on the nonlawyer's employment should be held to the minimum necessary to protect confidentiality of client information." (cite omitted) Respondents' suggested rule could easily result in nonlawyer employees becoming "Typhoid Marys," unemployable by firms practicing in specialized areas of the law where the employees are most skilled and experienced.

Protecting Confidentiality—The Rule for Disqualification

Absent written consent, the proper rule and its application for disqualification based on nonlawyer employee conflicts of interest should be as follows. The party seeking disqualification must show that its present or past attorney's former employee possesses confidential attorney-client information materially related to the proceedings before the court. The party should not be required to disclose the actual information contended to be confidential. However, the court should be provided with the nature of the information and its material relationship to the proceeding. (cite omitted)

Once this showing has been made, a rebuttable presumption arises that the information has been used or disclosed in the current employment. The presumption is a rule by necessity because the party seeking disqualification will be at a loss to prove what is known by the adversary's attorneys and legal staff. (cite omitted) To rebut the presumption, the challenged attorney has the burden of showing that the practical effect of formal screening has been achieved. The showing must satisfy the trial court that the employee has not had and will not have any involvement with the litigation, or any communication with attorneys or co-employees concerning the litigation, that would support a reasonable inference that the information has been used or disclosed. If the challenged attorney fails to make this showing, then the court may disqualify the attorney and law firm.

The Trial Court Properly Exercised Its Discretion

* * *

The Harrison firm's primary contention on appeal is that respondents failed to show that Vogel possessed any specific client confidences. The Harrison firm's repeated invocation of specific confidences misses the point and underscores the futility of its factual argument. Vogel admitted reviewing the Harrison firm's cases on Brobeck's computer to see "what kind of cases [the Harrison firm] had filed." The plain inference is that Vogel used his training in asbestos litigation to make a rough analysis of his prospective employer's cases. Vogel acknowledged that because of his experience in looking at SEAR forms, he knew that some cases have more value than others. He also testified that the SEAR forms are used as the basis for evaluating cases. The SEAR form information Vogel obtained about the Harrison firm's cases was part of a system of attorney-client communications.

There can be no question that Vogel obtained confidential attorney-client information when he accessed the Harrison firm's case files on Brobeck's computer. Respondents need not show the specific confidences Vogel obtained; such a showing would serve only to exacerbate the damage to the confidentiality of the attorney-client relationship. As discussed above, respondents had to show only the nature of the information and its material relationship to the present proceedings. They have done so.

To blunt the impact of Vogel's misconduct, the Harrison firm argues that the cases on the computer were newly filed and that no evidence showed the computer information to be more than appeared on the face of the complaints, which are public records. The argument is wrong on both points. While many of the cases were entered on the computer little more than a week earlier, others were entered weeks or months before Vogel looked at them. Moreover, the fact that some of the same information may appear in the public domain does not affect the privileged status of the information when it is distilled for an attorney-client communication. (cites omitted) Therefore, there was substantial evidence that Vogel possessed confidential attorney-client information materially related to the cases for which the trial court ordered disqualification.

Remember: Confidential information is all information relating to the representation of the client. The court uses a tortured analysis: "public information becomes attorney/client privileged information when it is distilled . . ." but misses the point. The information on the SEAR forms was confidential, so a conflict arises. The information doesn't have to be attorney/client privileged for the conflict to arise.

The Harrison firm also argues that there was no evidence that Vogel disclosed any confidences to any member of the firm, or that any such information was sought from or volunteered by Vogel. Harrison testified that he never asked Vogel to divulge anything other than impressions about three Brobeck attorneys. Harrison and his office manager also testified that Vogel was not involved in case evaluation or trial tactics discussions at the Harrison firm. However, this evidence is not sufficient to rebut the presumption that Vogel used the confidential material or disclosed it to staff members at the Harrison firm. Moreover, there was substantial evidence to support a reasonable inference that Vogel used or disclosed the confidential information.

Despite Harrison's own concern over an appearance of impropriety, Harrison never told Vogel not to discuss the information Vogel learned at Brobeck and did not consider screening Vogel even after Brobeck first inquired about Vogel's work on asbestos cases. The evidence also amply supports the trial court's observation that Vogel was "a very talkative person, a person who loves to share information." Further, Vogel's willingness to use information acquired at Brobeck, and the Harrison firm's insensitivity to ethical considerations, were demonstrated when Vogel was told to call respondent Fibreboard Corporation and Vogel knew the person to contact there.

The trial court did not apply a presumption of disclosure, which would have been appropriate under the rule we have set forth. The evidence offered by the Harrison firm is manifestly insufficient to rebut the presumption. Beyond that, though, substantial evidence established a reasonable probability that Vogel used or disclosed to the Harrison firm the confidential attorney-client information obtained from Brobeck's computer records. Accordingly, the trial court was well within a sound exercise of discretion in ordering the Harrison firm's disqualification.

Equitable Considerations for Disqualification Motions

[The court's discussion of the consideration of the possibility that Brobeck brought the motion as a tactical device is omitted.] [On their cross-appeal, Brobeck asked the court to disqualify the Harrison firm from *all* asbestos cases. The court declined, luckily for Mr. Harrison. The court ruled that disqualification was a case-by-case decision and could only be made by the court having jurisdiction over each case. Those discussions are omitted.]

Conclusion

We realize the serious consequences of disqualifying attorneys and depriving clients of representation by their chosen counsel. However, we must balance the important right to counsel of one's choice against the competing fundamental interest in preserving confidences of the attorney-client relationship. All attorneys share certain basic obligations of professional conduct, obligations that are essential to the integrity and function of our legal system. Attorneys must respect the confidentiality of attorney-client information and recognize that protecting confidentiality is an imperative to be obeyed in both form and substance. A requisite corollary to these principles is that attorneys must prohibit their employees from violating confidences of former employers as well as confidences of present clients. Until the Legislature or the State Bar choose to disseminate a different standard, attorneys must be held accountable for their employees' conduct, particularly when that conduct poses a clear threat to attorney-client confidentiality and the integrity of our judicial process.

The order of the trial court is affirmed.

CASE QUESTIONS

1. Review the preceding case where it says Question 1 Issue. Notice that in this section the court blurs the distinction between "confidential information" and "attorney/client privileged information." Can you explain to the court what the differences between the two concepts are?
2. Review the preceding case where it says Question 2 Issue. The court does not properly address the issue of the complaints as "public record." What do you know about public records and their effect on the duty of confidentiality?
3. Review the preceding case at the Question 2 Issue. What can you tell the court about the status of the SEAR forms information as "confidential" and the effect of possession of confidential information on conflict of interest?
4. If there is a lesson to be learned from this case, what is it?

CASE 2

Johnson v. Continental Casualty Co.
57 Wash. App. 359, 788 P.2d 598
(1990)

Continental Casualty Company appeals a summary judgment requiring it to pay the fees of the attorney Ivan Johnson independently hired in a professional negligence action. We reverse and direct the entry of summary judgment for Continental.

Continental issued a legal professional's liability policy to Johnson, an attorney. The policy excluded coverage for "any dishonest, fraudulent, criminal, or malicious act or omission of the insured." In the underlying action, Joan Tice sued Johnson for negligence but also alleged, among other things, that Johnson had suborned perjury.

Continental referred Johnson's defense to Robert Thomas of Lane Powell Moss & Miller, indicating, however, that it would defend under a reservation of rights because some of the allegations, if proved, would be covered and some would not. In a letter to Johnson, Continental suggested that, because the policy had a $250,000 liability limit and the damages claimed were unspecified, he might want to retain counsel at his own expense for protection of his interests beyond that limit. Johnson retained Patrick Comfort; Comfort in turn notified Continental that, in his opinion, Continental was responsible for his fees.

Johnson brought this declaratory action, praying that Continental be required to pay the fees of Comfort, whom he had retained to represent him on noncovered claims, or that Continental be required to defend him without reservation of rights. In due course, the parties filed cross motions for summary judgment.

Meanwhile, Thomas, with Johnson's knowledge and consent, negotiated a settlement of the underlying action. Continental paid the entire amount of the settlement ($20,000), and that action was dismissed. The trial court in the declaratory action then granted Johnson's and denied Continental's summary judgment motion. By the order, Comfort was "appointed" Johnson's attorney, and Continental was ordered to pay Comfort's fees because Johnson was not found liable for any noncovered claim.

Johnson contends essentially that when an insurer defends under a reservation of rights, a conflict of interest automatically arises requiring that the insurer pay for independent counsel chosen by the insured. Continental contends that no such conflict necessarily arises, that there was none in this case, and that Johnson is responsible for the fees he incurred to protect his noninsured interests. *See Farmers Ins. Co. v. Rees*, 96 Wash.2d 679, 638 P.2d 580 (1982). We agree with Continental.

Johnson relies on California authority. [*San Diego Navy Fed. Credit Union v. Cumis Ins. Soc'y, Inc.*, 162 Cal. App. 3d 358, 208 Cal. Rptr. 494 (1984) (if insured does not give informed consent to representation by counsel hired by insurer, then insurer pays reasonable fees of insured's independently hired attorney when conflict of interest exists in that multiple theories are alleged, some within and some outside the scope of coverage).]

The rule in Washington, however, is not that a conflict arises automatically in these cases, but that an insurer, defending under a reservation of rights, has an "enhanced obligation of fairness toward its insured." *Tank v. State Farm Fire & Cas. Co.,* 105 Wash.2d 381, 383, 715 P.2d 1133 (1986). The obligation comes about because of "*[P]otential* conflicts between the interests of insurer and insured, inherent in a reservation of rights defense, ..." (Italics ours.) *Tank*, 105 Wn. 2d at 383. In other words, no actual conflict of interest necessarily exists in a reservation of rights defense. In fact, such a defense is frequently a "valuable service to the insured." *Tank*, 105 Wash.2d at 390.

Nonetheless, an insurer must fulfill this "enhanced obligation of fairness" in a reservation of rights defense by meeting specific criteria: (1) the company must thoroughly investigate the claim; (2) it must retain competent defense counsel for the insured, and both retained defense counsel and the insurer must understand that only the INSURED is the client; (3) the company must inform the insured of the reservation of rights defense and ALL developments relevant to policy coverage and progress of the lawsuit; (4) the company must refrain from any activity that would show a greater concern for its monetary interest than for insured's financial risk. *Tank,* 105 Wash.2d at 388.

Moreover, specific criteria must be met by the defense counsel hired by the insurer. First, the attorney must understand that he represents the insured, not the company. [As the *Tank* court noted, this obligation stems from an attorney's obligation under RPC 5.4(c) not to "permit a person who recommends, employs, or pays the lawyer to render legal services for another to direct or regulate the lawyer's professional judgment in rendering such legal services." *Tank*, 105 Wn. 2d at 388. *See also RPC* 1.8(f).]

Second, the attorney owes an ongoing duty to the insured to disclose (1) conflicts of interest under RPC 1.7; (2) all information relevant to the insured's defense; and (3) all offers of settlement as they are presented. *Tank*, 105 Wash.2d at 388–89.

None of the materials Johnson submitted to the court shows any facts supporting his allegation of conflict of interest.

Johnson's affidavit in support of summary judgment only asserts, "I feel that the refusal of the defendant to provide coverage for certain of the above referenced claims creates a conflict of interest for the attorney selected by the defendant to defend against the above referenced claims." Such bare allegations are not sufficient to raise a genuine issue of material fact for the purpose of a summary judgment motion. *Meissner v. Simpson Timber Co.*, 69 Wash.2d 949, 955, 421 P.2d 674 (1966).

On the contrary, the record shows that Continental complied with the criteria announced in *Tank*.

Continental's reservation of rights letter and the documents concerning settlement reveal that a full investigation of the claim was made. The firm Continental employed to defend Johnson stayed fully in touch with him, and cooperated with and provided materials to his independent attorney, Comfort. Moreover, that firm ultimately settled the underlying claim with Johnson's knowledge and consent and for his benefit. There was no showing that Continental acted in its own monetary interests to Johnson's detriment, or that the attorney hired for Johnson did not inform or disclose as required.

In Washington, there is simply no presumption, as Johnson urges, that a reservation of rights situation creates an automatic conflict of interest. Therefore, the insurer has no obligation *before the fact* to pay for its insured's independently hired counsel. Any breach of the "enhanced obligation of fairness" in a reservation of rights situation might lead to after-the-fact liability of the insurer, retained defense counsel, or both. *Tank*, 105 Wn. 2d at 387–88. That, however, is not the situation here; Continental's efforts in meeting its obligation to Johnson led to the settlement of the underlying claim.

We do agree with the trial court that the summary judgment record discloses no triable fact issue. We conclude, however, that the legal issue presented should have been resolved by granting Continental's, not Johnson's, summary judgment motion.

Reversed.

CASE QUESTIONS

1. What was it that triggered Johnson's necessity for a lawyer in addition to his representation by his insurance carrier's lawyer (Thomas)? In other words, why did Johnson have to hire Comfort?
2. Explain a "reservation of rights" letter. What did it mean when Johnson's insurance company sent him this letter?
3. Why does a reservation of rights letter create a conflict of interest?
4. Johnson's lawyer relied on California law, but the case was in Washington. What is the difference between the law in California and the law in Washington? What was it about this difference that caused Johnson to lose this case?

ADVERTISING AND SOLICITATION

HYPOTHETICAL

At a cocktail party, March, a law firm employee, is listening to a woman give a play-by-play account of her car accident. She details various aches and pains she suffered as a result of the accident and adds, "I can't even get my insurance company to listen to me." March, who does not know the woman, pulls her employer's business card from her purse and says, "It sounds to me like you've got a bad faith claim against your insurance carrier. Here, take this card and call the lawyer I work for. I'm sure he can get everything worked out for you." The woman takes the card.

What Is "Access to Justice"?

There is an ever-widening gap between the need for legal representation and the satisfaction of that need. The primary reason for this problem is the inability of many people to pay for legal assistance. In fact, only about 15 percent of the people who need a lawyer can afford one. The secondary reason is the ignorance of the need for legal assistance. Because the law appears mysterious and frightening to the layperson, the uneducated and the impoverished are those who are the least likely to receive legal help, although it is these people who need help the most.

> Comment 2 to Rule 6.1 says that the rights and responsibilities of people and entities in this country are increasingly defined in legal terms and, therefore, legal assistance in coping with the complexity of the law is increasingly important.

All of us are obligated to continually rethink the efficiency of the practice of law and make it better suited to aid the public. The expanded use of paralegals and technology are two important components of the solution to the problem of providing *competent legal services to the public at affordable prices.*

ABA Opinion No. 320 (dating all the way back to 1968) states that it is the duty of the legal profession to devise methods that will improve the systems for bringing legal services to those people who need them "so long as this can be done ethically and with dignity." According to former Chief Justice Warren Burger, the use of paralegals is one effective method of bringing competent legal assistance to the public at a reasonable cost. There probably aren't any lawyers remaining who don't believe that the effective use of paralegals is one of the best ways to make legal services affordable and more accessible. Check your state bar's Web site and see if you can find the bar opinion on this issue.

The Unsavory Client

The question of the unsavory client is one that is the topic of heated discussion in ethics classes. The question "Must the female lawyer defend the rapist simply because he wants to hire her?" is a terrific class discussion topic. But the rapist is not the only unpopular client out there. Tobacco companies, paint manufacturers, drug companies, and gun manufacturers are at the top of the list in modern history. The paralegal doesn't have much input in what clients a law firm will take but should have some say in what cases he or she will work on. Here's the rule: Each and every client is entitled to the very best work product and consideration regardless of one's personal likes or dislikes. The duties of competency and integrity do not change for different types of cases or clients. If you think you can't do your best work, your duty of zealous representation work, on a case because of your personal beliefs, talk to a supervising lawyer about being reassigned.

The lawyer has a duty to not "avoid appointment" of representation (Model Rule 6.2). A lawyer is not *obligated* to accept a client whose character or cause is repugnant. It has traditionally been argued that lawyers must not accept representation of such a person if their distaste for the client or cause is so great that they are unable to render adequate representation.

In reality, lawyers are often appointed to cases for which they will not get paid or for which they are not competent. The lack of lawyers for poor people who have

> One of the highest services the lawyer can render to society is to appear in court on behalf of clients whose causes are in disfavor with the general public.

been accused of crimes has necessitated the "forcible" appointment of lawyers, rather like indentured servitude. A story coming out of Massachusetts in 2004 is that the lawyers who had been accepting court appointments refused to accept any new clients because the pay for this representation was so low. As a result, one superior court judge used an emergency rule to appoint the lawyers without their permission. The lawyers, of course, brought a lawsuit to stop this practice. The Massachusetts legislature responded by making changes to the system so that lawyers could be paid a reasonable fee.

Why Do Law Firms Need to Advertise?

Because the legal problems of laypeople are not always obvious to them, Rule 6.1 says that members of the legal profession should assist laypeople in recognizing their legal problems. In many instances, it is important that the legal problem be recognized and attended to within a certain time period. Therefore, legal professionals should encourage and participate in educational and public relations programs for members of the general public. These programs inform the public and provide them with an opportunity to meet with conscientious lawyers. Sometimes making that first call to a lawyer is too scary for people. Meeting a lawyer in a more informal setting, such as an informative seminar, helps people recognize their legal needs and get help.

Part of the job of protecting the public is assisting members of the public in recognizing their legal problems—and a part of responding to this responsibility is advertising. A limited form of advertising, that is, letting the public know the lawyer or law firm's name, phone number, and address, has always been permitted. If this were not true, members of the public would not be able to find a lawyer when they needed one. However, *Bates & O'Steen v. Arizona*[1] changed the laws prohibiting lawyers from advertising more than just their names and whereabouts in the late 1970s. Since *Bates,* those of you who are old enough will notice, lawyers advertise on television and radio (and now the Internet), using paid actors, scripts, and explanations about the legal services offered. This sort of advertising to the general public is no longer considered the improper solicitation of clients.

In *Bates & O'Steen,* the U.S. Supreme Court held that prohibiting advertising by lawyers and law firms was a violation of their First Amendment right to free speech. The Court ruled that because the speech can be regulated by the integrated bar and because such advertising serves to reduce the cost of legal services to the public, it benefits the administration of justice. The advertising in question was a newspaper advertisement that announced the legal work and prices of a legal clinic. It was not improper because it could not be classified as "in-person solicitation."

NFPA *EC* 1.7(b): A paralegal's title shall be included if the paralegal's name appears on business cards, letterhead, brochures, directories, and advertisements.

Although the Supreme Court's decision in *Bates & O'Steen* should have ended the controversy about lawyer advertising, it did not. In 1984, Attorney Zauderer was publicly reprimanded by the Ohio Supreme Court after running an advertisement entitled "Did You Use This IUD?" that depicted a larger-than-life Dalkon Shield. The advertisement, which ran in thirty-six Ohio newspapers, mentioned that the shield had led to infertility and spontaneous abortions and invited readers to telephone Zauderer with regard to his representation in a class action against the manufacturer and other parties. The U.S. Supreme Court reviewed the restrictions on lawyer advertising in *Zauderer v. Disciplinary Counsel.*[2] Zauderer's defense argued that the Ohio regulation violated his First Amendment right of free speech. The Supreme Court upheld the reprimand on the basis that the advertisement was misleading but affirmed the lawyer's right to advertise in what many 1980s legal professionals thought was a less-than-tasteful manner. Even the Supreme Court cannot regulate good taste. And, Zauderer had alerted many women to the dangers of that particular IUD, something they would not have otherwise known.

In the 1980s and 1990s television advertising became increasingly popular. Most states have passed laws regarding television advertising. For example, Virginia passed an ethics rule addressing the use of actors in law firm advertising. If an actor is portraying the lawyer, the commercial must specify that it is a dramatization so that the public is not fooled into thinking that the particular person in the commercial is the lawyer who will be handling their case.[3] What do you think about that argument?

What Is Good Lawyer Advertising?

In this area, as so many others, there are general guidelines we can study, but the states differ in the specifics. Most states adopted ABA Model Rule 7.2, but amended the rule in some way. In the boxes on this page and the next you'll find some examples. What you need to know is the law in your state. You won't find any ABA Model Code equivalents as the Model Code prohibited most forms of advertising except for the most basic name, address, phone number, and areas of practice.

In Pennsylvania subparagraph (b) of the Rule is expanded by providing examples of prohibited communications that create unjustified expectations about results "such as the amount of previous damage awards, the lawyer's record in obtaining favorable verdicts, or client endorsements. . . ." And Pennsylvania added a subparagraph that codifies Pennsylvania case law by prohibiting subjective claims as to the quality of the lawyer's services or his or her credentials. See *Spencer v. Honorable Justices of the Supreme Court,* 579 F.Supp. 880 (E.D. Pa. 1984), where the court ruled that a lawyer may not use inherently subjective terms such as "experienced," "expert," "highly qualified," or "competent" to describe his services.

Maryland Rule 7.2 looks very much like ABA Model Rule 7.2 but added paragraphs (e) and (f). Maryland Rule 7.2(e) requires that if an advertisement says that no fee will be charged if there is no recovery, it must specifically disclose if the client will be liable for expenses. Maryland Rule 7.2(f) requires that any lawyer, including a participant in an advertising group or lawyer referral services or other program, "shall be personally responsible for compliance with the provisions of Rules 7.1, 7.2, 7.3, 7.4 and 7.5 . . . ."

South Carolina adopted Model Rule 7.2 but added a few paragraphs. One of them is this:

(f) A lawyer shall not make statements in advertisements which are merely self-laudatory or which describe or characterize the quality of the lawyer's services; provided that this provision shall not apply to information furnished to a prospective client at that person's request or to information supplied to existing clients.

And this one:

(g) Every advertisement that contains information about the lawyer's fee shall disclose whether the client will be liable for any expenses in addition to the fee and, if the fee will be a percentage of the recovery, whether the percentage will be computed before deducting the expenses.

For some of the most restrictive rules on advertising, take a look at Louisiana's rules. LPRC 7.2. You can find all of Louisiana's professional responsibility rules in pdf format on the website of the Louisiana Attorney Disciplinary Board.
http://www.ladp.org

New York has more restrictive advertising rules starting in 2007. The amendments include the following:

- A ban on using testimonials by current clients or paid endorsements.
- An expansion of rules to cover computer and Internet-based advertising and solicitation, including restrictions on websites and e-mail, and bans on "pop-up" ads and chat-room solicitation.
- A ban on using nicknames, mottos or trade names that suggest an ability to obtain results.
- A requirement that ads stating "no fee will be charged if no money is recovered" disclose that client will remain liable for other expenses regardless of the case outcome.
- A ban on fictionalized portrayals of clients, judges or lawyers or re-enactments of events that are not authentic.

You can find the new rules at http://www.nycourts.gov

How Can There Be Both Good and Bad Solicitation?

Bad Solicitation

Although advertising is now permitted, solicitation is not. Well, most of the time it isn't. All states have rules that prohibit in-person "soliciting":

Sample Rule 7.3

a. A lawyer shall not by in-person, live telephone or real-time electronic contact solicit professional employment from a prospective client when a significant motive for the lawyer's doing so is the lawyer's pecuniary gain, unless the person contacted:

   (1) is a lawyer; or
   (2) has a family, close personal, or prior professional relationship with the lawyer.

b. A lawyer shall not solicit professional employment from a prospective client by written, recorded or electronic communication or by in-person, telephone or real-time electronic contact even when not otherwise prohibited by paragraph (a), if:

   (1) the prospective client has made known to the lawyer a desire not to be solicited by the lawyer; or
   (2) the solicitation involves coercion, duress or harassment.

Simply put, the difference between solicitation and advertising is that solicitation is in person, by telephone, or by written communication that is directed to a specific individual. Advertising, on the other hand, is directed to the public at large.

What's the difference to the public? Well, pressure is typically cited for the difference between advertising—general, not targeted, and the public is fairly immune to most forms of advertising—and solicitation—specific, targeted, and pressure driven. People have less trouble saying "no" to a typical advertisement than to a letter addressed to them on law firm stationery.

The rules prohibiting solicitation are the same for the paralegal. That "in-your-face" attempt to get a client is impermissible no matter what law firm employee is doing it. Furthermore, if a paralegal is found soliciting clients at the request of the lawyer, the lawyer will be held responsible.

In *Idaho State Bar v. Jenkins,*[4] the Idaho Supreme Court held that a lawyer could not be held liable for his paralegal's solicitation of professional employment absent clear and convincing evidence that the lawyer either ordered her to solicit business or, with knowledge of the paralegal's specific conduct, ratified her actions.

> Prior to her employment with the Jenkins' law firm as a legal assistant, Landeros was involved in providing social services to members of the Hispanic community in east Idaho. When the funding for that program ceased, Landeros obtained employment with Jenkins' law firm as a legal assistant. The hearing committee found . . . that Gordon Jenkins . . . hired

Landeros because of her close contacts with the Mexican community and for the sole purpose of bringing in new clients to the firm in the areas of personal injury, workmen's compensation, and immigration.

The court discussed the incidents involving contact of prospective clients by Landeros for the purpose of soliciting them for her employer. In one such incident, Landeros contacted the parents of a young man who had been killed in an automobile accident. She went to their home:

> The record indicates that Landeros told the Martinez family that Jenkins was the best lawyer in the firm and that he has sent her out to their home to ". . . see what she could do to help the family."

The court applied Idaho's Rule 5.3,[5] Responsibilities Regarding Nonlawyer Assistants:

> As a preliminary observation, there is no question or doubt that the conduct of Landeros in the Martinez incident constituted blatant solicitation of professional employment from a prospective client clearly in violation of Rule 7.3(a) of the Idaho Rules of Professional Conduct. However, the precise issue presented to us is not whether Landeros' conduct was unethical solicitation, which we deem it to be, but rather as expressly required under Rule 5.3(b)(1) the issue is whether Jenkins "ordered" the conduct, or "with knowledge of the specific conduct involved" ratified the conduct of Landeros.

Making a decision in favor of Attorney Jenkins, the court said:

> While one might characterize Francis Landeros as a loose cannon rolling around the deck of Jenkins' law office, the overwhelming evidence established a firm policy, supported by frequent staff meetings, aimed at educating Mr. Jenkins' non-lawyer staff about impermissible in-person solicitations. This program is precisely the kind of action a lawyer must take to assure himself that the impermissible conduct itself, as well as the consequences of an in-person solicitation, can be avoided or mitigated.

What Paralegal Landeros was doing was clearly solicitation because it was in person, initiated by her, for the purpose of securing a client for her employer for profit. Note that it was the lawyer who was on the hook for the improper conduct of his employee because there was no penalty that the court could impose on the paralegal. The court has the authority to issue an *injunction* to prohibit her from similar conduct in the future; but, as there is no regulatory body that licenses her, no penalty could be imposed upon her personally. Again, it is likely that Landeros was just trying to help the Martinez family and the Jenkins law office. She could not have been motivated by money because she would not have received anything for bringing the case into the office. But her good intentions did not mitigate the impropriety of her conduct.

Good Solicitation

Here's some more American history. It's interesting stuff so hang in there!

On the other hand, some good intentions do matter in the world of solicitation. Case on point is *In re Primus*.

In the 1960s, some of the states in the southern part of the United States enacted laws requiring women who applied for welfare to be sterilized in order to maintain their eligibility for Medicare. This is a shocking fact, but true. The ACLU decided to test the constitutionality of these laws, but in order to do that, they needed a client—or a victim of this practice. Mrs. Primus was a volunteer lawyer for the ACLU. She went to Aiken, South Carolina, and met with women there for the specific purpose of getting them to sign up with the ACLU as clients. She later wrote a letter to one of the women asking her to agree to sue. As a result of these activities, Mrs. Primus was disciplined by the State Bar of South Carolina for improper solicitation. From the state bar's perspective, her activities were illegal solicitation of clients. The U.S. Supreme Court, however, differentiated *Primus* from typical solicitation cases:

> Unlike the situation in *Ohralik,* however, appellant's act of solicitation took the form of a letter to a woman with whom appellant had discussed the possibility of seeking redress for an allegedly unconstitutional sterilization. This was not in-person solicitation for pecuniary gain. Appellant was communicating an offer of free assistance by attorneys associated with the ACLU, not an offer predicated on entitlement to a share of any monetary recovery. And her actions were undertaken to express personal political beliefs and to advance the civil liberties objectives of the ACLU, rather than to derive financial gain.

So, there's bad solicitation (*Ohralik*) and good solicitation (*Primus*).

What Is Direct Mail?

Somewhere in between traditional advertising and solicitation is *direct mail*. Sometimes it is referred to as "direct mail advertising," sometimes "direct mail solicitation." In either case, it is wise to follow the rules of your state regarding this form of prospective client contact. Direct mail is used in foreclosure matters, mass disaster cases, and in many other types of legal matters in which a list of prospective clients can be obtained. For instance, many courts make the list of upcoming residential foreclosures available. A law firm purchases this list and sends out a mass mailing to everyone on the list touting that firm's ability to relieve the homeowner from the foreclosure.

Whereas advertising to the general public is permitted because it is subject to scrutiny by the public, these direct and private communications to a prospective client are not open to review in the same manner. The fear that these private statements are misleading is tempered with the public's need to be informed about legal services and the lawyer's right to free speech.

Direct mail is not a new way of attracting clients. In 1981, *Matter of Discipline of Appert & Pyle*[5] upheld the right of two Minnesota lawyers to prepare and distribute brochures and letters concerning possible litigation stemming from the use of the contraceptive device, the Dalkon Shield. At the time, neither the suit against the manufacturer of the Dalkon Shield nor the state bar's action against the law firm attracted much attention.

In recent years, as direct mail has become a more prevalent advertising tool, it has received a corresponding amount of attention from the state bars and other disciplinary bodies. Several states have enacted statutes that prohibit any contact for a certain amount of time with people who have been charged with crimes or people who are related to victims of mass disasters. These statutes are designed to protect people from making choices about legal representation while they are especially vulnerable. Although these statutes have been challenged, most have been upheld.[6]

In-person solicitation is still improper, whether by a lawyer or paralegal. The line between solicitation and helping a member of the public understand a legal problem is not a clear one, but the motivation of the legal professional is a guide: if the in-person communication is motivated by the desire to make money, it is probably improper solicitation. If it is motivated by a desire to assist a member of the public in recognizing a legal problem, it is more likely proper.

Solicitation of legal work from people who are already clients of the firm is permitted. You can solicit your family members, too. Go check out your state's Rule 7.3.

So, Can Paralegals Advertise?

> NFPA *EC* 1.7(c): A paralegal shall not use letterhead, business cards or other promotional materials to create a fraudulent impression of his/her status or ability to practice in the jurisdiction in which the paralegal practices.

The short answer to this question is: paralegals cannot deliver legal services directly to the public, so they cannot advertise directly to the public.

But! Paralegals may advertise their services to lawyers and law firms through letters, advertisements in legal directories, and legal periodical publications.

Check to see if your state has an opinion on this issue. Those bar associations that have written opinions on this subject say that to allow paralegals to advertise their services directly to the public may mislead the public.[7] To the layperson, these advertisements imply that the paralegal can practice law. Doing so, however, constitutes the unauthorized practice of law in most states, as discussed in Chapter 2.

If you're reading this in California, you know that California has a definition of the word "paralegal" and only those people who qualify can use that term as a designation or title. California does have two categories of people who can deliver limited legal services directly to the public: Unlawful Detainer Assistants (UDAs) and Legal Document Assistants (LDAs). When you see listings for "Paralegals" in the yellow pages directory offering to help with your bankruptcy, immigration, or divorce, these people are not "paralegals" as the term is now defined. They are more likely LDAs. Unfortunately, the public doesn't know the term *Legal Document Assistant,* so if these people were listed in telephone directories under that name, no one would ever find them. As a result, they list themselves as "Paralegals," which is technically against the law. If they are delivering legal services directly to the public, they have the right to advertise, but beware! Both Unlawful Detainer Assistants and Legal Document Assistants are

Job Wanted
Entry level paralegal position. Recent grad with great people skills. Knowledge of law office software and procedures. Can supply writing samples. Please email: newparalegal@yahoo.com

regulated by very strict and precise advertising rules. Before striking out on your own in this area, read the rules carefully. California paralegals who do not work directly for the public may not advertise to the public.

A paralegal will be held to the same regulations as a lawyer with regard to solicitation of clients as we saw earlier with Paralegal Landeros (p. 150). In discussions with laypeople, it is important to be aware of allowing the layperson to lead the discussion. In other words, the layperson should ask the paralegal for a referral to a lawyer or firm before such a referral is offered. Although it is not improper solicitation to give the business card of your law firm to laypeople if they ask for it, it is improper solicitation to put the card in the pocket of an accident victim or to offer the card to a stranger.

Most state professional responsibility rules and codes require the lawyers to refrain from actively seeking out people who may have legal claims and to refrain from "convincing" laypeople that they do have a legal claim. The problem that arises, of course, is that laypeople may be irreparably injured if they do not seek legal assistance to pursue their claims or refuse to believe they have a claim. Unfortunately, the ethical course is to let them make their own decisions and refer them to a lawyer only if they ask for that kind of assistance. Many people, remember, will choose not to pursue a legal claim for reasons that are logical only to themselves.

Pablo, a recent graduate of a paralegal program, was hired by a sole practitioner on an "as-needed" basis. Pablo was promised a full-time job as soon as the lawyer had enough work to keep them both busy. Pablo tried to think of ways to increase the number of clients for his employer and came up with the following list:

1. Do excellent work for existing clients to get their repeat business and referrals.
2. Get involved in community services and meet new people. If these people ask for a referral to a lawyer, Pablo may refer them to his employer.
3. Write an informative pamphlet in Spanish that gives general information about tenant rights for the Spanish-speaking community. In Pablo's state, the law firm was permitted to print its name, address, and telephone number on such a pamphlet. Pablo also confirmed the contents of the pamphlet with the state bar association. In distributing the pamphlet, Pablo provided a community service and brought several tenants' rights cases to his employer.
4. Place an informative advertisement in the telephone directory under the name of the law firm with a description of the firm's areas of practice in accordance with his state's rules on advertising.

NFPA *EC* 1.7(d): A paralegal shall not practice under color of any record, diploma, or certificate that has been illegally or fraudulently obtained or issued or which is misrepresentative in any way.

NALS Code of Ethics Canon 6. Members of this association shall not solicit legal business on behalf of a lawyer.

5. Create an informative Web site for the law firm with the name and contact information as well as descriptions of the type of law the lawyer practices. Before listing any current clients on the Web site, Pablo should be sure to get written permission from the client.

Are There Times When Potential Clients Cannot Be Contacted?

As mentioned earlier, some states have laws that prohibit lawyers from contacting people who have been charged with crimes or victims or families of victims for a period of time after a mass disaster. These statutes are designed to "protect the personal privacy and tranquility of recent accident victims and their relatives and in ensuring that these individuals do not fall prey to undue influence or overreaching" while they are especially vulnerable. Although these statutes have been challenged, most have been upheld. Cases of note include *Ficker v. Curran*[8] from 1996 (striking down a statute banning written solicitation of persons charged with jailable traffic offenses for thirty days because of the short time frame for prosecuting these offenses) and *Florida Bar v. Went For It, Inc.,*[9] a U.S. Supreme Court case (upholding a statute banning contact with victims and families of victims of mass disasters for thirty days). The Supreme Court based much of its decision on a two-year study done by the Florida Bar. The study showed that the public's view of the legal profession was adversely affected as shown in this small section of the Court's opinion:

> The purpose of the 30-day targeted direct mail ban is to forestall the outrage and irritation with the state licensed legal profession that the practice of direct solicitation only days after accidents has engendered. The Bar is concerned not with citizens' "offense" in the abstract, . . . but with the demonstrable detrimental effects that such "offense" has on the profession it regulates.

> NALA Canon 1:
> A legal assistant must not perform any of the duties that attorneys only may perform nor take any actions that attorneys may not take.

> Pennsylvania has an additional prohibition against contacting prospective clients when "the lawyer knows or reasonably should know that the physical, emotional or mental state of the person is such that the person could not exercise reasonable judgment in employing a lawyer." Penn. Rule 7.3(b)(1).

New York began a reexamination of its solicitation laws after the TWA 800 crash in 1996. After the *Went-For-It* case, many other states began to incorporate the thirty-day moratorium into their state ethics rules.

Are Corporate Clients Treated Differently?

The in-person solicitation rules do not apply to corporate counsel in some states. The nonsolicitation rules exist to protect members of the public. There has never been a rule that says a lawyer can't take the corporate counsel of a business out to lunch and solicit the company's legal business. The rules are really meant to protect the unsophisticated user of legal services, not corporations. Some states (for example, Kansas' Ethics Opinion E-352 (1992)) specifically rejected this position. In the redraft of Model Rule 7.3, the ABA specifically excluded from the nonsolicitation rule people who are lawyers.

Can We Pay Someone for Referring a Case or Client to Us?

Most lawyers will tell you that the best way to get a client is through a referral. However, the ABA and most states agree that a lawyer should not be paid any more than the "responsibility assumed or work performed is worth." In other words, if a lawyer didn't work on the case, the lawyer shouldn't get paid.

If this is the law, why is it that we hear so much about lawyers and nonlawyers alike being paid *referral fees*? What is a referral fee and when is it permissible? The ABA apparently disapproves of referral fees but doesn't mind dividing fees. Comment 4, Model Rule 1.5, says:

> A *division of fee* is a single billing to a client covering the fee of two or more lawyers who are not in the same firm. A division of fee facilitates association of more than one lawyer in a matter in which neither alone could serve the client as well, and most often is used when the fee is contingent and the division is between a referring lawyer and a trial specialist.

In other words, the lawyers who do the work or assume responsibility for the case should get paid accordingly. But this is not a "referral fee" in the traditional sense. A referral fee is a fee paid for doing nothing other than bringing the client to the lawyer. In many instances, getting paid for bringing a case to a lawyer is *champerty*—the purchasing of a claim or a client. "Runners and cappers" are typically nonlawyers. They are people who get paid for bringing a case to a lawyer or law firm, or a patient to a doctor or hospital. Paying a runner or capper for bringing a case to a law firm is the illegal practice of *champerty*, or the purchasing of a claim, as we discussed in Chapter 4.

However, in California, referral fees to other lawyers are allowed under the Rules of Professional Conduct so long as the client has consented in writing, the total fee charged to the client is not increased, and the money is a "gift" for making a recommendation that later results in employment. It cannot be a "fee" or a "reward," and it cannot be made with the understanding that more such "gifts" will be made in the future for future referrals.

Why does California have a rule that is diametrically opposite of the law in all the other states? California's logic is that it is better to have a lawyer who is

> **Rule 7.2(b):** A lawyer shall not give anything of value to a person for recommending the lawyer's services. . . .

> A "runner" is "a person whose business it is to solicit patronage or trade." A "capper" is "a lure, decoy, or steerer especially in some illicit or questionable activity."

competent to handle a case take that case than have a lawyer who isn't competent take the case. Rather than have lawyers who don't know how to litigate, for example, take a litigation case, it is better to give that lawyer some "reward" for passing the case on to a lawyer who does know how to do litigation. Logically, lawyers are in business to make money. If you can make a little bit of money for referring a case to someone who is more competent to handle it, rather than make no money at all, this is a good thing and is likely to lead to less malpractice. (This is discussed again in Chapter 7.)

Paralegals, even California paralegals, should not accept referral fees from lawyers or agree to share a fee with a lawyer. This is addressed in Chapter 2 in the discussion of improper division of fees.

How Has Technology Changed the Rules of Advertising?

Perhaps it is not technology that has changed the rules of advertising so much as it is technology that has helped a more sophisticated user of legal services evolve. People are more used to high-pressure sales than they were in the 1970s. Because of television they are more familiar with lawyers and concepts of law. They are more aware of their legal rights. As a result, the state bars are not so protective of "the public" and are more aware of people as "consumers of legal services."

And then, of course, there is the Internet with its panoply of ethical issues.

> Florida became the first state expressly to regulate lawyer advertising on the Internet when its bar published an advisory statement January 1, 1996. It has updated its Computer-Accessed communications and Internet Guidelines. You can find the Guidelines on the bar's website: http://www.floridabar.org.

Here's a question: if my law firm Internet site can be viewed by people in all states across America, does it have to comply with the advertising rules of every state bar? Apparently not. Compliance with the rules of the states where the firm has offices should be sufficient. A reasonable analogy is a newspaper like the *New York Times*. That newspaper is sold in every state, but the lawyer ad isn't held up to the standards of every state's laws so it is unreasonable to believe that the lawyer Web site would. (Your lawyers can't practice law in those others states, anyway. How would a state have jurisdiction over them?)

If we have a page listing our clients, have we stepped out of the boundaries? Most states require a lawyer to have written permission from the client to list the client as a reference. In Opinion 33 (2005), New Jersey prohibited the use of endorsements from happy clients regarding the effectiveness of the representation. Virginia proscribes the use of endorsements by celebrities.

If we link to other Web sites, are we responsible to their content? No, but if there is false or misleading information on those other Web sites and we give the appearance that we are endorsing that false information, we probably violate state regulations on false advertising. Many law firm Web sites have links to their state bar association Web site or other sites of interest to the public.

What about referrals from the Internet? In June 2006, the State Bar of Texas opined that Texas lawyers cannot pay a fee to be listed on a for-profit Internet site that gets information from potential clients about their legal problems and forwards that information to lawyers who pay for listings.

If your firm's Web site has a method for the public to communicate with you, you may have created a confidentiality problem for yourself according to an ethics opinion from California. Visitors to the Web site have a reasonable belief that communication with the firm creates an attorney/client relationship that protects their secrets unless your disclaimer is clear and in plain language so it overcomes that presumption.

Luckily, the ABA has stepped into the fray pretty much right on the heels of each new ethical issue. Model Rule 7.3 addresses "real-time electronic contact" such as Internet chat rooms in its prohibition against in-person solicitation as of 2002.

SUMMARY

In this chapter we have discussed making legal services available to all of the members of the public, a concept we call "access to justice." Access to justice includes advertising that has to be honest and truthful and direct mail that is also proper. Access to justice, oddly enough, includes "good solicitation"; but "bad solicitation" is, well, bad, and we don't do it. Contacting corporate counsel is exempt from the solicitation rules. If it's an in-house lawyer, solicit away. Paralegal advertising is one of those subjects that will vary from state to state. The conservative view is that paralegals can only advertise to lawyers, to get a job, for instance. We know, however, that people calling themselves "paralegals" are advertising to the public directly, and that's just plain UPL in most states. There are a few states that have created a new classification of legal professional that can deliver limited legal assistance directly to members of the public and the rules of advertising are very strict so as not to mislead anyone. Even if you can't advertise in your state, the firm you work for can use your name and paralegal designation in its advertising in most states. We also learned in this chapter that mass disaster victims and families of victims cannot be contacted for a certain amount of time after the disaster. Paying someone for referring a case to your law firm is bad, unless you're a lawyer living in California. And we finish up the chapter with an application of the rules of advertising and solicitation in our Internet age. Rules about advertising vary from state to state so, as with much of ethics, you want to check with your state law before putting pen to paper.

CHAPTER REVIEW AND ASSIGNMENTS

CRITICAL THINKING

1. Let's go back to March at the party. What has she done that might be considered unethical? March had the best of intentions. She was trying to help. How could she have helped the woman with the legal problem and not crossed any ethical boundaries?

2. What do you think about representing the unsavory client. What if someone you loved died of lung cancer? Could you work on a case defending the tobacco company?

3. In order to generate more clients, a law firm mailed letters to the two largest real estate companies in town. In the letters, the firm set forth the prices routinely charged for basic real estate–related services and the length of time such services ordinarily require. Is the firm guilty of "solicitation"?

4. In order to generate more business for his law firm, a law clerk got a list of homes subject to foreclosure from the local courthouse. She then programmed an office computer to telephone these residences and give information about her law firm, which specializes in bankruptcy. Is this practice improper?

5. A week after a city housing project was destroyed by fire, several lawyers from one large law firm contacted the former residents and invited them to a meeting where a lawyer spoke and offered the people free legal assistance in recovering from the insurance company that insured the building. Are the lawyers guilty of improper solicitation?

6. What kind of information pamphlet would be ethical for a law firm in your state to distribute? How must the name, address, and telephone number of the law firm be listed on the pamphlet? Would it be ethical for a paralegal in your state to write and *sell* such a pamphlet?

ASSIGNMENTS

1. Do some research on your state law. Would it violate your state's lawyer advertising rules if a law firm adopted a vanity phone number such as 1-800-GR8-LWYR? Can your firm create a website address that looks like this: www.greatlawyer.com?

2. Does your state prohibit the use of actors portraying lawyers in television advertising? What do you personally think about this? Is the public confused or fooled by this practice.

3. How about a jingle? Can your firm's telephone ad include a clever jingle?

COLLABORATIVE ASSIGNMENTS

1. There is a disconnect between what you see in the telephone directory and what is permitted by the law. Students always want to know how it can be that people blatantly break the law. What do you think? Why is it that the authorities of each state don't stop this improper advertising of not-legal legal services? Use fifteen minutes of class time to review some local telephone directories and contact the companies who are advertising "paralegal services." What do they do there? Whom do they represent? Is what they are doing legal? If you think they are breaking the law, devise a four-step plan of what can be done about it.

2. If you haven't seen *Erin Brockovich*, now would be the time to see it and keep an eye on her contact with potential clients. Individually, take a minute to write down your legal opinion about whether her contact was improper solicitation or something else. After a minute, turn to your neighbor and discuss your opinions together. One of you should be ready to share with the rest of the class what you have decided.

REVIEW QUESTIONS

Multiple Choice

Select the best answer for each of the following questions.

1. The Model Rules say that members of the legal profession should assist laypeople in recognizing their legal problems because
   a. It provides needed income to the news and advertising media.
   b. Legal problems are not always obvious to laypeople.
   c. It is a good idea to keep lawyers' names out in the public.
   d. It doesn't harm anyone.
   e. This is not a true statement. The Model Rules advise against this sort of activity.

2. Lawyers and paralegals should participate in educational and public relations programs for members of the general public because
   a. These programs inform the public about their legal rights.
   b. Programs such as these provide the public with opportunities to meet conscientious lawyers.

   c. These programs may provide an opportunity to meet a lawyer in a situation that is not intimidating.
   d. Informational meetings are part of fulfilling our duty to help the public.
   e. All of the above are true.

3. Advertising for lawyers
   a. is illegal in most states.
   b. is illegal unless permission is obtained from the state bar in advance.
   c. was illegal before *Bates & O'Steen v. Arizona.*
   d. is a right protected by the First Amendment.
   e. both *c* and *d* above.

4. In *Zauderer v. Disciplinary Board of Ohio,* Lawyer Zauderer's advertising depicted a larger-than-life birth control device. The U.S. Supreme Court
   a. held that the advertisement could be disallowed by Ohio because it was distasteful.

b. held that the Ohio State Supreme Court was an inappropriate body to discipline lawyers in that state.

c. upheld the reprimand because the advertising was misleading.

d. affirmed Zauderer's right to advertise in a distasteful manner.

e. both *c* and *d* above.

5. Lawyer solicitation of clients

   a. may be permitted when the motivation is informing the public of their rights.

   b. is not permitted when the motivation is profit.

   c. is typically in person and pressure driven.

   d. may be targeted at a particularly vulnerable person or group.

   e. all of the above.

6. Rules about solicitation

   a. say that neither paralegals nor lawyers may solicit clients.

   b. are strict for lawyers but much more permissive when it comes to paralegals.

   c. have changed since technology has made it easier to solicit clients.

   d. say that a lawyer can be held liable for an employee's solicitation of clients.

   e. both *a* and *d* above.

7. Lawyers or paralegals who solicit clients

   a. may be prohibited from future solicitation by injunction.

   b. will most likely be jailed.

   c. are always motivated by money and should therefore be prohibited from further employment in the practice of law.

   d. can be fined by the court.

   e. None of the above are accurate statements.

8. Direct mail advertising

   a. is used to contact people whose homes are facing foreclosure.

   b. is illegal in most states.

   c. can be viewed as a good way of informing the public of legal rights.

   d. is usually determined to be improper solicitation.

   e. is an old-fashioned way to contact prospective problems but is seldom used modernly.

9. Paralegals

   a. may advertise their services to lawyers and law firms.

   b. may be listed with other legal professionals in the Martindale Hubbell directory.

   c. may not use solicitation in all situations when lawyers may not.

   d. should not offer legal services to clients.

   e. All of the above are true statements.

10. Some states have laws that prohibit lawyers from contacting victims or families of victims for a period of time after a mass disaster. These laws

   a. have been held an unconstitutional invasion of lawyers' First Amendment rights in many states.

   b. are supported by a study done by the Florida Bar that showed the the public's view of the legal professional is often outrage and irritation when lawyers solicit clients days after a mass disaster.

   c. are designed to protect the personal privacy of recent accident victims.

   d. are typically overturned by state supreme courts.

   e. Both *b* and *c* above are true statements.

Fill in the Blank

Complete each of the following sentences with the best word(s) or phrase(s).

1. Technology and paralegals are two important components of the solution to the problem of _____.

2. _____ is a legal way of getting clients, but _____ is not.

3. *Bates & O'Steen v. Arizona* is a U.S. Supreme Court case that held _____.

4. The ABA Model rule that covers the lawyer's responsibilities for nonlawyer assistants is _____.

5. A court order that might be issued to prevent a law firm from using improper solicitation or advertising is called _____.

6. An example of "good solicitation" is _____.

7. A method of attracting clients that is somewhere in between solicitation and advertising is called _____.

8. One place that a paralegal may advertise is _____.

9. Some states have enacted laws that prevent contacting potential clients for a certain amount of time after a _____.

10. Paying someone for referring a client to a law firm is called a _____.

True/False

Decide whether each of the following statements is true or false and write your answer on the line provided.

____ 1. More than 80 percent of Americans will not be able to afford a lawyer when they need one.

____ 2. There is no legal, ethical, or moral obligation for legal professionals to work for free.

____ 3. There is case law supporting the position that when lawyers and their firms provide free legal services, it is a violation of the Thirteenth Amendment. (Of course, to answer this question, you have to know what the Thirteenth Amendment says.)

____ 4. Lawyers are obligated to accept every client who wants to hire them.

____ 5. The U.S. Supreme Court held in the 1980s that lawyers have no constitutional right to advertise because the First Amendment does not apply to the legal profession.

____ 6. The National Federation of Legal Assistants has a rule that prohibits including paralegal names on letterhead stationery.

____ 7. There is case law that says that advertisements may include the attorney's win/loss ratio, for example, won the last three murder cases tried in the Superior Court of *X* state.

____ 8. In some areas of the country, a paralegal advertising that he or she is a "Notary Public" might be misunderstood or misinterpreted to mean that he or she is an attorney.

____ 9. There is good solicitation and bad solicitation.

____ 10. If a lawyer is not aware that his or her paralegal is soliciting clients, the lawyer will be held responsible anyway, under the doctrine of *respondeat superior*.

CASES FOR CONSIDERATION

CASE 1

Gideon v. Wainwright
372 U.S. 335, 83 S. Ct. 792
(1963)

MR. JUSTICE BLACK delivered the opinion of the Court.

Petitioner was charged in a Florida state court with having broken and entered a poolroom with intent to commit a misdemeanor. This offense is a felony under Florida law. Appearing in court without funds and without a lawyer, petitioner asked the court to appoint counsel for him, whereupon the following colloquy took place:

> "The COURT: Mr. Gideon, I am sorry, but I cannot appoint Counsel to represent you in this case. Under the laws of the State of Florida, the only time the Court can appoint Counsel to represent a Defendant is when that person is charged with a capital offense. I am sorry, but I will have to deny your request to appoint Counsel to defend you in this case.
>
> "The DEFENDANT: The United States Supreme Court says I am entitled to be represented by Counsel."

Put to trial before a jury, Gideon conducted his defense about as well as could be expected from a layman. He made an opening statement to the jury, cross-examined the State's witnesses, presented witnesses in his own defense, declined to testify himself, and made a short argument "emphasizing his innocence to the charge contained in the Information filed in this case." The jury returned a verdict of guilty, and petitioner was sentenced to serve five years in the state prison. Later, petitioner filed in the Florida Supreme Court this habeas corpus petition attacking his conviction and sentence on the ground that the trial court's refusal to appoint counsel for him denied him rights "guaranteed by the Constitution and the Bill of Rights by the United States Government." Treating the petition for habeas corpus as properly before it, the State Supreme Court, "upon consideration thereof" but without an opinion, denied all relief.

Since 1942, when *Betts v. Brady,* 316 U.S. 455, was decided by a divided Court, the problem of a defendant's federal constitutional right to counsel in a state court has been a continuing source of controversy and litigation in both state and federal courts. To give this problem another review here, we granted certiorari. 370 U.S. 908. Since Gideon was proceeding in forma pauperis, we appointed counsel to represent him and requested both sides to discuss in their briefs and oral arguments the following: "Should this Court's holding in *Betts v. Brady,* 316 U.S. 455, be reconsidered?"

I.

The facts upon which Betts claimed that he had been unconstitutionally denied the right to have counsel appointed to assist him are strikingly like the facts upon which Gideon here bases his federal constitutional claim. Betts was indicted for robbery in a Maryland state court. On arraignment, he told the trial judge of his lack of funds to hire a lawyer and asked the court to appoint one for him. Betts was advised that it was not the practice in that county to appoint counsel for indigent defendants except in murder and rape cases. He then pleaded not guilty, had witnesses summoned, cross-examined the State's witnesses, examined his own, and chose not to testify himself. He was found guilty by the judge, sitting without a jury, and sentenced to eight years in prison. Like Gideon, Betts sought release by habeas corpus, alleging that he had been denied the right to assistance of counsel in violation of the Fourteenth Amendment. Betts was denied any relief, and on review this Court affirmed. It was held that a refusal to appoint counsel for an indigent defendant charged with a felony did not necessarily violate the Due Process Clause of the Fourteenth Amendment, which for reasons given the Court deemed to be the only applicable federal constitutional provision. The Court said:

> "Asserted denial [of due process] is to be tested by an appraisal of the totality of facts in a given case. That which may, in one setting, constitute a denial of fundamental fairness, shocking to the universal sense of justice, may, in other circumstances, and in the light of other considerations, fall short of such denial." 316 U.S., at 462.

Treating due process as "a concept less rigid and more fluid than those envisaged in other specific and particular provisions of the Bill of Rights," the Court held that refusal to appoint counsel under the particular facts and circumstances in the *Betts* case was not so "offensive to the common and fundamental ideas of fairness" as to amount to a denial of due process. Since the facts and circumstances of the two cases are so nearly indistinguishable, we think the *Betts v. Brady* holding if left standing would require us to reject Gideon's claim that the Constitution guarantees him the assistance of counsel. Upon full reconsideration we conclude that *Betts v. Brady* should be overruled.

II.

The Sixth Amendment provides, "In all criminal prosecutions, the accused shall enjoy the right . . . to have the Assistance of Counsel for his defence." We have construed this to mean that in federal courts counsel must be provided for defendants unable to employ counsel unless the right is competently and intelligently waived. Betts argued that this right is extended to indigent defendants in state courts by the Fourteenth Amendment. In response the Court stated that, while the Sixth Amendment laid down "no rule for the conduct of the States, the question recurs whether the constraint laid by the Amendment upon the national courts expresses a rule so fundamental and essential to a fair trial, and so, to due process of law, that it is made obligatory upon the States by the Fourteenth Amendment." 316 U.S., at 465. In order to decide whether the Sixth Amendment's guarantee of counsel is of this fundamental nature, the Court in *Betts* set out and considered. "[r]elevant data on the subject . . . afforded by constitutional and statutory provisions subsisting in the colonies and the States prior to the inclusion of the Bill of Rights in the national Constitution, and in the constitutional, legislative, and judicial history of the States to the present date." 316 U.S., at 465. On the basis of this historical data the Court concluded that "appointment of counsel is not a fundamental right, essential to a fair trial." 316 U.S., at 471. It was for this reason the *Betts* Court refused to accept the contention that the Sixth Amendment's guarantee of counsel for indigent federal defendants was extended to or, in the words of that Court, "made obligatory upon the States by the Fourteenth Amendment." Plainly, had the Court concluded that appointment of counsel for an indigent criminal defendant was "a fundamental right, essential to a fair trial," it would have held that the Fourteenth Amendment requires appointment of counsel in a state court, just as the Sixth Amendment requires in a federal court.

We think the Court in *Betts* had ample precedent for acknowledging that those guarantees of the Bill of Rights which are fundamental safeguards of liberty immune from federal abridgment are equally protected against state invasion by the Due Process Clause of the Fourteenth Amendment. This same principle was recognized, explained, and applied in *Powell v. Alabama,* 287 U.S. 45 (1932), a case upholding the right of counsel, where the Court held that despite sweeping language to the contrary in *Hurtado v. California,* 110 U.S. 516 (1884), the Fourteenth Amendment "embraced" those " 'fundamental principles of liberty and justice which lie at the base of all our civil and political institutions,' " even though they had been "specifically dealt with in another part of the federal Constitution." 287 U.S., at 67. In many cases other than *Powell* and *Betts,* this Court has looked to the fundamental nature of original Bill of Rights guarantees to decide whether the Fourteenth Amendment makes them obligatory on the States. Explicitly recognized to be of this "fundamental nature" and therefore made immune from state invasion by the Fourteenth, or some part of it, are the First Amendment's freedoms of speech, press, religion, assembly, association, and petition for redress of grievances. For the same reason, though not always in precisely the same terminology, the Court has made obligatory on the States the Fifth Amendment's command that private property shall not be taken for public use without just compensation, the Fourth Amendment's prohibition of unreasonable searches and seizures, and the Eighth's ban on cruel and unusual punishment. On the other hand, this Court in *Palko v. Connecticut,* 302 U.S. 319 (1937), refused to hold that the Fourteenth Amendment made the double jeopardy provision of the Fifth Amendment obligatory on the States. In so refusing, however, the Court, speaking through Mr. Justice Cardozo, was careful to emphasize that "immunities that are valid as against the federal government by force of the specific pledges of particular amendments have been found to be implicit in the concept of ordered liberty, and thus, through the Fourteenth Amendment, become valid as against the states" and that guarantees "in their origin . . . effective against the federal government alone" had by prior cases "been taken over from the earlier articles of the federal bill of rights and brought within the Fourteenth Amendment by a process of absorption." 302 U.S., at 324–325, 326.

We accept *Betts v. Brady's* assumption, based as it was on our prior cases, that a provision of the Bill of Rights which is "fundamental and essential to a fair trial" is made obligatory upon the States by the Fourteenth Amendment. We think the Court in *Betts* was wrong, however, in concluding that the Sixth Amendment's guarantee of counsel is not one of these fundamental rights. Ten years before *Betts v. Brady*, this Court, after full consideration of all the historical data examined in *Betts*, had unequivocally declared that "the right to the aid of counsel is of this fundamental character." *Powell v. Alabama*, 287 U.S. 45, 68 (1932). While the Court at the close of its *Powell* opinion did by its language, as this Court frequently does, limit its holding to the particular facts and circumstances of that case, its conclusions about the fundamental nature of the right to counsel are unmistakable. Several years later, in 1936, the Court reemphasized what it had said about the fundamental nature of the right to counsel in this language:

> "We concluded that certain fundamental rights, safeguarded by the first eight amendments against federal action, were also safeguarded against state action by the due process of law clause of the Fourteenth Amendment, and among them the fundamental right of the accused to the aid of counsel in a criminal prosecution." *Grosjean v. American Press Co.,* 297 U.S. 233, 243–244 (1936).

And again in 1938 this Court said:

> "[The assistance of counsel] is one of the safeguards of the Sixth Amendment deemed necessary to insure fundamental human rights of life and liberty. . . . The Sixth Amendment stands as a constant admonition that if the constitutional safeguards it provides be lost, justice will not 'still be done.'" *Johnson v. Zerbst,* 304 U.S. 458, 462 (1938). To the same effect, see *Avery v. Alabama,* 308 U.S. 444 (1940), and *Smith v. O'Grady,* 312 U.S. 329 (1941).

In light of these and many other prior decisions of this Court, it is not surprising that the *Betts* Court, when faced with the contention that "one charged with crime, who is unable to obtain counsel, must be furnished counsel by the State," conceded that "[e]xpressions in the opinions of this court lend color to the argument . . . ." 316 U.S., at 462–463. The fact is that in deciding as it did—that "appointment of counsel is not a fundamental right, essential to a fair trial"—the Court in *Betts v. Brady* made an abrupt break with its own well-considered precedents. In returning to these old precedents, sounder we believe than the new, we but restore constitutional principles established to achieve a fair system of justice. Not only these precedents but also reason and reflection require us to recognize that in our adversary system of criminal justice, any person haled into court, who is too poor to hire a lawyer, cannot be assured a fair trial unless counsel is provided for him. This seems to us to be an obvious truth. Governments, both state and federal, quite properly spend vast sums of money to establish machinery to try defendants accused of crime. Lawyers to prosecute are everywhere deemed essential to protect the public's interest in an orderly society. Similarly, there are few defendants charged with crime, few indeed, who fail to hire the best lawyers they can get to prepare and present their defenses. That government hires lawyers to prosecute and defendants who have the money hire lawyers to defend are the strongest indications of the widespread belief that lawyers in criminal courts are necessities, not luxuries. The right of one charged with crime to counsel may not be deemed fundamental and essential to fair trials in some countries, but it is in ours. From the very beginning, our state and national constitutions and laws have laid great emphasis on procedural and substantive safeguards designed to assure fair trials before impartial tribunals in which every defendant stands equal before the law. This noble ideal cannot be realized if the poor man charged with crime has to face his accusers without a lawyer to assist him. A defendant's need for a lawyer is nowhere better stated than in the moving words of Mr. Justice Sutherland in *Powell v. Alabama:*

> "The right to be heard would be, in many cases, of little avail if it did not comprehend the right to be heard by counsel. Even the intelligent and educated layman has small and sometimes no skill in the science of law. If charged with crime, he is incapable, generally, of determining for himself whether the indictment is good or bad. He is unfamiliar with the rules of evidence. Left without the aid of counsel he may be put on trial without a proper charge, and convicted upon incompetent evidence, or evidence irrelevant to the issue or otherwise inadmissible. He lacks both the skill and knowledge adequately to prepare his defense, even though he has a perfect one. He requires the guiding hand of counsel at every step in the proceedings against him. Without it, though he be not guilty, he faces the danger of conviction because he does not know how to establish his innocence." 287 U.S., at 68–69.

The Court in *Betts v. Brady* departed from the sound wisdom upon which the Court's holding in *Powell v. Alabama* rested. Florida, supported by two other States, has asked that *Betts v. Brady* be left intact. Twenty-two States, as friends of the Court, argue that *Betts* was "an anachronism when handed down" and that it should now be overruled. We agree.

The judgment is reversed and the cause is remanded to the Supreme Court of Florida for further action not inconsistent with this opinion.

CASE QUESTIONS

1. Take a look at the U.S. Constitution and specifically the Sixth Amendment. What do you see there that contradicts the actions of the Florida State court in refusing to appoint an attorney to Mr. Gideon? Why is the Fourteenth Amendment necessary to Mr. Gideon's argument?
2. Why do you think this case went all the way to the U.S. Supreme Court? What would Gideon keep fighting? What would motivate the State of Florida to keep fighting?
3. The Court discusses *Betts v. Brady,* another U.S. Supreme Court case but from an earlier time (1942). Why would the Court take up the issue of the right to counsel again, as it had earlier decided the issue? What would possess the Court to overrule its earlier decision?

Ohralik v. Ohio State Bar Association
436 U.S. 447, 98 S.Ct. 1912, 56 L.Ed.2d 444
(1978)

Mr. Justice POWELL delivered the opinion of the Court.

In *Bates v. State Bar of Arizona,* 433 U.S. 350, 97 S.Ct. 2691, 53 L.Ed.2d 810 (1977), this Court held that truthful advertising of "routine" legal services is protected by the First and Fourteenth Amendments against blanket prohibition by a State. The Court expressly reserved the question of the permissible scope of regulation of "in-person solicitation of clients—at the hospital room or the accident site, or in any other situation that breeds undue influence—by attorneys or their agents or 'runners.'" Id., at 366, 97 S.Ct., at 2700. Today we answer part of the question so reserved, and hold that the State—or the Bar acting with state authorization—constitutionally may discipline a lawyer for soliciting clients in person, for pecuniary gain, under circumstances likely to pose dangers that the State has a right to prevent.

I.

Appellant, a member of the Ohio Bar, lives in Montville, Ohio. Until recently he practiced law in Montville and Cleveland. On February 13, 1974, while picking up his mail at the Montville Post Office, appellant learned from the postmaster's brother about an automobile accident that had taken place on February 2 in which Carol McClintock, a young woman with whom appellant was casually acquainted, had been injured. Appellant made a telephone call to Ms. McClintock's parents, who informed him that their daughter was in the hospital. Appellant suggested that he might visit Carol in the hospital. Mrs. McClintock assented to the idea, but requested that appellant first stop by at her home. During appellant's visit with the McClintocks, they explained that their daughter had been driving the family automobile on a local road when she was hit by an uninsured motorist. Both Carol and her passenger, Wanda Lou Holbert, were injured and hospitalized. In response to the McClintocks' expression of apprehension that they might be sued by Holbert, appellant explained that Ohio's guest statute would preclude such a suit. When appellant suggested to the McClintocks that they hire a lawyer, Mrs. McClintock retorted that such a decision would be up to Carol, who was 18 years old and would be the beneficiary of a successful claim.

Appellant proceeded to the hospital, where he found Carol lying in traction in her room. After a brief conversation about her condition, appellant told Carol he would represent her and asked her to sign an agreement. Carol said she would have to discuss the matter with her parents. She did not sign the agreement, but asked appellant to have her parents come to see her. Appellant also attempted to see Wanda Lou Holbert, but learned that she had just been released from the hospital. He then departed for another visit with the McClintocks.

On his way appellant detoured to the scene of the accident, where he took a set of photographs. He also picked up a tape recorder, which he concealed under his raincoat before arriving at the McClintocks' residence. Once there, he re-examined their automobile insurance policy, discussed with them the law applicable to passengers, and explained the consequences of the fact that the driver who struck Carol's car was an uninsured motorist. Appellant discovered that the McClintocks' insurance policy would provide benefits of up to $12,500 each for Carol and Wanda Lou under an uninsured-motorist clause. Mrs. McClintock acknowledged that both Carol and Wanda Lou could sue for their injuries, but recounted to appellant that "Wanda swore up and down she would not do it." The McClintocks also told appellant that Carol had phoned to say that appellant could "go ahead" with her representation. Two days later appellant returned to Carol's hospital room to have her sign a contract, which provided that he would receive one-third of her recovery.

In the meantime, appellant obtained Wanda Lou's name and address from the McClintocks after telling them he wanted to ask her some questions about the accident. He then visited Wanda Lou at her home, without having been invited. He again concealed his tape recorder and recorded most of the conversation with Wanda Lou. After a brief, unproductive inquiry about the facts of the accident, appellant told Wanda Lou that he was representing Carol and that he had a "little tip" for Wanda Lou: the McClintocks' insurance policy contained an uninsured-motorist clause which might provide her with a recovery of up to $12,500. The young woman, who was 18 years of age and not a high school graduate at the time, replied to appellant's query about whether she was going to file a claim by stating that she really did not understand what was going on. Appellant offered to represent her, also, for a contingent fee of one-third of any recovery, and Wanda Lou stated "O. K."

In explaining the contingent-fee arrangement, appellant told Wanda Lou that his representation would not "cost [her] anything" because she would receive two-thirds of the recovery if appellant were successful in representing her but would not "have to pay [him] anything" otherwise.

Wanda's mother attempted to repudiate her daughter's oral assent the following day, when appellant called on the telephone to speak to Wanda. Mrs. Holbert informed appellant that she and her daughter did not want to sue anyone or to have appellant represent them, and that if they decided to sue they would consult their own lawyer. Appellant insisted that Wanda had entered into a binding agreement. A month later Wanda confirmed in writing that she wanted neither to sue nor to be represented by appellant. She requested that appellant notify the insurance company that he was not her lawyer, as the company would not release a check to her until he did so. Carol also eventually discharged appellant. Although another lawyer represented her in concluding a settlement with the insurance company, she paid appellant one-third of her recovery in settlement of his lawsuit against her for breach of contract.

Both Carol McClintock and Wanda Lou Holbert filed complaints against appellant with the Grievance Committee of the Geauga County Bar Association. The County Bar Association referred the grievance to appellee, which filed a formal complaint with the Board of Commissioners on Grievances and Discipline of the Supreme Court of Ohio. After a hearing, the Board found that appellant had violated Disciplinary Rules (DR) 2-103(A) and 2-104(A) of the *Ohio Code of Professional Responsibility*. The Board rejected appellant's defense that his conduct was protected under the First and Fourteenth Amendments. The Supreme Court of Ohio adopted the findings of the Board, reiterated that appellant's conduct was not constitutionally protected, and increased the sanction of a public reprimand recommended by the Board to indefinite suspension.

The decision in *Bates* was handed down after the conclusion of proceedings in the Ohio Supreme Court. We noted probable jurisdiction in this case to consider the scope of protection of a form of commercial speech, and an aspect of the State's authority to regulate and discipline members of the bar, not considered in *Bates*. 434 U.S. 814, 98 S.Ct. 49, 54 L.Ed.2d 69 (1977). We now affirm the judgment of the Supreme Court of Ohio.

II.

The solicitation of business by a lawyer through direct, in-person communication with the prospective client has long been viewed as inconsistent with the profession's ideal of the attorney-client relationship and as posing a significant potential for harm to the prospective client. It has been proscribed by the organized Bar for many years. Last Term the Court ruled that the justifications for prohibiting truthful, "restrained" advertising concerning "the availability and terms of routine legal services" are insufficient to override society's interest, safeguarded by the First and Fourteenth Amendments, in assuring the free flow of commercial information. *Bates,* 433 U.S., at 384, 97 S.Ct., at 2709; see *Virginia Pharmacy Board v. Virginia Citizens Consumer Council,* 425 U.S. 748, 96 S.Ct. 1817, 48 L.Ed.2d 346 (1976). The balance struck in *Bates* does not predetermine the outcome in this case. The entitlement of in-person solicitation of clients to the protection of the First Amendment differs from that of the kind of advertising approved in *Bates,* as does the strength of the State's countervailing interest in prohibition.

A

Appellant contends that his solicitation of the two young women as clients is indistinguishable, for purposes of constitutional analysis, from the advertisement in *Bates*. Like that advertisement, his meetings with the prospective clients apprised them of their legal rights and of the availability of a lawyer to pursue their claims. According to appellant, such conduct is "presumptively an exercise of his free speech rights" which cannot be curtailed in the absence of proof that it actually caused a specific harm that the State has a compelling interest in preventing. But in-person solicitation of professional employment by a lawyer does not stand on a par with truthful advertising about the availability and terms of routine legal services, let alone with forms of speech more traditionally within the concern of the First Amendment.

Expression concerning purely commercial transactions has come within the ambit of the Amendment's protection only recently. In rejecting the notion that such speech "is wholly outside the protection of the First Amendment," *Virginia Pharmacy, supra,* at 761, 96 S.Ct., at 1825, we were careful not to hold "that it is wholly undifferentiable from other forms" of speech. 425 U.S., at 771 n. 24, 96 S.Ct., at 1830. We have not discarded the "common-sense" distinction between speech proposing a commercial transaction, which occurs in an area traditionally subject to government regulation, and other varieties of speech. To require a parity of constitutional protection for commercial and noncommercial speech alike could invite dilution, simply by a leveling process, of the force of the Amendment's guarantee with respect to the latter kind of speech. Rather than subject the First Amendment to such a devitalization, we instead have afforded commercial speech a limited measure of protection, commensurate with its subordinate position in the scale of First Amendment values, while allowing modes of regulation that might be impermissible in the realm of noncommercial expression.

Moreover, "it has never been deemed an abridgment of freedom of speech or press to make a course of conduct illegal merely because the conduct was in part initiated, evidenced, or carried out by means of language, either spoken, written, or printed." *Giboney v. Empire Storage & Ice Co.,* 336 U.S. 490, 502, 69 S.Ct. 684, 691, 93 L.Ed. 834 (1949). Numerous examples could be cited of communications that are regulated without offending the First Amendment, such as the exchange of information about securities, *SEC v. Texas Gulf Sulphur Co.,* 401 F.2d 833 (CA2 1968), cert. denied, 394 U.S. 976, 89 S.Ct. 1454, 22 L.Ed.2d 756 (1969), corporate proxy statements, *Mills v. Electric Auto-Lite Co.,* 396 U.S. 375, 90 S.Ct. 616, 24 L.Ed.2d 593 (1970), the exchange of price and production information among competitors, *American Column & Lumber Co. v. United States,* 257 U.S. 377, 42 S.Ct. 114, 66 L.Ed. 284 (1921), and employers' threats of retaliation for the labor activities of employees, *NLRB v. Gissel Packing Co.,* 395 U.S. 575, 618, 89 S.Ct. 1918, 1942, 23 L.Ed.2d 547 (1969). See *Paris Adult Theatre I v. Slaton,* 413 U.S. 49, 61–62, 93 S.Ct. 2628, 2637, 37 L.Ed.2d 446 (1973). Each of these examples illustrates that the State does not lose its power to regulate commercial activity deemed harmful to the public whenever speech is a component of that activity. Neither *Virginia Pharmacy* nor *Bates* purported to cast doubt on the permissibility of these kinds of commercial regulation.

In-person solicitation by a lawyer of remunerative employment is a business transaction in which speech is an essential but subordinate component. While this does not remove the speech from the protection of the First Amendment, as was held in *Bates* and *Virginia Pharmacy,* it lowers the level of appropriate judicial scrutiny.

As applied in this case, the Disciplinary Rules are said to have limited the communication of two kinds of information. First, appellant's solicitation imparted to Carol McClintock and Wanda Lou Holbert certain information about his availability and the terms of his proposed legal services. In this respect, in-person solicitation serves much the same function as the advertisement at issue in *Bates.* But there are significant differences as well. Unlike a public advertisement, which simply provides information and leaves the recipient free to act upon it or not, in-person solicitation may exert pressure and often demands an immediate response, without providing an opportunity for comparison or reflection. The aim and effect of in-person solicitation may be to provide a one-sided presentation and to encourage speedy and perhaps uninformed decisionmaking; there is no opportunity for intervention or counter-education by agencies of the Bar, supervisory authorities, or persons close to the solicited individual. The admonition that "the fitting remedy for evil counsels is good ones" is of little value when the circumstances provide no opportunity for any remedy at all. In-person solicitation is as likely as not to discourage persons needing counsel from engaging in a critical comparison of the "availability, nature, and prices" of legal services, cf. *Bates,* 433 U.S., at 364, 97 S.Ct., at 2699, it actually may disserve the individual and societal interest, identified in *Bates,* in facilitating "informed and reliable decisionmaking." Ibid.

It also is argued that in-person solicitation may provide the solicited individual with information about his or her legal rights and remedies. In this case, appellant gave Wanda Lou a "tip" about the prospect of recovery based on the uninsured-motorist clause in the McClintocks' insurance policy, and he explained that clause and Ohio's guest statute to Carol McClintock's parents. But neither of the Disciplinary Rules here at issue prohibited appellant from communicating information to these young women about their legal rights and the prospects of obtaining a monetary recovery, or from recommending that they obtain counsel. DR 2-104(A) merely prohibited him from using the information as bait with which to obtain an agreement to represent them for a fee. The Rule does not prohibit a lawyer from giving unsolicited legal advice; it proscribes the acceptance of employment resulting from such advice.

Appellant does not contend, and on the facts of this case could not contend, that his approaches to the two young women involved political expression or an exercise of associational freedom, "employ[ing] constitutionally privileged means of expression to secure constitutionally guaranteed civil rights." *NAACP v. Button,* 371 U.S. 415, 442, 83 S.Ct. 328, 343, 9 L.Ed.2d 405 (1963); see *In re Primus,* 436 U.S. 412, 98 S.Ct. 1893, 56 L.Ed.2d 417. Nor can he compare his solicitation to the mutual assistance in asserting legal rights that was at issue in *United Transportation Union v. Michigan Bar,* 401 U.S. 576, 91 S.Ct. 1076, 28 L.Ed.2d 339 (1971); *Mine Workers v. Illinois Bar Assn.,* 389 U.S. 217, 88 S.Ct. 353, 19 L.Ed.2d 426 (1967); and *Railroad Trainmen v. Virginia Bar,* 377 U.S. 1, 84 S.Ct. 1113, 12 L.Ed.2d 89 (1964). A lawyer's procurement of remunerative employment is a subject only marginally affected with First Amendment concerns. It falls within the State's proper sphere of economic and professional regulation. See *Button, supra,* 371 U.S. at 439–443, 83 S.Ct. at 341–343. While entitled to some constitutional protection, appellant's conduct is subject to regulation in furtherance of important state interests.

> "Injured workers or their families often fell prey on the one hand to persuasive claims adjusters eager to gain a quick and cheap settlement for their railroad employers, or on the other to lawyers either not competent to try these lawsuits against the able and experienced railroad counsel or too willing to settle a case for a quick dollar." 84 S.Ct. at 1115.

In recognizing the importance of the State's interest in regulating solicitation of paying clients by lawyers, we are not unmindful of the problem of the related practice, described in *Railroad Trainmen,* of the solicitation of releases of liability by claims agents or adjusters of prospective defendants or their insurers. Such solicitations frequently occur prior to the employment of counsel by the injured person and during circumstances posing many of the dangers of overreaching we address in this case. Where lay agents or adjusters are involved, these practices for the most part fall outside the scope of regulation by the organized Bar; but releases or settlements so obtained are viewed critically by the courts. See, e. g., *Florkiewicz v. Gonzalez,* 38 Ill.App.3d 115, 347 N.E.2d 401 (1976); *Cady v. Mitchell,* 208 Pa.Super. 16, 220 A.2d 373 (1966).

B

The state interests implicated in this case are particularly strong. In addition to its general interest in protecting consumers and regulating commercial transactions, the State bears a special responsibility for maintaining standards among members of the licensed professions. See *Williamson v. Lee Optical Co.*, 348 U.S. 483, 75 S.Ct. 461, 99 L.Ed. 563 (1955); *Semler v. Oregon State Bd. of Dental Examiners*, 294 U.S. 608, 55 S.Ct. 570, 79 L.Ed. 1086 (1935). "The interest of the States in regulating lawyers is especially great since lawyers are essential to the primary governmental function of administering justice, and have historically been 'officers of the courts.' " *Goldfarb v. Virginia State Bar*, 421 U.S. 773, 792, 95 S.Ct. 2004, 2016, 44 L.Ed.2d 572 (1975). While lawyers act in part as "self-employed businessmen," they also act "as trusted agents of their clients, and as assistants to the court in search of a just solution to disputes." *Cohen v. Hurley,* 366 U.S. 117, 124, 81 S.Ct. 954, 958, 6 L.Ed.2d 156 (1961).

As is true with respect to advertising, see *Bates, supra,* 433 U.S., at 371, 97 S.Ct., at 2702, it appears that the ban on solicitation by lawyers originated as a rule of professional etiquette rather than as a strictly ethical rule. See H. Drinker, Legal Ethics 210–211, and n. 3 (1953). "[T]he rules are based in part on deeply ingrained feelings of tradition, honor and service. Lawyers have for centuries emphasized that the promotion of justice, rather than the earning of fees, is the goal of the profession." Comment, A Critical Analysis of Rules Against Solicitation by Lawyers, 25 U.Chi.L.Rev. 674 (1958) (footnote omitted). But the fact that the original motivation behind the ban on solicitation today might be considered an insufficient justification for its perpetuation does not detract from the force of the other interests the ban continues to serve. Cf. *McGowan v. Maryland*, 366 U.S. 420, 431, 433–435, 444, 81 S.Ct. 1101, 1109–1110, 1114, 6 L.Ed.2d 393 (1961). While the Court in *Bates* determined that truthful, restrained advertising of the prices of "routine" legal services would not have an adverse effect on the professionalism of lawyers, this was only because it found "the postulated connection between advertising and the erosion of true professionalism to be *severely* strained." 433 U.S., at 368, 97 S.Ct., at 2701 (emphasis supplied). The Bates Court did not question a State's interest in maintaining high standards among licensed professionals. Indeed, to the extent that the ethical standards of lawyers are linked to the service and protection of clients, they do further the goals of "true professionalism."

The substantive evils of solicitation have been stated over the years in sweeping terms: stirring up litigation, assertion of fraudulent claims, debasing the legal profession, and potential harm to the solicited client in the form of overreaching, overcharging, underrepresentation, and misrepresentation. The American Bar Association, as amicus curiae, defends the rule against solicitation primarily on three broad grounds: It is said that the prohibitions embodied in DR2-103(A) and 2-104(A) serve to reduce the likelihood of overreaching and the exertion of undue influence on lay persons, to protect the privacy of individuals, and to avoid situations where the lawyer's exercise of judgment on behalf of the client will be clouded by his own pecuniary self-interest.

We need not discuss or evaluate each of these interests in detail as appellant has conceded that the State has a legitimate and indeed "compelling" interest in preventing those aspects of solicitation that involve fraud, undue influence, intimidation, overreaching, and other forms of "vexatious conduct." We agree that protection of the public from these aspects of solicitation is a legitimate and important state interest.

III.

Appellant's concession that strong state interests justify regulation to prevent the evils he enumerates would end this case but for his insistence that none of those evils was found to be present in his acts of solicitation. He challenges what he characterizes as the "indiscriminate application" of the Rules to him and thus attacks the validity of DR 2-103(A) and DR 2-104(A) not facially, but as applied to his acts of solicitation. And because no allegations or findings were made of the specific wrongs appellant concedes would justify disciplinary action, appellant terms his solicitation "pure," meaning "soliciting and obtaining agreements from Carol McClintock and Wanda Lou Holbert to represent each of them," without more. Appellant therefore argues that we must decide whether a State may discipline him for solicitation per se without offending the First and Fourteenth Amendments.

Nor could appellant make a successful overbreadth argument in view of the Court's observation in *Bates* that "the justification for the application of overbreadth analysis applies weakly, if at all, in the ordinary commercial context." 433 U.S., at 380, 97 S.Ct. at 2707. Commercial speech is not as likely to be deterred as noncommercial speech, and therefore does not require the added protection afforded by the overbreadth approach.

Even if the commercial speaker could mount an overbreadth attack, "where conduct and not merely speech is involved, . . . the overbreadth of a statute must not only be real, but substantial as well, judged in relation to the statute's plainly legitimate sweep." *Broadrick v. Oklahoma,* 413 U.S. 601, 615, 93 S.Ct. 2908, 2918, 37 L.Ed.2d 830 (1973). The Disciplinary Rules here at issue are addressed to the problem of a particular kind of commercial solicitation and are applied in the main in that context. Indeed, the Bar historically has characterized impermissible solicitation as that undertaken for purposes of the attorney's pecuniary gain and as not including offers of service to indigents without charge. Compare American Bar Association, Committee on Professional Ethics and Grievances, Formal Opinion 148 (1935), with Formal Opinion 169 (1937); see H. Drinker, Legal Ethics 219 (1953). See also *NAACP v. Button, supra,* 371 U.S., at 440, n. 19, 83 S.Ct., at 341. Solicitation has been defined in terms of the presence of the pecuniary motivation of the lawyer, see *People ex rel. Chicago Bar Assn. v. Edelson,* 313 Ill. 601, 610–611, 145 N.E. 246, 249 (1924); Note, Advertising, Solicitation and Legal Ethics, 7 Vand.L.Rev. 677, 687 (1954), and ABA Formal Opinion 148 states that the ban on solicitation "was never aimed at a situation . . . in which a group of lawyers announce that they are willing to devote some of their time and energy to the interests of indigent citizens whose constitutional rights are believed to be infringed." We hold today in *Primus* that a lawyer who engages in solicitation as a form of protected political association generally may not be disciplined without proof of actual wrongdoing that the State constitutionally may proscribe. As these Disciplinary Rules thus can be expected to operate primarily if not exclusively in the context of commercial activity by lawyers, the potential effect on protected, noncommercial speech is speculative. See *Broadrick, supra,* 413 U.S., at 612, 615, 93 S.Ct., at 2915, 2917. See also Note, 83 Harv.L.Rev., supra, at 882–884, 908–910.

We agree that the appropriate focus is on appellant's conduct. And, as appellant urges, we must undertake an independent review of the record to determine whether that conduct was constitutionally protected. *Edwards v. South Carolina,* 372 U.S. 229, 235, 83 S.Ct. 680, 683, 9 L.Ed.2d 697 (1963). But appellant errs in assuming that the constitutional validity of the judgment below depends on proof that his conduct constituted actual overreaching or inflicted some specific injury on Wanda Holbert or Carol McClintock. His assumption flows from the premise that nothing less than actual proved harm to the solicited individual would be a sufficiently important state interest to justify disciplining the attorney who solicits employment in person for pecuniary gain.

Appellant's argument misconceives the nature of the State's interest. The Rules prohibiting solicitation are prophylactic measures whose objective is the prevention of harm before it occurs. The Rules were applied in this case to discipline a lawyer for soliciting employment for pecuniary gain under circumstances likely to result in the adverse consequences the State seeks to avert. In such a situation, which is inherently conducive to overreaching and other forms of misconduct, the State has a strong interest in adopting and enforcing rules of conduct designed to protect the public from harmful solicitation by lawyers whom it has licensed.

The State's perception of the potential for harm in circumstances such as those presented in this case is well founded. The detrimental aspects of face-to-face selling even of ordinary consumer products have been recognized and addressed by the Federal Trade Commission, and it hardly need be said that the potential for overreaching is significantly greater when a lawyer, a professional trained in the art of persuasion, personally solicits an unsophisticated, injured, or distressed lay person. Such an individual may place his trust in a lawyer, regardless of the latter's qualifications or the individual's actual need for legal representation, simply in response to persuasion under circumstances conducive to uninformed acquiescence. Although it is argued that personal solicitation is valuable because it may apprise a victim of misfortune of his legal rights, the very plight of that person not only makes him more vulnerable to influence but also may make advice all the more intrusive. Thus, under these adverse conditions the overtures of an uninvited lawyer may distress the solicited individual simply because of their obtrusiveness and the invasion of the individual's privacy, even when no other harm materalizes. Under such circumstances, it is not unreasonable for the State to presume that in-person solicitation by lawyers more often than not will be injurious to the person solicited.

The efficacy of the State's effort to prevent such harm to prospective clients would be substantially diminished if, having proved a solicitation in circumstances like those of this case, the State were required in addition to prove actual injury. Unlike the advertising in *Bates,* in-person solicitation is not visible or otherwise open to public scrutiny. Often there is no witness other than the lawyer and the lay person whom he has solicited, rendering it difficult or impossible to obtain reliable proof of what actually took place. This would be especially true if the lay person were so distressed at the time of the solicitation that he could not recall specific details at a later date. If appellant's view were sustained, in-person solicitation would be virtually immune to effective oversight and regulation by the State or by the legal profession, in contravention of the State's strong interest in regulating members of the Bar in an effective, objective, and self-enforcing manner. It therefore is not unreasonable, or violative of the Constitution, for a State to respond with what in effect is a prophylactic rule.

On the basis of the undisputed facts of record, we conclude that the Disciplinary Rules constitutionally could be applied to appellant. He approached two young accident victims at a time when they were especially incapable of making informed judgments or of assessing and protecting their own interests. He solicited Carol McClintock in a hospital room where she lay in traction and sought out Wanda Lou Holbert on the day she came home from the hospital, knowing from his prior inquiries that she had just been released. Appellant urged his services upon the young women and used the information he had obtained from the McClintocks, and the fact of his agreement with Carol, to induce Wanda to say "O. K." in response to his solicitation. He employed a concealed tape recorder, seemingly to insure that he would have evidence of Wanda's oral assent to the representation. He emphasized that his fee would come out of the recovery, thereby tempting the young women with what sounded like a cost-free and therefore irresistible offer. He refused to withdraw when Mrs. Holbert requested him to do so only a day after the initial meeting between appellant and Wanda Lou and continued to represent himself to the insurance company as Wanda Holbert's lawyer.

The court below did not hold that these or other facts were proof of actual harm to Wanda Holbert or Carol McClintock but rested on the conclusion that appellant had engaged in the general misconduct proscribed by the Disciplinary Rules. Under our view of the State's interest in averting harm by prohibiting solicitation in circumstances where it is likely to occur, the absence of explicit proof or findings of harm or injury is immaterial. The facts in this case present a striking example of the potential for overreaching that is inherent in a lawyer's in-person solicitation of professional employment. They also demonstrate the need for prophylactic regulation in furtherance of the State's interest in protecting the lay public. We hold that the application of DR2-103(A) and 2-104(A) to appellant does not offend the Constitution.

Accordingly, the judgment of the Supreme Court of Ohio is affirmed.

CASE QUESTIONS

1. What's the difference between direct, in-person communication with a prospective client and "truthful, restrained advertising concerning the availability and terms of routine legal services"? Why aren't both activities protected by the First Amendment?

2. From the Court's recitation of the facts, what gives the impression that Ohralik "exerted pressure" or "demanded an immediate response, without providing an opportunity for comparison or reflection"? Did Carol and/or Wanda have

an opportunity for reflection before agreeing to Ohralik's representation? Can you argue the facts from both positions?

3. Ohralik gave Wanda a "tip" about the uninsured-motorist clause in the McClintocks' insurance policy. Did he violate any ethical rules by doing that?

4. The Court compares Mr. Ohralik's behavior to the conduct of Mrs. Primus in *In re Primus*, (1978) 436 U.S. 412, 98 S.Ct. 1893. Take a look at that case and make your own comparison of the lawyers' conduct.

5. Ohralik argues that the State must prove that Carol or Wanda were harmed but the Court disagrees. What is the Court's position regarding disciplining Ohralik even if his clients were not harmed?

FAIR FEES AND CLIENT TRUST ACCOUNTS

HYPOTHETICAL

The State of Palalico has a large indigent population. When these people need legal representation or legal help with ordinary issues such as wills, they go to one of several free legal clinics. These clinics are state-sponsored. The funds for keeping these clinics open, paying rent, paying the salaries of the lawyers, paralegals, secretaries, and managerial personnel come from one specific state fund called the Trust Account Fund. That fund is filled each year from the interest generated by the money that is in the client trust accounts that Palalico lawyers are obligated to keep. State law requires each lawyer or law firm to have at least one interest-bearing bank account where money given to the firm in advance of a lawsuit or other legal matter is kept. As that money generates interest each month, Palalico banks collect that interest and send it to the Trust Account Fund. Some lawyers are getting ready to file a lawsuit against the Trust Account Fund on the ground that their clients are entitled to the interest generated by their money sitting in interest bearing bank accounts.

How Do We Begin the Relationship with a Client?

When the client finds the law firm (because in theory the law firm is not finding a client), the firm and client must come to an agreement about their relationship. Typically, we call this relationship a "fee agreement" or a "representation agreement" or "the attorney/client agreement." The agreement should include the scope of the representation, what is expected of both the firm and the client, and the fees that will be charged.

Even though we typically describe law as a "profession," it is also a business. A fee agreement with a client is the balancing of the cost of that client's case (including overhead costs) and the amount of money that can be generated by the case. As we learned earlier, cases are typically either taken on an hourly rate basis or a contingency fee basis. The client always wants to know "how long will my case take" so that the client can estimate the cost per month and the amount of time (typically years) that the cost will continue. This is almost impossible in most cases. There are instances in which the cost can be estimated either because the law includes time limits or because the lawyer's experience in the area allows him or her to know how long the case will take within certain parameters. Giving time estimates can be dangerous because it can lead to unreasonable expectations. Counseling the client on the vagaries of the legal system and not making any promises about how long the case will take are wise courses of action.

The relationship the firm has with the client must be one of trust—trust going in both directions. The lawyer trusts the client to tell the truth, cooperate in discovery, and pay the bills. The client trusts the lawyer to tell the truth, communicate with the client about the progress of the case, work diligently, have the skill and knowledge to handle the matter competently, and send fair and honest bills. You can see that the client is expecting much more from the lawyer than the other way around! Lawyer and client need to speak honestly and frankly to each other before signing a contract for representation. Getting into any sort of relationship with the wrong person is a recipe for unhappiness and oftentimes worse.

The paralegal's role in creating the relationship between lawyer and client is an important support role. The lawyer promises to keep the client current on

---

In its Arizona Ethics Opinion No. 98-08, the Committee on the Rules of Professional Conduct ("the Committee") held that an attorney may ethically contract with a paralegal to conduct initial interviews of estate planning clients, but cautioned that (1) the attorney must supervise and control the paralegal's activities to assure that the paralegal does not engage in the unauthorized practice of law; (2) there must be no fee sharing between the attorney and the paralegal; (3) the initial interviews may only be with existing clients of the attorney; and, (4) there could be no solicitation of new business from the clients by the paralegal.

NALA Canon 5:
A legal assistant must disclose his or her status as a legal assistant at the outset of any professional relationship with a client, attorney, a court or administrative agency or personnel thereof, or a member of the general public. A legal assistant must act prudently in determining the extent to which a client may be assisted without the presence of an attorney.

the events of the representation, but this can be done more efficiently by the paralegal . . . and at a lower cost to the client. Presenting it that way will make the client more amenable to communicating with the paralegal. The lawyer promises diligence, skill, and knowledge—all three are part of the paralegal's role. And, of course, fair and honest billing is part of the paralegal's job. The paralegal's hourly rate should be explained, just as the rate of each lawyer on the case. As many members of the public are (still) not familiar with the role of the paralegal, when you present yourself as a professional member of "the team" and explain your supporting role, the client is invariably happy to know you. Give the client your card with your direct line and e-mail address. Encourage the client to communicate directly with you. You and everyone else on the team will be glad you did!

The debate about paralegals conducting initial client interviews wages on. The paralegal's job is to collect facts, and that is usually what happens during that first client interview. But clients always have legal questions, as well, and it may be UPL for the paralegal to respond.

What Are the Different Types of Fee Agreements?

Fee agreements are negotiable; but, like fee agreements with doctors, we don't think of them that way. When the doctor's office says that a particular procedure costs $500, we take that as the same sort of cost as in the grocery store, where we don't negotiate the price of an item. Fee agreements with lawyers are negotiable. Years ago, when some lawyers tried to set certain fees for certain types of procedures, they were disciplined by their state bar association for illegal price-fixing.[1] Even when a firm says that divorces are $500, that number should be negotiable. The more open communication there is between lawyer and client at the beginning of the representation, the less likely there will be disputes later about the bills. The legal fee must not only be fully explained to the client, but it must be objectively fair. ("objectively fair" is explained on page 196)

> Rule 1.5 says that reasonable fees should be charged to the client in appropriate cases in which the clients are able to pay them. This has been interpreted to mean that fees must be "objectively reasonable."

Paralegals (and other nonlawyers) are not permitted to "negotiate" fee agreements with clients on behalf of a lawyer.[2] However, this rule should not prohibit you from *explaining* a routine fee agreement to a client after getting instructions from the lawyer. If the agreement is not "negotiated," that is, if the client agrees to the contract as it is written, the client may properly sign the agreement without discussing it with a lawyer. If you have been given instruction in the various elements of the contract and told to explain it to the client, this should not constitute "the unauthorized practice of law." You are doing nothing more than repeating what the lawyer told you to say. (This falls under the "conduit" theory discussed in Chapter 2.)

All fee agreements must be fully explained to the client. If there is something that the client does not understand, an explanation should be given. Just like any other contract, if the person who signs it does not understand it, the contract may not be enforced against him or her.

Paralegals in most firms are viewed as "billable"; that is, the time they spend on a case or other legal matter is billed to the client. All billable personnel should be aware of the fee agreement that their law firm has with each client so that they can bill in accordance with the agreement. It is not at all unusual for billable personnel to have different hourly rates for different kinds of cases or different clients. Keeping track of this information is typically not your job, but it is good information to know. At the end of the fiscal or calendar year, tally up your billable hours times the hourly rate on each matter to figure out your GPP (gross paralegal product).[3] (Fair paralegal rates are discussed on pages 194-195.)

Contingency Fees

The prosecution of most personal injury cases is taken on a "contingency fee basis." This means that the law firm's recovery of legal fees is contingent upon the outcome of the case. The law firm may advance the costs of the lawsuit as well as dedicate hours to it. At the end of the lawsuit, if the judgment (or settlement) is in favor of the plaintiff, the costs of the suit will be paid out of the judgment and the lawyer and client will each get a percentage of the money. Contingency fee agreements vary. Some provide that the costs that the firm advanced are paid first, and the remaining money is divided between the firm and the client. In other words, the law firm may get one-third and the client two-thirds of the money remaining after the expenses are paid. Expenses can include costs of litigation (such as deposition costs and expert witness fees) as well as costs pertaining to medical treatment of the plaintiff. Other agreements provide that the lawyer takes a percentage of the judgment or settlement, and the advanced fees and costs come out of the portion remaining for the client.

Rule 1.5(c)
A fee may be contingent on the outcome of the matter for which the service is rendered, except in a matter in which a contingent fee is prohibited by paragraph (d) or other law. A contingent fee agreement shall be in a writing signed by the client and shall state the method by which the fee is to be determined, including the percentage or percentages that shall accrue to the lawyer in the event of settlement, trial or appeal; litigation and other expenses to be deducted from the recovery; and whether such expenses are to be deducted before or after the contingent fee is calculated . . . and, if there is a recovery, showing the remittance to the client and the method of its determination. . . .

Lawyers have been known to "overreach" in contingency fee agreements so that they are getting more than their fair share. For example, a contingency fee agreement allocating 20 percent to the client and 80 percent to the lawyer is overreaching.

Let's see how contingency fee arrangements work. Suppose that the client and the defendant have agreed to a $100,000 settlement amount.

Assuming the lawyer has a 40 percent contingency fee, spent $10,000 in costs, and the client's hospital bills total $30,000, the $100,000 could be apportioned like this:

$40,000 to the lawyer.

$60,000 to the client, but out of the client's portion subtract $10,000 in costs (paid back to the lawyer) and hospital bills of $30,000. Now the client has $20,000 remaining for his pain and suffering.

The $100,000 could be apportioned like this:

$10,000 in costs (paid back to the lawyer).

$36,000 (40 percent of $90,000) to the lawyer, leaving $54,000 for the client from which he must pay $30,000 to the hospital. Now the client ultimately gets $26,000.

The $100,000 could be apportioned like this:

$30,000 to the hospital.

$10,000 in costs (paid back to the lawyer), leaving $60,000; the lawyer gets 40 percent of the $60,000 ($24,000), and the client gets the remaining $36,000.

As you can see, the method of calculating the fees can make a big difference in the amount the client will ultimately get from the lawsuit. This is why a careful explanation of the fee agreement is important. The more the client understood and agreed to, the more likely the contract will be affirmed.[4] Even if the fee agreement is completely and carefully explained to the client, a fee that is <u>objectively unfair</u> will be set aside if the client contests it. In determining the fairness of the contract, the court will look at the following factors:

1. the sophistication of the client,
2. how well the contract was explained to the client by the law firm, and
3. how acceptable the fee agreement would seem to the average person.

An infamous California civil rights lawyer, after winning $44,000 in punitive damages for his clients, asked for and received $378,000 in attorney's fees under the federal civil rights statute 42 U.S.C. 1988. But the lawyer did not tell the U.S. District Court that he had a fee agreement with his clients that entitled him to 45 percent of their damage award with the costs of the litigation deducted from the clients' 55 percent. This left the lawyer's clients, who had suffered a substantial loss, about $800 each. The State Bar of California found that the lawyer had taken an unconscionable fee.[5] The double fee was objectively unreasonable and unfair.

All states' Rules provide for contingent fee agreements to be in writing and to fully set forth who gets what and in what order under the agreement.[6] The law in most states also provides that a contingency agreement is not permitted in some domestic matters and all criminal matters.[7] If you're wondering why this is true, look at the public policy rationale. It would not seem right to say to a lawyer, "If you get me off of this charge of possessing drugs for sale, I'll give you 35 percent of the money I'll make when I sell the drugs." And it seems equally wrong to say, "I want 40 percent of all of the spousal support I get for you from your ex-husband." The purpose of spousal support is to support the former spouse, not to pay the lawyer.

Arizona's Rule of Professional Conduct 1.8(e) says that A lawyer shall not provide financial assistance to a client in connection with pending or contemplated litigation, except that:
(1) a lawyer may advance court costs and expenses of litigation, *the repayment of which may be contingent on the outcome of the matter*, and
(2) a lawyer representing an indigent client may pay court costs and expenses of litigation on behalf of the client.

Arizona's Rule of Professional Conduct 1.5
. . . The agreement must clearly notify the client of any expenses for which the client will be liable whether or not the client is the prevailing party. . . .

The use of the expression "No Recovery, No Fee" in contingency fee cases has been questioned by some states as being misleading because the client is obligated to pay litigation expenses and court costs regardless of whether any recovery is obtained. For example, the Virginia Bar's ethics committee determined that this language and other phrases like "we guarantee to win, or you don't pay," "we are paid only if you collect," and "no charge unless we win" are all misleading and deceptive.[8]

Go back to our discussion of champerty in Chapter 4 on pages 111–112. Champerty is the purchasing of a cause of action. If a law firms says, "We'll take your case and you never have to pay anything, win or lose," doesn't that sound like the purchase of a claim? This is why some states have said that the client must remain liable for court costs and expenses of the litigation unless the client is otherwise indigent.

Rule 1.5
. . . Upon conclusion of a contingent fee matter, the lawyer shall provide the client with a written statement stating the outcome of the matter.

Colorado's version of 1.8(e):
While representing a client in connection with contemplated or pending litigation, a lawyer shall not advance or guarantee financial assistance to the lawyer's client, except that a lawyer may advance or guarantee the expenses of litigation, including court costs, expenses of investigation, expenses of medical examination, and costs of obtaining and presenting evidence, *provided the client remains ultimately liable for such expenses*. A lawyer may forgo reimbursement of some or all of the expenses of litigation if it is or becomes apparent that the client is unable to pay such expenses without suffering substantial financial hardship.

And don't forget that at the conclusion of a contingency fee case, the client is entitled to an *accounting*.

An *accounting* is a document that shows the amount that was awarded (or settled upon) and all of the amounts that were charged against the award (such as doctors bills or expert witness fees), how much will go to the law firm and how much will go to the client.

Hourly Billing

Another method of billing, and probably the most widely used in personal injury defense and every other kind of legal representation, is hourly billing. When each billable person begins working at a law firm, he or she will be assigned a certain billing rate. You should ask what your billing rate will be just so that you will have an idea of what an hour of your time is worth (and so that you know, if you have an urge to cheat on your time sheets, how much you are cheating the client).

NFPA *EC* 1.2(c):
A paralegal shall ensure that all timekeeping and billing records prepared by the paralegal are thorough, accurate, honest, and complete.

NFPA *EC* 1.2(d):
A paralegal shall not knowingly engage in fraudulent billing practices. Such practices may include but are not limited to: inflation of hours billed to a client or employer; misrepresentation of the nature of tasks performed; and/or submission of fraudulent expense and disbursement documentation.

If your firm uses hourly billing, all billable employees (lawyers, law clerks, and paralegals, usually) will be asked to keep an account of the time spent on each task and for what client. For purposes of illustration, the smallest billable amount is one-tenth of an hour, or six minutes. The time sheet on the next page illustrates the different "matters" or client cases this paralegal worked on during this day, what work she did, and how much time she spent. Time sheets were traditionally kept by hand on a form. Now they are kept on your computer by a program designed for that purpose. Whether written on a pad of paper or input into the computer, the information is only as good as it is accurate. For that reason, we say that time records should be kept contemporaneously, thoroughly, and accurately. (See the "Collaborative Assignments" on timekeeping at the end of this chapter.)

These time records are compiled by an accounting staff member, a bookkeeper, or an outside service and sent to the client in a form that looks like the illustration on page 186.

At the end of the billing cycle, typically thirty days or one month, all of the time records from each billable person are compiled and charged to the client. Before the bill is sent to the client, however, some person who is responsible for that client, typically called the *billing partner,* goes though the bill item by item to ensure that the client is not being over- or undercharged for the work. The bills should be checked for human as well as computer error. If you wrote down 1.1 hours but that number

```
                    DAILY TIME SHEET
━━━━━━━━━━━━━━━━━━━━━━━━━━━━━━━━━━━━━━━━━━━━━━━━━━━━━━━━━━━

Date   06/24/08

Employee  Renee A. Marcus—Paralegal

TIME    MATTER      DESCRIPTION
─────────────────────────────────────────────────────────
 .3      Jones       telephone call to Secretary of State
                     for corporate status check

 .5      Dolan       draft letter to Dept. of Motor
                     Vehicles regarding Mr. Dolan's
                     driving record

 .7      Dolan       research case law on
                     driving/negligence

1.5      Smith       research client's employment record

2.0      Smith       track down previous students to
                     provide information/references of
                     Mr. Smith's teaching method
─────────────────────────────────────────────────────────
5.0      TOTAL
```

was accidentally changed to 11 hours, the difference in the bill will be enormous! Just as all work product should be checked before it is sent out, the client's invoice should be checked for errors.

Other Billing Methods

Another approach to billing is *value billing*. This describes an agreement with the client whereby the client will be charged a flat rate for certain tasks. For example, if your fee agreement says that the client will be billed $150 for each complaint that is drafted on his behalf, this is value billing. If the client knows that interrogatories are $200 and court appearances are $500, he has a better idea of how much each matter will cost because the value billing cost is not dependent upon the time it takes each individual to accomplish a task.

In some places, the term *value billing* refers to the contract under which the law firm gets paid a small amount for the work done (as in a reduced hourly rate) and a bonus for a good result. In other words, the client is willing to pay more when he wins. Some people also refer to this kind of arrangement as *bonus billing*. When someone throws one of these terms at you, you might want to be clear exactly what kind of billing arrangement the person is talking about.

ABA Model Code DR 2-106 (A): A lawyer shall not enter into an agreement for, charge, or collect an illegal or clearly excessive fee.

* The Model Codes of Professional Responsibility are presented here as a historical reference and are not currently used.

Law Office of John B. Davis

1234 Oak Avenue
Anytown, OH
404/555-1212

July 1, 2008
Mr. Charles J. Dolan
50 Tower Road
Anytown, OH

Re: Dolan v. State of Ohio—services through June 30, 2005

DATE	DESCRIPTION	INIT	TIME	RATE	TOTAL
06/24	draft letter to DMV	RAM	.5	$75	$37.50
06/24	research case law	RAM	.7	$75	$52.50
06/24	review files and arrest record	RAM	1.5	$75	$112.50
06/25	telephone call	JBD	.1	$150	$15.00
06/25	review of deposition summaries	JBD	3.5	$150	$525.00
06/25	draft letter to DMV	JBD	.6	$150	$90.00
06/30	depostion summary	JBD	1.5	$150	$225.00

TOTAL NOW DUE   **$1057.50**

If you have any questions or concerns about this bill, please call immediately and ask to speak with Janice in Accounting.

A cousin to value billing is *fixed fee billing*. This is an arrangement with the client whereby the client is charged one flat rate for the representation regardless of how long it takes or how much work is involved. In representations that are mass-produced, such as relief from stay in bankruptcy or consumer collection matters, fixed fee billing is very popular. It allows the client to budget legal fees from the beginning of the representation; it encourages efficiency; it encourages delegation of work to employees who are more suited to the tasks; and it provides training for new staff members in an atmosphere where "hours billed" is not the primary focus. In essence, the client is paying for a product.

A variation of the typical hourly billing system is *blended rate billing*. In this arrangement, rather than paying $250 an hour for the partner, $180 an hour for the associate, and $75 an hour for the paralegal, the client agrees to pay one hourly rate, a blended rate of, for example, $150 an hour, for all billing employees. This encourages the firm to utilize the lower-rate billers and to use the expensive partners sparingly. On the other hand, if you think about it, some tasks may take considerably longer if performed by a lower-rate biller. If this is true, the client does not save any money utilizing the blended rate system.

What Should Be in the Fee Agreement?

A well-written fee agreement will

1. identify the client(s);
2. identify the lawyer primarily responsible for handling the file;
3. describe the nature and the scope of the representation;
4. set out the objectives of the representation;
5. tell the client what you expect from the client, such as timely responses to your requests and absolute truthfulness;
6. set out the basis for calculating the fee;
7. make clear the responsibility for paying costs and give some examples of standard costs;
8. describe the method, manner, and frequency of billing, including how any retainer money held in trust will be used;
9. make a disclaimer about results;
10. set forth the process for dealing with unpaid bills (are you going to arbitrate disputes?);
11. tell the client what happens if the firm needs to terminate the representation;
12. make a disclosure about professional liability insurance (we discuss this in detail in Chapter 7); and
13. make a clear statement about what will happen to the files at the conclusion of the case (remember, you don't want to store those files!) and if the representation is terminated.

What Should Not Be in the Fee Agreement?

If you take a look at Model Rule 1.5, you'll see some things there that lawyers are not allowed to do. For example, it is improper to ask the client for a gift (c), to sign away the literary rights to the client's case (d), or to limit the lawyer's liability for professional negligence or malpractice (1.8(h)). You don't want to have any of those things in the fee agreement. You don't want to have a guarantee that the client will win or any sort of "odds" that the client will win.

What Is a Retainer?

Law firms will often require a *retainer* from the client. There are several types of retainers; and, just like other billing terms, the terms are used interchangeably and are easily confused. Whenever you're talking about a retainer, be sure which one you're talking about.

The *classic retainer* ensures the firm's availability over time—like a reservation fee. This kind of retainer is considered earned upon receipt, whether or not services are actually provided.[9] What the client is paying for is the reservation, not necessarily any work. The type of retainer that is earned upon receipt regardless of services actually rendered is sometimes called a *nonrefundable retainer*. Some courts have declared nonrefundable retainers *per se* unreasonable because they impair the client's right to discharge the lawyer for any reason at any time, a right that is vital to the lawyer/client relationship.[10] A nonrefundable retainer has also been condemned as an "unearned fee." Think about this situation: A woman is fired from her job. She goes to a lawyer who says he will try to get her job back or, if not, get her damages, and he asks for a nonrefundable retainer. Upon receiving the money, the lawyer calls the former employer and asks if the employer will take the woman back. The employer says no. Has the lawyer earned the fee? After all, the promise was to "try" to get the client's job back. This is why courts have said that nonrefundable retainers are unreasonable.

An *advance payment retainer* is a present payment compensating the lawyer for services to be performed in the future; it is considered earned upon receipt and may be a "flat fee" (in other words, it may be paid without expectation that the lawyer will ask for more compensation once the retainer is exhausted).

The purpose of a *security retainer* is to secure payment for future services; it remains the property of the client until applied to charges for services actually rendered, and any unused portion is refundable to the client.

When most people talk about a "retainer," what they're talking about is the security retainer. This is how a retainer typically works: Client comes into your law office with a problem. Client explains the problem to the lawyer and an agreement is made to take Client's case on an hourly basis. The lawyer estimates how many hours per month the case will take and comes up with an outside per month amount of costs and expenses. The lawyer should take into account how many months it might take to be released from the representation if Client stops paying the bills and refuses to find a new lawyer. If a motion to be relieved as counsel typically takes two months from start to hearing, the lawyer will estimate two months' worth of costs and expenses for Client and make that the retainer amount. The lawyer asks Client for that amount up front. Say it is $50,000. That amount goes into a client trust account and Client's bills are charged against that amount. When the $50,000 is depleted, the lawyer will ask Client to replenish it. What the lawyer is doing is "banking" enough money to ensure that the bills will be paid.

Of course, the amount will change depending upon the type of case and the credit-worthiness of the client. If the client is a nationally known and well-respected corporation like, say, Microsoft, the retainer may be very small or not required at all because one assumes that such a corporation pays its bills in a timely fashion.

How Does a Client Trust Account Work?

A *client trust account* is a separate bank account set up to hold any money the firm receives on behalf of a client or third party. Funds that are placed in a trust account are settlement proceeds or damages payments that have not yet been disbursed to the client, advances that the client has given the firm from which to pay future costs of litigation, or advance payments for fees the firm has not yet earned (retainers). Lawyers tend to use the terms "attorney trust account" or "lawyer trust account" but if we call it a "client trust account" we're more likely to remember that the money in there belongs to the client.

Client trust accounts must be interest-bearing accounts. That means it has to be an account that accrues interest. Where does that interest go? You would think that it rightfully belongs to the clients whose money is in the account accruing interest, but for the most part, you would be wrong. In the typical client trust account, the interest is accrued and put into a fund called IOLTA or Interest On Lawyer Trust Account. The bank collects all of the interest from all of its IOLTAs and sends the money to the state bar of each state (or an organization designated by the state bar for that purpose). The State Bar uses the IOLTA money to fund the free legal service providers throughout the state. The interest on these client trust accounts, then, is what makes free legal services possible—to the tune of $200 million per year.[11]

Some states have exceptions to the requirement that client funds be placed in IOLTAs. An example of an exception may be if one particular client is having you hold a large amount of money for a long period of time. In that case, your state may allow you to set up a separate interest-bearing account for that one client and the client would be entitled to the interest. If you are ever put in charge of trust accounts for your firm, be sure to check with your state bar association to ensure you know all of the rules.

The law firm is responsible for your client's money from the moment you receive it. The firm must take sensible precautions to avoid misplacing or misfiling checks or cash, and it is good practice to not hold the money any longer than necessary before depositing it into the trust account.

If the client has given the firm money as a retainer, the money goes into the client trust account until it is earned. At the end of each month, then, the client is sent a bill or invoice for that month's work. Hearing no objection from the client, the money becomes earned by the law firm and must be transferred out of the client trust account immediately. No law firm money should be kept in the client trust account. That's called "commingling," and it is bad. You may have to keep a small amount of money in the client trust account to cover bank fees, but it is better if you have your General Operating Account (GOA) at the same bank and you ask the bank to take any fees out of the GOA. Your General Operating Account is the account out of which firm expenses are paid, and payroll, and so forth. If you have

---

Exactly this type of behavior was addressed in a concurring opinion in *In re Choroszej*. Attorney Choroszej deposited insurance proceeds into his client trust account and, without paying the medical provider, began writing checks out of the account, erroneously believing that the remaining funds were only his legal fees. The District of Columbia Court of Appeals suspended Choroszej for six months based, in part, on a single instance of negligent misappropriation. The misappropriation occurred when the account balance dropped below the amount owed to the medical provider. 624 A.2d 434 (D.C. 1992)

earned money from a client, it must be taken out of the client trust account and deposited into the General Operating Account before it is spent on firm expenditures. In other words, just because the money belongs to the firm, don't write a check to pay for a firm expenditure out of the client trust account. Lawyers have been known to try to hide personal money in client trust accounts so that creditors won't find it. This is a mistake, too. Law firm money and lawyer money must be segregated from client money. To not do so is improper commingling.

It is important to keep accurate accountings of the money in the client trust accounts. If, for example, a check is bounced from the client trust account, the bank will notify the state bar or other disciplinary authority in your state. The balance in the client trust account must never be lower than $0, therefore. These offenses are the ones that most often trip up lawyers because they are obvious, reported by the bank, and almost impossible to explain away. If some accounting error causes a mistake in the client trust account, it is best for the firm to notify the state bar first, with assurances that the problem has been fixed, before the bank reports the problem to the state bar. You always want to have accurate and up-to-date accounting records for the client trust account. Each state has a requirement regarding the number of years you must keep these records. Be sure to check with your state bar association.

There was some argument about the interest on lawyer trust accounts going to fund free legal service providers. Take a look at the case at the end of this chapter for the history and resolution of this matter.

If you keep property in trust for a client or in any other fiduciary capacity, like potential exhibits in litigation, securities, or personal property, as surety for payment of your fees, you must also provide for its safekeeping. A safe deposit box is the best means of doing this. You want to label each item so that you can be sure that it is identified with the appropriate client. You want to have a list of everything in that safe deposit box. It's also a good idea to have a copy of the items in the client file with a note that they are in the safe deposit box.

How Does a Law Firm Get Paid?

When everything goes well, the law firm sends a bill to the client and the client pays it. When things are not going well, the client refuses to pay the bill but the law firm has a continuing obligation to represent the client. This can devolve into litigation between lawyer and client over money and the lawyer's continuing obligation to represent the client. As we learned in Chapter 3, the lawyer's obligations under the duty of confidentiality change slightly when fighting with the client over fees or malpractice claims. Certainly the duty of loyalty can be irreparably damaged when the client and the lawyer fight about fees.

The ABA Model Code took a firm position against "fee fights." Based on a 1943 ABA Opinion (No. 250),[12] the ABA's Model Code EC 2-23 says that a lawyer "should be zealous in his efforts to avoid controversies over fees with clients." Further, "[h]e should not sue a client for a fee unless necessary to prevent fraud or gross imposition by the client."

In the 1980s, however, the ABA's standards on fee fights slackened in the wake of a shift in the profession toward a new focus on profit. In reality, very few lawyers ignored the unpaid client bill for the sake of Canon 2. In fact, many law firms employ paralegals to handle the collection of delinquent bills for the firm. The Model Rules' Comment on this subject reads only:

> [i]f a procedure has been established for resolution of fee disputes, such as an arbitration or mediation procedure established by the bar, the lawyer should conscientiously consider submitting to it.[13]

California and other states mandate fee arbitration. California's Business & Professions Code, Sections 6200 to 6206 require that the lawyer give notice to the client of the client's right to elect to arbitrate any fee dispute. (Arbitration is not mandatory for the client, only for the lawyer.) If the parties agree after the dispute has arisen but before the arbitration, the arbitration is binding. The advantage of fee arbitration is that it can be done quickly (without getting tied up in the court system), inexpensively, and informally by local bar associations who provide volunteer lawyers to act as arbitrators. (And don't forget that arbitration is an option for all disputes between lawyer and client but if the lawyer wants the client to agree to arbitration, for example, a malpractice claim, this provision must be in the fee agreement signed by the client.)

Some courts held that the ABA Model Code Ethical Consideration on the issue of not suing a client for fees was never intended to be a rule of law so much as an aspiration.[14] These courts have held that the lawyer has a right to collect against the former client in *quantum meruit* for the reasonable value of his services. The factors set forth in Disciplinary Rule 2-106 (which prohibited the collection of "an illegal or clearly excessive fee" by a lawyer) are the legal elements of the law of *quantum meruit*. In other words, even if the fee demanded by the lawyer would have been excessive, the lawyer is still entitled to a fee that covers the value of the work performed.

> *Quantum meruit* is Latin for the "value of the thing" or, in this case, "the value of the work."

To recover the fee, of course, the lawyer must show that the client retained him, that the two have an enforceable contract, and that the services performed were with the client's informed consent.[15]

To avoid fee fights, a thorough explanation of the fees before beginning the representation and an honest discussion about the anticipated costs are called for. The person in charge of collecting fees from clients should also be aware that the Fair Debt Collection Practices Act (15 U.S.C. Section 1692 *et. seq.*) applies to activities collecting fees from clients. The Fair Debt Collection Practices Act mandates that debt collectors treat people fairly and prohibits certain methods of debt collection. It is this law that prevents debt collectors from calling you in the middle of the night or threatening you with bodily harm.

Last, whoever in the firm is in charge of collecting fees from clients should review the rules on conflicts of interest. Once the law firm sues the client for fees, the law firm is in an adverse position to the client and cannot continue representation. (See "Conflict of Interest," Chapter 4.)

How Do We Get Fees from the Other Side in Litigation?

In many other countries, the practice is that the losing party pays the attorneys fees of the winning party. In the United States, the prevailing party may recover fees from the other party in only limited circumstances: where attorneys' fees are

Is "reasonable attorneys' fees" referring to a "reasonable attorney" or a "reasonable fee"?

provided for in a statute and where they are provided for in the contract. This is aptly called "the American Rule" of attorneys' fees.[16] For example, at the conclusion of the lawsuit, the *prevailing* party can ask the court to award attorneys' fees under the Federal Rehabilitation Act[17] because the statute specifically provides that in cases of discrimination against handicapped individuals, the prevailing party is entitled to "reasonable attorneys' fees."[18] The prevailing party files a memorandum or declaration setting forth all of the time spent, hourly billing rates, tasks, and costs of the litigation. In order to justify the rates of the different billers, resumes, or declarations of qualifications are a part of this paperwork. Ordinarily, a separate motion will be heard on the issue of the reasonableness of the fees requested.

Are Paralegal Fees Awardable?

Statutes and contracts ordinarily provide for "attorneys' fees." Taken literally, that would mean that other legal professionals such as paralegals and law clerks would not be included—that the cost of having such assistants must be "overhead" and taken into account in determining the lawyers' hourly rates. The interpretation of the term "attorneys' fees" has been as far as the U.S. Supreme Court, as you know.

Even though it might seem that *Missouri v. Jenkins* squarely answered the question of whether paralegal time is included in the expression "attorneys fees" in 1989, many courts spent many pages debating the issue for many years to come. Four years after *Missouri v. Jenkins*, in *Baldwin v. Burton*,[19] the Utah Supreme Court addressed this issue for the first time. In *Baldwin*, the prevailing party's lawyer had hired an independent paralegal. Looking to an Arizona case[20] in which the paralegal was an employee of the firm, the Utah court wrote:

> Applying the reasoning of *Brockbank* to the facts of this case, it is clear that had Baldwin's attorney not retained [paralegal] Richins to perform services traditionally performed by legal assistants, the attorney would have had to perform these services himself at a presumably higher billing rate.[21]

See also NFPA's publication *Fees for Paralegal Services: Are They Recoverable*—An Update (rev. 1995), [http://www.paralegals.org/Development/fees.html] and *Recoverability of Legal Assistant Time in Attorney Fee Applications*, 9 J. PARA. ED. & PRAC. 1, April 1993.

In spite of what appears to be a clear message from the Supreme Court, the issue is still far from settled among the state courts. For example, the Idaho Supreme Court held that the rule from *Missouri v. Jenkins* was inapplicable without any explanation and denied paralegal fees to the applicant in 1997.[22] However, the U.S. District Court for New York's Southern District awarded paralegal fees of $60 per hour, finding "the hourly rates sought by defendant are reasonable in light of the skill and experience brought to bear by . . . legal assistants."[23] And, the U.S. District Court for Louisiana's Eastern District awarded paralegal fees at $55 per hour.[24] All of those cases took place between 1997 and 1999. Hourly rates for paralegals have varied from $25 per hour[25] to $250 per hour for a class action suit.[26]

Rather than relying on case law, many states have amended their codes or adopted rules on the issue of awarding paralegal fees along with attorneys' fees. For example, Alaska amended its rules to specifically allow for the award of paralegal fees in 1995.[27] Michigan adopted Court Rule 2.626 (January 2001) expressly allowing paralegal time in fee awards.

Ultimately, the court is looking for the same thing that the client is looking for: a reasonable fee. Courts will take different routes to get there. There are cases in which the court has reduced the amount of the lawyer' fees requested because the lawyer was performing tasks more properly performed by a paralegal.[28] And, you should know that judges will not necessarily award the hourly rate that is requested for lawyers or paralegals. If the judge finds that an hourly rate charged by the firm is too high, it is ordinarily within the judge's discretion to lower it.

The good news is that, for the most part, the courts agree that it is the task, not the title of the billing employee, that is determinative of recoverability. Here's the rule: Clerical tasks are not billable and will not be recoverable. Tasks that are non-clerical are billable and are usually recoverable at an hourly rate that is appropriate for the task. For a look at how a court might analyze the billable from the clerical, review *Blair v. Ing* at the end of this chapter.

What do we want to include in our application for attorneys' fees? *Multi-Moto v. ITT Commercial Finance*[29] provides some guidance:

A party may separately assess and include in the award of attorneys' fees compensation for a legal assistant's work, if that assistant performs work traditionally done by an attorney. In order to recover such amounts, the evidence must establish: (1) the qualifications of the legal assistant to perform substantive legal work; (2) that the legal assistant performed substantive legal work under the direction and supervision of an attorney; (3) the nature of the legal work performed; (4) the legal assistant's hourly rate; and (5) the number of hours expended by the legal assistant.

Whenever applying for fees, these factors are essential for any declaration or motion filed with the court.

What Is an Inappropriate Fee?

The overriding consideration in client billing is that the fee must be *objectively fair*. Profit margin on employees is not a proper inquiry in determining fairness,[30] but the sophistication and relative bargaining power of the lawyer and

Contrast *Boston & Maine Corp. v. Sheehand, Phinney*, 778 F.2d 890 (1st Cir. 1985), with *Brobeck, Phleger & Harrison v. Telex Corp.*, 602 F.2d 866 (9th Cir. 1979).

client are proper considerations. The requirement that the fee be reasonable will override the terms of the contract in appropriate cases.

Obviously, a client will not have to pay an objectively unfair fee. Moreover, there is some case law holding that charging an excessive fee is grounds for disciplinary action.[31] The controlling factor in determining the appropriate and fair legal fee will not always be limited to the time expended by the lawyer and the lawyer's staff.[32] Sometimes the result of the law firm's work is the most important factor. In the case of contingency fee cases, the controlling factor is the settlement amount or the amount awarded.

The hourly rate assigned by the law firm to lawyers and paralegals is ordinarily in line with what the local market will bear. Where the average paralegal in one community might be $70, it may be $120 in another community. The amount by itself does not make the rate appropriate or inappropriate. A court will look at the education and training of the paralegal, the number of years of work experience, the task, and the amount of time spent. In a recent case[33] in which a paralegal took several hours to complete a routine form and was billed at almost the same rate as a junior associate, the court disallowed the fees saying:

> . . . billing rates should appropriately reflect several factors, including education, competence, experience, accountability and risk. Most paralegals lack the training derived from the rigors of law school. Without a license to practice law, they have no duty to account professionally as an officer of the court. Nor do they share the same risks of liability for malpractice. For these reasons, the court will carefully review any proposal to compensate a firm for paralegal services at rates that approach those allowed for attorneys.
>
> [The law firm] proposes that the paralegal be billed at $130 per hour, a rate that almost matches that of the most junior attorney on this file. When a paralegal is billed at a rate significantly less than that of an attorney, his or her service may represent a net savings despite a somewhat lesser degree of efficiency. But if this court is to allow a paralegal to be billed near the firm's rate for attorneys, then the court will expect a correspondingly high level of productivity. In the present instance, however, the particular paralegal did not efficiently complete the assigned task.

And, as already mentioned, there are cases reducing the fee charged by lawyers when the court finds that the tasks should have been performed by paralegals.[34]

Can I Accept a Referral Fee?

In Chapter 5 we discussed the idea that the ABA and most states agree that a lawyer should not associate with another lawyer (outside of the law firm) at the expense of the client, without first making a full disclosure to the client and obtaining the client's consent. Even then, the outside lawyer may not be paid any more than the responsibility assumed or work performed is worth. This does not include hiring employees or independent contractors who work under the supervision of the lawyer.

Rule 1.5(e):
A division of a fee between lawyers who are not in the same firm may be made only if: (1) the division is in proportion to the services performed by each lawyer or each lawyer assumes joint responsibility for the representation; (2) the client agrees to the arrangement, including the share each lawyer will receive, and the agreement is confirmed in writing; and (3) the total fee is reasonable.

The ABA Code and Rules disapprove of referral fees but are fine with a division of fees in appropriate circumstances. Comment 4, Model Rule 1.5, says:

> A division of fee is a single billing to a client covering the fee of two or more lawyers who are not in the same firm. A division of fee facilitates association of more than one lawyer in a matter in which neither alone could serve the client as well, and most often is used when the fee is contingent and the division is between a referring lawyer and a trial specialist.

But Model Rule 7.2(b) says that a lawyer *shall not* give anything of value to a person for recommending the lawyer's services.

In other words, the lawyers who do the work or assume responsibility for the case should get paid accordingly. But this is not a "referral fee" in the traditional sense. A referral fee is a fee paid for doing nothing other than bringing the client to the lawyer. If a lawyer pays someone else for bringing the lawyer a case, it is *champerty*—the purchasing of a claim or a client. If this is the law, why is it that we hear so much about lawyers and nonlawyers alike being paid referral fees? What is a referral fee and when is it permissible?

The short answer is that referral fees are not legal unless you live in California and you are a lawyer. In California, referral fees to other lawyers are allowed under the Rules of Professional Conduct only so long as the client has consented in writing, the total fee charged to the client is not increased, and the money is a "gift" for making a recommendation that later results in employment. It cannot be a fee or a reward and it cannot be made with the understanding that more such "gifts" will be made in the future for future referrals. The public policy reason behind the California rule is this: we want to encourage lawyers to take only those cases they are competent to handle. However, we understand the lawyer's need to make a living. If, by getting a referral fee, one lawyer will refer a case he or she cannot handle to some other lawyer who is competent to handle the case, this is a good thing for everyone. The first lawyer gets "some" money, the second lawyer will make money working for the client, and the client gets a lawyer who is competent to handle the case.

No matter what strong public policy reason there could be to support paralegals receiving referral fees, we should not accept referral fees from lawyers or agree to share a fee with a lawyer. This is discussed in Chapter 2 under the topic, "Improper Division of Fees."

What Should the Fee Agreement Say about Client Files and Fees?

As we discussed in Chapter 3 on confidentiality, client files belong to the client. They cannot be "held hostage" to insure the payment of legal fees. This is true even if the fee agreement between the law firm and the client specifically says that the law firm is entitled to a retaining lien on the files.

Several cases have discussed the *common law retaining lien* or the idea that the attorney has an equitable right to assert a lien that attaches to all papers, books, money, and other property of the client that the attorney has in his possession in order to secure payment of legal fees.

A *retaining lien* is not the same as a *charging lien*. A charging lien secures the legal fees by attaching a lien to a future judgment or settlement in the case. For instance, if a law firm is hired on a contingency fee basis and does work for the client and then the client fires that firm and hires a second firm, the first firm may file a *charging lien* in the lawsuit. When the case is settled or a judgment is rendered by the court, the first law firm has a lien on the amount awarded to the client. There may well be a fight about how much the first law firm is entitled to, but money should not be disbursed to the client or the second law firm before the percentages are all decided upon.[35]

One of the benefits of doing contingency fee work is not having to keep track of billable hours. However, in the instance of a charging lien where Firm 1 must show how much work it performed on behalf of the client before the case was taken over by Firm 2, without a record of billable hours, what proof will it have?

As discussed in Chapter 3 on Confidentiality, the information in the client file is confidential. It can't just be thrown in the trash when the case is over. And the firm does not want to be responsible for storing client files for an eternity. To be prepared for this eventuality, then, it is wise to have a clause in the fee agreement about what will happen to the files at the conclusion of the case—such as the client is responsible for taking the files at the conclusion of the case. The firm should have digital copies of everything in the file, and there are certain items in some files that cannot be released to the clients; but other than that, the storage boxes filled with papers can go home with the client.

What Are the Advantages of Pro Bono Service?

Take a look at your state's Rule 6.1. It probably says that persons who are unable to pay reasonable fees should be able to obtain necessary legal services. To ensure that all people can get legal assistance, lawyers and paralegals should support and participate in ethical activities designed to achieve that objective. That means that we should all do our part in pro bono activities.

Pro bono work is a big part of our duty to make legal services available to the public. More than that, however, pro bono work gives you a terrific feeling of helping society and your community. Remember, more than 80 percent of the people who live in America will not be able to afford legal help when they need it. So, take a minute and think about the legal needs that ordinary people have. They need a will, or a trust, or an agreement about who will take their children if they die. They may need to file bankruptcy or get help with an immigration matter. Maybe they would like to adopt children or get a divorce. Maybe they have been cheated and need help getting their money back. (This happens so frequently to the elderly.) Even something that seems simple to us, such as getting the store to refund money for a faulty product, may be insurmountable by someone else. That person needs legal assistance. (Do not include people who are accused of crimes in this long list of people who cannot afford a lawyer when they need one. Remember that the Constitution guarantees a lawyer to the accused at no cost in any matter in which imprisonment is a possible penalty.)

> Alaska Rule 6.1:
> Every lawyer has a professional responsibility to provide legal services to those unable to pay. A lawyer should aspire to render at least 50 hours of *pro bono publico* legal services per year.

> NFPA Canon 1.4(d) says that every paralegal should aspire to contribute 24 hours of pro bono service annually.

> The comments to Guideline No. 4 of NALA's *Annotated Model Standards and Guidelines for Utilization of Legal Assistants* state: "The working relationship between the lawyer and the legal assistant should extend to cooperative efforts on public service activities where possible."

> Corporate Pro Bono:
> http://www.cpbo.org

It's not just traditional law firms that are doing pro bono work. The Association of Corporate Counsel has an organization dedicated to putting corporate counsel in the pro bono scene.

Here are some reasons to do pro bono work for indigent clients, provided by the volunteer lawyers of the Maine statewide pro bono project:

* It provides personal satisfaction.
* It makes you feel very fortunate for what you have.
* It enhances public opinion about lawyers.
* It can lead to "paying" clients through word-of-mouth referrals.

And think of all of the wonderful people you'll meet who feel the way you do about public service! Please don't ever think that pro bono work is only for lawyers. Whatever the lawyers are doing to help someone, you are needed there, too.

SUMMARY

In this chapter, we began our discussion with the beginning of a relationship with the client and, specifically, the paralegal's role in creating that relationship. Now that we have a client, we needed to look at the different types of fee agreements typically used in the law office. We split up a settlement agreement amount so that we could see how contingency fees work. This chapter included keeping accurate, thorough, and contemporaneous time records; learning what a time sheet looks like, and putting the time sheet information into a client's bill. We looked at what sorts of things should be in fee agreements and some things that should not. We learned about retainers and about how client trust accounts work. Then we took a look at getting paid by the client and getting paid by the other side in litigation, where the age-old question of the awardability of paralegal fees came up. We learned that billing should be objectively fair in addition to accurate. At the end of the chapter, we looked at two subjects that many people never look at: referral fees and what to put in the fee agreement about client files. We finished up the chapter with a few words about pro bono service—or working without a fee.

CHAPTER REVIEW AND ASSIGNMENTS

CRITICAL THINKING

1. Let's go back to the State of Palalico and the funding of free legal clinics. Knowing what you know now about client trust accounts, do you side with the lawyers who believe that their clients are entitled to the interest generated by their interest bearing bank accounts, or with the state's policy of funding free legal clinics with this money? See *Brown v. Legal Foundation of Washington* at the end of this chapter.
2. Discuss what you would do if you were a paralegal supervisor and you discovered that one of your paralegals was "padding" his time sheets, which resulted in overbilling certain clients. If you were not the supervisor, would your reaction to someone else's overbilling be the same? If the person overbilling was a lawyer, not a paralegal, would your reaction or course of action change?
3. What do you think the appropriate professional penalty should be for a paralegal who steals from a client trust account? Should the employing lawyer be disciplined or penalized? Should the penalty be different for the paralegal who commits a similar wrong (such as shoplifting) outside of his or her professional duties.

1. Print out *Brobeck, Phleger & Harrison v. Telex* from the publisher's Web site (this is an abbreviated version of the case) and answer the following questions:
   a. Trace the amount of money Telex would have recovered and would have owed to IBM under the original antitrust litigation judgment, the appellate court's judgment, and the settlement agreement.
   b. Why did Telex hire Moses Lasky after the appellate court's ruling?
   c. In your own words, what was the fee agreement Telex made with Lasky?
   d. Explain the "excessive fee" rationale that Telex used to not pay Lasky.
   e. What do you think about Telex's argument? Did Lasky "deserve" the $1 million?
2. Review a standard fee agreement and translate any "legalese" in the agreement into plain English. If you don't have access to a fee agreement, you'll find an example on the publisher's Web site.

COLLABORATIVE ASSIGNMENTS

1. Get into groups of four and design a time sheet for keeping track of your time. Keep track of your time for one entire day on the time sheet your team designed making adjustments to the time sheet where necessary. Note each activity—brush teeth, .2 hours; brush hair, .1 hour—that you do throughout the day. At the end of the day, add up your time and see if it matches the number of hours in the day.
2. As individuals, write a billing entry for the following "Fact Pattern" using the information you obtained in this chapter. Remember: Billing entries should be contemporaneous, thorough, and accurate. Exchange your billing entry with a classmate. Do you see any ethics rules violated in the billing entry you were given?

   Fact Pattern: A lawyer stops you in the hallway and asks you to research this point of law: Does a person suing a lawyer for malpractice for failure to file a claim within the statute of limitations have to prove that he or she would win the underlying case? You go to the library and spend several hours on the issue. While you are researching this issue, you come across a case that is relevant to another case on which you are working, so you take some time to read that case, Shepardize® it, and take some notes. You cannot find an answer to the question about malpractice, but you have to go back to your office to make a phone call. On your way back to your office, you stop and have a cup of coffee and chat with an office buddy about the research you were doing. Then you go to your office, and, in preparation for making the telephone call, you look at your watch. All together, you were out of your office for 4.5 hours. At the end of your workday, you try to reconstruct your time for the day.

Multiple Choice

Select the best answer for each of the following questions.

1. Contingent fees, value billing, and hourly billing are
   a. methods of charging clients for legal services.
   b. methods for law firms to ensure equal profit sharing among partners.
   c. requirements for attorneys to perform legal services for corporations.
   d. billing increments that justify time spent by attorneys and paralegals.
   e. methods by which the law firm accountant will bill the law firm.

2. A client's file may be held by a lawyer who is owed money by that client until
   a. The lawyer receives his or her money.
   b. The lawyer gets paid but only if allowed by the attorney/client agreement.
   c. The client signs a promissory note to the attorney.
   d. The state supreme court's fee arbitration committee decides otherwise.
   e. This is typically not allowed. The client's file belongs to the client and cannot be held.

3. If compensation for paralegal time is sought by a lawyer, the application to the courts for fees should include
   a. a detailed statement of the time spent and legally substantive tasks performed by the paralegal.
   b. the paralegal's resume showing past work experience.
   c. a statement showing the paralegal's education and training to perform the paralegal work.
   d. the market rate for paralegal services in that practice area and geographical location.
   e. all of the above.

4. All timekeeping and billing records prepared and maintained by paralegals must be
   a. thorough.
   b. accurate.
   c. honest.
   d. prepared contemporaneously with the work.
   e. all of the above.

5. "Contingency fee" means
   a. The lawyer gets paid regardless of the outcome of the case.
   b. The lawyer gets paid on an hourly basis if the case is won.
   c. The law firm's recovery of legal fees is contingent upon the outcome of the case.
   d. The law firm will probably not get paid.
   e. The law firm's costs must be paid by the client, but the legal fees will be a percentage of the money that the client wins or is entitled to by settlement.

6. "Hourly rate" fee agreements are
   a. illegal in most states.
   b. common but unethical.
   c. common in plaintiff's personal injury work.
   d. common in divorce cases.
   e. common in criminal prosecutions.

7. Fee agreements with clients
   a. should not be negotiated by paralegals.
   b. should be in writing.
   c. should be fully explained to the client.
   d. should be fair and reasonable.
   e. all of the above.

8. The money in the lawyer's "client trust account"
   a. belongs to the client.
   b. belongs to the lawyer.
   c. belongs to the client until the lawyer sends a bill to the client for services rendered and then becomes the lawyer's.

d. belongs to the client until the lawyer sends a bill to the client along with an accounting indicating how the funds are to be distributed and the client agrees.

e. belongs to the state bar.

9. You are going to work for a personal injury law firm. When you are negotiating your pay agreement, you should

   a. Ask to get one-third of the amount of money made by the law firm on each case you work on.

   b. Ask to get one-third of the amount of money made by the law firm on each case you refer to the law firm.

   c. Ask to get one-third of the amount of money made by the law firm whenever attorney's fees are recovered from the losing party.

d. Ask to get a wage based on the number of hours you work.

e. Ask to get both an hourly wage and one-third of any recovery from the cases you bring into the firm.

10. Fees charged for a paralegal's time are

    a. recoverable whenever lawyers' fees are recoverable.

    b. recoverable in most instances where lawyers' fees are recoverable.

    c. never recoverable.

    d. are recoverable, but only in cases against the government.

    e. are recoverable, but only in contingency cases.

Fill in the Blank

Complete each of the following sentences with the best word(s) or phrase(s).

1. The document that describes the monetary arrangements between an attorney and his or her client is called a _____.

2. The type of fee arrangement between an attorney and a client in which the attorney receives a percentage of the award or settlement amount is called a _____ fee agreement.

3. *Pro bono* means _____.

4. A law firm will often require a "retainer" from a client. A retainer is _____.

5. Champerty is _____.

6. A classic retainer's purpose is to _____.

7. IOLTA is short for _____.

8. *Quantum meruit* means _____.

9. The overriding consideration in client billing is that the fee must be _____.

10. A referral fee is _____. (I'm looking for a description.)

True/False

Decide whether each of the following statements is true or false and write your answer on the line provided.

____ 1. Fee agreements between lawyer and client are negotiable.

____ 2. Paralegals are not allowed to negotiate a fee agreement.

____ 3. Paralegals must never explain a fee agreement to a client.

____ 4. Paralegals in most firms are billable.

____ 5. Contingency fee agreements were permissible before the 1990s but are not permissible any longer.

____ 6. Paralegals should not be concerned with the number of hours they bill or the

amount of revenue they generate for their employing law firm.

____ 7. Value billing is not permissible in any state.

____ 8. It is not proper to ask the client to sign away the literary rights to the client's case.

____ 9. A fee agreement may contain a provision limiting the lawyer's liability for professional negligence so long as it is initialed by the client.

____ 10. Client retainers are not typically utilized now that banks permit electronic transfers.

CASE 1

Brown v. Legal Foundation of Washington
538 U.S. 216, 123 S.Ct. 1406
(2003)

Justice Stevens delivered the opinion of the Court.

The State of Washington, like every other State in the Union, uses interest on lawyers' trust accounts (IOLTA) to pay for legal services provided to the needy. Some IOLTA programs were created by statute, but in Washington, as in most other States, the IOLTA program was established by the State Supreme Court pursuant to its authority to regulate the practice of law. In *Phillips v. Washington Legal Foundation,* 524 U.S. 156 (1998), a case involving the Texas IOLTA program, we held "that the interest income generated by funds held in IOLTA accounts is the 'private property' of the owner of the principal." Id., at 172. We did not, however, express any opinion on the question whether the income had been "taken" by the State or "as to the amount of 'just compensation,' if any, due respondents." Ibid. We now confront those questions.

I.

As we explained in *Phillips,* id., at 160–161, in the course of their legal practice, attorneys are frequently required to hold clients' funds for various lengths of time. It has long been recognized that they have a professional and fiduciary obligation to avoid commingling their clients' money with their own, but it is not unethical to pool several clients' funds in a single trust account. Before 1980, client funds were typically held in non-interest-bearing federally insured checking accounts. Because federal banking regulations in effect since the Great Depression prohibited banks from paying interest on checking accounts, the value of the use of the clients' money in such accounts inured to the banking institutions.

In 1980, Congress authorized federally insured banks to pay interest on a limited category of demand deposits referred to as "NOW accounts." See 87 Stat. 342, 12 U.S.C. § 1832. This category includes deposits made by individuals and charitable organizations, but does not include those made by for-profit corporations or partnerships unless the deposits are made pursuant to a program under which charitable organizations have "the exclusive right to the interest.'"

In response to the change in federal law, Florida adopted the first IOLTA program in 1981 authorizing the use of NOW accounts for the deposit of client funds, and providing that all of the interest on such accounts be used for charitable purposes. Every State in the Nation and the District of Columbia have followed Florida's lead and adopted an IOLTA program, either through their legislatures or their highest courts. The result is that, whereas before 1980 the banks retained the value of the use of the money deposited in non-interest-bearing client trust accounts, today, because of the adoption of IOLTA programs, that value is transferred to charitable entities providing legal services for the poor. The aggregate value of those contributions in 2001 apparently exceeded $200 million.

In 1984, the Washington Supreme Court established its IOLTA program by amending its *Rules of Professional Conduct*. IOLTA Adoption Order, 102 Wash.2d 1101. The amendments were adopted after over two years of deliberation, during which the court received hundreds of public comments and heard oral argument from the Seattle-King County Bar Association, designated to represent the proponents of the Rule, and the Walla Walla County Bar Association, designated to represent the opponents of the Rule.

In its opinion explaining the order, the court noted that earlier Rules had required attorneys to hold client trust funds "in accounts separate from their own funds," id., at 1102, and had prohibited the use of such funds for the lawyer's own pecuniary advantage, but did not address the question whether or how such funds should be invested. Commenting on then-prevalent practice the court observed:

> "In conformity with trust law, however, lawyers usually invest client trust funds in separate interest-bearing accounts and pay the interest to the clients whenever the trust funds are large enough in amount or to be held for a long enough period of time to make such investments economically feasible, that is, when the amount of interest earned exceeds the bank charges and costs of setting up the account. However, when trust funds are so nominal in amount or to be held for so short a period that the amount of interest that could be earned would not justify the cost of creating separate accounts, most attorneys simply deposit the funds in a single noninterest-bearing trust checking account containing all such trust funds from all their clients. The funds in such accounts earn no interest for either the client or the attorney. The banks, in contrast, have received the interest-free use of client money." Ibid.

The court then described the four essential features of its IOLTA program: (a) the requirement that all client funds be deposited in interest-bearing trust accounts, (b) the requirement that funds that cannot earn net interest for the client be deposited in an IOLTA account, (c) the requirement that the lawyers direct the banks to pay the net interest on the IOLTA accounts to the Legal Foundation of Washington (Foundation), and (d) the requirement that the Foundation must use all funds received from IOLTA accounts for tax-exempt law-related charitable and educational purposes.

(Description of Washington's rules omitted here)

In its opinion the court responded to three objections that are relevant to our inquiry in this case. First, it rejected the contention that the new program "constitutes an unconstitutional taking of property without due process or just compensation." Id., at 1104. Like other State Supreme Courts that had considered the question, it distinguished our decision in *Webb's Fabulous Pharmacies, Inc. v. Beckwith,* 449 U.S. 155 (1980), on the ground that the new " 'program creates income where there had been none before, and the income thus created would never benefit the client under any set of circumstances.' " 102 Wash.2d, at 1108 (quoting *In re Interest on Trust Accounts,* 402 So.2d 389, 395 (Fla.1981)).

Second, it rejected the argument that it was unethical for lawyers to rely on any factor other than the client's best interests when deciding whether to deposit funds in an IOLTA account rather than an account that would generate interest for the client. The court endorsed, and added emphasis, to the response to that argument set forth in the proponents' reply brief:

'Although the proposed amendments list several factors an attorney should consider in deciding how to invest his clients' trust funds, . . . all of these factors are really facets of a single question: Can the client's money be invested so that it will produce a net benefit for the client? If so, the attorney must invest it to earn interest for the client. Only if the money cannot earn net interest for the client is the money to go into an IOLTA account.'

"Reply Brief of Proponents, at 14. This is a correct statement of an attorney's duty under trust law, as well as a proper interpretation of the proposed rule as published for public comment. However, in order to make it even clearer that IOLTA funds are only those funds that cannot, under any circumstances, earn net interest (after deducting transaction and administrative costs and bank fees) for the client, we have amended the proposed rule accordingly. See new CPR DR 9—102(C)(3). The new rule makes it absolutely clear that the enumerated factors are merely facets of the ultimate question of whether client funds could be invested profitably for the benefit of clients. If they can, then investment for the client is mandatory." 102 Wash.2d, at 1113–1114.

The court also rejected the argument that it had failed to consider the significance of advances in computer technology that, in time, may convert IOLTA participation into an unconstitutional taking of property that could have been distributed to the client. It pointed to the fact that the Rule expressly requires attorneys to give consideration to the capability of financial institutions to calculate and pay interest on individual accounts, and added: "Thus, as cost effective subaccounting services become available, making it possible to earn net interest for clients on increasingly smaller amounts held for increasingly shorter periods of time, more trust money will have to be invested for the clients' benefit under the new rule. The rule is therefore self-adjusting and is adequately designed to accommodate changes in banking technology without running afoul of the state or federal constitutions." Id., at 1114.

Given the court's explanation of its Rule, it seems apparent that a lawyer who mistakenly uses an IOLTA account as a depositary for money that could earn interest for the client would violate the Rule. Hence, the lawyer will be liable to the client for any lost interest, however minuscule the amount might be.

In 1995, the Washington Supreme Court amended its IOLTA Rules to make them applicable to Limited Practice Officers (LPOs) as well as lawyers. LPOs are non-lawyers who are licensed to act as escrowees in the closing of real estate transactions. Like lawyers, LPOs often temporarily control the funds of clients.

II.

This action was commenced by a public interest law firm and four citizens to enjoin state officials from continuing to require LPOs to deposit trust funds into IOLTA accounts. Because the Court of Appeals held that the firm and two of the individuals do not have standing, *Washington Legal Foundation v. Legal Foundation of Washington*, 271 F.3d 835, 848–850 (CA9 2001), and since that holding was not challenged in this Court, we limit our discussion to the claims asserted by petitioners Allen Brown and Greg Hayes. The defendants, respondents in this Court, are the justices of the Washington Supreme Court, the Foundation, which receives and redistributes the interest on IOLTA accounts, and the president of the Foundation.

In their amended complaint, Brown and Hayes describe the IOLTA program, with particular reference to its application to LPOs and to some of the activities of Recipient Organizations that have received funds from the Foundation. Brown and Hayes also both allege that they regularly purchase and sell real estate and in the course of such transactions they deliver funds to LPOs who are required to deposit them in IOLTA accounts. They object to having the interest on those funds "used to finance the Recipient Organizations" and "to anyone other than themselves receiving the interest derived from those funds." App. 25. The first count of their complaint alleges that "being forced to associate with the Recipient Organizations" violates their First Amendment rights, id., at 25, 27–28; the second count alleges that the "taking" of the interest earned on their funds in the IOLTA accounts violates the Just Compensation Clause of the Fifth Amendment, id., at 28–29; and the third count alleges that the requirement that client funds be placed in IOLTA accounts is "an illegal taking of the beneficial use of those funds." Id., at 29. The prayer for relief sought a refund of interest earned on the plaintiffs' money that had been placed in IOLTA accounts, a declaration that the IOLTA Rules are unconstitutional, and an injunction against their enforcement against LPOs. See id., at 30.

Most of the pretrial discovery related to the question of whether the 1995 Amendment to the IOLTA Rules had indirectly lessened the earnings of LPOs because LPOs no longer receive certain credits that the banks had provided them when banks retained the interest earned on escrowed funds. Each of the petitioners, however, did identify a specific transaction in which interest on his escrow deposit was paid to the Foundation.

Petitioner Hayes and a man named Fossum made an earnest money deposit of $2,000 on August 14, 1996, and a further payment of $12,793.32 on August 28, 1996, in connection with a real estate purchase that was closed on August 30, 1996. Id., at 117–118. The money went into an IOLTA account. Presumably those funds, half of which belonged to Fossum, were used to pay the sales price, "to pay off liens and obtain releases to clear the title to the property being conveyed." Id., at 98. The record does not explain exactly how or when the ultimate recipients of those funds received or cashed the checks issued to them by the escrowee, but the parties apparently agree that the deposits generated some interest on principal that was at least in part owned by Hayes during the closing.

In connection with a real estate purchase that closed on May 1, 1997, petitioner Brown made a payment of $90,521.29 that remained in escrow for two days, see id., at 53; he estimated that the interest on that deposit amounted to $4.96, but he did not claim that he would have received any interest if the IOLTA Rules had not been in place. The record thus suggests, although the facts are not crystal clear, that funds deposited by each of the petitioners generated some interest that was ultimately paid to the Foundation. It also seems clear that without IOLTA those funds would not have produced any net interest for either of the petitioners.

After discovery, the District Court granted the defendants' motion for summary judgment. As a factual matter the court concluded "that in no event can the client-depositors make any net returns on the interest accrued in these accounts. Indeed, if the funds were able to make any net return, they would not be subject to the IOLTA program." *Washington Legal Foundation v. Legal Foundation of Washington,* No. C97–0146C (WD Wash., Jan. 30, 1998), App. to Pet. for Cert. 94a. As a legal matter, the court concluded that the constitutional issue focused on what an owner has lost, not what the " 'taker' " has gained, and that petitioners Hayes and Brown had "lost nothing." Ibid.

While the case was on appeal, we decided *Phillips v. Washington Legal Foundation,* 524 U.S. 156 (1998). Relying on our opinion in that case, a three-judge panel of the Ninth Circuit decided that the IOLTA program caused a taking of petitioners' property and that further proceedings were necessary to determine whether they are entitled to just compensation. The panel concluded: "In sum, we hold that the interest generated by IOLTA pooled trust accounts is property of the clients and customers whose money is deposited into trust, and that a government appropriation of that interest for public purposes is a taking entitling them to just compensation under the Fifth Amendment. But just compensation for the takings may be less than the amount of the interest taken, or nothing, depending on the circumstances, so determining the remedy requires a remand." *Washington Legal Foundation v. Legal Foundation of Washington,* 236 F.3d 1097, 1115 (2001).

The Court of Appeals then reconsidered the case en banc. 271 F.3d 835 (CA9 2001). The en banc majority affirmed the judgment of the District Court, reasoning that, under the ad hoc approach applied in *Penn Central Transp. Co. v. New York City,* 438 U.S. 104 (1978), there was no taking because petitioners had suffered neither an actual loss nor an interference with any investment-backed expectations, and that the regulation of the use of their property was permissible. Moreover, in the majority's view, even if there were a taking, the just compensation due was zero.

The three judges on the original panel, joined by Judge Kozinski, dissented. In their view, the majority's reliance on Penn Central was misplaced because this case involves a "per se" taking rather than a regulatory taking. 271 F.3d, at 865–866. The dissenters adhered to the panel's view that a remand is necessary in order to decide whether any compensation is due.

In their petition for certiorari, Brown and Hayes asked us not only to resolve the disagreement between the majority and the dissenters in the Ninth Circuit about the taking issue, but also to answer a question that none of those judges reached, namely, whether injunctive relief is available because the small amounts to which they claim they are entitled render recovery through litigation impractical. We granted certiorari. 536 U.S. 903 (2002).

III.

While it confirms the state's authority to confiscate private property, the text of the Fifth Amendment imposes two conditions on the exercise of such authority: the taking must be for a "public use" and "just compensation" must be paid to the owner. In this case, the first condition is unquestionably satisfied. If the State had imposed a special tax, or perhaps a system of user fees, to generate the funds to finance the legal services supported by the Foundation, there would be no question as to the legitimacy of the use of the public's money. The fact that public funds might pay the legal fees of a lawyer representing a tenant in a dispute with a landlord who was compelled to contribute to the program would not undermine the public character of the "use" of the funds. Provided that she receives just compensation for the taking of her property, a conscientious pacifist has no standing to object to the government's decision to use the property she formerly owned for the production of munitions. Even if there may be occasional misuses of IOLTA funds, the overall, dramatic success of these programs in serving the compelling interest in providing legal services to literally millions of needy Americans certainly qualifies the Foundation's distribution of these funds as a "public use" within the meaning of the Fifth Amendment.

(The Court's discussion on "the type of taking" (physical v. regulatory) is omitted.)

IV.

"The Fifth Amendment does not proscribe the taking of property; it proscribes taking without just compensation." *Williamson County Regional Planning Comm'n v. Hamilton Bank of Johnson City*, 473 U.S. 172, 194 (1985). All of the Circuit Judges and District Judges who have confronted the compensation question, both in this case and in Phillips, have agreed that the "just compensation" required by the Fifth Amendment is measured by the property owner's loss rather than the government's gain. This conclusion is supported by consistent and unambiguous holdings in our cases.

Most frequently cited is Justice Holmes' characteristically terse statement that "the question is what has the owner lost, not what has the taker gained." *Boston Chamber of Commerce v. Boston,* 217 U.S. 189, 195 (1910). Also directly in point is Justice Brandeis' explanation of why a mere technical taking does not give rise to an obligation to pay compensation:

> "We have no occasion to determine whether in law the President took possession and assumed control of the Marion & Rye Valley Railway. For even if there was technically a taking, the judgment for defendant was right. Nothing was recoverable as just compensation, because nothing of value was taken from the company; and it was not subjected by the Government to pecuniary loss." *Marion & Rye Valley R. Co. v. United States,* 270 U.S. 280, 282 (1926).

A few years later we again noted that the private party "is entitled to be put in as good a position pecuniarily as if his property had not been taken. He must be made whole but is not entitled to more." *Olson v. United States,* 292 U.S. 246, 255 (1934). In *Kimball Laundry Co. v. United States,* 338 U.S. 1 (1949), although there was disagreement within the Court concerning the proper measure of the owner's loss when a leasehold interest was condemned, it was common ground that the government should pay "not for what it gets but for what the owner loses." Id., at 23 (Douglas, J., dissenting). Moreover, in his opinion for the majority, Justice

Frankfurter made it clear that, given "the liability of all property to condemnation for the common good," an owner's nonpecuniary losses attributable to "his unique need for property or idiosyncratic attachment to it, like loss due to an exercise of the police power, is properly treated as part of the burden of common citizenship." Id., at 5.

Applying the teaching of these cases to the question before us, it is clear that neither Brown nor Hayes is entitled to any compensation for the nonpecuniary consequences of the taking of the interest on his deposited funds, and that any pecuniary compensation must be measured by his net losses rather than the value of the public's gain. For that reason, both the majority and the dissenters on the Court of Appeals agreed that if petitioners' net loss was zero, the compensation that is due is also zero.

V.

(The Court's discussion of a lawyer mistakenly depositing funds in an IOLTA account when those funds might have produced net earnings for the client is omitted.)

VI.

To recapitulate: It is neither unethical nor illegal for lawyers to deposit their clients' funds in a single bank account. A state law that requires client funds that could not otherwise generate net earnings for the client to be deposited in an IOLTA account is not a "regulatory taking." A law that requires that the interest on those funds be transferred to a different owner for a legitimate public use, however, could be a per se taking requiring the payment of "just compensation" to the client. Because that compensation is measured by the owner's pecuniary loss—which is zero whenever the Washington law is obeyed—there has been no violation of the Just Compensation Clause of the Fifth Amendment in this case. It is therefore unnecessary to discuss the remedial question presented in the certiorari petition. Accordingly, the judgment of the Court of Appeals is affirmed.

It is so ordered.

CASE QUESTIONS

1. What did the resolution of this case mean for state bar associations all over the United States?
2. How would you explain this decision to a client who kept a large sum of money in your firm's trust account? Can you think of a way to explain it that would make the client feel better about not getting interest on his/her money?

Blair v. Ing
95 Hawai'i 247, 253, 21 P.3d 452
(2001)

In this case, plaintiffs-appellants Leslie Blair and Laura Bishop (Plaintiffs) sued defendant/cross-claimant appellee Thomas Thayer for professional negligence and breach of implied contract. Plaintiffs claimed that Thayer, an accountant, had breached a duty to them as intended third-party beneficiaries to an agreement between their mother, Joan Hughes, and Thayer for the preparation of the estate tax return for decedent Lloyd Hughes. After the trial court granted Thayer's motion to dismiss the complaint, Plaintiffs appealed. On February 27, 2001, this court upheld the dismissal in favor of Thayer because: (1) Thayer was alleged to have been hired to prepare tax returns—not to give estate planning advice—and, thus, Plaintiffs were merely incidental beneficiaries; and (2) as merely incidental beneficiaries, Thayer owed Plaintiffs no duty. *Blair v. Ing*, 95 Hawai'i 247, 21 P.3d 452, reconsideration denied, 95 Hawai'i 247, 21 P.3d 452 (2001).

Thayer then filed request for compensation for necessary expenses and attorneys' fees pursuant to Hawai'i Revised Statutes (HRS) §§ 607–14 (Supp. 2000) and 607–9 (1993), (1) and Hawai'i Rules of Appellate Procedure (HRAP) Rules 39(d) (2000) and 53(b) (2000). In his motion, Thayer requests reimbursement of attorneys' fees in the amount of $21,570.00, general excise tax in the amount of $898.82, and costs in the amount of $756.92, for a total request of $23,225.74.

(In its discussion, the court found that Thayer was entitled to fees and then discussed the appropriateness of awarding Thayer's request for paralegal fees.)

B. REASONABLENESS OF THE FEES

In his motion, Thayer requests $21,570.00 for attorneys' fees incurred in this appeal. Plaintiffs oppose those fees that are attributable to "legal assistants," arguing that "[n]othing in the statute purports to allow paralegal or secretarial fees." This court has never directly addressed whether paralegal or other non-attorney fees are allowable as part of a "reasonable attorneys' fees" award.

In *Missouri v. Jenkins*, 491 U.S. 274 (1989), the United States Supreme Court upheld compensation awarded for the work of law clerks and paralegals under the Civil Rights Attorneys' Fees Act, 42 U.S.C. § 1988, which provided for "a reasonable attorney's fee as part of the costs." Id. at 288. Further, the Supreme Court recognized the "increasingly widespread custom of separately billing for the services of paralegals and law students who serve as clerks" and determined that "the prevailing practice [of] bill[ing] paralegal work at market rates [including paralegal fees in a fee request] is not only permitted by [the statute], but also makes economic sense." *Jenkins,* 491 U.S. at 287–88 (citations omitted). The Supreme Court explained that, "[b]y encouraging the use of lower cost paralegals rather than attorneys wherever possible, permitting market-rate billing of paralegal hours, encourages cost-effective delivery of legal services[.]" Id. at 288 (citations and internal quotation marks omitted). A number of other states are in accord. See, e.g., *Cline v. Rocky Mountain, Inc.,* 998 P.2d 946, 950–51 (Wyo. 2000); *Barker v. Utah Pub. Serv. Comm'n,* 970 P.2d 702, 712 (Utah 1998); *Taylor v. Chubb Group of Ins. Cos.,* 874 P.2d 806, 809 (Okla. 1994); *First NH Banks Granite State v. Scarborough,* 615 A.2d 248, 281 (Me. 1992); *Continental Townhouses East Unit One Ass'n. v. Brockbank,* 733 P.2d 1120, 1127–28 (Ariz. Ct. App. 1986) [hereinafter, *Continental Townhouses*]; *Gill Sav. Ass'n v. International Supply Co., Inc.,* 759 S.W.2d 697, 704–05 (Tex. Ct. App. 1988).

In *Continental Townhouses,* the Arizona Court of Appeals stated:

> Lawyers should not be required to perform tasks more properly performed by legal assistants or law clerks solely to permit that time to be compensable in the event an attorneys' fees application is ultimately submitted. Requiring such a misallocation of valuable resources would serve no useful purpose and would be contrary to the direction to interpret the Rules of Civil Procedure to serve the "just, speedy, and inexpensive determination of every action." Instead, proper use of legal assistants and law clerks should be encouraged to facilitate providing the most cost-effective legal services to the public. If compensation could not be obtained for legal assistant and law clerk services *in appropriate cases,* the fee-shifting objective of [mitigating the burden of the expense of litigation] would also not be accomplished.

733 P.2d at 1127 (internal citations omitted) (emphasis added). The Arizona court then proceeded to comment on the billing of paralegals on a separate fee basis, as opposed to including the "costs" of paralegals within an attorney's hourly billing rate:

> It also cannot be assumed legal assistant services are automatically included in lawyers' hourly billing rates as a standard law office operating expense. Instead, such services are often itemized and billed separately. Moreover, lawyers should not be required to inflate their hourly rates to include legal assistant time as a general overhead component. Doing so would make fair allocation of the cost of such services impossible, since some clients and matters may require a much higher proportion of legal assistant and law clerk services than others.

Id. at 1127–28.

Based on the foregoing authority, we hold that, *in appropriate cases,* a request or award of attorneys' fees may include compensation for separately billed legal services performed by a paralegal, legal assistant, or law clerk [hereinafter, collectively, legal assistant].

In discussing the categories of persons and tasks that should be considered under the term "legal assistant" for purposes of attorneys' fees applications, the court in *Continental Townhouses* held that, in order to be included within an attorneys' fee award, the work performed by the legal assistant must be legal work, supervised by an attorney, and the fee application must contain enough details to demonstrate to the court that these requirements have been met. Id. at 1128.

We agree and, therefore, hold that the reasonableness of legal assistant fees be reviewed on a case-by-case basis for the value of services rendered and that an award of such fees be limited to charges for work performed that would otherwise have been required to be performed by a licensed attorney at a higher rate. See id.; *Taylor,* 874 P.2d at 809. Such a holding is consistent with the purpose of encouraging cost-effective delivery of legal services. See *Jenkins*, 491 U.S. at 288.

In his fee request, Thayer has asked for the following compensation for "legal assistants":

Sandy Takenaka (1.4 hours × $50.00 = $70.00)

Patty Yukawa (2.6 hours × $50.00 = $130.00)

Kevin Chang, Esq (3.9 hours × 25.00 = $97.50)

We analyze the tasks performed by each in turn.

The worksheets submitted with respect to Ms. Takenaka document short telephone calls to clients regarding depositions and the transmission of documents to the court. Every one of the services performed were services ordinarily considered secretarial and would not "otherwise have had to have been performed by a licensed attorney at a higher rate." Thus, none of the services performed by Ms. Takenaka are compensable in the attorneys' fees award. Accordingly, we deny the $70.00 requested for fees associated with tasks performed by Ms. Takenaka.

The worksheets submitted with respect to Ms. Yukawa document the following:

8/24/99	*Preparation of record on appeal* at Supreme Court Clerk's Office	2.6 hours

(Emphasis added.) We note that the record on appeal is actually prepared by the clerk of the court or agency from which the appeal is taken prior to being transmitted to the supreme court. See Hawai'i Rules of Appellate Procedure (HRAP) Rule 11(a) (2000) (providing that "[e]ach appellant, shall comply with the provisions of HRAP Rule 10(b) (2000) [designating the composition of the record on appeal] and shall take any other action necessary to enable the clerk of the court to assemble and transmit the record"). In preparing the record on appeal, the clerk of the court or agency consecutively numbers the court or agency file and prepares a numbered index of all the pages therein. A copy of the index is thereafter provided to all parties to the appeal. See HRAP 11(b) (2000). Thus, Ms. Yukawa could not have "prepar[ed]" the record on appeal. Consequently, the request of 2.6 hours is denied.

The worksheets submitted with respect to Mr. Chang document the following:

6/21/00	Retrieve cases and articles on third party beneficiary and accountant liability issues Search all West General Digest 36+ account liability	1.7 hours
6/26/00	Shepardize Plaintiffs cases retrieve any pertinent negative history. Make sure we have	

	copies of all our cited cases. Go to First Circuit Court retrieve Storm case. Go to Supreme Court retrieve accountant case.	4 hours
6/27/00	Shepardize our cases on Keycite. Go to Supreme Court and retrieve all our missing cases from outside our jurisdiction	1.8 hours
	Total	3.9 hours

The nature of the work performed by Mr. Chang is clearly of a legal nature. Legal research, including Shepardizing cases, is a task that would undoubtedly have been performed by a licensed attorney at a higher rate, in the absence of Mr. Chang's services. Thus, the tasks performed by Mr. Chang are compensable.

No other challenges to the attorneys' fees request have been raised. Accordingly, we grant the amount of $21,370 as reasonable attorneys' fees, which includes fees charged for legal assistant services, in this appeal.

(The remainder of this case is omitted.)

CASE QUESTIONS

1. What was the Court's rationale for allowing Thayer to recover attorneys' fees at all?
2. What was the Court's rationale for not allowing the Takenaka and Yukawa paralegal fees but allowing the Chang fees?
3. What policies would you institute in your Hawaii law firm based on this decision?

CASE 3

Mullens v. Hansel-Henderson
65 P.3d 992
(2002)

I. INTRODUCTION

We granted certiorari to decide whether the court of appeals erred in holding that an attorney must return fees received for legal services when the services were successfully completed but the agreement was not in writing. The court of appeals ordered attorney Steven Mullens to return fees earned during representation of Victoria Hansel-Henderson in claims against her former employer because the underlying contingent fee agreement did not comply with the requirements of

Colorado Rules of Civil Procedure Chapter 23.3, and was therefore unenforceable. We hold that an attorney is entitled to fees under quantum meruit when the agreed upon services are successfully completed but the contingent fee agreement is not in writing. Therefore, we reverse and remand the case to the court of appeals with directions to decide any remaining issues in accordance with the views expressed in this opinion.

II. FACTS AND PROCEDURAL HISTORY

In 1990, respondent Victoria Hansel-Henderson entered into a written contingent fee agreement with petitioner Steven Mullens, a Colorado attorney with over twenty years experience in Workers' Compensation claims. Under the terms of this initial contract, Mullens agreed to represent Hansel in a Workers' Compensation claim against her employer Public Service Company for injuries sustained on the job. In exchange for representation, Mullens would receive twenty percent (20%) of any monies received by him on her behalf. Mullens agreed to carry all costs related to this litigation.

As Mullens worked on the Workers' Compensation claim over the next two years, he learned of attempts by Public Service Company to influence medical diagnoses being made for purposes of evaluating Hansel's injuries. Mullens recognized that these tactics supported a potential Bad Faith claim for the intentional mishandling and manipulation of the Workers' Compensation claim. Mullens discussed this potential claim with Hansel and the two agreed that he would also represent her in this Bad Faith claim for an additional fee. Although testimony regarding the precise fee to be paid under this new agreement varied somewhat, the trial court found that Mullens and Hansel had an agreement for a fee of forty percent (40%) of any monies received for this new claim. This separate agreement was never committed to writing.

In 1993, after three years of work, Mullens settled the two claims. The employer agreed to pay Hansel $37,560 to settle the Workers' Compensation claim and $262,440 to settle the Bad Faith claim for a total on the two claims of $300,000. From the settlement amounts Mullens retained thirty-three percent (33%) of the total settlement amount, instead of twenty percent (20%) of the Workers' Compensation claim and forty percent (40%) of the Bad Faith claim. This arrangement allowed Hansel to receive $12,488 more than she could have expected to receive under the terms of the oral contingent fee agreement. Hansel accepted the amounts and signed two documents, one for each claim, releasing the employer from further liability. The trial court found that at disbursement Hansel was very pleased with the outcome of the claims and did not object to the amounts of attorney's fees. Hansel negotiated the settlement checks.

In 1995, two years after Mullens received his attorney's fees and Hansel accepted the settlement money, Hansel initiated action against Mullens to recover all of the attorney's fees paid for the Bad Faith settlement. Hansel asserted in her complaint that Mullens was not entitled to attorney's fees from the Bad Faith settlement because the contingent fee agreement for the Bad Faith claim was not in writing as required by Colorado Rules of Civil Procedure Chapter 23.3, and was therefore not enforceable. Hansel argued that because Mullens was not entitled to payment under an oral contingent fee agreement, Mullens should be required to return to Hansel all of the attorney fees that she paid for the Bad Faith claim.

After finding an oral agreement for forty percent (40%) of all settlement monies on the Bad Faith claim, the trial court held that the agreement was not enforceable because it was never reduced to writing as required by Chapter 23.3. However, the court determined that the fees collected by Mullens were reasonable for the services performed and allowed Mullens to retain fees under quantum meruit. Hansel appealed the trial court holding allowing Mullens to retain the fees acquired from the settlement of the Bad Faith claim.

On appeal, the court of appeals decided that *Dudding v. Norton Frickey & Assoc.,* 11 P.3d 441 (Colo. 2000), controlled. According to the court of appeals, *Dudding* holds that under Chapter 23.3, Rule 5(d), there can be no recovery under quantum meruit where the underlying contingent fee agreement fails, unless the agreement contains a statement clearly giving the client notice that she may be liable to pay compensation to the attorney under quantum meruit. Because the court of appeals found no evidence of any notification that recovery under quantum meruit might be possible, the court of appeals reversed the trial court's judgment.

Since we have not had the opportunity to examine whether quantum meruit recovery is available for unenforceable contingent fee agreements where the agreed upon legal services have been completed, and because Chapter 23.3 does not specifically answer this question, we granted certiorari. After considering this issue we conclude that the rule in *Dudding* applies only to those situations where the attorney-client relationship terminates before the agreed upon legal services are completed. Because the court of appeals' application of *Dudding* is overly broad, we reverse.

III. ANALYSIS

This case requires us to examine whether an attorney may keep attorney's fees paid for services performed pursuant to an unenforceable oral contingent fee agreement when the services were successfully completed. Our examination of this issue is broken into three areas. First, we consider how attorney's fees under unenforceable contingent fee agreements are limited by our rules. Specifically, we examine the Rule 5(d) notice requirement found in Chapter 23.3 of Colorado Rules of Civil Procedure, and the example of this notice provided in Rule 7. Second, we address whether our earlier decisions resolve the issue now before us. Finally, we examine quantum meruit and the function of the Rule 5(d) limitation in the context of a contingent fee agreement where the legal services were successfully completed.

A. Rules Governing Contingent Fees

Whether or not the terms of a contingent fee agreement are enforceable is controlled by Chapter 23.3 of Colorado Rules of Civil Procedure. Rule 6 of Chapter

23.3 states that "no contingent fee agreement shall be enforceable by the involved attorney unless there has been substantial compliance with all of the provisions of this chapter." C.R.C.P. Ch. 23.3, Rule 6. Hence, if a contingent fee agreement fails to substantially comply with the rules of Chapter 23.3, it is unenforceable.

According to Rule 1, a contingent fee agreement must be in writing. C.R.C.P. Ch. 23.3, Rule 1; *Beeson v. Indus. Claim Appeals Office*, 942 P.2d 1314, 1316 (Colo.App.1997). Therefore, an oral contingent fee agreement is not enforceable and the attorney cannot recover the fee amount specified in the oral agreement. This, however, does not necessarily preclude the attorney from recovering fees altogether. Generally attorneys may recover on an unenforceable contract on the basis of quantum meruit. Restatement (Third) of the Law Governing Lawyers § 39 (2002) (If a client and lawyer have not made a valid contract providing for another measure of compensation, a client owes a lawyer who has performed legal services for the client the fair value of the lawyer's services); 7 Am.Jur.2d § 289 (attorneys may recover on a quantum meruit basis even where the parties have entered an unenforceable fee contract).

Although recovery under quantum meruit is generally allowed for unenforceable fee agreements, Chapter 23.3 limits such recovery. *Elliott v. Joyce*, 889 P.2d 43, 46 (Colo.1994). Chapter 23.3 limits compensation under quantum meruit through a notice requirement detailed in Rule 5(d). Rule 5(d) mandates that contingent fee agreements contain "a statement of the contingency upon which the client is to be liable to pay compensation otherwise than from amounts collected for him by the attorney." C.R.C.P. Ch. 23.3, Rule 5(d). If the client is to be required to pay the attorney from monies not obtained for the client by the attorney through settlement or judgment, the fee agreement must contain a statement giving the client notice of such a possibility.

The limitation that Rule 5(d) imposes on quantum meruit is central to our discussion. Hansel argues that Rule 5(d) requires that for there to be any compensation under quantum meruit, there must be notice of the possibility of liability under quantum meruit in the contingent fee agreement. Hansel argues that without such notice of potential quantum meruit recovery, Mullens cannot receive any payment under quantum meruit for legal services that resulted in a settlement of the Bad Faith claim. Thus, the initial question before us is whether Rule 5(d) broadly applies to limit any compensation of attorney's fees under quantum meruit when the agreed upon legal services have been completed. In answering this question we look to Form 2 in Rule 7 to enhance our understanding of Rule 5(d).

Chapter 23.3, Rule 7, entitled Forms, offers two examples of conforming contingent fee agreements. Form 2, subsection 3 is an example of how the quantum meruit notice statement should be drafted in order to allow for quantum meruit recovery. C.R.C.P. Ch. 23.3, Rule 7, Committee Comment. The example is significant in that by stating when compensation under quantum meruit is allowed, it demonstrates that the Rule 5(d) notice requirement applies to situations where the attorney-client relationship terminates before the agreed upon legal services are completed. Subsection 3 states in pertinent part:

The client is not to be liable to pay compensation otherwise than from amounts collected for the client by the attorney, except as follows:

In the event that the client terminates this contingent fee agreement without wrongful conduct by the attorney . . . or if the attorney justifiably withdraws from the representation, the attorney may ask the court . . . to order the client to pay the attorney a fee based upon the reasonable value of the services provided by the attorney.

As stated, this example of a notice statement demonstrates that the Rule 5(d) notice requirement applies when the client terminates the agreement without wrongful conduct by the attorney, or the attorney justifiably withdraws from representation, before the agreed upon legal services are completed.

Form 2 of Rule 7 has no application where the attorney-client relationship is not terminated prematurely. Where the attorney-client relationship is not terminated prematurely and the agreed upon services are completed, as is the case here, the notice requirement as given in Form 2 of Rule 7, does not notify the client whether the attorney is entitled to compensation. Rather, it is the contingent fee agreement itself that provides the client notice that compensation is expected when the legal services are completed. Specifically, the language in both Rule 5(d) and Form 2 of Rule 7, " . . . otherwise than from amounts collected for him by the attorney," serves to limit the application of Rule 5(d) to cases where the attorney-client relationship is terminated before the attorney collects a recovery for the client. The client, under the contingent fee agreement itself, has notice that once the attorney obtains a recovery for the client, the client must compensate the attorney for his services. Thus, the example in Rule 7 helps to explain that the Rule 5(d) notice requirement does not apply to situations where the agreed upon legal services have been completed.

(The court's discussion of two earlier cases is omitted.)

C. Quantum Meruit When the Legal Services Are Completed

We have never before examined whether the Rule 5(d) notice requirement applies to situations where the agreed upon legal services, such as a settlement or judgment, have been completed. However, the court of appeals explored such a situation in *Beeson v. Indus. Claim Appeals Office,* 942 P.2d 1314 (Colo.App.1997).

In *Beeson,* the contested fees arose from an oral contingent fee agreement where attorney Fogel had obtained a settlement for client Beeson, thereby completing the contingency of the contract. *Beeson,* 942 P.2d at 1315. Two years after accepting the distribution of funds, Beeson sought to retrieve her payment of attorney's fees because the fee agreement failed to comply with Chapter 23.3, and hence the contract was unenforceable. Id. at 1315–16. Under the unenforceable contract, Beeson reasoned, Fogel should not have received the bargained-for amount. Id. at 1315. In Beeson, the court of appeals agreed that the underlying contingent fee agreement was unenforceable, however, the court allowed Fogel to be compensated for his services under a quantum meruit analysis. Id. at 1316.

The *Beeson* court determined that fees may be recovered on the basis of quantum meruit so long as the attorney shows that a benefit was conferred, appreciated, and accepted by the client under such circumstances that it would be inequitable for the benefit to be retained without payment of its value. Id. Because the services agreed upon in the unenforceable oral agreement were completed, the Rule 5(d) notice requirement was not applicable. Id. Specifically, the *Beeson* court reasoned that because Fogel was not seeking fees after having been terminated by the client;

because Fogel had not unilaterally withdrawn while the claim was pending; and because he had fully performed the requested services, completely resolving the matter, he was entitled to reasonable compensation for his work. Id. We agree with the analysis of the court of appeals in *Beeson* in light of the nature of contingent fee agreements and the function the Rule 5(d) notice requirement serves.

The notice requirement fulfills an important function. The purpose of Rule 5(d) is to assure that the client knows whether she will be liable for attorney's fees under quantum meruit when there is not already an expectation to pay. In a contingent fee relationship, the client is put on notice by the nature of the contingent fee agreement itself that should the attorney fulfill his end of the bargain to the benefit of the client, the client will be required to pay the attorney from the funds the attorney receives for the client. Hence, where the agreed upon legal services are completed, the client has the expectation that she must pay the attorney. This expectation exists even if the fee agreement is later found unenforceable because it is not in writing. Since the client already has an expectation that she must pay the attorney from the monies the attorney recovers for her, requiring a statement expressing such does not advance the essential function of Rule 5(d) of giving the client notice as to her potential liability.

In contrast, if the agreed upon legal services are not completed, the client will have no notice that she may be expected to pay the attorney. The expectation to pay for services that have not been completed will arise only if there is express notice of such an obligation. Only in situations where the attorney fails to complete the agreed upon services, and the client therefore has no expectation of needing to pay, is the presence of the notice statement meaningful.

(The court's discussion of "money had and received" is omitted.)

IV. CONCLUSION

We hold that Mullens earned reasonable attorney fees, despite an unenforceable contingency agreement, under quantum meruit. Thus, we reverse the judgment of the court of appeals and remand for the court to decide any remaining issues consistent with this opinion.

CASE QUESTIONS

1. Why do you think contingency fee cases require written agreements?
2. What logical reason could Mullens have had for not getting his client to sign a new fee agreement?
3. One of the advantages of representing clients on a contingency fee basis is not having to keep time sheets. But if you don't keep accurate daily time records, how could you prove your quantum meruit case?
4. After reading this case, what policies would you adopt for your law firm?

CHAPTER

7

COMPETENCE AND NEGLIGENCE

HYPOTHETICAL

Perry has been working as a bankruptcy paralegal for three years for the same firm. He interviews clients, prepares bankruptcy forms, arranges for these forms to be filed, communicates with the clients, and sees their cases through to the end. As most cases only require one appearance by a lawyer, Perry does 90 percent of the work on each case. His supervising lawyer reviews his work but, as of the last year, never has to make any corrections. When Perry's supervising lawyer takes a four-month medical leave of absence, Perry continues working on bankruptcy cases. He prepares a lawyer (one who is not familiar with bankruptcy cases) to make the required appearances. The clients and the firm are happy with Perry's work.

How Is Competence Measured for the Lawyer?

It stands to reason that if a lawyer does competent work, that lawyer has not committed negligence. What does a lawyer have to do to be competent? The answer to that question is in two parts: the civil liability of the lawyer and the criminal liability. A lawyer may be sued by the former client for incompetence and/or prosecuted by the state bar or other regulatory authority. Here we focus on the lawyer's civil liability. We take up the lawyer's criminal liability in Chapter 9.

The modern trend has been to speak in terms of "professional negligence" rather than "malpractice" because that "mal" part of malpractice seems to imply a bad intent.

Rule 1.3:
A lawyer shall act with reasonable diligence and promptness in representing a client.

Rule 1.1
A lawyer shall provide competent representation to a client. Competent representation requires the legal knowledge, skill, thoroughness, and preparation reasonably necessary for the representation.

A lawyer's relationship with a client is that of a *fiduciary*. A fiduciary is a person that stands in a special relation of trust, confidence, or responsibility in certain obligations to another person. That place as a fiduciary means that the lawyer (and the paralegal!) must always act with complete loyalty and good faith toward the client. The good faith part means that the lawyer (and the paralegal!) must act with an amount of skill and care that is befitting a person who is a member of the legal profession. When the level of skill and care goes below that standard, the lawyer may be said to be negligent.

By now you must know a little something about torts. If so, you will recognize that "professional negligence" is, in essence, a negligence case (duty, breach, causation, damages) but the "duty" part is that of a professional. Historically, the plaintiff in a legal professional negligence case had to establish that the lawyer acted in a "grossly negligent" manner toward the client.[1] More recently, however, the plaintiff in a professional negligence case need only establish simple negligence as in any other tort/negligence action. To review: the elements of a negligence cause of action are (1) the existence of the attorney/client relationship (which gives rise to a duty); (2) acts that constitute negligence or the lack of use of reasonable skill and care; (3) that the acts or omissions are the proximate cause of the damage to the client, or "but for" such negligence, the client would have been successful in his or her action; and (4) actual damages.[2]

If we take a simple case in which the client comes to the lawyer with an automobile accident case and the lawyer forgets to file the case within the statute of limitations, we can see how the negligence case against the lawyer will work.

The "duty" part is simply to act as the reasonable lawyer would have under the circumstances. Typically, expert testimony is given as to the standard of care ordinarily used by lawyers in the community, but in this case it seems obvious that the reasonable lawyer would have filed the claim on time. The breach part is when the lawyer fails to file the claim on time. The causation part is going to get a little tricky. In order to prove the "but for" part of the negligence claim, the client/plaintiff must prove that he or she would have won the underlying case (the auto crash case). How can the client/plaintiff prove he or she would have won the underlying case when that case was never filed and no discovery was ever taken in that case? Without any evidence, it's going to be pretty hard to do. The states don't agree on this issue, so this is one of those areas for which you need to look up the law in your state. For example, in one California case, the court held that the lawyer's failure to file a suit before the statute of limitations has run on the action is "plainly malpractice where the attorney can show no reasonable justification for his inaction."[3]

....

CHAPTER OBJECTIVES (CONT.)

How Do These Rules Apply to the Paralegal?
What Is Professional Liability Insurance and Can I Get It?
What's the Best Way to Avoid Professional Negligence?

Prima facie is Latin. It means on its face, on first sight, without closer inspection.

The Illinois Appellate Court, however, held that the plaintiff has to show that "but for" the attorneys' negligence in allowing the statute to run, the plaintiff would have won his or her case.[4]

Where the underlying matter is not a "case" that would have been won or lost by that negligent lawyer, the client/plaintiff's *prima facie* case must show (1) the existence of the attorney/client relationship giving rise to a duty, (2) negligent giving of advice or exercise of judgment on which the client detrimentally relies, and (3) damage to client proximately caused by negligent advice or judgment.[5]

Lack of knowledge or nonobservance of local statutes, rules, and case law can in itself justify a finding by the court of professional negligence.[6] A good way to look at this is that the lawyer "is not an insurer, nor is he answerable to client for every error in judgment or mistake" but the lawyer does "contract to use the reasonable knowledge and skill in the transaction of business which lawyers of ordinary ability and skill possess and exercise."[7]

ABA Model Code EC 6-1: Because of his vital role in the legal process, a lawyer should act with competence and proper care in representing clients. He should strive to become and remain proficient in his practice and should accept employment only in matters which he is or intends to become competent to handle.

The Model Codes of Professional Responsibility are presented here as a historical reference and are not currently used.

Although lawyers will be liable to the client for damages caused by their failure to use care, skill, and diligence, the lawyer will typically not be held liable for new law or indefinite law.[8]

What is "new" will be determined just as the standard of care: what do typical lawyers in the area know? This means that lawyers must take continuing education courses and read about current developments in the law in legal literature. In addition, as we discussed in Chapter 6, the lawyer has the ethical obligation to assist in improving the legal profession and may do so by participating in bar activities intended to advance the quality and standards of members of the profession.

What Is "Mental Competence"?

Many lawyers are disciplined by their state regulatory forces or sued by former clients for lack of competence—but not for the reasons you may be thinking. Competence is the legal knowledge and skill reasonably necessary for the representation but it is also thoroughness and preparation, and those require the right state of mind. There is no rule that says that lawyers must be free from alcohol, drugs, or mental problems. There are several rules, however, requiring the lawyer be diligent in representation of and communication with the client. These rules are violated by lawyers who are suffering from drug or alcohol abuse or mental instability.

NFPA *Model Code EC* 1.3(c)
Should a paralegal's fitness to practice be compromised by physical or mental illness, causing that paralegal to commit an act that is in direct violation of the *Model Code*/*Model Rules* and/or the rules and/or laws governing the jurisdiction in which the paralegal practices, that paralegal may be protected from sanction upon review of the nature and circumstances of that illness.

Millions of Americans suffer from depression, anxiety, and other health problems. Millions more struggle with alcohol and other drug dependency. The law is a stressful place to be. And it is undeniable that people who are stressed often turn to drugs and alcohol. The American Bar Association recognized this problem long ago when it established its Commission on Impaired Attorneys. The commission works as an informational bureau for lawyer-impairment issues and programs. The commission has published surveys of lawyer assistance programs, including each state's opinions on the confidentiality of information about lawyer impairment and rules about immunity from prosecution. These surveys clearly show that the states differ radically on these issues. For example, in the 1980s, one state held that drug addiction may be considered a mitigating factor in lawyer discipline[9] while another court in the same year refused to recognize drug and alcohol addiction as mitigating factors.[10]

In the 1990s, there was a movement among state bars to treat alcoholism and drug dependency as diseases that need to be medically treated. Many states created diversion programs to take the lawyer off the disciplinary track and into a program for counseling, treatment, and monitoring. This would be a good time for you to check your own state's current beliefs in this area.

There is no doubt that drug and alcohol abuse impairs a person's ability to do competent work. What you may not be aware of, however, is the pervasiveness

Rule 5.1
(a) A partner in a law firm, or a lawyer who individually or together with other lawyers possesses managerial authority in a law firm, shall make reasonable efforts to ensure that the firm has in effect measures giving reasonable assurance that all lawyers in the firm conform to the Rules of Professional Conduct.
(b) A lawyer having direct supervisory authority over another lawyer shall make reasonable efforts to ensure that the other lawyer conforms to the Rules of Professional Conduct.
(c) A lawyer shall be responsible for another lawyer's violation of the Rules of Professional Conduct if:
    (1) the lawyer orders or, with knowledge of the specific conduct, ratifies the conduct involved; or
    (2) the lawyer is a partner or has managerial authority in the law firm in which the other lawyer practices, or has direct supervisory authority over the other lawyer, and knows of the conduct at a time when its consequences can be avoided or mitigated but fails to take reasonable remedial action.

of the problem. Take a minute to ponder these statistics: In 2002, 120 million Americans twelve years old and older reported drinking within thirty days of the survey. That's 51 percent of our population. Fifty-four million people reported binge drinking. In 2002, the Substance Abuse and Mental Health Services Administration estimated that 9.4 percent of Americans age twelve and older could be classified as substance abusers or substance dependent. According to the American Bar Association, the corresponding estimate for lawyers is nearly double—15 to 18 percent.

The American Bar Association issued Formal Opinion 03-429 in 2003. This opinion addresses the obligations of lawyers under ABA Model Rule 5.1. The nutshell version is this: impaired lawyers have the same obligations under the ethics rules as other lawyers. Mental impairment does not lessen a lawyer's obligation to provide clients with competent representation. A firm's paramount obligation is to protect the interests of its clients. It is obligated to take all of the necessary steps. We discuss what those steps are in Chapter 9. For purposes of this chapter on competence, however, what you need to know is that impaired professionals are not "competent" within the context of the client who will sue the lawyer under tort, contract, or other theories. The state bar may consider an impairment a mitigating factor in determining an appropriate discipline. Where the lawyer has committed negligence, however, a civil court will look to the harm caused to the client so that the client can be recompensed. The reason for the negligence will not be a factor in assessing damages.

Are There Other Causes of Action against Negligent Lawyers?

Remember that the client and the lawyer signed a contract at the beginning of their relationship. That means that a breach of contract claim is usually brought against the negligent lawyer.

The lawyer clearly breaches his part of the contract when he, for example, fails to file a claim within the statute of limitations. So why bother with all of that proving negligence stuff if it is so obvious that the contract has been breached? Punitive damages are not ordinarily available in contract actions, so the wise plaintiff includes the tort cause of action and tries to prove "gross negligence."

There are even more causes of action and violations of law used in cases against negligent lawyers. For an example of the use of the federal Deceptive Trade Practices Act, read the *Latham* case at the end of this chapter.

What Does It Mean to Be Competent in a Specific Area?

Law is becoming increasingly specialized. As the law becomes more complex, it becomes harder to keep up with the many and varied changes. Gone are the days of the "general practitioner." Lawyers are obligated to only take those cases that they are "competent" to take on. Taken to an extreme, of course, if the lawyer has to know how to do a certain type of matter before taking the first one, the new practitioner could practice nothing and the user of legal services would have to go to a different lawyer for each of his or her different needs. But the Comments to Model Rule 1.1 say that some of the most important skills for the legal practitioner don't have anything to do with knowledge of specific laws. The most important skills are analysis of precedent, evaluation of facts, and legal drafting. To be competent, then, does not mean the memorization of great bodies of law but, rather, those fundamental skills such as being able to determine what kinds of legal problems a situation may involve. Once having analyzed the problems, all of the answers are in the library (either the one down the hall or the virtual one). Diligence and thoroughness, coupled with analytical and drafting abilities, are the keys to competence in the field of law whether you are a lawyer or a paralegal.

To be competent in a specialized area of the law, say tax, more training and more preparation are necessary. To maintain that higher level of competence, continuing education is a must. Continuing education should be more than reading in your chosen area; it should include sharing ideas with others so that you have the opportunity to see how others are interpreting the law. Anyone who wants to know if he or she is truly knowledgeable in an area of the law should try teaching it. Teaching is one of the best ways to learn.

To become competent in a specific area, the new lawyer will have to start with that first case, some extra reading and studying, and talking to others who specialize in that field. Some sage advice given to new lawyers: never be afraid to ask a question; never take on a case unless you are qualified, unless you can get qualified or get assistance. Oh. And have malpractice insurance.

Lawyers who start out on their own take the most risks because they don't have those older lawyers around to train them. Here's a story from California: Attorney Lewis was a solo practitioner who had been admitted to practice in 1972. In 1974, he accepted the representation of a prisoner and, when the prisoner's wife died, he appointed himself administrator of her estate even though he had no previous probate experience. (He initially associated an experienced probate attorney but released him after a short time.) An investigation in 1977 showed that he had not prepared an inventory of the estate nor filed any state, federal, or estate taxes. He had sold the assets of the estate to pay his attorney's fees on the prisoner-client release motions and failed to put the money in an interest-bearing client trust account. The court found, among other things, that attorney Lewis was in violation of a multitude of California ethics rules.[11] Not a good way to start one's career.

Look at some lawyer or law firm advertising and find an advertisement that says "Specializing in . . ." or "Specialist in . . . ." Lawyers who hold themselves out to the public as specialists in areas of law will be held to the standard of care and skill as other specialists of ordinary ability who specialize in the same fields.[12] So, for example, in the case of some lawyers who held themselves out to the public as specialists in maritime law, the court ruled that they should be held to the standard of care of a "reasonably prudent specialist" in that particular and very special field.[13] To prove that standard of care, the court allowed expert testimony of other maritime law specialists in order to determine if the defendant/lawyer breached the duty he owed to his clients.

How Is Negligent Disregard for the Client Different?

We've talked about this before, haven't we? Some lawyers have this irritating habit of ignoring the client. In addition to leading to a complaint against the lawyer with the state's lawyer-regulatory authority, disregard for the client can lead to a professional negligence claim. In *Wells v. State Bar,*[14] the client needed legal help because he had been indicted when he refused to submit to the military draft regulations. His lawyer (Wells) persuaded him to enlist in the military and subsequently file a petition for "conscientious objector" status. Although criminal charges against the client were dropped when he enlisted, they were reinstated shortly thereafter when he was absent without leave in order to prepare his own conscientious objector petition, after having gotten no cooperation from Wells. The client was in constant communication with the lawyer, but each contact resulted in the lawyer's litany of excuses for why the petition had not been prepared. The client eventually submitted his own petition and was released from military service three weeks later. The Supreme Court of California held that Wells's habitual disregard of his client's needs and his virtual abandonment of his client were clearly professional negligence.

Lack of communication with clients is a problem of growing concern to the state bars. Recent polls show that the top client complaint is: "My lawyer doesn't communicate with me." An increasing number of lawyers accept the representation of more clients than they can conceivably represent competently, and that often means neglecting some clients in favor of others. This is where you come in: paralegals can assist their lawyer employers, help the clients, and promote good public relations by keeping clients informed. Clients need to know the important developments in their cases. They need the procedural steps explained to them. They are entitled to explanations for delays. Their telephone calls, e-mail, and letters should be responded to in a timely fashion. With proper supervision and direction, paralegals can and should do all of these tasks. What can be done about the lawyer who isn't doing the legal work, like Mr. Wells? The paralegal can do that part, too, as you know. A paralegal can draft the petition for the lawyer's signature. There is an argument to be made that the lawyer who is negligently not representing the client will also not bother to review the paralegal's work. Proper supervision, including reviewing the paralegal's work, is a mandate under Model Rule 5.3, discussed in Chapter 2. The lawyer who does not properly supervise the paralegal's work assists the paralegal in UPL.

What about Negligent Preparation of Documents?

An excellent resource for case law and articles on negligence is ATLA's *Professional Negligence Law Reporter.*

As we have already discussed, a lawyer is clearly not accountable for the consequences of every act that may later be determined by a court to be an error.[15] It is not possible to draft "litigation proof" documents. (Remember, there is a "reasonably foreseeable" part to that negligence claim.) However, clients have been awarded damages because of a lawyer's negligence in failing to advise the client about the possible effect of a contract,[16] for failing to advise a client that a proposed transaction required a permit,[17] and for not advising clients/purchasers that the business they negotiated for and purchased was subject to liens of creditors that were unknown to them.[18] Drafting documents includes thinking through the possible interpretations of that document sometime in the future when someone tries to enforce it in a court of law and including contingencies for misinterpretation of the parties' intent.

What Are Some Defenses to a Negligence Claim?

In the world of torts, as you have probably already discovered, different states recognize different defenses. Some of these are comparative fault, contributory negligence, and assumption of the risk. You should look at which of these are available in professional negligence cases in your state. Good faith is a defense to professional negligence claims that is typically not found in other negligence cases. The good faith defense says that if the legal professional acts in good faith with an honest belief that his or her acts and advice are in the client's best interest and they are based on accurate information and adequate research, the legal professional will not be liable for mere errors in judgment. For an example, see *In re Watts*,[19] where the U.S. Supreme Court specifically held that innocent error does not violate the lawyer's fiduciary duty.

What Is the Statute of Limitations in Negligence Actions?

The statute of limitations on ordinary negligence cases ordinarily begins to run at the time of the negligent act. With professional negligence, however, it is conceivable that the injured party will not become aware of the problem until many years after the lawyer's representation has ended. For that reason, some courts have held that in cases of negligent drawing of a will, the statute should begin to run at the time of the testator's death when the error will come to light.[20] Problems arise with this theory when it takes many years for a will to be probated. The statute could run without the injured party ever having discovered the professional negligence.

> This is the *discovery rule.*

Check your state law on this. Some states have held that the "discovery" theory for beginning the statute of limitations in lawyer negligence cases is most appropriate.[21] In other words, the statute of limitations on the action does not begin to run until the client has discovered, or a reasonable person should have discovered, the negligence, error, or omission. So, for example, in a case in which the client brought an action against a lawyer for legal malpractice claiming that the lawyer did not ensure that adequate security existed for a debt owed to client arising out of the sale of the client's dry-cleaning business, the court held that the statute of limitations began to run at the time of the buyer's default.[22] The court said:

> The doctrine of *privity* in contract law provides that a contract cannot give rights to or impose obligations on anyone except the parties to the contract.

> The statute of limitations in a legal malpractice action does not begin to run until the client discovers, or should have discovered, the attorney's negligence and the client has sustained actual and appreciable harm. (at 207)

Likewise, when the client is unable to bring a cause of action against the lawyer because the malpractice claimant is in prison or has some other legal or physical problem, the statute will not begin to run until after the claimant is released or is physically well.[23]

Who Can Sue for Professional Negligence?

Another problem in this area is that of the age-old question: to whom is the duty owed? We know that the lawyer owes a duty of due care to the client. In that case, the lawyer and client are also in *privity of contract.* Where the person bringing the negligence claim has actually employed the lawyer or has consulted with the lawyer in contemplation of retaining that lawyer, the privity of contract is clear. The problem arises, for example, where the legal services were the drafting of a will. In that case, the person in privity of contract with the lawyer is dead. That person can't bring a negligence claim. It is the heirs (or the people who claim they should have been heirs!) of the client who want to bring the negligence claim. We have already learned about the discovery rule for these situations. What we have to find is that the lawyer's duty of due care extends beyond the client all the way to the client's heirs and would-be heirs.

Is There a Cause of Action for Negligent Referral?

All states have Lawyer Referral and Information Service (LRIS) organizations. These can be state or local bar associations that members of the public can call for a referral to a lawyer. A typical LRIS will, for a small fee, provide the name and contact information of three lawyers. The member of the public is then responsible for interviewing them and choosing. Lawyers who want to be part of this referral service (typically called "panel members") submit an application to the LRIS that includes information about areas of practice, years in practice, and the existence of professional liability insurance. A few negligent referral cases have been filed against LRIS organizations, but all have been dismissed before trial. In one claim, filed against the Chicago Bar Association,[24] the court ruled that the taking of a referral fee does not make the LRIS and insurer somehow vicariously accountable for any mistakes the lawyer may later make.[25]

Who Will Be Responsible for the Lawyer's Negligence?

A law partnership, as well as all its members, is liable for the negligent acts of the individual members of the firm performed within the scope of their authority[26] but not for acts committed outside of the course of business.[27] In *Nuka v. Williamson,*[28] a New York court did not hold the lawyer's firm liable for his negligence where his negligent acts were committed while the lawyer was acting as counsel for the municipality and were outside of his position with the firm. Limited liability partnerships (LLPs) have proliferated in the 1990s in an attempt to narrow the scope of liability. A limited liability partnership combines some elements of partnerships and corporations. The idea, as the name implies, is to give each partner limited liability while still allowing everyone an active role in the management of the firm. Every state has its own law governing LLPs. The intent of the law is that each partner is not liable for the negligence of the others but most states agree that all partners are liable for contract and intentional tort claims brought against the LLP.[29]

How Do These Rules Apply to the Paralegal?

For paralegals who work under the supervision of a lawyer, the key term here is *respondeat superior*. That's another Latin term we learn in torts, and it means "let the master answer." Because paralegals work under the supervision of a lawyer, and the lawyer is responsible for properly supervising the paralegal and adopts the paralegal's work "as his own," any mistakes the paralegal makes will be the lawyer's responsibility.

Model Rule 5.3(a) advises the lawyer to exercise due care in the selection of competent and trustworthy persons to conduct the affairs of the lawyer's clients. Additionally, that model rule mandates proper delegation and supervision. The lawyer must maintain a relationship with the client, so complete delegation of a client's matter to the paralegal is improper. Under the doctrine of *respondeat superior,* lawyers will be held liable for the negligent acts of all of their nonattorney employees if those acts occur during the course and within the scope of their employment. Further, lawyers will be held negligent themselves for improperly supervising their nonattorney personnel. Obviously, no lawyer can be held to have knowledge of every small detail of his office; he must accept responsibility for the work of his staff.[30]

> **NALA Canon 2**
> A legal assistant may perform any task that is properly delegated and supervised by an attorney, as long as the attorney is ultimately responsible to the client, maintains a direct relationship with the client, and assumes professional responsibility for the work product.

> **NALA Canon 4:**
> A legal assistant must use discretion and professional judgment commensurate with knowledge and experience . . . .

This isn't new. Since the beginning of the use of nonlawyer employees, the lawyer has been held responsible for the errors of employees. In a 1921 case, California held that although a nonlawyer assistant may draft all the pleadings and papers necessary to be drawn for the lawyer's practice, the lawyer is still responsible for examining those papers, approving them, or altering them to meet the standards of due care and diligence of an ordinary attorney of like skill and knowledge.[31] Now that California has adopted law defining paralegals and restricting the use of that designation to people with certain qualifications, the California legislature took the opportunity to spell out that lawyers that use the services of paralegals are expressly responsible for their acts of negligence.[32]

For those paralegals who are delivering legal services directly to the public, there are three choices for the standard of care. The first is that of a reasonable paralegal under the circumstances. When persons represent themselves as having even greater skill than that of the ordinary person, they are typically held to that higher standard. Because paralegals are engaged in a specific profession, they will be held to the standard higher than that of the ordinary person: that of a person of their training and abilities and of the type of professional they hold themselves out to be. The second choice is to hold paralegals to the standard of lawyers. Where paralegals seek to do the same work that lawyers do, they should be held to the same standard of care as lawyers. There is case law to support this theory. Read *Tegman v. Accident & Medical Investigations, Inc.* at the end of this chapter.

To illuminate yet a third way to look at paralegal negligence, take the example of the paralegal who may be found to be engaging in the unauthorized practice of law. If the court finds that a violation of prescribed standards amounts to negligence *per se,* then this paralegal may be found negligent *per se.* On the other hand, many courts have been reluctant to use the *per se* theory when the standard breached is one of licensing. It can be reasoned, then, that if a license is the only thing between a paralegal and a lawyer, these courts would find that license insufficient for a *per se* holding.

However, courts have found that the difference between a layperson and a lawyer is not only the license but also the specialized training and skill. The paralegal is somewhere in between the two, with some specialized training and skill but not quite that of a lawyer. The answer to the *per se* question, then, is: maybe.

Some jurisdictions have held that the compelling reason for licensing statutes is protecting the public from exactly the sort of injury that will be caused by a person who is unlicensed; thus, the incompetence of the particular defendant is of no consequence. That the person is unlicensed is enough. In *Biakanja v. Irving*,[33] a famous California case, a layman improperly prepared certain documents that were subsequently declared unenforceable. His conduct was clearly negligent, but the court muddied the issues by making the point that the defendant was practicing law without a license, which may have led them to a negligence *per se* holding. In New York, however, a court held that representation by an unlicensed person did

> *Per se* is Latin. It means "without more."

NALA Canon 6
A legal assistant must strive to maintain integrity and a high degree of competency through education and training with respect to professional responsibility, local rules and practice, and through continuing education in substantive areas of law to better assist the legal profession in fulfilling its duty to provide legal service.

NFPA *Model Code* EC 1.1
Ethical Considerations
EC 1.1(a) A paralegal shall achieve competency through education, training, and work experience.
EC 1.1(b) A paralegal shall aspire to participate in a minimum of twelve (12) hours of continuing legal education, to include at least one (1) hour of ethics education, every two (2) years in order to remain current on developments in the law.
EC 1.1(c) A paralegal shall perform all assignments promptly and efficiently.

not *per se* void all proceedings.[34] The court remanded the issue for an investigation into the adequacy of the representation.

Paralegals have to be competent just as lawyers must. You can always improve your level of competence by getting more legal training and education and staying current with your legal specialty by reading professional publications and attending continuing legal education programs. Participating in legal and professional associations dedicated to the advancement of the paralegal profession will also increase your competence.

The lawyer who tries to blame his or her incompetence on staff members will not be looked upon favorably by the courts.[35] Remember, Model Rule 5.3 and all of the different ways that Model Rule has been adopted in the various states make the lawyer responsible for appropriate hiring, delegation, and supervision.

What Are Some Specific Acts or Omissions as Negligence?

> ABA Model Code EC 6-6 A lawyer should not seek, by contract or other means, to limit his individual liability to his client for malpractice.
>
> * The Model Codes of Professional Responsibility are presented here as a historical reference and are not currently used.

Legal professionals will be liable for any loss sustained by their client as a result of their negligent failure to prepare, file, or serve the appropriate pleadings.[36] A lawyer can even be found negligent for not taking a case. In *Dogstad v. Veseley, Otto, Miller & Keefe,*[37] a lawyer failed to do the minimum research before assessing the merits of a claim and before telling the client that there was no cause of action in her complaints. Further, he failed to inform the client about the impending running of the statute of limitations. The court had first to find that the attorney/client relationship had been established during the initial client interview in spite of the lack of formal contract and lack of evidence that the client paid anything to the lawyer. It then held that the lawyer's omissions were negligent.

Parker v. Carnahan[38] was a summary judgment case from Texas in which the court found a triable issue of whether lawyers were negligent in failing to advise an individual that they were not representing her. The duty arises "if the fact finder determines that attorneys were aware or should have been aware that their conduct would have led a reasonable person to believe that she was being represented by the attorneys." We discussed this in Chapter 6 when we were talking about creating the relationship with the client. If your firm decides not to take a case, clear written communication should be made with that person to inform them of your "we're not representing you" position.

In *Rice v. Forestier,*[39] the lawyer was held to be negligent for failing to tell a client that he refused to handle a case. The lawyer had represented the client in a voluntary bankruptcy proceeding. When the client was served with a complaint by a creditor and the client had the papers delivered to his lawyer, the lawyer had the complaint placed in the client's file but failed to notify the client that he did not intend to file an answer or take other responsive action. The court found that the lawyer's negligent failure to communicate with his client caused a default to be taken against the client personally, instead of against his corporation, and that had the client not retained another lawyer, he would have lost his home to the creditors of the corporation.

A law firm that had been retained by a physician's insurer to defend a medical malpractice action was held liable for damages incurred by the physician when it settled the action contrary to his specific instructions.[40] On the other hand, holding that a lawyer cannot be held liable for a mistake in judgment, the court in *Glenna v. Sullivan*[41] found that the lawyer who recommended that his client accept a settlement from the insurance company when the client's medical record indicated that her injuries may have been caused by a previous accident was not negligent. His advice was given in good faith after diligent study of the information available to him.

What Is Professional Liability Insurance and Can I Get It?

Lawyers' professional liability insurance became available after World War II. Before that time, only Lloyds of London would underwrite a policy for any professional other than a doctor. Because of the increasingly complex nature of the law and legal practice, compounded by the fact that cases handled by lawyers involve increasingly large amounts of money, professional liability insurance has become a standard expense of the practicing lawyer. Some states require that a lawyer disclose his or her liability insurance (or lack thereof) in each retainer agreement so that the client can make an informed choice.

If you are a Legal Document Assistant or Unlawful Detainer Assistant in California, you had to post a $25,000 bond. The bond is your promise to pay if you are found to owe a client money for any reason. If you don't pay, the money will be paid by the company that bonded you. Then the bond company comes after you for the money. Before giving you the bond (which usually costs a small percentage of the bond value), the bonding company asked you for a source of collateral such as your house or money in a bank account. It would work this way: say you are found to be negligent to the tune of $10,000. The bond company will pay that amount to the plaintiff. Then the bond company will look to you for the $10,000. If your house was listed as collateral and you cannot pay the debt any other way, the bond company has the right to have your house sold so that you can pay them back the $10,000. Insurance doesn't work that way. Say you want a $1 million policy. You pay the insurance company an amount for the policy. This is called a premium. The amount of the premium is based on the insurance company's estimate of your risk as a customer. When the court awards your former client a $10,000 judgment, the insurance company will have to pay the money you owe to the plaintiff but it will not come looking to you for reimbursement. That was the risk that the insurance company took when it sold you the insurance policy. Of course, it has the right to refuse to insure you anymore after the expiration of the policy you paid for or it may increase the amount of your premium because it has determined that you are a bigger risk than it originally thought.

Professional liability insurance is available to paralegals through a number of companies that you can find on the Internet or through your paralegal association.

Policies look very much like policies for lawyers and have similar coverage. The premiums, however, are substantially less. This may be because the potential liability of a paralegal, who primarily works for a lawyer, is lower than the potential liability of the lawyer. If, indeed, the doctrine of *respondeat superior* still protects the negligent paralegal, what is the need for insurance? There's this one: many lawyers don't have professional liability insurance. If the paralegal is negligent, the paralegal may well be sued. Even if not found liable, professional liability insurance will protect the paralegal from prohibitively high defense costs. As there have been instances of paralegals being named as defendants in professional liability suits, this type of insurance is something to think about.

NALS Code Canon 1. Members of this association shall maintain a high degree of competency and integrity through continuing education to better assist the legal profession in fulfilling its duty to provide quality legal services to the public.

Freelance paralegals may have a more likely potential liability, as they may not be covered by a lawyer's policy and the lawyer-employer may not have liability insurance (also known as *errors and omissions* or *E&O* insurance). Those who walk the dangerous line of practicing law without a license should also think seriously about this kind of insurance. Legal technicians, authorized to practice in limited areas, should look at professional liability insurance. You can be held liable for legal malpractice even if you are not licensed to practice law,[42] although it is unlikely that you can be insured for malpractice if you are not authorized to engage in the activity in which the malpractice was committed.

Additionally, independent insurance coverage may make you more desirable when you are looking for a job. In any case, it is a good idea to find out if your employer has liability insurance and look into your own if you are not otherwise covered.

Ordinarily, professional liability insurance covers direct financial loss and expense to the legal professional or a firm that arise from claims of neglect, omissions, or errors. This type of insurance does not cover bodily injury or property damage and will compensate only for loss that actually "arises from" the conduct of professional legal services. Professional liability insurance also usually does not compensate for intentional torts, only negligence.

Chuck Herring, a Texas attorney who authored a textbook called *Texas Legal Malpractice and Lawyer Discipline,* says that the average lawyer can expect to be sued for professional negligence three times during a career. Real estate lawyers are more prone to attract claims than are their colleagues in other specialties. A survey done by the American Bar Association a few years ago found that malpractice claims involving real estate were second only to claims involving personal injury law.

What's the Best Way to Avoid Professional Negligence?

Some rules of thumb for the successful legal professional follow:

1. Keep abreast of changes in the law. Take continuing education classes. Read legal journals and periodicals.

2. Hold yourself out as a specialist in a field only if you have worked in that field for a substantial length of time or have a specialist certificate in that field.

3. Be completely honest about what you know how to do and what you do not know how to do. If you are unsure of your skills, be sure that you are working in a place where you will get training and supervision.

4. Keep in mind that your loyalties must be to your firm, supervising attorney, paralegal supervisor, and your firm's clients. Don't let outside influences affect the quality of your work.

5. As soon as you notice a problem, such as a missed statute of limitations or other error, bring it to the attention of your supervisor.

6. Never, under any circumstances, try to hide a potential ethical or legal problem.

When we were discussing making contracts with the client, we discussed ABA Model Rule 1.8(h). It says that legal professionals must not attempt to limit their liability for professional negligence by contract with their client. In other words, you can't put a clause in the engagement contract that says that the client agrees to never hold the lawyer responsible for negligence. That makes sense. Otherwise, everyone would include that clause and no client would ever be able to sue a lawyer for negligence.

SUMMARY

In this chapter, we took a hard look at what it means to be a competent legal practitioner. Although the rule seems clear and simplistic (competence is the legal skill, knowledge, preparation, and thoroughness required for each matter), in practice the rule is far from clear. Alcohol and drug abuse will render the practitioner "not competent." Although a lawyer will not be held to guarantee every action, document, or procedure, the lawyer is primarily expected to have the skills of analysis of precedent, evaluation of facts, and legal drafting. The lawyer who purports to be a specialist, however, will be held to the standards of a specialist. The biggest problem, the one most commonly complained about, is lack of communication—an area in which the paralegal can be of great value to the lawyer. The doctrine of *respondeat superior* will shield the traditional paralegal from personal liability for errors, but there is at least one recent case that stands for the proposition that the paralegal who works as a lawyer will be held to the standards of a lawyer and will suffer the same consequences. People who are in privity of contract may sue the lawyer for negligence, breach of contract, and other causes of action. Professional liability insurance is available to lawyers and paralegals to pay for attorney's fees and damages in many instance of incompetence.

CHAPTER REVIEW AND ASSIGNMENTS

CRITICAL THINKING

1. Go back to the "Hypothetical" at the beginning of this chapter. Is Perry doing the right thing representing the firm's bankruptcy clients? Will Perry or the firm incur any liability for any mistakes he makes? If Perry makes a mistake, can he be sued for negligence? To what standard will Perry be held? Is his firm in any trouble? What actions, if any, may be brought against the firm by the regulatory authority in Perry's state? To help you with your answer, review the *Tegman* case at the end of this chapter.

2. Wilson, an office manager for a very busy sole practitioner, notices a dormant file that has slipped down in back of a file cabinet. When he investigates the file, he notes that the statute of limitations runs out at the end of the day and the complaint has not been filed. Wilson does not have enough time to draft a complaint and get the rest of his work done. He does not know if this case was settled, if the plaintiff is still a client, or if the lawyer intended to file a complaint. His employer lawyer is out of town. What steps should Wilson take?

3. Senior Paralegal Kathy has been asked to draft a type of document that is unfamiliar to her. She researches some old firm files and finds a printed document published by a bank, which is the document she has been asked to draft. Kathy copies most of the printed form and presents her document to the supervising attorney as her own work. Is Kathy liable for plagiarism? See *Federal Intermediate Credit Bank of Louisville v. Kentucky Bar Assn.*, 540 S.W.2d 14 (Ky. 1976).

4. Stanford, a paralegal, is assisting his employer with a pro bono matter. Because the time spent on this matter is not "billable," Stanford does not give it his full attention. Is Stanford correct in his belief that a pro bono case is not entitled to the same diligence and competence as a paying client's matter? See *Franko v. Mitchel,* 762 P.2d 1345 (Ariz. 1988).

ASSIGNMENTS

1. You're interviewing for a job. How can you find out if the law firm has professional liability insurance? How would this question/discussion go?

2. Each state has its own statute of limitations on malpractice actions. Research your state statute on the time within which an action must be brought. When does the statutory time begin to run? What events might "toll" the statute in your state?

3. Is professional liability insurance mandated in your state? Is there an obligation to inform potential clients about professional liability insurance? Before you research the answer to those questions, write a paragraph about what you think the answer is and why. What are some reasons for requiring insurance? Why is it important (or is it?) for the client to be aware of whether the firm has insurance?

4. Where can you get insurance? How much will it cost? What are the insurance policy limits? Download an insurance policy and read through it so that you have an understanding of what is covered and what is not.

COLLABORATIVE ASSIGNMENT

1. This is a perfect place for some role-play. One student (or the teacher) can be the supervising lawyer. The other students can be paralegals who have discovered a missed statute of limitations or other error.

REVIEW QUESTIONS

Multiple Choice

Select the best answer for each of the following questions.

1. Competence means
   a. diligence, thoroughness, adequate preparation, knowledge, and skill.
   b. complying with requests from the client for information.
   c. doing the job as well as possible.
   d. getting the proper education.
   e. none of the above.

2. The most common complaint by clients about lawyers is regarding
   a. the lawyer's failure to communicate.
   b. the price of legal representation.
   c. the length of the wait for a trial.
   d. the rude behavior by lawyers and staff members.
   e. the slow pace of the court system.

3. Delegation by a lawyer to a paralegal of legal tasks is proper if
   a. The lawyer maintains a direct relationship with his or her client.
   b. The lawyer supervises the delegated work.
   c. The lawyer takes responsibility for the work product.
   d. All of the above.
   e. None of the above. Delegation is improper.

4. All states' codes of professional conduct applicable to legal professionals
   a. prohibit incompetent, unethical, or irresponsible individuals from practicing law.
   b. tell legal professionals about their duties toward their clients.
   c. are minimum guidelines of ethical conduct.
   d. all of the above.
   e. none of the above.

5. Paralegals can improve their level of competence through
   a. obtaining additional legal training and/or education.
   b. reading legal and professional publications to remain current with news of the legal specialty in which they practice and related professional issues.

c. participating in legal and professional associations dedicated to the advancement of the paralegal profession.

d. *a* and *b*, but not *c*.

e. all of the above.

6. Paralegals are obligated to perform work for the client competently because

a. The employing lawyer will be liable if they do not.

b. They have an ethical obligation to perform competently.

c. They have potential tort liability for incompetence.

d. All of the above.

e. None of the above.

7. The person (or people) who can sue the lawyer for incompetence is (are)

a. only the client who paid the lawyer.

b. the client who paid the lawyer and that person's family.

c. all of the people in privity of contract with the client.

d. all of the people to whom the lawyer owed a fiduciary duty.

e. all of the people in privity of contract with the lawyer.

8. When the lawyer attributes all or part of his or her negligence to a staff member (secretary, clerk, or paralegal),

a. The lawyer will be viewed more favorably by the disciplinary authorities.

b. The lawyer will not be viewed more favorably by the disciplinary authorities.

c. The lawyer's penalty will be reduced.

d. The lawyer's penalty will be reduced if the responsible staff person has been fired.

e. The lawyer will probably avoid liability altogether.

9. The doctrine of *respondeat superior* means

a. The employer is responsible for the wrongs of the employee.

b. It's okay for the paralegal to be negligent.

c. The lawyer will be solely responsible for the paralegal's negligence.

d. The lawyer is responsible for the intentional torts of his or her staff members.

e. The partners of the law firm will have to pay the employees of the law firm.

10. One of the biggest problems facing the paralegal in the area of competence is

a. There are not enough good schools.

b. Lawyers are not adept at delegating.

c. A paralegal has inadequate liability insurance.

d. There is insufficient case law to determine paralegal competence.

e. Lawyers are not competent.

Fill In the Blank

Complete each of the following sentences with the best word(s) or phrase(s).

1. Under the doctrine of _____, attorney employers are liable for the dishonest acts of their paralegal employees under the course and scope of the paralegal's employment.

2. ABA *Model Rules of Professional Conduct* numbers _____ and _____ apply to competence.

3. A fiduciary is _____ _____.

4. Another term for "malpractice" is _____.

5. Two ways to stay competent in your area of the law are _____ and _____.

6. The statute of limitations in a professional liability case ordinarily begins to run _____ (I'm looking for "when").

7. The rule referred to in Question 6 is called the _____ Rule.

8. The people who can sue the lawyer for malpractice are everyone _____.

9. Insurance that lawyers and law firms typically get to cover them for negligence is called_____.

10. Being competent requires _____.

True/False

Decide whether each of the following statements is true or false and write your answer on the line provided.

____ 1. A lawyer's relationship with a client is that of a fiduciary.

____ 2. Negligence is a tort.

____ 3. Lawyers will be held liable for damages caused by their lack of knowledge about the law regardless of how new that law may be.

____ 4. There is no such thing as mental competence.

____ 5. Negligent lawyers may also be sued on a breach of contract claim.

____ 6. Negligent disregard for a client is not something that we need to worry about since the inventions of e-mail and cell phones.

____ 7. The statute of limitations in negligence claims is typically four years.

____ 8. Paralegals should encourage their employers to sponsor paralegal attendance and participation in continuing legal education opportunities as part of maintaining and improving paralegal competence.

____ 9. The doctrine of *superior intelligencia* will protect paralegals from liability for incompetence.

____ 10. Only people in privity of contract with the lawyer have standing to sue for malpractice.

CASES FOR CONSIDERATION

CASE 1

Latham v. Castillo
972 S.W.2d 66
(Tex. 1998)

In this case, we consider whether an attorney's affirmative misrepresentations to his clients that cause the clients to lose their day in court can constitute unconscionable action under the Deceptive Trade Practices–Consumer Protection Act (DTPA). The court of appeals answered in the affirmative. We affirm the court of appeals' remand of the DTPA claim, and we reverse and render judgment that the Castillos take nothing on their remaining claims.

I.

On January 3, 1986, Audona Castillo prematurely gave birth to twin daughters, Kay and Sara, at Taft Hospital. Born with birth defects, the girls were immediately transferred to Driscoll Foundation Children's Hospital where both underwent surgery. Sara died approximately one week later. The Castillos then filed a medical malpractice suit against Driscoll Hospital on Sara's behalf and received a $6,000,000 default judgment. Later, their attorney, Rene Rodriguez, settled the case for $70,000.

Kay Castillo, the surviving twin, died on February 14, 1988. In December 1989, the Castillos hired B. Mills Latham to file a legal malpractice claim against Rodriguez for settling the default judgment and to pursue a medical malpractice claim against Driscoll Hospital for Kay's death. While Latham settled the legal malpractice claim against Rodriguez for $400,000, the statute of limitations ran on the Castillos' medical malpractice claim on February 14, 1990 without suit being filed. The Castillos then sued Latham for legal malpractice because Latham failed to file the medical malpractice action for Kay's death within the two-year statute of limitations. The Castillos also sued Latham for unconscionable action under the DTPA because Latham affirmatively represented to them that he had filed and was actively prosecuting the medical malpractice claim. Finally, the Castillos alleged that Latham wrongfully misrepresented himself, breached the contract of employment, and was negligent.

After the Castillos presented their case to a jury, the trial court granted a directed verdict for Latham that the Castillos take nothing. The court of appeals reversed and remanded, holding that the Castillos had presented some evidence to prevent a directed verdict on their DTPA claim. The court of appeals also remanded the "remaining theories of recovery"—fraudulent misrepresentation and breach of contract—without discussion. The court of appeals affirmed the directed verdict on the negligence claim, however, because the Castillos did not present evidence that but for Latham's negligence, the medical malpractice suit would have been successful.

The central question before us is whether the Castillos have presented some evidence to support each element of their DTPA cause of action. We hold that they have done so.

II.

The trial court granted a directed verdict against the Castillos on all claims. Accordingly, we must view the evidence in the light most favorable to them and indulge every reasonable inference in their favor. *Harbin v. Seale,* 461 S.W.2d 591, 592 (Tex. 1970). If reasonable minds could differ on controlling facts, the trial court errs in refusing to submit the issues to the jury. *Collora v. Navarro,* 574 S.W.2d 65, 68 (Tex. 1978). We consider the DTPA claim first.

A.

The Castillos alleged Latham's conduct constituted an "unconscionable action or course of action" that violated the DTPA. *Tex. Bus. & Com. Code* § 17.50(a)(3). Under section 17.45, "unconscionable action or course of action" means "an act or practice which, to a person's detriment: (A) takes advantage of the lack of knowledge, ability, experience, or capacity of a person to a grossly unfair degree; or (B) results in a gross disparity between the value received and consideration paid, in a transaction involving transfer of consideration." Id. § 17.45(5). The Castillos have relied only on subsection (A) in asserting that Latham's actions were unconscionable. To be actionable under subsection (A), the resulting unfairness must be "glaringly noticeable, flagrant, complete and unmitigated." *Chastain v. Koonce,* 700 S.W.2d 579, 584 (Tex. 1985).

The Legislature's stated public policy in enacting the DTPA is to "protect consumers against false, misleading, and deceptive business practices [and] unconscionable actions." *Tex. Bus. & Com. Code* § 17.44. To achieve that goal, the Legislature has mandated that the Act shall be "liberally construed and applied." Id. Therefore, we must view Latham's actions with this legislative directive in mind.

Attorneys can be found to have engaged in unconscionable conduct by the way they represent their clients. See, e.g., *DeBakey v. Staggs,* 605 S.W.2d 631, 633 (Tex. Civ. App.—Houston [1st Dist.] 1980), writ ref'd n.r.e. per curiam, 612 S.W.2d 924 (Tex. 1981) (finding an attorney unconscionably took advantage of a client to a grossly unfair degree when the attorney knowingly failed to obtain in a timely manner a name change for the client's minor child). The Castillos assert that Latham acted unconscionably in representing that he was actively prosecuting their medical malpractice claim for Kay's death when in fact he was not.

The Castillos depended on Latham to file suit against the hospital for Kay's death. As Mrs. Castillo testified, "You trust in a professional because they know more than you." The record reveals, and Latham's attorney conceded at oral argument before this Court, that there is some evidence that Latham told the Castillos he had filed the medical malpractice claim when in fact he had not. Although he affirmatively represented to them that he was actively pursuing the claim, Latham never did file the suit and limitations ran. As a result, the Castillos lost the opportunity to prosecute their claim against the hospital for Kay's death.

Viewing Latham's actions in the light we must, his actions are similar to the attorney's conduct in *DeBakey.* Latham took advantage of the trust the Castillos placed in him as an attorney. Therefore, the Castillos have presented some evidence that they were taken advantage of to a grossly unfair degree.

Latham argues, however, that the Castillos' DTPA claim is essentially a dressed-up legal malpractice claim. Therefore, he asserts, the Castillos must prove that they would have won the medical malpractice case for Kay's death in order to recover. Because they did not present any evidence on this, Latham argues, the Castillos cannot recover. We disagree.

The legislative intent in enacting the DTPA was to provide plaintiffs a remedy where the common law fails. See *Woo v. Great Southwestern Acceptance Corp.,* 565 S.W.2d 290, 298 (Tex. Civ. App.—Waco 1978, writ ref'd n.r.e.). Section 17.43 states that the remedies provided by the Act "are in addition to any other procedures or remedies provided for in any other law." *Tex. Bus. & Com. Code* § 17.43 (emphasis added). Moreover, the Legislature mandates that the DTPA is to be "liberally construed and applied to promote its underlying purposes." Id. § 17.44. Recasting the Castillos' DTPA claim as merely a legal malpractice claim would subvert the Legislature's clear purpose in enacting the DTPA—to deter deceptive business practices.

If the Castillos had only alleged that Latham negligently failed to timely file their claim, their claim would properly be one for legal malpractice. However, the Castillos alleged and presented some evidence that Latham affirmatively misrepresented to them that he had filed and was actively prosecuting their claim. It is the difference between negligent conduct and deceptive conduct. To recast this claim as one for legal malpractice is to ignore this distinction. The Legislature enacted the DTPA to curtail this type of deceptive conduct. Thus, the DTPA does not require and the Castillos need not prove the "suit within a suit" element when suing an attorney under the DTPA. The Castillos have presented some evidence of unconscionable action.

It is not enough that the Castillos merely prove an unconscionable action or course of action by Latham, however. Latham's unconscionable action must have been the producing cause of actual damages. *Tex. Bus. & Com. Code* § 17.50(a). Latham argues that the Castillos cannot recover mental anguish damages under the DTPA without first proving an economic injury. We disagree.

Section 17.50(a) of the DTPA, as it appeared when this suit was filed, indicated that "[a] consumer may maintain an action where any of the following constitute a producing cause of actual damages." *Tex. Bus. & Com. Code* § 17.50(a) (emphasis added). We have stated that the term "actual damages," as used in the DTPA, means those recoverable at common law. *Brown v. American Transfer & Storage Co.,* 601 S.W.2d 931, 939 (Tex. 1980). It is axiomatic that mental anguish damages are actual damages recoverable at common law for "some common law torts . . . , and by analogy for knowing violations of certain statutes such as the Deceptive Trade Practices Act." *City of Tyler v. Likes,* 962 S.W.2d 489, 495 (Tex. 1997) (citations omitted).

Therefore, the Castillos do not have to first prove that they have suffered economic damages in order to recover mental anguish damages. The Castillos have satisfied their burden on the damages element of a DTPA cause of action if they have presented some evidence of mental anguish.

In *Parkway Co. v. Woodruff,* 901 S.W.2d 434 (Tex. 1995), we established the evidentiary requirements for recovery of mental anguish damages. To survive a legal sufficiency challenge, plaintiffs must present "direct evidence of the nature, duration, and severity of their mental anguish, thus establishing a substantial disruption in the plaintiffs' daily routine." Id. at 444. If there is no direct evidence, the Court will apply "traditional 'no evidence' standards to determine whether the record reveals any evidence of 'a high degree of mental pain and distress' that is 'more than mere worry, anxiety, vexation, embarrassment, or anger' to support any award of damages." Id. (citation omitted).

The plaintiffs in *Parkway* alleged that they were "hot," "very disturbed," "not pleased," and "upset." Id. at 445. We held that these allegations were "mere emotions" that did not rise to a compensable level. Id.; see also *Saenz v. Fidelity & Guar. Ins. Underwriters,* 925 S.W.2d 607, 614 (Tex. 1996) (holding that plaintiff's allegations that she "worried . . . a lot" did not rise to a compensable level under *Parkway*); *Republic Ins. Co. v. Stoker,* 903 S.W.2d 338, 342 (Tex. 1995) (Spector, J., concurring) (stating that plaintiff's allegations that she was "very upset" by the offending conduct did not rise to the level of any evidence of compensable mental anguish required under *Parkway*). In each of these cases, the plaintiffs' evidence of mental anguish amounted to "mere emotions." The mental anguish testimony in this record, however, exceeds that in *Parkway, Saenz,* and *Stoker.*

For example, at trial Ernest Castillo testified that because Latham told them he had filed the medical malpractice suit when in fact he had not:

A   Well, it made me throw up.

Q   Made you sick?

A   Sick, nervous, mad.

Q   Tell the jury how you felt about that, what it did to you.

A   It just—it just hurt me a lot because I trusted in him and I—and if I had known, I would have looked for more lawyers. And he promised me he was going [to] do it, and I trusted him to do it. Because of what they had done to my daughters, I would have never stopped; what the doctors done, I would have never stopped.

      Audona Castillo testified at trial:

A   I—my heart was broken. I was devastated, I felt physically ill.

In sum, there is some evidence that Latham's conduct caused the Castillos a "high degree of mental pain and distress" that a jury could consider. We are confident that the trial judge will instruct the jury to differentiate between the mental anguish the Castillos suffered because of their daughters' deaths, which is not compensable in this suit, and that they may have suffered because of Latham's actions, for which the Castillos may be compensated.

The Castillos have presented some evidence of each element of their DTPA cause of action and the trial court erred in directing a verdict against them on the DTPA claim. We therefore remand this claim to the trial court for a new trial.

B.

The Castillos also complained in the court of appeals that the trial court erred in granting a directed verdict on their fraudulent misrepresentation and breach of contract claims. The court of appeals sustained these points of error without discussion and remanded them to the trial court. The court of appeals erred by not discussing issues necessary to final disposition of the appeal. See *Tex. R. App.* P. 47.1. Upon our consideration of these issues, we find no evidence to support these claims.

Under common law, two measures of damages are available for fraudulent misrepresentation: (1) the "out of pocket" measure, which is the "difference between the value of that which was parted with and the value of that which was received"; and (2) the "benefit of the bargain" measure, which is the difference between the value represented and the value actually received. *Formosa Plastics Corp. USA v. Presidio Eng'rs & Contractors, Inc.,* 960 S.W.2d 41, 49 (Tex. 1997); *W.O. Bankston Nissan, Inc. v. Walters,* 754 S.W.2d 127, 128 (Tex. 1988) (citing *Leyendecker & Assocs., Inc. v. Wechter,* 683 S.W.2d 369, 373 (Tex. 1984)). A plaintiff may recover either the out of pocket or the benefit of the bargain damages, whichever is greater. *Arthur Andersen & Co. v. Perry Equip. Corp.,* 945 S.W.2d 812, 817 (Tex. 1997). The Castillos have not pleaded or proved either of these types of damages.

The Castillos presented no evidence of the amount they expected to recover on the medical malpractice claim for Kay's death but for Latham's actions. See *Cosgrove v. Grimes,* 774 S.W.2d 662, 665–66 (Tex. 1989). Accordingly, they presented no evidence to support benefit of the bargain damages. The Castillos also did not demonstrate any out of pocket expenses paid to Latham. Therefore, the Castillos have not presented any evidence of recoverable common-law fraudulent misrepresentation damages, and the trial court correctly granted a directed verdict on this claim.

C.

Finally, the Castillos have alleged a breach of contract claim against Latham for his failure to prosecute the medical malpractice claim for Kay's death. However, because the only damages alleged, mental anguish, are not recoverable under a breach of contract cause of action, this claim also fails. See *Stewart Title Guar. Co. v. Aiello,* 941 S.W.2d 68, 72 (Tex. 1997).

III.

We hold that the Castillos have presented some evidence to support each element of their DTPA cause of action. Therefore, we affirm the court of appeals' remand of the DTPA cause of action. We nevertheless reverse and render judgment that the Castillos take nothing on their fraudulent misrepresentation and breach of contract claims.

CASE QUESTIONS

1. What was the effect of using the Deceptive Trade Practices Act rather than an ordinary claim of negligence for the case Latham neglected to file?
2. Why didn't the Castillos' claim for fraudulent misrepresentation work? Why was it dismissed by the court?
3. Why did the breach of contract claim fail? Do you think the Castillos have a cause of action in negligence against the lawyer who prosecuted this malpractice claim?
4. What actions could attorney Latham have taken to avoid this professional negligence?

CASE 2

Tegman v. Accident & Medical Investigations, Inc.
107 Wn.App. 868, 30 P.3d 8
(2001)

Becker, J.—When a paralegal performs legal services with knowledge that there is no supervising attorney responsible for the case, the paralegal will be held to an attorney's standard of care. Attorneys have a duty to keep their clients informed about material developments in their cases. The trial court found that Deloris Mullen, a paralegal, and Lorinda Noble, an attorney, while employed by a non-lawyer who represented accident victims, breached this duty and caused harm to the plaintiffs when they failed to advise them of the risk involved with allowing a nonlawyer to settle their cases. We affirm the judgments.

The trial court's findings of fact present the following account of the events surrounding this dispute. Between 1989 and 1991, plaintiffs Maria Tegman, Linda Leszynski, and Daina Calixto were each injured in separate and unrelated automobile accidents. After their accidents, each plaintiff retained G. Richard McClellan and Accident & Medical Investigations, Inc. (AMI), for legal counsel and assistance in handling their personal injury claims. McClellan and AMI purported to represent each plaintiff in seeking compensation from insurance companies for their injuries. Each plaintiff signed a contingency fee agreement with AMI, believing that McClellan was an attorney and AMI a law firm. McClellan has never been an attorney in any jurisdiction.

McClellan and AMI employed Camille Jescavage and Lorinda Noble, both licensed attorneys. Jescavage and Noble learned that McClellan entered into contingency fee agreements with AMI's clients and that McClellan was not an attorney. They settled a number of cases for AMI, and learned that McClellan processed settlements of AMI cases through his own bank account. Noble resigned from AMI in May 1991, after working there approximately six months.

In July 1991, McClellan hired Deloris Mullen as a paralegal. Mullen considered Jescavage to be her supervising attorney though Jescavage provided little supervision. Jescavage resigned from AMI in the first week of September 1991. McClellan told Mullen that her new supervising attorney would be James Bailey. Mullen did not immediately contact Bailey to confirm that he was her supervising attorney. He later told her he was not.

While at AMI, Mullen worked on approximately 50–60 cases, including those of plaintiffs Tegman, Leszynski and Calixto. Mullen was aware of some of McClellan's questionable practices and knew that there were substantial improprieties involved with his operation. Mullen stopped working at AMI on December 6, 1991, when the situation became personally intolerable to her and she obtained direct knowledge that she was without a supervising attorney. When she left, she did not advise any of the plaintiffs about the problems at AMI.

After Mullen left, McClellan settled each plaintiff's case for various amounts without their knowledge or consent, and deposited the funds in his general account by forging their names on the settlement checks.

In 1993, Calixto, Leszynski, and Tegman each individually sued McClellan, AMI, Mullen, and Jescavage. Tegman also sued Noble. Their complaints sought damages on various theories. The cases were consolidated. Discovery took place between 1993 and 1998. In the interim, McClellan pleaded guilty to mail fraud in United States District Court in 1997 and was sentenced to two years imprisonment. Also, this court affirmed a judgment by the same trial court in another case where McClellan settled a client's case without authorization and stole the proceeds. *Bullard v. Bailey,* 91 Wn.App. 750, 959 P.2d 1122 (1998). That judgment apportioned

20 percent fault to attorney James Bailey who, like Noble and Jescavage, had associated himself with AMI and failed to warn his clients of McClellan's improprieties.

In the present matter, the court entered summary judgment against McClellan and AMI on the issue of liability. After a six-day trial, the court held Mullen, Noble, and Jescavage liable for negligence and legal negligence, and awarded damages. Only Mullen and Noble appeal. Their appeals have been consolidated.

STANDARD OF REVIEW

An appellate brief must include argument in support of issues presented for review, together with citations to legal authority. See RAP 10.3(a)(5). Assignments of error not argued in a brief are deemed abandoned. *Valley View Indus. Park v. City of Redmond,* 107 Wn.2d 621, 630, 733 P.2d 182 (1987); *Pappas v. Hershberger,* 85 Wn.2d 152, 153, 530 P.2d 642 (1975). Accordingly, we review only those assignments of error that are supported by argument in appellants' briefs.

Our review of a trial court's findings of fact and conclusions of law is a two-step process. We first determine whether the trial court's findings of fact were supported by substantial evidence in the record. *Landmark Dev., Inc. v. City of Roy,* 138 Wn.2d 561, 573, 980 P.2d 1234 (1999). Substantial evidence is evidence which, viewed in the light most favorable to the party prevailing below, would persuade a fair-minded, rational person of the truth of the finding. *State v. Hill,* 123 Wn.2d 641, 644, 870 P.2d 313 (1994). If the findings are adequately supported, we next decide whether those findings of fact support the trial court's conclusions of law. *Landmark Dev.,* 138 Wn.2d at 573.

PARALEGAL NEGLIGENCE

Mullen, a paralegal, contends the court erred in finding her negligent. To establish the elements of an action for negligence, a plaintiff must show: (1) the existence of a duty owed, (2) breach of that duty, (3) a resulting injury, and (4) a proximate cause between the breach and the injury. *Iwai v. State,* 129 Wn.2d 84, 96, 915 P.2d 1089 (1996).

Nonattorneys who attempt to practice law will be held to the same standards of competence demanded of attorneys and will be liable for negligence if these standards are not met. *Bowers v. Transamerica Title Ins. Co.,* 100 Wn.2d 581, 586-89, 675 P.2d 193 (1983); *Hogan v. Monroe,* 38 Wn.App. 60, 65, 684 P.2d 757 (1984) (realtor who drafted addendum that substantially altered the rights of property buyers held to the standard of care of a reasonably prudent attorney).

In Bowers, sellers sold property to buyers who had persuaded a nonattorney escrow agent to prepare an unsecured promissory note in favor of the sellers. After the deed was delivered to the buyers, the sellers learned the significance of the fact that the note was unsecured. They discovered that the buyers had departed for places unknown after using the property as security for a substantial loan. The sellers sued the escrow agent and obtained summary judgment on liability for negligence. Our Supreme Court affirmed, holding the escrow agent to an attorney's standard of care. The escrow agent breached a duty to inform the sellers of the advisability of obtaining independent counsel. *Bowers,* 100 Wn.2d at 590. That duty was owed because the escrow agent, by preparing the closing documents, was engaging in the practice of law.

The "practice of law" clearly does not just mean appearing in court. In a larger sense, it includes "legal advice and counsel, and the preparation of legal instruments and contracts by which legal rights are secured." *In re Droker & Mulholland,* 59 Wn.2d 707, 719, 370 P.2d 242 (1962). See also *Bowers,* 100 Wn.2d at 586; *Wash. State Bar Ass'n v. Great W. Union Fed. Sav. & Loan Ass'n,* 91 Wn.2d 48, 54, 586 P.2d 870 (1978); *State v. Hunt,* 75 Wn.App. 795, 801–02, 880 P.2d 96 (1994).

Mullen contends that her status as a paralegal precludes a finding that she was engaged in the practice of law. She argues that a paralegal is, by definition, someone who works under the supervision of an attorney, and that it is necessarily the attorney, not the paralegal, who is practicing law and owes a duty to the clients. Her argument assumes that she had a supervising attorney. The trial court's determination that Mullen was negligent was dependent on the court's finding that Mullen knew, or should have known, that she did not have a supervising attorney over a period of several months while she was at AMI. "Had Mullen been properly supervised by an attorney at all times during her employment with AMI, plaintiffs presumably would have no case against her. Rather, her supervising attorney would be responsible for any alleged wrongdoing on her part."

We agree with the trial court's observation. The label "paralegal" is not in itself a shield from liability. A factual evaluation is necessary to distinguish a paralegal who is working under an attorney's supervision from one who is actually practicing law. A finding that a paralegal is practicing law will not be supported merely by evidence of infrequent contact with the supervising attorney. As long as the paralegal does in fact have a supervising attorney who is responsible for the case, any deficiency in the quality of the supervision or in the quality of the paralegal's work goes to the attorney's negligence, not the paralegal's. In this case, Mullen testified that she believed James Bailey was her supervising attorney after Jescavage left. The court found Mullen was not justified in that belief. Mullen assigns error to this finding, but the evidence supports it. Mullen testified that she had started to distrust McClellan before he informed her that Bailey would be her supervising attorney. Mullen also testified that she did not contact Bailey to confirm that he was supervising her. Bailey testified at a deposition that he did not share Mullen's clients and she did not consult him regarding any of her ongoing cases. He also said that one of the only conversations he remembers having with Mullen with respect to AMI is one where he told her that he was not her supervising attorney after she raised the issue with him. This testimony amply supports the trial court's finding that Mullen was unjustified in her belief that Bailey was her supervising attorney.

In *Hunt,* a paralegal appealed a criminal conviction for the unauthorized practice of law based on his conduct in running a claim settlement company. Among other things, Hunt failed to inform his clients of his activities, did not

inform clients of the full amount of settlements, reached settlements without consulting his clients, and filed incomplete or improper documents in court. In a constitutional challenge to the unauthorized practice of law statute, RCW 2.48 180, Hunt argued that his status as a paralegal prevented a finding that he was engaged in the practice of law. The Court of Appeals disagreed and affirmed his conviction: "'It is the nature and character of the service performed which governs whether given activities constitute the practice of law,' not the nature or status of the person performing the services." *Hunt,* 75 Wn. App. 802 (quoting *Wash. State Bar Ass'n,* 91 Wn.2d at 54). As in *Hunt,* Mullen's status as a paralegal did not preclude the trial court from concluding that Mullen had engaged in the practice of law.

Contrary to Mullen's argument, such a conclusion does not require evidence that the paralegal called herself an attorney, entered appearances, or charged fees. Mullen testified that she negotiated settlements on behalf of the plaintiffs. She sent a letter rejecting, without Tegman's knowledge, a settlement offer made to Tegman. She continued to send out demand and representation letters after Jescavage left AMI. Letters written by Mullen before Jescavage's departure identify Mullen as a paralegal after her signature, whereas letters she wrote after Jescavage's departure lacked such identification. Even after Mullen discovered, in late November 1991, that Bailey was not her supervising attorney, she wrote letters identifying "this office" as representing the plaintiffs, neglecting to mention that she was a paralegal and that no attorney was responsible for the case. This evidence substantially supports the finding that Mullen engaged in the practice of law.

Mullen contends that she cannot be held liable for negligence because the statute that prohibits the unauthorized practice of law was not in effect at the time she worked for AMI. The trial court dismissed the plaintiffs' claims that were based on the alleged statutory violation, but this does not prevent Mullen from being liable on the negligence claim. Under *Bowers,* the duty arises from the practice of law, not from the statute.

Mullen points out that an attorney-client relationship is an element of a cause of action for legal malpractice. *Daugert v. Pappas,* 104 Wn.2d 254, 704 P.2d 600 (1985). The trial court did not find that she had an attorney-client relationship with any of the plaintiffs, and she contends that as a result it is illogical to hold her to the standard of care of an attorney.

Mullen, because she is not an attorney, could not have attorney-client relationships. Nevertheless, as *Bowers* demonstrates, a layperson can logically be held to the standard of care of an attorney in a negligence action. The duty arises from the attempt to engage in the practice of law rather than from the professional status of the defendant. The trial court, covering all bases, held Mullen liable both for negligence and legal negligence. While the "legal negligence" label may have been incorrect, any such error is immaterial because the negligence theory produces the same result and, as the trial court observed, for practical purposes the allegations are the same.

Accordingly, we conclude the trial court did not err in following *Bowers* and holding Mullen to the duty of an attorney. The duty of care owed by an attorney is that degree of care, skill, diligence, and knowledge commonly possessed and exercised by a reasonable, careful, and prudent lawyer in the practice of law in Washington. *Hizey v. Carpenter,* 119 Wn.2d 251, 261, 830 P.2d 646 (1992).

Mullen challenges, as unsupported by the evidence, the trial court's key finding as to the duties that Mullen owed and breached. The court found that the standard of care owed by an attorney, and therefore also by Mullen, required her to notify the plaintiffs of:

> (1) the serious problems concerning the accessibility of their files to persons who had no right to see them, (2) the fact that client settlements were not processed through an attorney's trust account, but rather McClellan's own account, (3) the fact that McClellan and AMI, as non-lawyers, had no right to enter into contingent fee agreements with clients and receive contingent fees, (4) the fact that McClellan was, in fact, engaged in the unlawful practice of law, and that, generally, (5) the clients of McClellan and AMI were at substantial risk of financial harm as a result of their association with AMI. Mullen breached her duty to her clients in all of these particulars.

The finding rests on the testimony of attorney Charles Nelson Berry III, an expert witness for the plaintiffs. The trial court found Berry's testimony to be "thoughtful and well-considered" and, significantly, unrebutted.

Mullen argues that the finding must be stricken because Berry improperly derived the standard of care from the Rules of Professional Conduct. In testifying that an attorney's conduct violated the legal standard of care, an expert witness may base an opinion on an attorney's failure to conform to an ethics rule, and may testify using language found in the Rules of Professional Conduct, as long as the jury is not led to believe that the ethical violations were actionable. *Hizey,* 119 Wn.2d at 265. Berry's testimony, phrased in terms of breach of the standard of care, stayed within this constraint. We conclude the finding is supported by substantial evidence. Accordingly, the trial court did not err in concluding that Mullen was negligent.

The trial court's findings on damages, unchallenged by Mullen on appeal, are verities. See *Cowiche Canyon Conservancy v. Bosley,* 118 Wn.2d 801, 808, 828 P.2d 549 (1992). Mullen does, however, challenge the trial court's findings on proximate cause. Like the defendant attorney in *Bullard v. Bailey,* 91 Wn. App. 750, 959 P.2d 1122 (1998), she essentially contends this element is unsupported because McClellan's improper settlement of the cases would have caused the plaintiffs' damages regardless of her failure to warn them. She emphasizes that by the time she left AMI, the plaintiffs had already signed invalid contingency fee agreements with McClellan and that he was well on his way to converting their funds.

Proximate cause consists of two elements: cause in fact and legal causation. *Bullard,* 91 Wn.App. at 755. Cause in fact is the "but for" consequence of the injury. *Bullard,* 91 Wn.App. at 755 (citing *City of Seattle v. Blume,* 134 Wn.2d 243, 251, 947 P.2d 223 (1997)). It is a matter of what has in fact occurred and is generally for the trier of fact to decide. *Bullard,* 91 Wn.App. at 755. As in *Bullard,* we conclude the trial court did not err in its determinations of proximate cause.

All three plaintiffs testified that they hired McClellan and AMI to legally represent them and believed that McClellan was an attorney whom they trusted and relied upon to handle their respective claims. They found out that he was not an attorney only after their claims had been settled. Mullen did not advise any of the plaintiffs that McClellan was not a lawyer; that AMI was not a law firm; that she, as a paralegal, had no real supervision; or that client funds did not go through

(quoting *King v. City of Seattle,* ~~...~~
contends that her connection to the plai~~...~~
not render direct legal advice and that it is unjust ~~...~~
gal, responsible for the criminal, intentional acts of her employer. The Bullard court
rejected a similar argument asserted by Bailey, an attorney who allowed himself to
become associated with McClellan:

> Under the circumstances presented, particularly McClellan's financial diffi-
> culties, unlawful legal practice, and Bailey's failure to correct Bullard's mis-
> apprehensions, ordinary human experience should have led Bailey to expect
> Bullard would suffer some harm at McClellan's hands, regardless whether it
> was the precise harm suffered.

Bullard, 91 Wn.App. at 759.

Although Mullen was a paralegal, she is held to an attorney's standard of care
because she worked on the plaintiffs' cases during a period of several months when
she had no supervising attorney. The fact that she did not render legal advice directly
does not excuse her; in fact, her failure to advise the plaintiffs of the improper arrangements at AMI is the very omission that breached her duty. Under these circumstances
it is not unjust to hold her accountable as a legal cause of the plaintiffs' injuries.

As all the elements of negligence have been established, we affirm the judgment against Mullen.

JOINT AND SEVERAL LIABILITY

This part of the court's opinion is omitted. It was overturned on appeal. *Tegman v.
Accident & Med. Investigations, Inc.,* 150 Wn.2d 102 (2002).

CASE QUESTIONS

1. Why was the paralegal Mullen held to the standard of an attorney?
2. In addition to the standard of care, what else did the court believe Mullen was
   required to do once she discovered that McClellan was not a licensed lawyer?

CHAPTER

8

....

THE DUTY OF ZEALOUS REPRESENTATION

....

CHAPTER OBJECTIVES

By the end of this chapter, you will know the answers to these questions:

What Does Zealous
  Representation Mean?
What Is the Penalty for
  Tampering with Evidence?
How Are We Accidentally
  Deceitful?
What Is Pretexting and Why
  Is It Impermissible?
How Can I Avoid Being Told
  to Be Deceitful?
How about Overpaying
  Expert Witnesses?
  Or Giving Gifts to Judges?
Do I Really Have to Do the
  Other Guy's Job?
What Makes a Claim
  Frivolous?
What Does It Mean to Be a
  Fiduciary?

HYPOTHETICAL

Elianna is a paralegal employed by a large corporation in the Human Resources department. She receives approximately 200 e-mails per day. The process of sorting them and storing them in the appropriate electronic folders is beginning to take an hour or more per day. Elianna decides, as a result, that she doesn't need to keep all of the employee-related e-mails and so she deletes many of them as soon as she reads them. Her corporation, as Elianna knows, does not have an organized or routine method for backing up the e-mails from the server. The company has experienced server crashes that have had the effect of erasing all of the stored e-mails.

What Does Zealous Representation Mean?

When we think about our system of due process, we think about the right to counsel. The U.S. Supreme Court wrote:

> The right to be heard would be, in many cases, of little avail if it did not comprehend the right to be heard by counsel... [The layman] requires the guiding hand of counsel at every step in the proceedings against him.[1]

The defendant in a criminal case has the right to counsel, but not just plain vanilla counsel. The right is to loyal, diligent, skilled, thorough, competent, and zealous counsel. What does *zealous* mean,

ABA Model Code
EC 7-2
The bounds of
the law in a given
case are often
difficult to
ascertain.

* The Model Codes
of Professional
Responsibility are
presented here as a
historical reference
and are not
currently used.

exactly? It means trying hard. Think of *competent* as a fellow just sort of walking along. Then think of *zealous* as someone running really hard.

The word "zeal" appears in bold type in the ABA Model Codes. Canon 7 says that the lawyer shall represent the client *zealously* within the bounds of the law. That part about the bounds of the law confounded folks a bit, however, so we don't see the word "zeal" so much in the ABA Model Rules.

CHAPTER OBJECTIVES (CONT.)

How Is the Prosecutor Like a
    Boy Scout?
What Exactly Is an Ex Parte
    Communication and Why
    Is It Bad?

ABA Model Rule 3.1 discusses at length the adversary system and its interdependence on the evidentiary and procedural regulations of the courts. These considerations advise and admonish us to zealously prepare and present the facts and the law to the court so that it may make the most just decision. They request that we maintain a dignified manner in order to expedite the legal process. They ask us to have respect for the courts and the complexity of their task. We need to be diligent in our efforts to avoid even the unintentional violation of our ethical duties. So, we're looking at *diligent* rather than *zealous* in the Model Rules. Diligent doesn't give the image of the fanatic—the zealot. When we hear lawyers talk about this duty, and when we hear them talk about "zealous representation," we should think diligent. The public is entitled to more than simple competence.

Where Is That "Boundary of the Law"?

In the following sections, we'll look at some of the more obvious "zeal" violations and some that are not so obvious. Although you should know that many of these fact patterns will present themselves in real life, we should not be concerned or intimidated. The ethical path is there for us to choose.

Suppressing Evidence

We are specifically prohibited from *suppressing* (hiding) *evidence* that we or our clients have a legal obligation to reveal. This prohibition extends to hiding witnesses as well. Lawyers who know suppression or secreting and do not notify the court will be responsible for these illegal acts of their clients. The reasoning behind these regulations is that the proper administration of justice requires that the tribunal be made aware of all evidence. Without it, it cannot make an educated and just decision.

In *In re Ryder,*[2] the defendant's lawyer, formerly a U.S. Attorney (who presumably knew better), took the weapon used in the robbery, and the loot, and tried to hide it. His intent was to keep the evidence from the government and destroy the chain of custody required for the government to put the weapon and money into evidence at defendant's trial. The court rejected Ryder's argument that the items were protected under attorney/client privilege (covered in Chapter 5) because it was the lawyer, not the client, who initiated the secreting of the evidence. The weapon, by the way, is not "confidential information," either, because it is an instrument of a crime. It is not "information" of any sort. What is confidential, however, is where the weapon came from. So, with those two things in mind, what could Ryder have done with the weapon? According to the case, Ryder consulted with other lawyers before he took these actions. (They apparently had not studied the Virginia codes of professional responsibility either.) Because Ryder made an effort to discover his ethical responsibilities, the penalty for suppression of evidence was suspension for eighteen months instead of disbarment.

ABA Canon (1908) 15

The lawyer owes "entire devotion to the interest of the client, warm zeal in the maintenance and defense of his rights and the exertion of his utmost learning and ability," to the end that nothing be taken or be withheld from him, save by the rules of law, legally applied. No fear of judicial disfavor or public unpopularity should restrain him from the full discharge of his duty. In the judicial forum the client is entitled to the benefit of any and every remedy and defense that is authorized by the law of the land, and he may expect his lawyer to assert every such remedy or defense. But it is steadfastly to be borne in mind that the great trust of the lawyer is to be performed within and not without the bounds of the law. The office of attorney does not permit, much less does it demand of him for any client, violation of law or any manner of fraud or chicane. He must obey his own conscience and not that of his client.

In *Sullins v. State Bar,*[3] the lawyer for the executor of an estate received a letter from a relative indicating that the relative renounced all interest in the decedent's estate. The lawyer hid the letter and then told the remaining heir that the estate would probably be in litigation for a long time. In its finding that the lawyer had misled the heir for his own gain, the California Supreme Court quoted from an earlier California case:

> It has been uniformly held that the purpose of a disciplinary proceeding is not to punish the attorney but to inquire into the moral fitness of an officer of the court to continue in that capacity and to afford protection to the public, the courts and the legal profession. [citing *Demain v. State Bar,* 475 P.2d 652 (Cal. 1970)]

Hiding evidence and lying to the client does not speak very highly of Mr. Sullins' moral fitness.

And suppression of evidence, failing to make it available to the prosecutor, will likely result in a mistrial for your client. In *Quinones v. State,*[4] the defendant's lawyer hid a weapon the defendant used but later showed it to the jury in his case to prove self-defense. The judge wrote:

> During the course of what should have been a simple case, defense counsel achieved unprecedented levels of attorney misconduct. Indeed, it is arguable that his intent was not to try the case at all but, rather, to sabotage it. Counsel's misconduct is best addressed as presented by the state in its motion for mistrial: first, repeated disobedience of the trial court's orders, and second, the suppression of physical evidence. His misbehavior unquestionably had a significant impact on the jury. Defense counsel's disregard for the court's orders was not only unethical but contumacious.

> *Contumacious:* Obstinately disobedient or rebellious; insubordinate.

Fabricating Evidence

Legal professionals who deliberately *fabricate evidence* or knowingly allow the client to *fabricate evidence* for the purpose of putting it before the court are guilty of perpetrating a fraud upon the court and *obstructing justice.*[5] This fabrication can take several forms.

Inducing a Witness to Lie

Attorney Wright was disbarred by the Supreme Court of Nevada for obstruction of justice when he was found guilty of *subornation of perjury* and *tampering with witnesses.* Wright had entered into an agreement with his client whereby they would pay a witness to testify that the client had satisfied the six-week residency requirement for obtaining a divorce. What Wright did not know was that the "client" was a private investigator who had been hired by members of the local bar to catch Wright in the illegal and unethical act.[6]

> *Subornation:* To induce a person to commit an unlawful or evil act.

You wouldn't want to tell your client to lie about the date on which her accident occurred to avoid a problem with the statute of limitations.[7] And you wouldn't want to advise the client to "play dumb" and, if questioned about certain past convictions, to deny them.[8]

You also wouldn't want to bribe police officers to influence their testimony, whether to induce them to testify truthfully or falsely.[9] In fact, you don't even want to suggest that bribing a police officer would be the right thing to do or take any steps to go about doing that.[10]

Lawyers facing disciplinary action make a big mistake by offering false testimony or false documents at a disciplinary hearing.[11] As if it weren't bad enough that the lawyer is in trouble with the disciplinary body of the state, unethical behavior in the disciplinary proceeding may have tornado-esq impact on an already dark and stormy circumstance.

Allowing a Witness to Lie

If it is obvious that it is improper to tell a witness to give false testimony, perhaps it is almost as obvious that it is also improper to allow a witness to testify falsely. Oregon's Rule 3.3(a)(3) addresses this issue. The Comments following the Rule discuss the problem of the client who will offer perjurious testimony or already had offered false testimony and the possible solutions. Ultimately, according to the Comments, the best course of action is to convince the client to admit to the perjured testimony and, failing that, the lawyer must withdraw from the representation "if that will remedy the situation."

Oregon's Rule 3.3
(a) A lawyer shall not knowingly: . . . (3) offer evidence that the lawyer knows to be false. If a lawyer, the lawyer's client, or a witness called by the lawyer, has offered material evidence and the lawyer comes to know of its falsity, the lawyer shall take reasonable remedial measures, including, if necessary, disclosure to the tribunal. A lawyer may refuse to offer evidence, other than the testimony of a defendant in a criminal matter, that the lawyer reasonably believes is false.

If it will not, the lawyer should make a disclosure to the court. This is not reconciled with the duty of confidentiality. That puts us in the unenviable position of having to tell the court something that would be in all other instances confidential. How do we do that? Very cautiously. Any disclosure of confidential information should be limited in scope to the tiniest bit of information that can be told while still getting the point across, and limited in direction to the judge. Perjured statements themselves are not protected by the attorney/client privilege so we can be compelled to testify as to them.[12] That means, then, that when everything goes bad, the client has committed perjury and the client's counsel is an accessory.

Making False Affidavits

Filing a declaration or affidavit with the court that contains lies, even when they seem inconsequential, is misconduct. Mr. Bishop filed an affidavit with the court requesting an extension of time. In it he stated that he had the flu and was unable to work. The court held that the filing of a false statement in an affidavit was grounds for public reprimand. Although Bishop could not be sanctioned for "secreting" himself, the court could find him guilty of obstructing the adjudicative process.[13] (The court refers the reader to 40 ALR3d 169 for more cases on similar misconduct.)

Stop and read that paragraph again. The lie the lawyer told was that he had the flu. How bad of a lie could that be? It's such a small thing and so very unlikely to be proven false. Make a photocopy of this case, frame it and hang it in your office. When anyone asks you to tell this itty bitty sort of lie, you can simply point to your framed explanation of why you're not going to do that.

Making False Documents

Technology has given us many benefits—and an equal number of temptations. Years ago, the best available was ... tape, white-out, and a photocopier. "Now it is a relatively easy matter to create false documents using any of several readily available software." It's still misconduct. It's just easier to do. In a 2006 case from Washington, a lawyer (Poole) created an invoice, backdated it to May 28th, and presented it to opposing counsel as evidence that the client was on notice about the amounts owed from that time.[14] The hearing officer determined that the lawyer never sent the client an invoice in May but manufactured it later. Technology played an important role in bringing Poole's deception to light. During the investigatory process and at the hearing, Poole gave two potential explanations for why the disputed May 28 credit failed to appear on any subsequent invoice. Poole alternatively claimed (1) that the credit was never "finalized" in the "TimeSlips" program and (2) that a "date-restrictor" may have been applied that would have allowed only certain activity to be reflected in subsequent statements. The State Bar had a TimeSlips expert, however, who refuted all of Poole's explanations. A word to the wise: don't underestimate the regulatory body's ability to use technology.

What Is the Penalty If I Create or Preserve False Evidence?

In *Anatomy of a Murder,*[15] the defendant's recently retained lawyer lectures the defendant on the various defenses to first degree murder, eliminating each possibility for the defendant's case throughout the instruction. At the end of the lecture, the defendant comes to recognize through his own deductive reasoning that his only possible defense is that of temporary insanity. At that moment, he suddenly "realizes" that he has no recollection of the actual shooting or any occurrences surrounding the shooting. The attorney has successfully led his client to the development of his own defense.

Although this book is fictional, it contains methods used by lawyers that are not far from the truth.[16] ABA Model Code EC 7-6 talks about how perplexing situations can be for lawyers when they cannot determine the state of mind of their client or the intentions of the client. Legal professionals clearly cannot encourage a client to take a course of action that will defraud the judicial system or a private individual. When asked to aid the client in developing evidence relevant to the client's state of mind, we are obligated to construe the situation in the client's best interests. In *Anatomy of a Murder,* the lawyer was obligated to construe his client's state of mind as having been temporarily insane at the time of the crime. If there is any doubt, the lawyer should resolve the doubt in favor of the client. But we must not falsify evidence in our zealousness.

This is what the penalty may look like: In *Matter of Morris,*[17] the lawyer was convicted of the felony of "misprision of felony," failure to disclose to the authorities that his client had committed a felony. The lawyer was suspended from practice for six months, even though he did not intend to interfere with the administration of justice, he did not attempt to actively deceive or defraud a tribunal, and he had no dishonest or selfish motive or desire for pecuniary gain.

The disciplinary board acknowledged that Morris was "between a rock and a hard place" because his knowledge of his client's felonious activities was confidential information. How could the lawyer report the client while maintaining his duty of confidentiality? This problem was resolved when the IRS asked Morris directly about the client's activities and Morris responded truthfully. Check your state law right now. What exceptions exist to the duty of confidentiality when the client is committing a crime?

In *Matter of Wines*,[18] Wines primarily handled plaintiff's personal injury work. He engaged in "selective quoting" in reports he made to opposing counsel and their medical experts. Although Wines argued that his reports were intended only to be summaries and, therefore, they were not supposed to be complete, the court found that his summaries omitted only information that was damaging to his clients' cases. In its opinion, the court set forth several examples of Wines' summaries where he misquoted and misconstrued the information to the point where the original facts were unrecognizable. The court found that he was in violation of the state disciplinary rules that prohibit representation of a client in "any manner of fraud or chicane."

> Chicane means trickery.

The majority quoted at length from the opinion of the State Bar Commissioner's Report:

> An attorney does not have the duty to do all and whatever he can that may enable him to win his client's cause or to further his client's interest. His duty and efforts in these respects, although they should be prompted by his "entire devotion" to the interest of his client, must be within and not without the bounds of the law.... His conduct should be characterized by candor and fairness. He should not knowingly misquote the contents of a paper, nor willfully commit any act against the interest of the public. His conduct always should be in harmony with justice, honesty, modesty and good morals.

In *Carter v. Jones*,[19] the lawyer was suspended from practice for three months for the intentional forgery of signature of a party and of the signature of a notary public. These were flagrant violations of rules of conduct that "cannot be excused by a misguided desire for expediency, even in the absence of any actual intent to deprive another of money or valuable assets." This is a good lesson for any of you who are also a notary public.

Here's another one: The lawyer in *In re Berberian*[20] notarized a legal document by signing his partner's name in full view of the court clerk. The lawyer claimed at his disciplinary hearing that his partner had notarized the copy but forgotten to notarize the original so he was simply writing in the name for him to save time for the client. The lawyer apologized at length for his misconduct but was nevertheless suspended from practice until the court saw fit to reinstate him. This sort of conduct, the court felt, would lead to more severe breaches of ethical duties.

What do you think about the "slippery slope" theory of discipline? Does it move us closer to our goal of protecting the public to discipline a lawyer for what he might be on his way to doing?

This is my personal favorite: In *State ex rel Nebraska State Bar v. Fisher*,[21] a defense attorney who enlarged the bullet hole in state's evidence (a leather belt) by forcing a dowel through it, thereby ruining the probative value of the evidence, was disbarred. What was he thinking?

ABA Model Code DR 7-102(A)(4) In his representation of a client, a lawyer shall not participate in the creation or preservation of evidence when he knows or it is obvious that the evidence is false. (Closing your eyes won't help.)

* The Model Code of Professional Responsibility are presented here as a historical reference and are not currently used.

What Is Spoliation of Evidence?

A party has a duty to preserve evidence under its control. To destroy evidence is *spoliation*. There is an inference that destroyed evidence would have been bad news for the party that destroyed it if the destruction was intentional. Therefore, the factfinder may construe the use of that evidence against the spoliator. An example may be where a person claims to have been injured by a defective product but the person has disgarded or lost it. In that case, the defendant may move the court to dismiss the case.

Plain old ordinary common law spoliation has a technological counterpart. In *Zubulake v. UBS Warburg LLC*,[22] the court outlined a party's duty to preserve electronic evidence in the face of current or anticipated litigation. The *Zubulake* court also set forth a new legal standard for determining the cost allocation among parties for producing inaccessible electronic data.[23] The e-mails had been deleted but could be reconstructed from backup files. The reconstruction was going to be costly, however (over $200,000), and so the cost had to be allocated between the party that had control of the backup files and the party that wanted them reconstructed. In a third decision about the evidence, the court applied the time-honored standard that a party has a duty to preserve evidence when the party knows or should know that the evidence is relevant to pending or anticipated litigation. It was irrelevant that the evidence was e-mail.

How Are We Accidentally Deceitful?

Being deceitful seems to be an everyday event in some form or another. It is so easy to lie. Sometimes it is easier to lie than tell the truth and bear the consequences. Do you commute to work? How many times have you told your employer you got stuck in traffic, or the train was delayed, rather than say "I decided to sleep in an extra half hour"? Well, *you* probably haven't done that, but do you know someone who has?

There are many cases that speak of the "materiality" of the deceit. Cases about legal practitioners deceiving beneficiaries about the amount of their inheritance or

> **Rule 4.1** In the course of representing a client, a lawyer shall not knowingly make a false statement of material fact or law to a third person.
>
> * Full Model Rule and commentary can be found in Appendix E.

about lawyers simulating clients' signatures on settlement checks, or participating in other obvious connivance aimed at the court, opposing counsel, or their own clients litter the reports. All of these are examples of "material" deceit. The kind of deceit that is not reported is the potentially immaterial deceit.

What Is Material?

The materiality of the deceit must go to the task at hand and not to the ultimate outcome of the case. In other words, how material was the deception to accomplishing the task? If the deceptive representation was crucial to the accomplishment of the task, it is a "material fact" for purposes of Rule 4.1.

As a common example, the task is "find the defendant who is evading service of process." It can be a simple matter to call the defendant's employer and say that you are an old girlfriend of the defendant and would like to look him up. "Could I please have his home address?" The task has been accomplished. The cost was a small lie.

In this instance, the lie was told clearly within the "representation of the client." Although the misrepresentation was immaterial to the outcome of the case, it was enormous when analyzed to the task at hand (getting the defendant served). This is where the average legal professional fails in the analysis. We tend to think of "materiality" as going to some ultimate issue in the case and not to the task at hand.

How Are We Deceitful in Discovery?

Over the years, some stories of outrageous deceit have circulated in the legal community. One person who works for a large, well-known firm tells a story of a complex leveraged buyout negotiation process that was going on between his firm and another. An associate of his firm, as the story goes, was told to dress up like a messenger and retrieve a package from opposing counsel. The package was to go to the opposing counsel's client, but before it went, the "messenger" was to make a copy of all of the pertinent documents in order to gain an advantage in the negotiations.

It is easy to see that this deceptive practice took place during the representation of a client, albeit in a nonlitigation setting but during representation nonetheless. Even though the deception might not have affected the ultimate outcome of the representation, the goal was to get a copy of documents belonging to someone else and the deceptive practice was material in accomplishing that goal.

A more believable instance of deceit in the law office has to do with the in-house postage meter. Interrogatory response deadlines come and go, but if the missed deadline is only a day or so old, can't we just change the date on the postage meter so that it will appear that the envelope was mailed on the correct day? Again, if the task at hand is mailing in a timely fashion under the rules of discovery, changing the date on the envelope is not "material" to the outcome of most cases, but it is a false statement of material fact regarding the mailing.

Another example of common law office deceit is the law office employee who signs the client's name to a discovery document or attestation. It does not seem such a horrible thing if the law firm has the client's permission to sign the document in the client's absence for the sake of expediency. Several courts, however, have strongly disagreed with that position. A better idea is to get opposing counsel's agreement to allow the lawyer to sign for the client as "attorney-in-fact" until such time as the client returns and can sign the document or attestation personally. If the other counsel has knowledge and has agreed to it, it should not be a problem explaining the situation to a judge later. It is not a misrepresentation of material fact if the lawyer signs his or her name in place of the client's name and is therefore beyond reproach.

What Is Pretexting and Why Is It Impermissible?

Here is another example of the practice of law changing with new technology. *Pretexting* is the use of impersonation or fraud to trick another person into releasing personal information about themselves or others. There are online brokers of personal information who offer, for a price, personal information such as cell phone records, the identities of people who use P.O. boxes, and the identities of people who use dating services. Anyone can purchase pretexted information online. It has become increasingly obvious that lawyers are major consumers of pretexted information. In this way, lawyers are purchasing private information about people that they know was obtained through illegal means.

The truth is, lawyers have used illegally obtained information for generations. The difference is that the popular methodology used to be private investigators. Anthony Pellicano's name has been in the press often since the federal government filed an indictment against him and some of the high-priced lawyers he worked for.

ABA Model Rule 4.1 prohibits lawyers from lying to others during the course of representation but, as the lawyer is responsible for agents and employees, these people are not allowed to lie either. In other words, telling the agent to lie will not absolve the lawyer from a violation of the duty not to lie. If we know that the information was obtained by using false information, we know we must not use that information. It was always true of private investigators, and it is true now of pretexting.

How Can I Avoid Being Told to Be Deceitful?

Does this sound familiar? The lawyer instructs the paralegal to notarize a document indicating that the signer was present when, in fact, he is not. Now what? First, point to your framed copy of *In re Bishop*. Next, tell the lawyer about Lawyer Robinson who was suspended for six months and had to pay all of the court costs for exactly this behavior.[24] This case is from 2006, so it isn't out of date. Don't let anyone tell you that's an "old fashioned point of view." This is real life. It is happening today. Now we are prepared.

Even lawyers who recognize that a deceptive act is improper if they do it commonly believe that they can shield themselves by getting someone else to do it. Model Rule 5.3 on the supervision of nonlawyer employees makes it clear that the lawyer is on the hook for all activities of employees that would be a violation of professional ethics if engaged in by a lawyer.

In a 2004 New York discipline case, a lawyer instructed her secretary to sign the paralegal's name to a document and file it with the court, all without the paralegal's knowledge. Result? It's hard to tell exactly because of all of the lawyer's misconduct over a period of several years. It included creating false documents, which she then submitted to a court; counseling a client to lie in a certification and to disobey a court order; directing an employee to work on a client's case and charge the client after the client had fired her; eliciting false testimony from a witness during trial; making misrepresentations to clients, the court, and third parties; failing to refund the unearned portion of a retainer; directing a paralegal in her employ, who formerly worked for respondent's adversary in a pending case, to work on that case, even questioning the paralegal about her adversary's litigation strategy; and billing clients for work done by paralegals at a higher (lawyer) billable rate. She was suspended for three years in New Jersey and disbarred in New York.[25] What was the result for the secretary and paralegal employees? It looks like they lost their jobs. Maybe we should frame this case instead of *In re Bishop*.

By the way, we have already discussed the illegal nature of padding time sheets but the issue comes up again here. If you have been told to pad your time sheets, you have been instructed to deceive the client. This is true even if you are working on a contingency fee case and the time sheets are not used to bill the client.[26] In a 2004 case from Louisiana, an associate tells this familiar story:

> There was often not enough for me to do. When I brought my concern to the partners, I was "encouraged, both specifically and by implication, to 'pad my bills.'" I believe it is wrong to bill clients for work that is not done, but I was also afraid of losing my job if I didn't do what I was told. My decision was to "pad" my bills in the plaintiff's personal injury contingency fee cases on which I was working by logging time that I did not actually work. I felt this was the most acceptable solution to my dilemma, because (a) bills in plaintiff's personal injury contingency fee cases are not paid by the client, so there was no real damage done to anyone by a "padded bill," and (b) when my total hours were checked by the partners of the firm, the amount would be high enough to keep my job.

The result? This young lawyer was suspended for three months. Was this fellow really in a no-win situation? Perhaps his declaration would have been more complete if he had said that he, upon learning of the deceitful practices of the firm, immediately began to look for a new job and intended to leave this firm as soon as he could secure new employment. Everyone has bills to pay but we can pay those bills with the salary of honest employers who have ethical practices.

ABA Model Code EC 7-30
Vexatious or harassing investigations of veniremen or jurors seriously impairs the effectiveness of our jury system. For this reason, a lawyer or anyone on his behalf who conducts an investigation of venirement or jurors should act with circumspection and restraint.

* The Model Codes of Professional Responsibility are presented here as a historical reference and are not currently used.

Is It Improper to Investigate Jurors?

If you've seen *Runaway Jury,* you know that members of a jury can be investigated by the parties for possible interest in the outcome of the case, unauthorized communications about the case, or other reasons that would cause the jury members to be disqualified from serving.[27] These investigations, however, must not be "vexatious or harassing," and any improper conduct by or toward a jury member must be reported to the court promptly. Of course, you probably wouldn't know that last rule from *Runaway Jury,* but it is, in fact, the law.

Is It Improper to Talk to the Press?

Here's another one you probably wouldn't believe from what we see in the news every day. Model Rule 3.6 makes it clear that it is improper for lawyers or their employees to discuss an active case with members of the press,[28] the public, or the jury. In 1966, the U.S. Supreme Court ruled:

> The undeviating rule of this Court was expressed by Mr. Justice Holmes over half a century ago: "The theory of our system is the conclusions to be reached in a case will be induced only by evidence and argument in open court, and not by any outside influence, whether of private talk or public print."[29]

There are what are supposed to be *limited* exceptions to this rule, also found in ABA Model Rule 3.6, including the right to respond to a statement made to the

Rule 3.6(a)
A lawyer who is participating or has participated in the investigation or litigation of a matter shall not make an extrajudicial statement that the lawyer knows or reasonably should know will be disseminated by means of public communication and will have a substantial likelihood of materially prejudicing an adjudicative proceeding in the matter.

press that may have the effect of prejudicing the case against your client. You can see how this exception could produce an avalanche of accusations about who said what to the press.

Courts cannot completely prohibit talking to the media. In *United States v. Salameh*,[30] the court's blanket prohibition directed to counsel not to make statements to the media having "anything to do with this case" was held to be overbroad. And in *National Broadcasting Company v. Cooperman*,[31] the court's directive to lawyers not to communicate with news media on any issues relating to case was held to be unconstitutional prior restraint.

Nevertheless paralegals should never offer their opinion on a current case (to anyone other than those in the need-to-know circle). Regardless of what you may see on television, trial publicity is improper under your state's rules of professional conduct with few exceptions.

How about Overpaying Expert Witnesses?

A lawyer may reimburse witnesses for their expenses but must not pay non-experts more than an amount that reimburses them for loss incidental to having been a witness.[32] Expert witnesses may ordinarily be paid a reasonable amount for their services over the nominal witness fee, but not an excessive amount. It was traditionally held that witnesses should not be paid a contingency fee because such an arrangement may influence their testimony. In light of the many times an expert is needed in contingency cases, however, this tradition is being eroded. Lawyers are responsible for ensuring that their clients and employees adhere to these rules as well.

Or Giving Gifts to Judges?

Model Rule 3.5 admonishes that we should not seek to influence a judge by any improper means. This includes gifts. Some judicial positions are now filled by way of election, however. How much of a campaign contribution can a practitioner or law firm make to a judge's campaign? Under the 1980 ABA *Code of Judicial Conduct,* campaign contributions could not be made to a judge but could be made to a committee organized in the candidate's name. Under the 1990 ABA *Code of Judicial Conduct,* contributions to a campaign fund of a judge in any form are not permitted.

The rules that apply to judges specifically prohibit accepting gifts or loans to avoid the appearance of impropriety as well as to avoid bias and prejudice. An exception may be where the judge and lawyer (or lawyer employee) are family friends, in which case small exchanges of gifts during the holidays are probably not within the meaning of the consideration. Another exception may be where a judge has performed a marriage or other special ceremony for the lawyer (or employee), in which case a small token of appreciation is fine.

When contemplating making such a gift to a judge or other official, bear in mind that the purpose for the prohibition is to ensure impartiality. A gift or loan, therefore, must not be of such importance or size such that it would blemish "public confidence in the integrity and impartiality of the judiciary in the administration of the adversary system of justice."[33]

Do I Really Have to Do the Other Guy's Job?

Probably the most overlooked duty to the court is our duty to disclose law that is contrary to the position of our client. If opposing counsel doesn't find the law that is in his client's favor, you are obligated to provide it to the court. Does that mean that you have to do your opponent's job? Yes, that's exactly what Model Rule 3.3(a)(2) requires.[34] If you know of controlling law that is directly opposed to your position, the correct tactic is to cite it for the court, be up-front, and distinguish it on its facts or another way. Trying to hide the controlling law is never a good idea.

Is There a Law That Says I Have to Be Nice to Opposing Counsel?

Clients, not their legal representatives, are the litigants, and they may have ill feelings toward one another. Legal professionals, however, should not allow the client's feelings to influence their attitude toward the opposing counsel. (See Model Rule 3.4, Fairness to Opposing Counsel.) No matter how tough litigation gets, a legal professional must always maintain his or her professionalism.

Mr. Clarke, a lawyer from New York, made the following comments to a female lawyer in front of other lawyers, the court reporter, and the witness at a deposition in 1992:

"I don't have to talk to you, little lady."

"Tell that little mouse over there to pipe down."

"What do you know, young girl?"

"Be quiet, little girl."

"Go away, little girl."

This abusive behavior cost Mr. Clarke $500.[35] He was ordered to pay it himself, to not pass the cost on to his employing law firm or the client, and to pay the money to the Clients' Security Fund, a fund maintained by New York to "maintain the integrity and protect the good name of the legal profession, protect law clients from dishonest conduct in the practice of law, and promote public confidence in the administration of justice in New York State."

A criminal defense attorney was held in direct criminal contempt for making personal attacks against the prosecutor, accusing the prosecutor of "lying and cheating," even though the trial judge had not cautioned or warned counsel that his conduct could result in contempt, because his conduct was facially contemptuous. There were nine pages of trial transcript that showed repeated personal attacks against the prosecutor: "[l]et's see if we can cheat some more today…cheat, cheat, cheat."[36]

> "The conduct of attorneys is not measured by how close to the edge of thin ice they skate . . . but how much honor can be poured into the generous spirit of lawyer-client relationships."
> —*Matter of Cooperman*, 83 N.Y.2d 465 (1994)

> The "terminating sanction" is throwing your client's case (or defense) out of court. Try explaining that to your client!

More than courtesy is required. Cooperation is required. Lawyers who fail to extend common courtesies to their opposition, who fail voluntarily to comply with proper discovery requests and instead obstruct discovery, and who act in defiance of courts must be sanctioned accordingly.[37] What are some possible penalties? Some courts have used "the terminating sanction" against counsel who abused the system.[38]

The natural animosity that arises between counsel in litigation is no excuse for the failure to act in good faith.[39] And, there is no requirement that you show that opposing counsel's abuses are willful before sanctions will be imposed.[40]

Some other specific instances of conduct that have been grounds for disciplinary action include calling opposing counsel "a sneak and a snitch" in open court[41]; accusing opposing counsel of bribing a witness and threatening physical violence[42]; accusing opposing counsel of "playing dirty pool," using "smear tactics," "sandbagging witnesses," and a myriad of other colloquialisms[43]; and unjustified filings of bankruptcy petitions in attempts to cause delay and harass opposing counsel.[44]

It is important for all legal professionals to maintain composure at all times during communications with opposing counsel and others in the judicial system. Personal attacks, rude comments, snide remarks, or statements made in anger will rarely, if ever, serve to help a situation and will more often than not exacerbate problems. Sometimes being calm can be of invaluable assistance.

> Rule 3.5(d)
> A lawyer shall not engage in conduct intended to disrupt a tribunal.

Frank often attended court hearings with his supervising lawyer. After one particularly heated argument in court, Frank's employer met the opposing counsel on the courthouse steps where the two continued their argument. Frank was angry, too, but he saw that the argument was getting louder, neither lawyer would back down, and a crowd was beginning to gather to watch the battle. Sensing that the best course of action was to separate the two lawyers, he politely but insistently interrupted their argument and "reminded" his employer about a fictitious urgent matter. This allowed both lawyers to escape what could have been an embarrassing and destructive situation.

Is There a Duty to Show Courtesy to the Court?

The lawyer may stand firm against abuse by a judge but should not reciprocate, in the manner of two wrongs not making a right. The judge has the power of contempt and the lawyer does not. The best thing the lawyer can do is protect the record for review by a higher court and refrain from belligerence or theatrics.

Here are some things you should not say to a judge—probably not anywhere, but definitely not in New York:

"This is rampant corruption. I don't know what else to say. This is a sham."

"This is blatantly corrupt. You are sticking it to me every way you can."

"I'm not rude to them [a reference to the court's staff], I'm rude to you, because I think you deserve it. You are corrupt and you stink. That's my honest opinion, and I will tell you to your face."[45]

And here's a tactic no one should take—in California, at the very least; these are comments to a municipal court judge:

"I will not move on."

"I will not move on in this issue until you haul me away."

"You're not going to convict my client."

"You're not my mother."

"If you're going to convict my client, I'm going to react."[46]

The court has the inherent power to punish for contempt.[47] Contempt is committed when the lawyer or any other person impugns the integrity of the court. This impugnation can be oral or written, in or out of court.

When the court sanctions the lawyer for improper conduct, it is improper for the lawyer to pass the cost of the sanctions on to the client.[48]

In *In re Buckley*,[49] the lawyer, after a long and heated argument with the judge and opposing counsel, stated: "This court obviously doesn't want to apply the law." He was held in contempt of court, fined $500, and sentenced to five days in jail, even after a complete and heartfelt apology. The court ruled that his outburst was an accusation of judicial dishonesty.

Here are other examples of language that the court has held to be contemptuous:

Gillen v. Municipal Court[50]—a statement that opposing counsel had won the case before it began; *U.S. v. Schiffer*[51]—a statement that the court was rife with "Stalinism, Hitlerism, Mussolinism, and all these isms"; *U.S. v. Sacher*[52]—a statement that the trial had been a sham and a pretense.

In *State v. Caffrey*,[53] a lawyer who had repeatedly been asked to sit said, "It won't be necessary, Your Honor. I'm getting out of this court, if you can call it a court." In *In re Cohen*,[54] the lawyer used foul language and called the court "a circus."

Paralegals and laypeople arguing in their own behalf are subject to contempt of court rules. They are not, however, entitled to any less freedom of speech than a lawyer would be simply by virtue of their not belonging to the bar. In *In re Little*,[55] petitioner, who was denied a continuance and whose counsel was unavailable, argued his own case. When he made statements insinuating that the court was biased, he was not in contempt of court according to the U.S. Supreme Court. It held that he was "entitled to as much latitude in conducting his defense as we have held is enjoyed by counsel vigorously espousing a client's cause."[56]

Keep in mind that all states' rules require the legal professional to inform the appropriate authority about wrongdoing by a judicial officer that would raise a question about the judge's fitness. This is in line with the constitutional rights of free speech and the legal professional's duty to protect the public. (The "appropriate authority" is probably the authority in your state that disciplines judges.) Regardless of what may be considered improper behavior by the judge, the legal professional must be "temperate and dignified" at all times in dealing with the court, the clients, opposing counsel, and the public at large. Those in the legal profession are held to a higher standard.

Is It Deceitful to Cite Dicta in Court Briefs?

Rule 3.1, Comment 1, says that legal professionals can urge any permissible construction of the law in representing the client.[57] Law schools and paralegal training institutions spend a great deal of time discussing *dicta,* or that part of a judicial decision or opinion that is not directly related to the holding of the court.[58] Some instructors admonish that it is wholly improper to use anything other than the holding or rule in court briefs. In practice, however, this is not the case. A more user-friendly rule is that dicta is entitled to consideration as being a persuasive authority, but it is not binding as authority within the confines of *stare decisis.* So long as something that is not the *rule of the case* is not misrepresented as being the rule of the case, it is safe to use it. In other words, whatever you are using is fair game so long as it is properly identified. It should be cited or quoted in a fashion that is appropriate and not misleading. If you are quoting from the dissenting opinion, simply identify it as taken from the dissenting opinion. It is not at all unusual for the law that was once a dissenting position to become the majority opinion.

What's So Bad about a Loophole?

Many laypersons accuse legal professionals of using deceptive devices, loopholes in the law, and confusing legal terms in order to win. What these individuals fail to realize is that, with the exception of the criminal prosecutor, the lawyer is duty bound to win. Clients have confidence in and pay that lawyer who they feel is best equipped to win. Canon 7 from the old ABA Model Codes instructs all members of the legal profession that it is their ethical duty to win for their client, if at all legally possible. Legal professionals who do not use all of their faculties to do so betray a sacred and long-held trust.

What Makes a Claim Frivolous?

Whereas there is no definitive regulation that mandates that lawyers take every client who seeks their legal assistance (for instance, where lawyers find the cause so repugnant that they could not provide diligent legal assistance; see Chapter 5), once they have accepted the client, lawyers are compelled to argue any legal points on behalf of that client that have merit. The advocate role requires that the lawyer argue for any claim that the lawyer does not, after due consideration and investigation, consider to be without merit or frivolous.

Model Rule 3.1 says that a lawyer *shall not* bring or defend a frivolous claim or contention. A frivolous action is one that is brought primarily for the purpose of harassment or where there is no good faith argument to support the action. This, of course, does not mean that only suits over existing law should be brought or defended against. Were that the case, new law would seldom be forged. What it does mean is that the lawyer must believe that the claim or cause has merit, even if it requires modification or reversal of existing law. Sometimes those are the best cases. The legal practitioner has a duty to use the legal system, not abuse it. This means both the substantive and procedural part of the law.

Abuse of process, use of the process of the law for improper means, can be brought as a cross-complaint or counter suit in civil cases in many states. If the lawyer is named as a cross-complainant, it may mean that he or she must hire independent counsel to represent him or her. In addition, a malicious prosecution suit can be brought after the conclusion of the frivolous suit. Therefore, it is the wise practitioner who considers all of the consequences of the lawsuit that teeters on the edge of frivolity.

In awarding sanctions against a lawyer for frivolous or bad faith tactics, the court should not look at one or two things but, rather, the totality of the circumstances. In one case that looked at this rule of law, the plaintiff's law firm brought a claim that was worth $32 in the Superior Court by inflating the value with frivolous causes of action to meet the statutory minimum for Superior Court.[59] As the suit was brought on a mechanics lien that had already expired, the court had no problem finding that it was frivolous and brought for the sole purpose of harassment. The penalties were severe.

What Does It Mean to Be a Fiduciary?

The legal professional is in a *fiduciary* relationship with the client. This means that he or she must work with the client in good faith and to the best of his or her ability. This duty is derived from the lawyers's membership in the profession that pledges itself to assist members of the public in advocating their legal rights and securing legal benefits. In the old ABA Model Codes, Canon 7 advises lawyers that they must not step outside of the law in their zealous best efforts to assist the client. The bounds of the law, according to *EC* 7-1, are set forth in the Model Codes as well as in the enforceable professional regulations set forth by the states.

The corresponding Model Rule 2.1, says that the bounds of the law may not be what they seem. In representing the client, lawyers should look not only to what the law says but "to other considerations such as moral, economic, social and political factors."

The "bounds of the law" in many individual cases will be hard to determine. The rules are broad, are difficult to apply, and change continually. Where the line between the lawful and the unlawful is difficult to find, we should look to see whether our role is one of an adviser or an advocate. Advocates must take the facts as they find them. They may interpret the facts but must not try to change them in their own or their client's mind. They should, however, interpret factual situations in their client's favor while working as advocates.

While working for the client as an adviser, legal professionals should assist the client by using their professional judgment in predicting the probable decisions of judiciary or administrative bodies. Further, part of doing the best we can for the client is assisting the client in understanding the consequences of future conduct. Although paralegals cannot "give legal advice," paralegals can convey advice to the client that they have been instructed to convey.

How Bad Is It to Encourage or Aid a Client to Break the Law?

It is never proper to encourage or aid a client in a violation of the law.[60] The legal professional as adviser can appropriately counsel a client as to the probable outcome of a course of action. It is also appropriate to continue to represent the client after the client has unilaterally taken action that the legal professional has advised against or knows will not be the most beneficial for the client. It is not appropriate, however, for the legal professional to knowingly assist a client in taking illegal action or making frivolous claims. It is misconduct for the professional to encourage the client to commit a criminal act or to advise the client about how to avoid the consequences of a criminal act.

> Rule 2.1
> In representing a client, a lawyer shall exercise independent professional judgment and render candid advice. In rendering advice, a lawyer may refer not only to law but to other considerations such as moral, economic, social and political factors, that may be relevant to the client's situation.

> Code EC 7-5
> A lawyer as adviser furthers the interest of his client by giving his professional opinion as to what he believes would likely be the ultimate decision of the courts on the matter at hand and by informing his client of the practical effect of such decision.

If you assist a client in illegal action, you will not be able to hide behind the "my client made me" excuse. For example, in *Young v. Rosenthal,*[61] the court stated that a lawyer has an affirmative duty to refuse to make false declarations and statements to the court. The court found that the members of the law firm "willfully and knowingly made false declarations and statements in an attempt to deceive the court" and that such conduct could not be excused "by claiming that their client had 'insisted' upon it." In this case, the lawyers "knowingly lied to the court, acquiesced in their client's demands, and actively supported frivolous motions. An award of sanctions against the attorneys in this situation was absolutely mandatory. This is an example of the clearest of cases." If the client demands such conduct, the wisest course for the lawyer is to withdraw from further representation.[62] Because the duty of confidentiality continues, the lawyer cannot warn the client's next lawyer about this potential danger.

It seems so obvious that counseling clients to hide their assets and to give sworn testimony misrepresenting their financial position is illegal, but lawyers do it anyway. It was held to be grounds for suspension from practice in *Florida Bar v. Beaver*.[63]

In *Matter of Kerr*,[64] the Washington Supreme Court held that the lawyer's knowing participation in a client's plan to suborn perjury is an offense involving moral turpitude and is grounds for disbarment. A lawyer, ruled the court, has the affirmative duty to notify the court of perjured testimony regardless of the lawyer's pledge of confidentiality. In not notifying the court of the client's plan to bribe witnesses, the lawyer knowingly aided and encouraged the crime.

How Is a Prosecutor Like a Boy Scout?

Unlike other lawyers, the prosecutor's duty is not to win but to reach a just result or to "do justice."[65] Prosecutors' clients are the public, the state, and the government, so they must use their best efforts to see that the guilty are convicted and the innocent do not suffer. While representing the public and the government, prosecutors must often make decisions that would be made by the client if the client were a private lawyer. For that reason, prosecutors must always act in the best interests of their client: the public. The law says that they should construe all reasonable doubts in favor of the accused. This duty also encompasses the prosecuting attorney's duty to refrain from tactics that would be unethical if used by the accused's lawyer.

If you saw *My Cousin Vinny*, you learned the law that Vinny didn't know: prosecutors have the duty to make timely disclosure of any evidence or witnesses known to them that may help the defendant's case.[66] The role of prosecuting lawyers, then, is more than that of an advocate; their duty is not to obtain convictions but to fully and fairly present to the court the evidence material to the charge on which defendant stands trial.

The prosecution must disclose all substantial material evidence favorable to an accused; this includes evidence of bad acts of the alleged victim.[67] For example, in a California case, the prosecutor did not disclose that the alleged victim was himself accused of filing false reports until after the preliminary hearings were held. Because the reports were "favorable to an accused" and pertinent to the credibility of a material witness, the prosecutor had a duty to provide the reports to the accused.

What Exactly Is an *Ex Parte* Communication and Why Is It Bad?

Rule 4.2 says that the legal professional must not communicate with an opposing party except through that party's counsel. This is because the legal professional who is speaking directly to the opposing party may be seen to be taking an unfair advantage. Of course, opposing counsel may give permission for you to speak with the client. Another exception in California is where a lawyer is also a party to the action. In that case, the lawyer is considered a party, not counsel, and therefore may speak directly with the other party.[68] The Comments to Model Rule 4.2 suggest that the lawyer/party's fundamental rights as a litigant outweigh the state's interest in preventing direct communication with the opposing party. In other states, however, even the pro se lawyer may not communicate with the other party if the other party is represented by counsel.[69]

Here is a case in which the *ex parte* communication rule was put into action: A lawyer's *ex parte* communication with defendant's management-level employees, director of corporate security, its director of human resources, and its chief of uniformed security about plaintiff's case caused the District Court to disqualify the lawyer from representing the plaintiff, even though the lawyer did not intentionally violate the prohibition against *ex parte* communications. Additionally, the lawyer presented to the court substantial credible evidence that defendant was systematically destroying relevant evidence. It didn't matter. The lawyer was disqualified anyway.[70] *Ex parte,* then, means without the other lawyer there.

Model Rule 4.3 warns us not to allow an opposing party who is not represented by counsel to believe that the legal professional is a disinterested person. Often, the Comment says, unrepresented people assume that a lawyer is simply a disinterested authority on the law. The lawyer should correct that misunderstanding and should not give any legal advice to the unrepresented person other than the advice to obtain legal representation. These rules have few exceptions. The best course is to not communicate with any party to an action who may have a conflicting interest except through that party's lawyer. If the party does not have counsel, explain that your position is only to do your best for your own client, not to help the adverse party, and that the unrepresented person should seek the assistance of counsel. It is not the unauthorized practice of law to advise an unrepresented person to obtain counsel. Further, it would not be considered giving the opposing party legal advice to suggest some places where that person may be assisted at no cost, such as referring the unrepresented person to a free legal clinic.

Furthermore, lawyers and their employees must not communicate with the court during the pendency of a case unless a copy of the communication is promptly given to opposing counsel.[71] This rule typically applies to communications about the merits of the case and not to clerical issues; but to be sure, you should check your state law.[72] Any attempt to solicit information on the merits of a case pending before that court from court personnel is prohibited.[73] Being courteous and even friendly with court staff is a good thing; asking them for "inside information" is not allowed.

SUMMARY

Our duty to act zealously in the representation of clients is tempered with our obligation to act only within the bounds of the law. In the practice of law, you may be involved in a case or a cause that is distasteful to your friends, for example, the representation of the defense of an abhorrent criminal or the defense of a corporation that has defrauded or physically harmed the public. Your friends will criticize you for taking up this representation: "How can you *do* that?" they will ask. Your answer is that the Constitution guarantees each person the right to counsel and the rules that govern our profession make it an obligation to represent each client zealously. As legal professionals, our job is to render zealous representation, not to become the client or the cause.

On the other hand, sometimes in our zeal to represent our client to the best of our ability, we may be tempted to step outside of the boundaries of the law: suppress or tamper with evidence, say inappropriate things about the judicial system or opposing counsel, purchase an untrue expert opinion, or bribe a witness or juror. Some of these temptations will be obvious; others will not be. Before you act, get information about the propriety of your intentions. Ultimately, staying within the bounds of the law will be the best for us, our clients, and the legal profession.

CHAPTER REVIEW AND ASSIGNMENTS

CRITICAL THINKING

1. Go back to Elianna at the beginning of the chapter. Knowing what you know now, do you think there is anything wrong with her new e-mail practices? Can you foresee a time when deleting e-mail could be a problem? What are some steps she could take to protect herself and her employer? To aid you in your answer, see *In re Napster, Inc.,* __ F.Supp.2d__, 2006 WL 3050864 (N.D.Cal. 2006)

2. Sam is a legal professional with the district attorney's office. While working on a case in which the apartment of the accused had been searched pursuant to a warrant, leading to four pounds of heroin being found in the apartment and the accused making a complete confession, Sam notices that the warrant was not authorized for service at night, when the search had been made. Sam believes that if he brings this to the attention of the District Attorney, the search will be declared invalid and the heroin pusher will be set free. What should Sam do? To aid you in your answer, see *Lee v. State,* 324 So.2d 694 (Fla. 1976).

3. Lupe Legal Professional suspects that the judge who will be hearing a case that she is working on is an alcoholic. In order to get proof, she arranges to speak to him on some matter and record their conversation so that she will have evidence of his incoherent and slurred speech. Is Lupe protecting the public? Is this a proper method? To aid you in your answer, see *People v. Selby*, 606 P.2d 46 (Colo. 1975).

4. While representing Husband in a divorce action, Joan's firm discovers that Husband has not established residency and thus his divorce decree will be invalid. Joan convinced her roommate to testify falsely to establish that Husband had lived in state for the requisite amount of time. Was Joan's action unethical? Would it make a difference if Joan had been an attorney? See *In re Griffith*, 219 So.2d 357 (Ala. 1969).

ASSIGNMENTS

1. Ask ten people (people who are not classmates, lawyers, paralegals, or otherwise associated with the law) if they think that lawyers are ethical on a scale of one to five, with five being the most ethical and one meaning not at all ethical. Ask each of the ten people to name one thing that lawyers do that is unethical. Keep track of your answers to combine with the answers of other students in the class.
2. Visit the Web site of your state bar association and find the place where the lawyer discipline cases are. Find the cases against lawyers for representation that crossed the boundary of the law.

COLLABORATIVE ASSIGNMENTS

1. This chapter is just chock-full of fun stuff to do! *Runaway Juror* comes to mind as a terrific movie. For unethical handling of evidence, see *Class Action*, if you haven't watched it before. There was a wonderful *L.A. Law* episode about the young lawyer whose client tells him the location of his murder victim, a child. What is the ethical thing to do with that information?
2. Brainstorm in class. How many truly outrageous things can you think of that lawyers have done in the "zealous representation" of their clients?
3. Try some spontaneous role-play with unethical conduct. One team makes up the situation and a person from the other team plays the unsuspecting paralegal. How would you react to this situation?

REVIEW QUESTIONS

Multiple Choice

Select the best answer for each of the following questions.

1. Another expression for hiding evidence is
   a. secreting.
   b. suppressing.
   c. suborning.
   d. both *a* and *b*.
   e. *a*, *b* and *c*.

2. If a client comes to your office with the weapon he used to commit a crime, that weapon is
   a. covered by the attorney/client privilege.
   b. covered by the duty of confidentiality.
   c. covered by both the duty and the privilege.

d. neither privileged nor confidential.

e. covered by the work product privilege.

3. In *Sullins v. State Bar,* when the lawyer hid a letter in order to mislead his client into believing that an estate would be in litigation for a long time, he was found guilty of

a. misprision of evidence.

b. spoliation of evidence.

c. violating his duty of confidentiality.

d. misleading the client for personal gain.

e. violating the attorney/client privilege.

4. Subornation of perjury is

a. allowing the client to testify falsely.

b. inducing a person to testify falsely.

c. paying a juror to vote in your favor.

d. tampering with evidence.

e. bribing the judge.

5. Spoliation of evidence is

a. destroying evidence.

b. allowing the evidence to go rotten.

c. hiding evidence.

d. inducing a client to create false evidence.

e. forgetting to introduce something into evidence.

6. The use of impersonation or fraud to trick another person into releasing personal information about other people is called

a. impersonation of evidence.

b. spoliation of evidence.

c. misprision of evidence.

d. pretexting.

e. suborning evidence.

7. Legal professionals are in a _____ relationship with the client.

a. fiduciary

b. financial

c. personal

d. theoretical

e. irrational

8. It is proper to aid your client in a violation of the law

a. when it is necessary to win.

b. when it is in the client's best interests.

c. when you get paid extra for it.

d. when you can be sure no one will ever find out about it.

e. never.

9. The prosecutor is like a Boy Scout because

a. He has to wear a green uniform.

b. He is always kind in thought and deed.

c. He is not obligated to win but to find the just result.

d. He is obligated to win and always tries hard to win.

e. He isn't at all like a Boy Scout.

10. An ex parte communication is

a. an improper communication you have at a social event.

b. a communication between lawyer and the opposing party.

c. a communication between a lawyer and the judge without the other party's lawyer.

d. both *b* and *c*.

e. *a*, *b*, and *c*.

Fill in the Blank

Complete each of the following sentences with the best word(s) or phrase(s).

1. _____ is inducing a witness to testify falsely.

2. Perjurious evidence is _____.

3. A party has a duty to preserve evidence under its control. Destroying or changing evidence is called _____.

4. _____ is the use of impersonation or fraud to trick another person into releasing personal information.

5. Paying an expert witness the value of his/her time is acceptable but _____ is not.

6. Model Rule 3.5 admonishes that we should not seek to influence a judge by any improper means. This means we can't _____.

7. The most overlooked duty to the court is the duty to _____.

8. The part of an opinion that is not directly related to the holding of the court is called _____.

9. The legal professional is in a _____ relationship with the client.

10. The legal professional must not communicate with the opposing party except through that party's lawyer. To do otherwise is to have a(n) _____ communication.

True/False

Decide whether each of the following statements is true or false and write your answer on the line provided.

____ 1. The defendant in a criminal case has the right to complete loyalty and good faith best efforts of a competent lawyer at every stage of the trial.

____ 2. You are obligated to suppress evidence when it is detrimental to your client's case.

____ 3. Fabricating evidence is perpetrating a fraud on the court and obstruction of justice.

____ 4. Subornation of perjury is inducing a person to lie on the witness stand by bribery or fear of harm.

____ 5. A lawyer has the duty to do all and whatever he can that may enable him to win his client's cause or to further his client's interest.

____ 6. It is okay to destroy the original documents, even if they will be used as evidence, so long as you have a copy that is just as legible.

____ 7. If something is illegal for a lawyer to do, it is okay to have the paralegal do it.

____ 8. Telling a little, bitty lie in order to get some information about the opposing side is okay.

____ 9. Using pretexted information is perfectly legal so long as you purchase it at full price.

____ 10. Talking to the press about an ongoing case is OK so long as you tell the truth.

CASES FOR CONSIDERATION

CASE 1

Easton Sports, Inc. v. Warrior LaCrosse, Inc.
2006 WL 2811261
(E. D. Mich. 2006)

ORDER GRANTING IN PART EASTON SPORTS, INC.'S MOTION REGARDING NEWLY DISCLOSED EVIDENCE AND FOR SANCTIONS

This cause is before the magistrate judge on Plaintiff Easton Sports, Inc.'s Motion Regarding Newly Disclosed Evidence and for Sanctions. The parties appeared, by counsel, for hearing on January 10, 2006. Having reviewed Plaintiff's motion, together with Defendants' Response, and having had the benefit of argument and extensive post-hearing briefing, I find that the motion should be, and the same is hereby granted in part.

Upon review of the record and the evidence presented in connection with Plaintiff's motion, I make the following findings of fact:

1. In late November 2004, David Morrow, President of Warrior Lacrosse, Inc. ("Warrior") contacted Homayoun "Holmes" Ghassemi, Director of Hockey Marketing for Easton Sports, Inc. ("Easton") regarding his possible employment by Warrior. (Ghassemi Dep. at pp. 69–70; Morrow Dep. at p. 60).

2. In January 2005, Ghassemi arranged and attended a meeting between Morrow and Ron Kunisaki of Innovative Hockey ("Innovative"). The subject of the meeting was the potential acquisition of Innovative by Warrior. (Ghassemi Dep. at pp. 93–96).

3. In February 2005, Ghassemi used his personal Yahoo computer service account to forward a "Hockey Business Model" to Morrow and Nicole LeCuyer of New Balance. The attachment includes a projection attributed to "Holmes" that he could build Innovative's sales to $50M in five years. (Plaintiff's Ex. C).

4. Between February 22 and March 7, 2005, Ghassemi forwarded several Easton files from his office e-mail account to his personal Yahoo account. Included were e-mails entitled "Stealth Pants Concept" and "EMX & SHS Cross Sections," the attachments to which were later found to have been downloaded to Ghassemi's Warrior computer. (Plaintiff's Ex. D and Ex. E).

5. On March 20, 2005 (a Sunday), Ghassemi accessed approximately 200 Easton files on his office computer. (Plaintiff's Ex. F and Ex. G).

6. On March 21, 2005, Ghassemi informed Easton of his resignation. (Plaintiff's Ex. F; Ghassemi Dep. at p. 152). He accepted Warrior's offer of employment on the same date. (Ex. E to Defendant's Post-Hearing Brief of 2/9/06).

7. On March 29, 2005, Ghassemi accessed at least 90 files on his Easton computer. An additional 46 files were introduced into the software. On the same date, Ghassemi met with Easton officials for the last time and departed the premises. (Plaintiff's Exs. H, I and J; Goldsmith Dep. at pp. 38–39; Ghassemi Dep. at p. 175).

8. On April 26, 2005, Easton's attorney notified David Morrow of Warrior by letter that Easton had reason to believe Ghassemi had stolen trade secrets. (Plaintiff's Ex. K).

9. On April 28, 2005, Warrior's counsel replied by letter, stating that the firm was "in the process of examining the facts underlying this matter," and that it would "continue to investigate." (Defendant's Ex. 2).

10. On April 28, 2005, Warrior amended Ghassemi's offer of employment letter, adding language that Ghassemi should not bring anything from Easton to his employment with Warrior. (Defendant's Ex. 3).

11. On May 4, 2005, Warrior's counsel issued a letter denying that "Ghassemi, Wensley or Bankoske had retained any documents" from Easton. (Plaintiff's Ex. L).

12. On May 9, 2005, Easton's counsel disclosed screenshots of Ghassemi's Easton computer to Warrior's attorneys. The screenshots reflected Ghassemi's access to 100 files on March 20, 2005. (Plaintiff's Ex. M).

13. Upon receipt of Easton's May 9, 2005 letter, Morrow inquired of Ghassemi as to whether he had taken any Easton confidential information. Ghassemi denied doing so. (Morrow Dep. at pp. 135–36).

14. On May 11, 2005 and May 18, 2005, Ghassemi submitted affidavits denying the theft of Easton documents. (Plaintiff's Ex. N).

15. On May 23, 2005, Easton filed its Complaint in this action. The Complaint alleged Ghassemi's misappropriation of Easton documents as well as his use of his Yahoo account to communicate with Defendants. The Complaint was served upon Defendants' attorneys by facsimile copy. (Complaint at ¶ 11; Proof of Service).

16. On May 24, 2005, Ghassemi canceled his Yahoo account, which resulted in the destruction of Yahoo records concerning his computer use. (Plaintiff's Exs. O and P).

17. On May 24, 2005, Easton requested forensic inspection of Warrior computers. (Easton's Brief in Support of Its Motion for Expedited Discovery, p. 8).

18. On June 7, 2005, the district judge indicated that he would be inclined to permit a forensic review of the computer hard drives of Ghassemi, Bankoske and Wensley, but did not definitively rule on Plaintiff's motion. (Plaintiff's Ex. Q).

19. On June 10, 2005, the Court issued a Document Preservation Order, including "documents or files that are possessed by Homayoun Ghassemi, among others." (Docket No. 15).

20. On June 10, 2005, Easton served its First Request for Production of Documents, which included requests for "all documents which originated at Easton," all documents "referring to Easton" and "all documents referring to document destruction, modification or deletion." (Easton's Request for Production # 2, 11, 14).

21. On July 15, 2005, Defendants produced documents in response to Plaintiff's requests. None of the documents from Ghassemi evidenced his possession or misappropriation of Easton documents. (Defendant's Ex. 9).

22. On August 24, 2005, Easton moved to compel inspection of the computers of Ghassemi, Wensley, Bankoske and Morrow. (Docket Entry 46).

23. On September 8, 2005, Ghassemi testified under oath that he "didn't take any information" and that, other than some documents he found in his apartment and returned, he did not "leave Easton with any Easton documents of any kind." (Ghassemi Dep. at pp. 190–191).

24. On September 14, 2005, the magistrate judge ordered an inspection of the Ghassemi, Wensley and Bankoske hard drives. (Docket No. 61).

25. On October 7, 2005, Ghassemi executed yet another declaration that he did not take or transfer any confidential Easton information. (Defendant's Ex. 14).

26. On November 2, 2005, forensic examination of the unallocated space on Ghassemi's Warrior computer revealed that it had "experienced" a CD which appeared to have been produced on March 19, 2005, and which contained six Easton file names. It could not be determined whether any files were opened, copied, printed or transmitted. (Defendant's Ex. 18).

27. On December 22, 2005, Defendant produced documents revealing that two additional Easton file names traceable to Ghassemi's Yahoo account were found on his Warrior hard drive. (Plaintiff's Exs. B and E).

It is clear from the evidence that Defendants participated in a series of communications to and from Homayoun Ghassemi during the term of his employment with Easton. Plaintiff characterizes those communications as part of an effort by Defendants to recruit Ghassemi and to exploit his disloyalty to Easton by securing access to the Plaintiff's trade secrets and other confidential business information. Defendants deny any effort on their part to gain access to Easton's confidential information. They maintain that their efforts to persuade Ghassemi and others to leave Easton's employ and to work for Warrior constituted a normal and perfectly legitimate business practice. Those opposing positions constitute the merits of this case, and are beyond the scope of this motion. The only issue for determination here is whether Defendants wilfully, or negligently, destroyed evidence or otherwise permitted it to be lost, such that a default judgment or other sanction should be imposed against them.

I am persuaded that Homayoun Ghassemi inappropriately accessed numerous confidential electronic documents in Easton's computer record system. I am satisfied that Ghassemi transferred at least a portion of those records to his personal Yahoo computer service account. I find that Ghassemi corruptly terminated his Yahoo computer service contract with the intent to bring about the destruction of any information or data compiled or stored through that service. I further find that Ghassemi inappropriately copied confidential Easton business information to a compact disc ("CD"); that he retained control of the disc following the termination of his employment with the Plaintiff; and that he thereafter accessed the contents of the disc through the computer assigned to him by Warrior. That information, however, was deleted (apparently by Ghassemi) after the filing of this lawsuit, but prior to the court ordered examination of the computer hard drive.

Subsequent forensic examination of computers utilized by other relevant employees of the Defendants has yielded no evidence of access by them to Plaintiff's confidential information. Nor is there evidence that Ghassemi, or anyone else, disseminated hard copies of any Easton document.

I find the evidence on the issue of whether Defendants acted promptly enough, or aggressively enough, in acting to preserve relevant and discoverable information to be sufficient to warrant a finding of at least negligence, and to justify the imposition of a sanction. I am satisfied, however, that Plaintiff has not met its burden of establishing a breach of Defendants' discovery obligations so severe as to warrant the striking of their defenses and the imposition of a default judgment.

A party has a duty to preserve evidence where it is reasonably foreseeable that it is material to a potential legal action and properly discoverable. Spoliation of evidence occurs when a party intentionally alters or destroys relevant evidence before an imposing party has an opportunity to examine it. If a threshold showing of spoliation is made, the burden shifts to the possessor of the evidence to prove that the opponent was not prejudiced by the alteration or destruction. The test for prejudice is whether there is a reasonable possibility, based upon concrete evidence, that access to the destroyed or altered evidence, which is not otherwise obtainable, would produce evidence favorable to the objecting party. *Nationwide Mutual Fire Insurance Company v. Ford Motor Company,* 174 F.3d 801, 804 (6th Cir.1999). Our Circuit has held that "[t]he rules that apply to the spoiling of evidence and the range of appropriate sanctions are defined by state law." Id.

Under Michigan law, "[a] trial court has the authority, derived from its inherent powers to sanction a party for failing to preserve evidence that it knows or should know is relevant before litigation is commenced. *MASB-SEG Prop./Cas. Pool, Inc. v. Metalux,* 231 Mich.App. 393, 400 (1998). A sanction may be appropriate "regardless of whether the evidence is lost as the result of a deliberate act or simple negligence, [as] the other party is unfairly prejudiced · · · ·" *Brenner v. Colk,* 226 Mich.App. 149, 161 (1997).

The evidence here clearly establishes that Homayoun Ghassemi, while in the employ of Easton, engaged in a series of communications with the Defendants, and that he acted in Defendants' behalf in facilitating negotiations by Warrior for the purchase of Innovative Hockey. The evidence further establishes that Ghassemi, on the eve of his departure from Easton, accessed a large number of that company's confidential electronic documents. A substantial amount of confidential Easton information was transferred to Ghassemi's personal Yahoo account, and several confidential documents were downloaded to a disc.

The contents of the disc were thereafter "experienced" by a computer assigned to Ghassemi by Warrior. The evidence further discloses that Ghassemi terminated his Yahoo contract for computer services immediately after Warrior received notice of Plaintiff's lawsuit. The inevitable, and fully foreseeable result of that contract termination was the loss of relevant evidence which would otherwise have been recoverable.

Ghassemi's destruction of that evidence, and the introduction of the contents of the disc to his Warrior computer occurred during his agency relationship with Warrior, long after Easton's suspicions were communicated to him by Warrior, and immediately after the filing of this action. Furthermore, Ghassemi has not produced the CD, despite clear evidence of his access to it subsequent to his departure from Easton.

The Court must consider the reasons for destruction of evidence and determine if they support an inference of bad faith. I am satisfied that Ghassemi's several sworn declarations regarding his departure from Easton with confidential information were false. Defendants have essentially conceded that Ghassemi's conduct supports an inference of bad faith. They simply maintain that the wrongful conduct of Ghassemi was not solicited by them and should not expose them to sanctions. There is evidence, however, suggesting that Ghassemi's lack of loyalty to Easton was known, if not solicited, by Warrior. Ghassemi actively facilitated the efforts of

Warrior (an Easton competitor) to negotiate with Kunisaki. The business plan which Ghassemi and Morrow (and LeCuyer) transmitted clearly referenced Innovative Hockey, and "Holmes" (Ghassemi) materially assisted in evaluating and effectuating Warrior's acquisition of that company while he was still in Easton's employ. The lack of recollection experienced by both Morrow and Ghassemi on this subject is, to say the least, incredible. No innocent explanation for Ghassemi's destruction of his Yahoo account has been presented. Nor has he explained the fact that data from a CD he admitted making but denied taking from Easton was found on his Warrior computer. There is definite evidence that Easton information was transmitted to a Warrior computer both from that CD and from Ghassemi's Yahoo account. Ghassemi unquestionably knew that, and a case can be made that Warrior should have done more to detect and preserve relevant data under Ghassemi's control.

Defendants argue that Easton is unable to prove that any relevant communication of its confidential information was made beyond Ghassemi's Warrior computer. Similarly, Plaintiff is unable to present definitive evidence as to whether the documents "experienced" by Ghassemi's Warrior computer were viewed on Ghassemi's computer by other agents of the Defendants. I find those facts insufficient to forestall the imposition of some sanction. It is impossible for Plaintiff to identify communications from Ghassemi's Yahoo account which have been lost, and it would be unfair to insist upon a clear and definite showing of prejudice in light of the fact that Ghassemi, who clearly rendered assistance to Warrior long before his resignation was submitted to Easton, destroyed the most likely sources of corroborative proof. Based upon the presentations of the parties, I am not unalterably persuaded that Defendants' failure to ensure the preservation of Ghassemi's electronic data was the result of bad faith on their part. I am satisfied, however, that the evidence available could persuade a reasonable and unbiased fact finder that Morrow (at least) was aware of Ghassemi's abuse of Easton's confidential records, and not the least bit interested in ensuring their preservation on Ghassemi's or Warrior's computer systems. Even the negligent destruction of evidence is prejudicial to an opposing party, and undermines the litigation process. I conclude that the standard has been met. Thus, I find that a sanction is appropriate in this case.

Justice requires that any sanction imposed be proportionate to the circumstances. Dismissal of a claim or defense is an extreme sanction and should be imposed only in extreme situations where there is evidence of wilfulness, bad faith, or substantial fault by a non-complying party. While I find that the evidence in this case might support a finding of wilfulness, I do not find that it compels such a conclusion. Accordingly, a lesser sanction is appropriate.

** A special instruction advising the jury that destroyed evidence may be presumed to be unfavorable to the party who is responsible for its destruction has been held to be an appropriate sanction for the spoiling of evidence. *Beck v. Haik,* 337 F.3d 624, 641 (6th Cir. 2004). I find that an appropriate sanction for Defendants' failure to prevent the spoliation of evidence by its agent, Ghassemi, in this instance would be: (a) an Order allowing Plaintiff to present evidence of the Defendants' failure to preserve the electronic data; (b) an instruction to the jury that it may presume, based upon the spoliation, that the evidence destroyed would have been favorable to Plaintiff; and (c) an Order permitting counsel for Easton to argue in favor of the negative inference. The ultimate decision in such matters, however, should be reserved to the trial judge.

I further find that the reasonable attorney fees and costs associated with Easton's preparation and prosecution of the motion regarding newly disclosed evidence and for sanctions should be imposed upon Defendants.

IT IS THEREFORE ORDERED that Easton Sports, Inc.'s Motion Regarding Newly Disclosed Evidence and For Sanctions is Granted in Part. I recommend that the district court judge permit Plaintiff to offer evidence and argument relating to the Defendants' spoliation of evidence and that an appropriate jury instruction be given with regard to the same.

IT IS FURTHER ORDERED that Plaintiff, Easton Sports, Inc., shall document to the magistrate judge, within twenty-one (21) days, the attorney fees and costs incurred in connection with the preparation, filing and prosecution of the within motion. Defendant may file a response to the documentation within fourteen (14) days after it is served.

CASE QUESTIONS

1. This is a truly awesome case that demonstrates that even people who are very knowledgeable about computers cannot outwit the forensic experts. What advice would you have given Ghassemi after he told you (pretend for a moment you are his lawyer) that he had downloaded information from his former employer's computer system and burned it to a CD?
2. Why did the court order sanctions against Warrior and not just Ghassemi?
3. Re-read at ** near the end of the case text. What would that special instruction look like? Write a jury instruction for this case.

CASE 2

Midwest Motor Sports v. Arctic Sales, Inc.
347 F.3d 693
(8th Cir. 2003)

This case arose out of a dispute between Arctic Cat Sales, Inc. (Arctic Cat), a snowmobile manufacturer, and two South Dakota Arctic Cat dealers, Midwest Motor Sports, Inc., d/b/a/ Elliott Power Sports (Elliott), and A-Tech Cycle Service, Inc. (A-Tech). Elliott sued Arctic Cat, asserting that Arctic Cat had violated South

Dakota franchise law when it terminated Elliott's Arctic Cat franchise and established A-Tech as a new franchisee in the same city as Elliott. During discovery, Arctic Cat's counsel hired a private investigator to visit the Elliott and A-Tech franchises and to surreptitiously record conversations with each dealer's employees. Subsequently, the district court entered an order sanctioning Arctic Cat's attorneys for unethically tape recording parties represented by opposing counsel. As a sanction, the district court excluded from evidence the tape recordings taken by the investigator, as well as any evidence obtained as a result of the recordings. The parties settled the franchise termination case prior to trial; however, they reserved the question of whether additional sanctions should be imposed. The district court then entered a written order denying further sanctions and explaining in detail the basis for its exclusionary order. We affirm the imposition of the evidentiary sanctions, and we decline to hold that monetary sanctions should have been imposed as well.

I.

During the pendency of the franchise litigation suit, the attorneys for Arctic Cat, Roger Damgaard and Timothy Shattuck, retained the services of a private investigator, Adrian Mohr. Mohr was formerly a special agent with the FBI for nearly 30 years. The attorneys requested that Mohr visit the Elliott showroom to determine what products Elliott's salespersons were promoting and what equipment was on display in the showroom in order to ascertain which brand of snowmobile was selling best, and to determine whether Elliott had been financially burdened by the loss of the Arctic Cat franchise. Mohr wore a recording device to memorialize the conversations. The Arctic Cat attorneys did not provide Mohr with a script of what to ask during his showroom visits but indicated certain topics that they wanted Mohr to cover in the conversations. Mohr had written in his notes of this meeting with the attorneys the phrases "ADMIT SKIDOO & OR YAMAHA BEST" and "bad mouth A-Tech" as possible subjects to elicit during his conversations. (Elliott's App. at 150.) He was also provided the name of "Jim LeTendre," who was identified by the Arctic Cat attorneys as Elliott's sales manager. Mohr's deposition testimony reveals that while he was not supposed to try to talk to LeTendre, if he encountered LeTendre, he was supposed to ask LeTendre whether Elliott could service an Arctic Cat snowmobile if Mohr bought one elsewhere. This evidence demonstrates that Arctic Cat's attorneys were willing to let their investigator talk with one who had managerial responsibility in the organization represented by opposing counsel and substantially undercuts Arctic Cat's assertion that the investigator was instructed only to talk to low-level employees. However, Mohr never encountered LeTendre during his visits to the Elliott showroom.

Mohr visited the Elliott showroom on November 12, 1999, and again on December 28, 1999, posing as a customer and intending to elicit admissions from an Elliott salesman. Mohr asked the salesman, "Bill," why Elliott no longer carried the Arctic Cat line of snowmobiles, if Elliott was allowed to sell a 1999 Arctic Cat that it had for sale, and if Elliott could obtain parts and provide service for an Arctic Cat.

On November 11, 1999, Mohr and his wife—who provided "companionship and cover"—visited A-Tech's showroom and posed as customers. The Arctic Cat attorneys instructed Mohr to record anything that an A-Tech representative might say about the lawsuit. Upon entry into the dealership, Mohr was approached by Jon Becker, the president and owner of A-Tech. Mohr knew that attorney Daniel Lias then represented Becker as one interested in the Arctic Cat/Elliott litigation, but Mohr was undeterred and proceeded to question Becker about the Arctic Cat snowmobile line. Mohr's interviewing of the president and owner of A-Tech raises a reasonable inference that he had not been instructed to avoid questioning management personnel.

Mohr provided Arctic Cat's attorneys with copies of his recordings and snowmobile brochures obtained during his several showroom visits. Contemporaneously with the time that Mohr was visiting Elliott and A-Tech, Arctic Cat's attorneys made a Federal Rule of Civil Procedure 34 Request for Inspection to Elliott's counsel, Steven Johnson, and to A-Tech's counsel, Daniel Lias, asking to inspect, photograph, and videotape the Elliott and A-Tech dealerships.

In his deposition, Mohr acknowledged that he was aware that a lawsuit was pending between Arctic Cat and Elliott, and that both Elliott and A-Tech were represented by counsel. However, Mohr failed to disclose to either Elliott or A-Tech that he was visiting both dealers' showrooms at the behest of Arctic Cat's attorneys or that he was wearing a recording device. Mohr further admitted that his purpose in visiting the snowmobile dealers was to "elicit evidence in a pending civil case on behalf of the lawyers that hired" him. (Arctic Cat's App. at 9.) Mohr questioned the Arctic Cat attorneys as to whether the tape recording of these conversations between represented parties was legal. They assured him that his conduct was legal but did not tell him whether his conduct was ethical, nor did they discuss with him the ethical rules governing his conduct as their agent.

Arctic Cat filed a motion to disqualify Elliott's counsel, Mr. Johnson, due to an alleged conflict of interest under Rule 1.7 of the Rules of Professional Conduct. Elliott and A-Tech filed motions for sanctions against Arctic Cat's attorneys for their use of Mohr to secretly obtain information about the dealerships in anticipation of trial. The district court denied Arctic Cat's motion to disqualify Mr. Johnson and granted the motions for sanctions. As a sanction, the district court excluded Mohr's audio recordings and any evidence gleaned from those recordings. Arctic Cat and its counsel appeal the district court's imposition of the evidentiary sanctions and its refusal to disqualify Mr. Johnson. Elliott and A-Tech appeal the district court's denial of their motions for monetary sanctions against Arctic Cat's counsel.

II.

A. COMMUNICATIONS WITH REPRESENTED PARTIES AND THE USE OF AUDIO RECORDINGS

Arctic Cat contends that the district court erred in imposing evidentiary sanctions for its counsel's violation of the South Dakota Rules of Professional Conduct. We review the district court's imposition of sanctions for violating the ethical rules for an abuse of discretion. *Cooter & Gell v. Hartmarx Corp.,* 496 U.S. 384, 405, 110 S.Ct. 2447, 110 L.Ed.2d 359 (1990).

Acts or omissions by an attorney, individually or in concert with any other person or persons, which violate the attorney's oath of office or the *Rules of Professional Conduct,* as adopted by rule by the Supreme Court, or any other disciplinary rules adopted by the Supreme Court, shall constitute misconduct and shall be grounds for discipline, whether or not the act or omission occurred in the course of an attorney-client relationship. S.D. Codified Laws § 16-19-32 (Michie 1995). South Dakota has adopted the American Bar Association's Model Rules of Professional Conduct. See *In re Discipline of Dorothy,* 605 N.W.2d 493, 499 (S.D.2000) (acknowledging the adoption of the ABA's *Model Rules of Professional Conduct*). Therefore, we turn to the *Model Rules* for guidance.

Rule 4.2 provides:

> In representing a client, a lawyer shall not communicate about the subject of the representation with a person the lawyer knows to be represented by another lawyer in the matter, unless the lawyer has the consent of the other lawyer or is authorized to do so by law or a court order.

Under the test set out in the Model Rules, an organization's employee is considered to be represented by the organization's lawyer, and is covered by the prohibition in Rule 4.2, if the employee meets any one of the following three criteria: (1) he has managerial responsibility in the represented organization, (2) his acts or omissions can be imputed to the organization for purposes of civil or criminal liability, or (3) his statements constitute admissions by the organization. Model Rules of Prof'l Conduct R. 4.2 cmt. 7.

Investigator Mohr made personal contact with Jon Becker, A-Tech's president and owner. Under the Rule, it clearly would have been unethical for Arctic Cat's attorneys to communicate with Becker, a "critical" nonparty witness with ultimate managerial responsibility for A-Tech, about A-Tech's sales volumes and practices without first obtaining permission from A-Tech's attorney, Daniel Lias. The subject of the representation was the Arctic Cat/Elliott litigation, of which a critical portion was Elliott's expert's million-dollar damages estimate. Because every Arctic Cat snowmobile sold by A-Tech was a machine not sold by Elliott, the damages estimate could have been challenged in part by how much Arctic Cat business A-Tech was actually doing.

Arctic Cat's attorneys attempt to shield themselves from responsibility by "passing the buck" to Mohr. They allege that they directed Mohr to speak only to low-level salespeople for the purpose of becoming familiar with the Arctic Cat line. Even if these factual assertions were true, lawyers cannot escape responsibility for the wrongdoing they supervise by asserting that it was their agents, not themselves, who committed the wrong. Although Arctic Cat's attorneys did not converse with Becker themselves, the Rules also prohibit contact performed by an investigator acting as counsel's agent. See Model Rules of Prof'l Conduct R. 5.3. "Since a lawyer is barred under Rule 4.2 from communicating with a represented party about the subject matter of the representation, she may not circumvent the Rule by sending an investigator to do on her behalf that which she is herself forbidden to do."

ABA Comm. on Ethic and Prof'l Responsibility, Formal Op. 95-396 ("[I]f the investigator acts as the lawyer's 'alter ego,' the lawyer is ethically responsible for the investigator's conduct."). In other words, an attorney is responsible for the misconduct of his nonlawyer employee or associate if the lawyer orders or ratifies the conduct. Model Rules of Prof'l Conduct R. 5.3. Accordingly, we conclude that Arctic Cat's attorneys are ethically responsible for Mohr's conduct in communicating with Becker as if they had made the contact themselves.

Mohr also made personal contact with Elliott's salesman, "Bill." This contact necessarily implicates the third criterion of Rule 4.2. We conclude, as the district court did, that the discussions with "Bill" were intended to elicit admissions to be used against Elliott at trial, the subject of both Arctic Cat's counsel's and Mr. Johnson's representation. Indeed, it is apparent to us that Arctic Cat's counsel would have attempted to present "Bill's" statement that Elliott made a business decision to drop the Arctic Cat line under the party admission exception to the hearsay rule. While we recognize that some courts have been hesitant to equate the ethical rules' use of "admissions" to the use of the same concept in Federal Rule of Evidence 801, we note that those courts were applying different state evidentiary rules or ethical rules than the ones that govern in South Dakota. Alternatively, the circumstances in those cases did not invoke the same threat to the attorney-client relationship protected by Rule 4.2 that exists in this case. Where, as here, attorneys elicit specific admissions from an opponent's low-level employees that the attorneys know would be advised against by the employer's counsel, we have no doubt that the ethical considerations in Rule 4.2 apply.

Although the violations of Rule 4.2 alone would be sufficient to impose the evidentiary sanctions at issue here, they are further justified by the specific circumstances surrounding those violations. While there is no evidence that Arctic Cat's counsel directly contacted Becker or "Bill," the Model Rules of Professional Conduct prohibit a lawyer from violating the *Rules* "through the acts of another." Model Rules of Prof'l Conduct R. 8.4(a). Mohr's interviews took place under false and misleading pretenses, which Mohr made no effort to correct. Not only did Mohr pose as a customer, he wore a hidden device that secretly recorded his conversations with Becker and "Bill."

Model Rule 8.4(c) prohibits "conduct involving dishonesty, fraud, deceit or misrepresentation." The district court found that Mohr's conduct in making secret recordings of his conversations with Becker and "Bill" necessarily involved deceit or misrepresentation. In reasoning that it is unethical for an attorney or investigator to record conversations without the consent of the other party, the district court relied on cases from other jurisdictions and on the ABA Committee on Ethics and Professional Responsibility's Formal Opinion 337 (1974) ("[N]o lawyer should record any conversation whether by tapes or other electronic device, without the consent or prior knowledge of all parties to the conversation.").

After the district court issued its opinion, the ABA published a new Formal Opinion which reverses its position in Formal Opinion 337 and states that a lawyer who electronically records a conversation without the knowledge of the other party or parties to the conversation does not necessarily violate the Model Rules of Professional Conduct.

See ABA Comm. on Ethics and Prof'l Responsibility, Formal Op. 422 (2001). The ABA advised that "[a] lawyer may not, however, record conversations in violation of the law in a jurisdiction that forbids such conduct without the consent of the parties, nor falsely represent that a conversation is not being recorded." Id. The laws of South Dakota permit recording by one party to a conversation without the knowledge or consent of the other party. *South Dakota v. Braddock,* 452 N.W.2d 785, 788 (1990).

Nevertheless, conduct that is legal may not be ethical. The ABA suggests that nonconsensual recordings be prohibited "where [the recording] is accompanied by other circumstances that make it unethical." ABA Comm. on Ethic and Prof'l Responsibility, Formal Op. 01-422. Mohr's unethical contact with Becker and "Bill" combined with the nonconsensual recording presents the type of situation where even the new Formal Opinion would authorize sanctions.

The duty to refrain from conduct that involves deceit or misrepresentation should preclude any attorney from participating in the type of surreptitious conduct that occurred here. As Mohr's deposition testimony makes clear, his covert recordings were conducted with Arctic Cat's attorneys' knowledge and approval. In addition, there is evidence in the record that the course of conduct by Mohr was not only ratified by Arctic Cat's counsel, but that it was directed by them. Arctic Cat's attorneys admit that the intent behind Mohr's retention was to determine whether Elliott was continuing to sell and service Arctic Cat snowmobiles in order to rebut Elliott's damages expert at trial. (Arctic Cat's Br. at 35.) Arctic Cat's counsel contends that Mohr's visit to A-Tech was merely to become familiar with the Arctic Cat snowmobile line. The evidence does not support this assertion. The record shows that while Mohr did indeed visit two other Arctic Cat dealers for purposes of familiarization, only his visit to A-Tech was recorded. We conclude that Mohr's purpose in visiting A-Tech was to elicit specific admissions from A-Tech's employees about A-Tech's sales of Arctic Cat snowmobiles because Elliott's damages were impacted by A-Tech's sales and service of the Arctic Cat line-information that could have been obtained properly through the use of formal discovery techniques.

Arctic Cat was using Mohr's undercover ruse to elicit damaging admissions from Elliott's employee and A-Tech's president to secure an advantage at trial. Such tactics fall squarely within Model Rule 8.4(c)'s prohibition of "conduct involving dishonesty, fraud, deceit or misrepresentation." Arctic Cat contends that it only retained Mohr after traditional means of discovery had failed. Arctic Cat's attorneys may have become frustrated with their opposing counsel's refusal to cooperate, but that frustration does not justify a self-help remedy. It is for this very reason that our system has in place formal procedures, such as a motion to compel, that counsel could have used instead of resorting to self-help remedies that violate the ethical rules.

[Section B on conflict of interest is omitted.]

C. FEES AND COSTS

Having determined that the district court properly disallowed Mohr's recordings or any evidence gleaned from those recordings to be introduced into evidence, we now turn to Elliott and A-Tech's argument advanced in their appeals that the district court abused its discretion by failing to award monetary sanctions. Prior to this case, the law in South Dakota was unsettled on the question of whether using an investigator to elicit admissions from opposing parties' employees was unethical. Furthermore, as demonstrated by the ABA's change in position, the ethical rules related to secret recording by lawyers and investigators were evolving. Thus, we conclude that the district court's imposition of solely evidentiary sanctions was appropriate and adequate. We remind all members of the Bar that the obligations and duties of lawyers in our society demand conduct of the highest moral character. We believe, as did the district court, that because South Dakota law was not fully developed, Arctic Cat's lawyers' error in determining what their investigator could do should not result in a monetary sanction against them or their client.

III.

The judgment of the district court is affirmed.

CASE QUESTIONS

1. If Arctic lawyers had questions for Elliott employees, why didn't they just schedule depositions for them?
2. Why didn't using the investigator "shield" Arctic's lawyers?
3. A-Tech personnel were not part of the lawsuit between Arctic and Elliott. Why was it unethical to send the investigator to speak to A-Tech's president and owner?

C H A P T E R

9

THE UMBRELLA DUTY OF INTEGRITY

HYPOTHETICAL

Marco, a paralegal with the District Attorney's office, is sitting at a bar with his best friend, George, who has just told him that he has terminal colon cancer. George has had a few drinks before he also tells Marco that five years earlier he hid a piece of exculpatory evidence in a murder trial.

What Does the Duty of Integrity Look Like?

Maybe our discussion should have begun here, with integrity. Without integrity, what do these other duties mean? They only have value when the people engaged in the profession have integrity. But what does that mean exactly? Integrity is one of those things that cannot be quantified.

The rules of legal ethics have as their goal protecting the lawyer/client relationship, maintaining public confidence in the legal profession, and ensuring the integrity of judicial proceedings.[1] In short, the rules are meant to *protect the public*.

As we discussed in Chapter 1, Rule 8.1[2] requires that before a lawyer recommends an applicant for admission to the bar, that

CHAPTER OBJECTIVES

By the end of this chapter, you will know the answers to these questions:

What Does the Duty of Integrity Look Like?
Is There a Duty to Report the Misconduct of Others?
Do I Have to Report My Own Misconduct?
Can I Just Threaten to Report Misconduct?
How Does That Apply to Paralegals?
Who Are the Appropriate Authorities?
Is There a Duty to Make the Law Better?
What Sorts of "General Misconduct" Are Prohibited?
What Is Involved in Protecting the Public Trust?

NFPA Canon 1.2
A paralegal shall
maintain a high
level of personal
and professional
integrity.

lawyer should be as certain as is possible that the applicant is of "*good moral character*." This refers to that part of the bar application in which applicants must name several persons, one of whom is a lawyer, who have known them for a certain length of time. The state bar then contacts these references and asks them for a statement about the "fitness" of the applicant as a lawyer.[3]

Do you think a person's integrity can be determined by the recommendations of other people? Is it reasonable to assume that because a person has an honorable past that we can expect integrity in the future? Perhaps. But we might analogize that question to, for example, being sober. If a person has a lifetime of sobriety, what is the likelihood of that person becoming an alcoholic? The world of law is stressful. Can it change a person's character? Maybe.

Is There a Duty to Report the Misconduct of Others?

NALS Canon 2.
Members of this
association shall
maintain a high
standard of
ethical conduct
and shall
contribute to the
integrity of the
association and
the legal
profession.

Chief Justice Cardozo, as early as 1928, recognized that it is each attorney's duty to police the profession for traces of impropriety. In *People ex rel. Karlin v. Culkin,*[4] he wrote: "If the house is to be cleaned, it is for those who occupy and govern it, rather than for strangers, to do the noisome work." His statement is a clear recognition that the legal profession does not want to be judged by laypeople and will, therefore, police itself and maintain a higher standard so that it is not vulnerable to outside scrutiny.

If we don't want other people watching and reporting, we need to give the public a sense of security that someone is ensuring the integrity of the profession by policing themselves. For that reason, your state's rendition of ABA Rule 8.3[5] is important for study. This rule requires lawyers to report ethics violations of other lawyers in order to maintain the integrity of the profession. This is what Chief Justice Cardozo was talking about, and it is called *self-policing*. Otherwise known as "Fink Rules,"[6] these rules require any legal professional who possesses unprivileged (i.e., not protected by the privileges recognized by the rules of evidence) knowledge or any evidence that is not confidential concerning the wrongdoing of any other legal professional to reveal that knowledge or evidence to the appropriate tribunal or authority when asked. The Model Rules and NFPA Model Code, however, go even farther than requiring disclosure when asked. They require the legal professional to report professional misconduct even when there is no inquiry. All of the so-called "Fink Rules" recognize that the legal professional should not report information that is protected by a privilege or is confidential.[7] The following sections consider some examples of this rule.

Does the Judge Have to Report Lawyer Misconduct?

In *Blacknell v. State*[8], defendant's counsel made improper statements to the press so the judge presiding over the criminal trial filed a disciplinary complaint against him. The judge thereafter refused to recuse himself from the case. Defendant's claim of bias was rejected by the Indiana Supreme Court: "Counsel's statement to the newspaper

> **Rule 8.3**
>
> (a) A lawyer who knows that another lawyer has committed a violation of the *Rules of Professional Conduct* that raises a substantial question as to that lawyer's honesty, trustworthiness, or fitness as a lawyer in other respects, shall inform the appropriate professional authority.
>
> (b) A lawyer who knows that a judge has committed a violation of applicable rules of judicial conduct that raises a substantial question as to the judge's fitness for office shall inform the appropriate authority.
>
> (c) This Rule does not require disclosure of information otherwise protected by Rule 1.6 or information gained by a lawyer or judge while participating in an approved lawyers assistance program.

was in direct violation of DR 7-107. Under DR 1-103, the trial judge was *obligated* to report the violation" [emphasis added].

Does Opposing Counsel Have to Report Lawyer Misconduct?

In *In re Appeal of Infotechnology, Inc.,*[9] the trial court ruled that opposing counsel had standing to enforce the Rules of Professional Conduct in its motion to disqualify, even though counsel did not represent the party that had the conflict. At the appellate level, however, this was reversed. The appellate court found that a nonclient third-party enforcement of conflict matters was not contemplated by the Model Rules, except where that party can prove some sort of personal harm or misconduct that taints the fairness of the proceeding. The court

> . . . 8.3 does *not* vest lawyers with the authority to bring ethical violations to the attention of the trial court for the purpose of having that court discipline counsel under the Rules. . . . The rule requires lawyers to report only violations raising "substantial" questions about a lawyer's "honesty, trustworthiness or fitness" . . . and report violations to "the appropriate professional authority" and not to a tribunal.

Probably the most oft-cited case in this area is *In re Himmel.*[10] Himmel represented a woman who claimed that another lawyer (Casey) had converted funds to which she was entitled as a result of a settlement. Himmel agreed to get the converted settlement amount from Casey for one-third of the recovery. The settlement agreement that Himmel drafted in settlement of the woman's claim against Casey included the woman's agreement not to initiate any criminal, civil, or disciplinary action against Casey. Himmel was later disciplined for failing to notify the appropriate authorities of Casey's misappropriation of client funds. The court found that Himmel possessed *unprivileged information* of another attorney's misconduct.

Himmel's argument that he did not report Casey because his client directed him not to do so was unacceptable to the court. The court pointed out that Himmel's primary duty is to *protect the public* and *assist in maintaining the integrity of the legal profession.* The lawyer cannot circumvent the rules by saying that he was instructed to do so.[11] The Supreme Court suspended Himmel for a year for violating Illinois' Rule 8.3. The *Himmel* decision has been criticized[12] and followed[13] by courts in Illinois.

Rule 8.3 is one of the rules in the ABA Model Rules that was left out or amended by many states as they were adopting the Model as their own. Some states made reporting certain situations mandatory. In Illinois' version of 8.3, only ethical breaches that specifically violate certain other professional responsibility rules are reportable. If you have nonprivileged[14] personal knowledge of unethical behavior by a secretary, office manager, paralegal, or attorney that could prove harmful to a member of the public, you should research the authority in your state and consider reporting that behavior to the appropriate authorities. Who those authorities are is discussed in the section called Who Are the Appropriate Authorities.

Do We Have to Report the Misconduct of Others in Our Law Firm?

The Rule does not protect the person who reports misconduct from a later lawsuit for defamation. Nor does it protect the lawyer who reports the misconduct to the wrong authority. In *Skolnick v. Kass,*[15] Ms. Kass, an associate with a firm where Mr. Skolnick was a partner, reported Skolnick to the trial court for allegedly forging and filing documents with that court. The appropriate authority, the Illinois Appellate Court later told her, was the Illinois Supreme Court as only that court and its designated agent (the ARDC[16]) have the authority to discipline lawyers in that state. Kass also created a problem for herself by entering into a protective order agreement in the trial court that prohibited her from disseminating the incriminating documents. After that agreement, she had no documents with which to support her disclosure to the Supreme Court or ARDC. This is an excellent case for the concept of what it means to "know" or "have knowledge of" someone else's conduct.

In *Bohatch v. Butler & Binion,*[17] Ms. Bohatch was made a partner of the firm. That entitled her to see the printouts of billable time charged to each client. After reviewing the billables of another partner, MacDonald, Bohatch discussed her belief that the other partner was overbilling one client in particular with managing partners of the firm. An investigation was initiated, and it was determined that there was no overbilling. In discussions with the client's in-house counsel, the firm was assured that everyone was happy with MacDonald's time records, and Bohatch was told to start looking for a new job. As the law does not guarantee anyone the right to continue being a partner, Bohatch's later lawsuit against the firm for improperly firing her did not garner her the damages she was looking for. Because the firm breached the partnership agreement with Bohatch by cutting off her draw and benefits, however, she was entitled to some compensatory damages. Bohatch followed the letter of the law by taking her concerns to the appropriate authority, but in doing so she lost the trust and confidence of her partners.

Do I Have to Report My Own Misconduct?

Some commentators say that as privileged information needs not be disclosed and one's own criminal conduct would be protected by the Fifth Amendment privilege against self-incrimination, one need not report oneself. Model Rule 8.3, you should note, says that the lawyer having knowledge of "another" lawyer's misconduct must report. In theory, that excludes the lawyer having to report knowledge of him or herself. For a case that decided the opposite, see *Office of Disciplinary Counsel v. Casety,*[18] in which the Supreme Court found that the lawyer's failure to report his conviction of voluntary manslaughter immediately after his conviction was grounds for disbarment. And note that California has no duty to report another person but does require self-reporting under Business & Professions Code, Section 6068. There also does not appear to be an equivalent under the NALA Code of Ethics; however, that Code does require "the legal assistant to avoid conduct which would cause the lawyer to be unethical or even appear to be unethical, and loyalty to the employer is incumbent upon the legal assistant."[19]

Can I Just Threaten to Report Misconduct?

It is improper for the legal professional to use the threat of disciplinary action to gain an advantage in his or her case. You will find this rule in, for example, Maine Ethics Opinion 100 (October 4, 1989) opining that when the legal professional is representing someone in a malpractice case against another lawyer, it is improper to use the threat of a disciplinary complaint to gain advantage in the civil matter. The lawyer may explain to the client how to go about filing such a disciplinary complaint, but the lawyer must not encourage the filing of such a complaint as a tactic. Further, the lawyer must withdraw from the representation if the client insists on using such a threat.[20]

Sometimes in the "heat of the battle," we might threaten to report opposing counsel to disciplinary authorities in order to bring it to his attention that he is acting unethically. Attorney Pyle did exactly that. Pyle represented the plaintiff in a personal injury case. Before the defendant was represented by counsel, he signed a complete admission of liability in the case. His insurance company hired a lawyer to defend the case nevertheless and that lawyer filed an answer and responded to discovery without paying any attention to the admission. Pyle wrote a lengthy letter specifying the action he would take if the defense did not settle the case immediately. Among his list of things to do was: "Turn the facts of the case over to the Disciplinary Administrator." Pyle was later found in violation of 8.3 for not reporting defense counsel when he had evidence of that lawyer's misconduct and two other disciplinary codes going to "prejudice to the administration of justice" for making the threat. The disciplinary panel, in a footnote to the final hearing report, also opined that Pyle may have committed blackmail. So, the lesson we learn from this case is that when we have the urge to threaten opposing counsel as a result of his unethical conduct, that is the time we should seriously think about the duty to report him to the disciplinary authority.

> Pyle reached the conclusion that the defendant was not being competently represented by his lawyer. Through his own client, he sent a new declaration to the defendant stating, among other things, that he had lost confidence in his lawyer. Pyle got in trouble for this as well. Lawyers cannot communicate with opposing parties when they are represented by counsel. (Rule 4.2) This prohibition includes having someone else (such as your client) make the communication for you.

How Does That Apply to Paralegals?

It has been theorized that, as nonlawyers such as law clerks and paralegals are governed by their states' rules governing lawyer professional responsibility, they have an affirmative duty to report unethical practices of an attorney or another legal professional. The NFPA Model Code EC-1.2(f) makes reporting an affirmative duty in the case of dishonesty pertaining to client trust accounts or other client assets. The NFPA Model Code EC-1.3(d) makes reporting fraud an affirmative duty regardless of the object of the fraud or who will be hurt. However, there is no statutory or case authority that specifically extends this duty to the nonlawyer legal professional.

> NFPA Model Code EC-1.2(f)
> A paralegal shall advise the proper authority of nonconfidential knowledge of any dishonest or fraudulent acts by any person pertaining to the handling of the funds, securities, or other assets of a client. The authority to whom the report is made shall depend on the nature and circumstances of the possible misconduct (e.g., ethics committees of law firms, corporations and/or paralegal associations, local or state bar associations, local prosecutors, administrative agencies, etc.). Failure to report such knowledge is in itself misconduct and shall be treated as such under these rules.

The NFPA's Model Code includes two ethical considerations that require the reporting of misconduct. EC-1.2(f) requires the advising of the proper authority of any trust fund violations, and EC-1.3(d) says:

> A paralegal shall advise the proper authority of any nonconfidential knowledge of any action of another legal professional which clearly demonstrates fraud, deceit, dishonesty, or misrepresentation.

Who Are the Appropriate Authorities?

Once the decision is made to report, to whom should the report be made? Who is the "proper authority"? A 1993 case from Pennsylvania suggests that the client is definitely not the proper authority for purposes of reporting misconduct. In that case, the paralegal had evidence of "fraudulent overbilling" of a client. (See Chapter 6 regarding Fees and the Client.) The paralegal told the client about the billing fraud and was fired from her job. In the paralegal's wrongful termination action against the employer, the Pennsylvania court implied that the paralegal should not have made "gratuitous disclosures" of the alleged misconduct to affected clients. The court mentioned that there were "proper authorities" and "persons responsible for reporting such conduct or for protecting the public interest" but did not elucidate on who those authorities might be.

NFPA EC-1.3(d)
A paralegal shall advise the proper authority of nonconfidential knowledge of any action of another legal professional that clearly demonstrates fraud, deceit, dishonesty, or misrepresentation. The authority to whom the report is made shall depend on the nature and circumstances of the possible misconduct (e.g., ethics committees of law firms, corporations and/or paralegal associations, local or state bar associations, local prosecutors, administrative agencies, etc.). Failure to report such knowledge is in itself misconduct and shall be treated as such under these rules.

Within a firm or corporation, the problem may well be solved within the confines of the employment. Perhaps there is a managing partner, office manager, or ethics committee in charge of allegations of improper conduct. If not, the state bar, district attorney, or attorney general may be the proper authority depending upon the severity of the wrongdoing and who the wrongdoer is.

The Pennsylvania court also drew a distinction between having evidence of others engaging in unethical billing practices and the paralegal being asked or required to engage in similar practices. The judge wrote that "no employee should be forced to choose between his or her livelihood and engaging in fraud or other criminal conduct." To the extent that the paralegal was required to engage in fraud in order to keep the job, the at-will employment doctrine would not apply to the paralegal. In other words, the Pennsylvania employment laws would offer some protection to the employee who is discharged for refusing to commit fraud but will not protect the employee discharged for blowing the whistle on the employer.

If asked by a proper tribunal, the legal professional must always tell the truth with regard to personal knowledge of the unethical practices of another legal professional. Bear in mind that the tribunal probably has the right to call a paralegal or other law firm employee as a witness in any ethics action before it or before a court. Responding truthfully to inquiry by a law enforcement agency is mandatory, assuming the information is not protected by some evidentiary privilege.

There is no authority that reporting unethical conduct is mandatory for the nonlawyer. There will be times, however, when you feel that reporting someone else's conduct is the right thing to do. When making a determination about reporting unethical or criminal behavior of another legal professional, consider the following (not exclusive) factors:

1. Do you have all of the facts?
2. Who is being harmed by the behavior? The public?
3. What are your motives for reporting the behavior?
4. Who is the "proper authority" in your law firm?
5. Who is the "proper law enforcement authority" in your state?
6. How much do you need your job? Can you risk retaliation?
7. In your state, is there an affirmative duty to report misconduct?
8. Are there laws in your state that protect "whistleblowers"?
9. Is there someone else with whom you can discuss the problem to get another perspective? A clergyman, doctor, or teacher?
10. Does anyone else have knowledge of the wrong behavior who could support your position?

Is There a Duty to Make the Law Better?

Changes in human affairs over time will necessitate changes in the law. Model Rule 6.3 and Model Rule 6.4[21] encourage the legal professional to be active in law reform and legal services organizations that are part of our changing world. The participation of legal professionals will work for the better of the legal system. An example of this can be found in the history of *Molien v. Kaiser Foundation Hospitals.* In the mid-1970s, Valerie Molien went to Kaiser Hospital for a routine physical examination. The examining physician diagnosed Valerie as having

---

Rule 6.3
A lawyer may serve as a director, officer or member of a legal services organization, apart from the law firm in which the lawyer practices, notwithstanding that the organization serves persons having interests adverse to a client of the lawyer. The lawyer shall not knowingly participate in a decision or action of the organization:

(a) if participating in the decision or action would be incompatible with the lawyer's obligations to a client under Rule 1.7; or

(b) where the decision or action could have a material adverse effect on the representation of a client of the organization whose interests are adverse to a client of the lawyer.

infectious syphilis and advised her to tell her family members about it because they might be infected as well. Valerie's husband underwent the testing, as did other members of her family and, when none of them was determined to have syphilis, discord broke out within the family. Husband and wife became suspicious of one another and finally divorced. All of the family members suffered severe emotional distress, but Valerie's husband Steve was the most severely affected. Eventually, it was discovered that the doctor's original diagnosis had been in error. Valerie had never had syphilis. The hospital had been mistaken.

At that time, California had no cause of action for "negligent infliction of emotional distress." *Dillon v. Legg*[22] was the nearest precedent, a case in which a mother alleged severe emotional distress after having witnessed a car run over her child. In *Dillon*, however, the California Supreme Court relied heavily on the fact that the mother witnessed the accident and suffered actual physical harm. It was questionable whether the California court would stretch the *Dillon* rule to allow Steve some compensation against Kaiser because he had not actually "witnessed" harm to Valerie.

Rule 6.4
A lawyer may serve as a director, officer or member of an organization involved in reform of the law or its administration notwithstanding that the reform may affect the interests of a client of the lawyer. When the lawyer knows that the interests of a client may be materially benefited by a decision in which the lawyer participates, the lawyer shall disclose that fact but need not identify the client.

> A demurrer is a pleading that says that even if the facts are as alleged by the opposite party, they do not sustain the cause of action based on them. It is the same as saying: even if everything you have alleged is true, so what?

The trial court in *Molien* sustained demurrers to the causes of action, stating that negligent infliction of emotional distress is not actionable in California where the plaintiff had not actually witnessed the harm to the loved one. On review, however, the California Supreme Court held that modern times demanded that a cause of action may be stated for the negligent infliction of emotional distress and further held that the unqualified requirement of physical harm is no longer justified. The lawyer for plaintiff Molien had carved new law in California and championed a good cause for his client.

As a person working in the legal field, you will come across case law that is bad or simply does not reflect current society's best interests. You will find statutes that are badly drafted or have unintended consequences. You have a duty to work toward remedying these problems for the good of the public.

What Sorts of "General Misconduct" Are Prohibited?

There are many violations of the rules of ethics that we have not been able to cover in this text that fall under the category of "general misconduct." Most of these rules fall under a bigger category of "common sense." For example, it is misconduct to yell at the court's personnel.[23] It is also not a good idea to, with reckless disregard for the truth, accuse a court of dishonest conduct.[24]

> **Rule 8.4**
> It is professional misconduct for a lawyer to
> (a) violate or attempt to violate the rules of professional conduct, knowingly assist or induce another to do so, or do so through the acts of another;
> (b) commit a criminal act that reflects adversely on the lawyer's honesty, trustworthiness or fitness as a lawyer in other respects;
> (c) engage in conduct involving dishonesty, fraud, deceit or misrepresentation . . .

There are those amorphous rules that prohibit conduct that is "prejudicial to the administration of justice" such as Attorney Pyle's conduct in threatening another lawyer.

> **Rule 4.4**
> In representing a client, a lawyer shall not use means that have no substantial purpose other than to embarrass, delay, or burden a third person, or use methods of obtaining evidence that violate the legal rights of such a person.

In *Grievance Administrator v. Fried,*[25] some lawyers came up with the following: they associated in certain lawyers who had conflicts with judges for the purpose of having those judges recuse themselves. In this way they conspired to get their criminal defendant clients in front of a judge who was known for giving lighter sentences. These lawyers, then, would get paid $1000 for simply associating in (and not doing any work) so that the judge (who was related to them) was forced to recuse himself. Both the lawyers using this trick and the lawyers related to the judges were disciplined for conduct that was prejudicial to the proper administration of justice.

Another example of conduct prejudicial to the administration of justice comes from Oklahoma where a lawyer filed a parental rights termination petition in one county and lost so she filed it in another county. The Uniform Child Custody Jurisdiction Act requires that the accompanying affidavit advise the court of any other litigation (pending or concluded) concerning the same child. The discipline panel found the second filing frivolous, designed to burden opposing party and counsel, and prejudicial to the administration of justice.[26]

As advocates for a client, we are not held to any rule that prevents or restricts justifiable criticism of the legal system or judges.[27] But criticism should be temperate and dignified and at the right time and place. The purpose of the criticism should be to protect the public and make the judicial system better, not in anger or retribution.

It is never a good idea to lie to a court, even about a personal matter. The lawyer who represented to the small claims court that an amount she owed to her

> **Rule 8.2**
> (a) A lawyer shall not make a statement that the lawyer knows to be false or with reckless disregard as to its truth or falsity concerning the qualifications or integrity of a judge, adjudicatory officer or public legal officer, or of a candidate for election or appointment to judicial or legal office.
> (b) A lawyer who is a candidate for judicial office shall comply with the applicable provisions of the code of judicial conduct.

landlord had been paid when the lawyer knew that there were insufficient funds in her bank account to cover the check engaged in conduct involving dishonesty, fraud, deceit, or misrepresentation as set forth in Rule 8.4.[28] This was true even though the improper conduct had to do with the lawyer's personal life as opposed to her representation of a client.

Remember: The dishonesty or level of wrongdoing will be viewed not from the vantage point of the lawyer or paralegal, but from the viewpoint of the public.[29] "Protect the public" is the legal professional's foremost duty.

Don't use the legal process and your superior knowledge to bully people or not pay your bills. In *Matter of Gemmer,*[30] the offending lawyer refused to pay a personal bill and filed repetitive motions and a malicious abuse of process action in response to a suit to collect the personal bill. Gemmer was suspended from practice for three years for this and other misconduct. The court said,

> Respondent simply avoided paying a just bill, once again using his legal skills to retaliate, harass and damage the plaintiffs. His conduct is beyond a mere violation of the *Code*; it is willful refusal to admit even the slightest error.

What Is Involved in Protecting the Public Trust?

We are required to maintain the high standards of professional conduct and encourage others to do so as well. It requests that every legal professional be "temperate and dignified" and "refrain from all illegal and morally reprehensible conduct" because people who are engaged in the practice of law are held high in the public esteem and are in the public eye at all times. For that reason, it contends, people in this profession have a higher standard to maintain than that of the average citizen.

SUMMARY

This chapter begins with a notion that perhaps we should have begun the entire book with the concept of "integrity." Integrity is such a large umbrella idea that it can, if we let it, dominate all of our discussions about professional responsibility. All of the rules of professional responsibility or rules of professional conduct or rules of ethics or whatever you have been calling them during your study—all of them have as their primary goal to protect the public. The public has a reasonable expectation that all of us who enter the field of law (in all capacities) will be people of good moral character. A wise man once said that if all people were angels, we wouldn't need laws; but we are not angels, so we ask ourselves if we have a responsibility for the ethical behavior of people other than ourselves. Do we have a duty to report other people's misconduct? And if we do, to whom should we report? Once again in this chapter we make a distinction between California law, where lawyers have a duty to report their own misconduct, and other states, where lawyers may have a duty to report the misconduct of other lawyers. We can be fairly sure that paralegals do not have this duty, but we do all have the duty to protect the public trust. So, in this chapter we have come full circle from protecting the public to protecting the public.

CHAPTER REVIEW AND ASSIGNMENTS

CRITICAL THINKING

1. Let's go back to Marco in the "Hypothetical" at the beginning of this chapter. What kind of information has George given him? Is it protected by the attorney/client privilege or duty of confidentiality? If not, does Marco have a duty to do something with the information? Does it make any difference if Marco and George are lawyers or paralegals? Does it make any difference that George is dying? What should Marco do with this information? To guide you in your answer, see *In re Riehlmann*, 891 So.2d 1239 (La. 2005).
2. Integrity is an amorphous quality. We all believe we are people of integrity, but what does that really mean? Give examples (from inside and outside the field of law) of having integrity. Give examples of not having integrity.

ASSIGNMENTS

1. Look for cases of lawyers disciplined for a violation of 4.4, conduct that is *prejudicial to the administration of justice*. You can use that phrase as your search query.
2. Check with your state's disciplinary authority. What is the most common reason for lawyer discipline in your state? What steps do you think you could take, as a paralegal for one of those lawyers, to prohibit the conduct that leads to discipline.

COLLABORATIVE ASSIGNMENTS

1. In this activity, each of you will decide if you are most like (1) a beachball, (2) a microscope, (3) a clipboard, or (4) a puppy. Choose a corner of the classroom for

each group. When students get together their groups (of beachballs, microscopes, clipboards, or puppies), discuss what it is about you that makes you think of yourself as a beachball (or microscope, or clipboard, or puppy). Each of these personality traits or beliefs should have something to do with how you view what you have just learned about the world of ethics or how you think you will use your knowledge in your work as a paralegal. On a piece of poster paper, each group should write a list of your traits/beliefs to share with the rest of the class.

2. In this final class activity, take fifteen minutes and write a letter to yourself completing these sentences: (1) at the ends of six months, I expect to have encountered the following ethical issue:_____. (2) I predict the circumstances of my encounter will be:_____. (3) And I will handle the situation by taking the following action:_____. Seal your letter in an envelope and come up with a delivery method for your letter so that you receive it in six months.

REVIEW QUESTIONS

Multiple Choice

Select the best answer for each of the following questions.

1. According to the NFPA Codes of Conduct, a paralegal shall maintain a high level of
   a. personal and professional integrity.
   b. octane fuel.
   c. credit.
   d. continuing education credits.
   e. ability.
2. The ABA Model Rules require that before a lawyer recommends an applicant to admission to the bar, the lawyer should be certain that the applicant
   a. has a high grade point average.
   b. has paid off all student loans.
   c. is of good moral character.
   d. is available to accept a job right away.
   e. has passed the bar exam.
3. The rule that requires lawyers to report ethics violations of other lawyers is called
   a. the finking rule.
   b. self-policing.
   c. tattle-telling.
   d. integrity checking.
   e. There is no such rule.

4. In *In re Himmel,* attorney Himmel was disciplined because he failed to
   a. help his client.
   b. contact opposing counsel before filing a motion.
   c. correctly draft the settlement agreement.
   d. report unprivileged information about another lawyer's misconduct.
   e. keep accurate records about his client trust account.
5. If your client insists on threatening disciplinary action against opposing counsel, the lawyer must
   a. Notify the state bar.
   b. Send a notice to the State Attorney General.
   c. Withdraw from representation.
   d. Assist the client through the complaint process.
   e. Warn opposing counsel that a disciplinary complaint is pending.
6. The rules regarding reporting the misconduct of other legal professionals
   a. does not apply to paralegals.
   b. only applies to paralegals in ABA Model Code states.

c. applies to paralegals who are members of NFPA in accordance with that organization's Model Code.

d. does not apply to paralegals who are employed by corporations.

e. applies to all paralegals.

7. Once you have made the decision to report the unethical conduct of another legal professional,

a. You must determine who the proper authority is.

b. You must report the conduct to the office manager.

c. You must report the conduct to the senior partner.

d. You must report the conduct to your immediate supervisor, whomever that person may be.

e. You must report the conduct to the state bar or other disciplinary organization in your state.

8. Although there is no absolute duty, there are two Model Rules that encourage the legal professional to

a. Participate in continuing legal education.

b. Be active in law reform.

c. Pay bar dues ahead of the time they are due.

d. Keep accurate records of client trust accounts.

e. Represent indigent criminals pro bono.

9. In *Matter of Gemmer*, the lawyer used his superior knowledge of the legal field and court system in order to

a. win a case for his client.

b. sue a client for fees.

c. escape paying a personal bill.

d. win the Nobel Peace Prize.

e. pass the bar exam.

10. A lawyer who cannot take some action because it is unethical, should

a. Ask the paralegal to do it.

b. Ask a secretary to do it because lawyers and paralegals are bound by codes of ethics but secretaries are not.

c. Order the paralegal to do it.

d. Contact the state bar to ask who would ethically do this unethical task.

e. Forget about it.

Fill in the Blank

Complete each of the following sentences with the best word(s) or phrase(s).

1. The rules of professional responsibility are meant to _____.

2. Before a lawyer recommends an applicant for admission to the bar, the lawyer should be certain that the applicant has _____.

3. The rule that requires lawyer to report ethical violations of other lawyers is called _____. (I'm not looking for "finking" here.)

4. Lawyers and paralegals have a duty to protect the public and assist in _____.

5. There are violations of the rules and then there is _____ misconduct.

6. Every legal professional should be _____ and _____.

7. A lawyer may report the misconduct of another lawyer so long as the information is _____.

8. Model Rule 8.3 requires lawyers to report violations that raise substantial questions about a lawyer's honesty, trustworthiness, or _____.

9. A legal professional who decides to report the unethical behavior of another legal professional should be sure to report to _____.

10. An example of unethical conduct that directly impacts the public is _____.

True/False

Decide whether each of the following statements is true or false and write your answer on the line provided.

____ 1. The rules of professional responsibility in each state are meant to keep the legal profession in a position of power in our society.

____ 2. State bar applications typically require good moral character.

____ 3. Paralegals have a statutory duty to report the misconduct of lawyers but not of other paralegals.

____ 4. Model Rule 8.3 requires lawyers to report violations that raise substantial questions about a lawyer's honesty, trustworthiness, or fitness to practice law.

____ 5. There are no cases holding that a lawyer has a duty to report the misconduct of other lawyers.

____ 6. If all of the knowledge you have about a lawyer's misconduct is privileged, there is still a duty to report that lawyer.

____ 7. California lawyers have a duty to report their own misconduct to the state bar.

____ 8. Making a threat of disciplinary action to gain an advantage in a case is appropriate to protect the interests of your client.

____ 9. The "appropriate authority" to whom ethical breaches should be reported is always the client because you have a duty to protect the client.

____ 10. Criticizing the judicial system is always a violation of a legal professional's ethical responsibilities.

CASE FOR CONSIDERATION

CASE 1

In re Landry
934 S.2d 694
La. (2006)

UNDERLYING FACTS

The underlying facts are largely undisputed. Respondent was admitted to the Louisiana bar in April 1996. In March 1997, respondent accepted a position as a title attorney with Authentic Title, Ltd.

In July 1997, respondent acted as the closing attorney for a transaction involving Walter Wallendorf ("Walter"), who wished to refinance his home. Because Walter's wife, Patsy Wallendorf ("Patsy"), had died several months earlier, respondent determined that it was necessary to open a succession to complete the refinancing. Walter informed respondent that he and Patsy had no children and no property other than the home and its furnishings. Walter also told respondent that "there was no will" when Patsy died. When respondent asked Walter for the names of witnesses who could verify these facts, Walter informed respondent that he and Patsy had not socialized much and that he could not think of any witnesses who could provide the information.

Thereafter, respondent prepared an affidavit of death and heirship based solely on the information provided by Walter. The affidavit stated that Patsy died intestate. Walter signed the affidavit and respondent notarized it. A second affidavit was executed by Kelly Jones and Heather St. Amant, two notarial secretaries employed by Authentic Title, repeating the information contained in Walter's affidavit. These secretaries swore in the affidavit that they were "well acquainted" with Patsy and knew that she had died intestate. Respondent reviewed the Jones/St. Amant affidavit and notarized it. The affidavits were included with a petition for possession signed by respondent and filed in the matter entitled Succession of Patsy Ruth Wallendorf, No. 513-162 on the docket of the 24th Judicial District Court for the Parish of Jefferson. In August 1997, the court rendered a judgment of possession in favor of Walter.

Approximately one year later, respondent learned that Patsy had in fact died testate. In 1994, Patsy had executed a will leaving all of her assets, including the Wallendorf home, to Michael Bradford Walker and Jennifer Brooke Walker ("Michael and Jennifer"), the children of Shirley Walker ("Shirley"). Walter apparently believed that his wife had rescinded that will shortly before her death in 1997, leaving her without a will. Subsequently, Shirley retained counsel and brought an action to annul the 1997 judgment of possession. Walter represented himself in the litigation. At the conclusion of the proceeding, the court set aside the earlier judgment of possession in Walter's favor and appointed Shirley as the testamentary executrix of Patsy's succession.

In July 2000, Michael and Jennifer filed a civil suit against respondent and others. During the course of the litigation, Heather St. Amant testified that neither she nor Ms. Jones knew Patsy at the time they executed the affidavit attesting that they were "well acquainted" with Patsy and knew she had died intestate. Ms. St. Amant testified that she signed the affidavit, even though she did not know Patsy, because she was told to do so. In October 2001, Michael and Jennifer settled their suit for $70,000, which sum was paid by Authentic Title.

DISCIPLINARY PROCEEDINGS

Following its investigation of a complaint filed by Shirley, the ODC filed one count of formal charges against respondent, alleging that his conduct violated Rules 3.3(a)(1) (knowingly making a false statement of fact or law to a tribunal), 8.4(c) (engaging in conduct involving dishonesty, fraud, deceit, or misrepresentation) and 8.4(d) (engaging in conduct prejudicial to the administration of justice) of the *Rules of Professional Conduct*. Respondent answered the formal charges, admitting most of the factual allegations and admitting that he violated the cited *Rules of Professional Conduct* "by virtue of his submission of affidavits in which the affiants declared personal knowledge of facts that they did not know, although in good faith believed to be true."[1]

This matter then proceeded to a formal hearing on the merits, at which respondent and Shirley Walker testified. In addition, respondent offered testimony, both in person and by letter and affidavit, attesting to his good character and reputation.

Hearing Committee Recommendation

After considering this matter, the hearing committee made factual findings as follows: Respondent relied upon Walter's representations that he and Patsy had no children and had no property other than their residence and its furnishings and contents. Respondent also relied upon Walter's representations that Patsy did not execute a will and died intestate. When respondent questioned Walter regarding witnesses who could verify these facts, Walter advised respondent that he could not think of anyone who could execute the appropriate affidavits of death and heirship. Assuming Walter's representations were accurate, respondent prepared an affidavit of death and heirship for Walter's signature. Respondent or another employee of Authentic Title prepared a second affidavit wherein employees of Authentic Title alleged to have personal knowledge of the facts that Walter represented to respondent. Respondent notarized the second affidavit even though he knew or should have known the employees did not have the requisite personal knowledge to execute the affidavit. When Patsy's succession was filed with the court, Walter was recognized as the sole heir and placed in possession of all of the property in the succession. Some two years later, Shirley brought an action to annul the judgment of possession in favor of Walter. Shirley represented to the court that Patsy had died testate and Shirley's children were the proper heirs to the succession. An ancillary litigation was filed seeking recovery against respondent and others for the errors outlined above. That litigation was settled in October 2001, giving the injured parties $70,000 in settlement of their claim.

Based on these factual findings and respondent's stipulations in his answer, the committee determined that respondent violated the *Rules of Professional Conduct* as alleged in the formal charges. The committee found mitigating factors to be present, namely "the relative inexperience of the respondent, the respondent's reliance upon the statements of his client, and the lack of any motive to do harm to any party." The committee determined that instead of taking the time to investigate Walter's statements, respondent gave into pressure to expedite the refinancing process. The committee further determined that in doing so, respondent made an error which was not motivated by financial gain and was probably made because respondent believed he was expediting a matter that was both truthful and accurate. Respondent's error caused financial loss, which has been resolved by the courts.

The committee was impressed by the character witness and character affidavits submitted by respondent for consideration. The committee also felt that respondent's error was "one that all people in all professions are confronted with at the beginning of their careers."

Under these circumstances, the committee recommended that respondent be publicly reprimanded. The ODC filed an objection to the hearing committee's recommendation.

Ruling of the Disciplinary Board

After review, the disciplinary board determined that the hearing committee's factual findings were not manifestly erroneous. Furthermore, the board determined the committee properly found that respondent had violated the *Rules of Professional Conduct* as alleged in the formal charges.

The board found that respondent's conduct was negligent as to the 8.4(c) and (d) violations; however, his violation of Rule 3.3(a)(1) was knowing. It determined his conduct caused harm to both Shirley's children and Walter, because Shirley's children were required to file a lawsuit to have the appropriate will recognized by the court, and Walter was forced to defend himself in the proceeding. It concluded the lawsuit might have been avoided had respondent investigated Patsy's succession issues. Nevertheless, it recognized Shirley's children received $70,000 in settlement of their malpractice claim against respondent and others.

The board determined that the baseline sanction in this matter is a public reprimand. It found no aggravating factors present. In mitigation, it noted the following: absence of a dishonest or selfish motive, timely good faith effort to make restitution or to rectify the consequences of the misconduct, full and free disclosure to the disciplinary board and a cooperative attitude toward the proceedings, inexperience in the practice of law (admitted 1996), character or reputation, and remorse.

Finding that the case law supports a public reprimand for the misconduct at issue, the board ordered that respondent be publicly reprimanded.[2] It further ordered that he be assessed with all costs and expenses of these proceedings.

Three members of the disciplinary board dissented on the issue of an appropriate sanction. Relying on *In re: Wahlder*, 98-2742 (La.1/15/99), 728 So.2d 837, the dissenting board members would recommend that respondent be suspended from the practice of law for six months, with all but thirty days deferred.[3]

The ODC sought review of the disciplinary board's ruling in this court. We ordered the parties to submit briefs addressing the issue of whether the record supports the board's report. After reviewing the briefs filed by both parties, we docketed the matter for oral argument.

DISCUSSION

Bar disciplinary matters come within the original jurisdiction of this court. La. Const. art. V, § 5(B). Consequently, we act as triers of fact and conduct an independent review of the record to determine whether the alleged misconduct has been proven by clear and convincing evidence. *In re: Quaid*, 94-1316 (La.11/30/94), 646 So.2d 343; *Louisiana State Bar Ass'n v. Boutall*, 597 So.2d 444 (La.1992). While we are not bound in any way by the findings and recommendations of the hearing committee and disciplinary board, we have held the manifest error standard is applicable to the committee's factual findings. See *In re: Caulfield*, 96-1401 (La.11/25/96), 683 So.2d 714; *In re: Pardue*, 93-2865 (La.3/11/94), 633 So.2d 150.

Based on the stipulations by respondent and other evidence in the record, we find respondent notarized and caused to be filed into a succession proceeding two affidavits that he knew or should have known contained false information. As respondent has admitted, there is clear and convincing evidence which establishes that he has violated Rules 3.3(a)(1), 8.4(c), and 8.4(d) of the *Rules of Professional Conduct*.

Having found evidence of professional misconduct, we now turn to a determination of the appropriate sanction for respondent's actions. In considering that issue, we are mindful that disciplinary proceedings are designed to maintain high standards of conduct, protect the public, preserve the integrity of the profession, and deter future misconduct. *Louisiana State Bar Ass'n v. Reis*, 513 So.2d 1173 (La.1987). The discipline to be imposed depends upon the facts of each case and the seriousness of the offenses involved considered in light of any aggravating and mitigating circumstances. *Louisiana State Bar Ass'n v. Whittington*, 459 So.2d 520 (La.1984).

With regard to the affidavit of death and heirship executed by Walter, stating that Patsy died without leaving a will, we find respondent's conduct was largely negligent. Although respondent probably should have undertaken a more detailed investigation to confirm the correctness of Walter's statement that Patsy died intestate, there was nothing in the statement to indicate it was false on its face.

The same cannot be said of the affidavit executed by respondent's office staff. It is undisputed that respondent knew his notarial secretaries were not "well acquainted" with Patsy, and that they had no personal knowledge of whether she died intestate. The only logical conclusion which can be drawn from respondent's actions is that he knowingly and intentionally filed this false affidavit into the court records. Respondent's actions caused actual harm to Walter and Shirley's children. In addition, respondent's actions caused harm to the court system, which must be able to rely on the truthfulness of representations made by counsel. The baseline sanction for respondent's misconduct is a suspension from the practice of law. See *In re: Wahlder*, 98-2742 (La.1/15/99), 728 So.2d 837.

In mitigation, we accept the hearing committee's finding that respondent did not file this affidavit with any improper motive. As the committee observed, respondent sincerely believed that Walter's representation that his wife died intestate was truthful and accurate, and his actions were undertaken with the intent of expediting the refinancing of Walter's home. We also recognize the absence of a prior disciplinary record, respondent's full and free disclosure to the disciplinary board and cooperative attitude toward the proceedings, inexperience in the practice of law at the time of the offense, good character and reputation, and remorse. We are unable to discern any aggravating factors from the record.

Considering all the circumstances, we find the appropriate sanction in this case is a six-month suspension from the practice of law. In light of the substantial mitigating factors present, and the absence of any aggravating factors, we will defer all but thirty days of the suspension, subject to the condition that any misconduct during a six-month period may be grounds for making the deferred portion of the suspension executory, or imposing additional discipline, as appropriate.

DECREE

Upon review of the findings and recommendations of the hearing committee and disciplinary board, and considering the record, briefs, and oral argument, it is ordered that Mitchell Reid Landry, Louisiana Bar Roll number 24147, be suspended from the practice of law for a period of six months. It is further ordered that all but thirty days of the suspension shall be deferred and respondent shall be placed on unsupervised probation for six months, subject to the condition that any misconduct during this period may be grounds for making the deferred portion of the suspension executory, or imposing additional discipline, as appropriate. All costs and expenses in the matter are assessed against respondent in accordance with Supreme Court Rule XIX, § 10.1, with legal interest to commence thirty days from the date of finality of this court's judgment until paid.

CASE QUESTIONS

1. The ODC filed one charge against Attorney Landry but then did not like the decision of the hearing committee. What were the specific reasons the ODC filed an objection to the hearing committee's recommendation?
2. What was the Disciplinary Board's decision? What was the argument of the dissenters on that Board?
3. Patsy's real heirs were awarded $70,000 in a civil action. What difference should that make in Attorney Landry's disciplinary action? What difference should it make that he is young and inexperienced?

NALA Code of Ethics and Professional Responsibility

Canon 1

A legal assistant must not perform any of the duties that attorneys only may perform nor take any actions that attorneys may not take.

Canon 2

A legal assistant may perform any task which is properly delegated and supervised by an attorney, as long as the attorney is ultimately responsible to the client, maintains a direct relationship with the client, and assumes professional responsibility for the work product.

Canon 3

A legal assistant must not: (a) engage in, encourage, or contribute to any act which could constitute the unauthorized practice of law; and (b) establish attorney-client

*Copyright 1975: Revised 1979, 1988, 1995. Reprinted with permission of NALA, 1516 S. Boston, #200, Tulsa, OK 74119, http://www.nala.org.

relationships, set fees, give legal opinions or advice or represent a client before a court or agency unless so authorized by that court or agency; and (c) engage in conduct or take any action which would assist or involve the attorney in a violation of professional ethics or give the appearance of professional impropriety.

Canon 4

A legal assistant must use discretion and professional judgment commensurate with knowledge and experience but must not render independent legal judgment in place of an attorney. The services of an attorney are essential in the public interest whenever such legal judgment is required.

Canon 5

A legal assistant must disclose his or her status as a legal assistant at the outset of any professional relationship with a client, attorney, a court or administrative agency or personnel thereof, or a member of the general public. A legal assistant must act prudently in determining the extent to which a client may be assisted without the presence of an attorney.

Canon 6

A legal assistant must strive to maintain integrity and a high degree of competency through education and training with respect to professional responsibility, local rules and practice, and through continuing education in substantive areas of law to better assist the legal profession in fulfilling its duty to provide legal service.

Canon 7

A legal assistant must protect the confidences of a client and must not violate any rule or statute now in effect or hereafter enacted controlling the doctrine of privileged communications between a client and an attorney.

Canon 8

A legal assistant must do all other things incidental, necessary, or expedient for the attainment of the ethics and responsibilities as defined by statute or rule of court.

Canon 9

A legal assistant's conduct is guided by bar associations' codes of professional responsibility and rules of professional conduct.

B

....

NALS Code of Ethics*

Members of NALS are bound by the objectives of this association and the standards of conduct required of the legal profession.

Every member shall

- Encourage respect for the law and the administration of justice;
- Observe rules governing privileged communications and confidential information;
- Promote and exemplify high standards of loyalty, cooperation, and courtesy;
- Perform all duties of the profession with integrity and competence; and
- Pursue a high order of professional attainment.

Integrity and high standards of conduct are fundamental to the success of our professional association. This Code is promulgated by the NALS and accepted by its members to accomplish these ends.

Canon 1

Members of this association shall maintain a high degree of competency and integrity through continuing education to better assist the legal profession in fulfilling its duty to provide quality legal services to the public.

---

*Reprinted by permission from NALS . . . the association for legal professionals.

Canon 2

Members of this association shall maintain a high standard of ethical conduct and shall contribute to the integrity of the association and the legal profession.

Canon 3

Members of this association shall avoid a conflict of interest pertaining to a client matter.

Canon 4

Members of this association shall preserve and protect the confidences and privileged communications of a client.

Canon 5

Members of this association shall exercise care in using independent professional judgment and in determining the extent to which a client may be assisted without the presence of a lawyer and shall not act in matters involving professional legal judgment.

Canon 6

Members of this association shall not solicit legal business on behalf of a lawyer.

Canon 7

Members of this association, unless permitted by law, shall not perform paralegal functions except under the direct supervision of a lawyer and shall not advertise or contract with members of the general public for the performance of paralegal functions.

Canon 8

Members of this association, unless permitted by law, shall not perform any of the duties restricted to lawyers or do things which lawyers themselves may not do and shall assist in preventing the unauthorized practice of law.

Canon 9

Members of this association not licensed to practice law shall not engage in the practice of law as defined by statutes or court decisions.

Canon 10

Members of this association shall do all other things incidental, necessary, or expedient to enhance professional responsibility and participation in the administration of justice and public service in cooperation with the legal profession.

National Federation of Paralegal Associations, Inc. Model Code of Ethics and Professional Responsibility*

PREAMBLE

The National Federation of Paralegal Associations, Inc. ("NFPA") is a professional organization comprised of paralegal associations and individual paralegals throughout the United States and Canada. Members of NFPA have varying backgrounds, experiences, education and job responsibilities that reflect the diversity of the paralegal profession. NFPA promotes the growth, development and recognition of the paralegal profession as an integral partner in the delivery of legal services.

In May 1993 NFPA adopted its *Model Code of Ethics and Professional Responsibility* ("*Model Code*") to delineate the principles for ethics and conduct to which every paralegal should aspire.

Many paralegal associations throughout the United States have endorsed the concept and content of NFPA's *Model Code* through the adoption of their own ethical codes. In doing so, paralegals have confirmed the profession's commitment to increase the quality and efficiency of legal services, as well as recognized its responsibilities to the public, the legal community, and colleagues.

Paralegals have recognized, and will continue to recognize, that the profession must continue to evolve to enhance their roles in the delivery of legal services. With increased levels of responsibility comes the need to define and enforce mandatory

---

*Reprinted by permission from the National Federation of Paralegal Associations, Inc., http://www.paralegals.org.

rules of professional conduct. Enforcement of codes of paralegal conduct is a logical and necessary step to enhance and ensure the confidence of the legal community and the public in the integrity and professional responsibility of paralegals.

In April 1997 NFPA adopted the *Model Disciplinary Rules* ("*Model Rules*") to make possible the enforcement of the Canons and Ethical Considerations contained in the NFPA *Model Code*. A concurrent determination was made that the *Model Code of Ethics and Professional Responsibility*, formerly aspirational in nature, should be recognized as setting forth the enforceable obligations of all paralegals.

The *Model Code* and *Model Rules* offer a framework for professional discipline, either voluntarily or through formal regulatory programs.

§1. NFPA MODEL DISCIPLINARY RULES AND ETHICAL CONSIDERATIONS

1.1 A PARALEGAL SHALL ACHIEVE AND MAINTAIN A HIGH LEVEL OF COMPETENCE

Ethical Considerations

EC-1.1(a) A paralegal shall achieve competency through education, training, and work experience.

EC-1.1(b) A paralegal shall aspire to participate in a minimum of twelve (12) hours of continuing legal education, to include at least one (1) hour of ethics education, every two (2) years in order to remain current on developments in the law.

EC-1.1(c) A paralegal shall perform all assignments promptly and efficiently.

1.2 A PARALEGAL SHALL MAINTAIN A HIGH LEVEL OF PERSONAL AND PROFESSIONAL INTEGRITY

Ethical Considerations

EC-1.2(a) A paralegal shall not engage in any ex parte communications involving the courts or any other adjudicatory body in an attempt to exert undue influence or to obtain advantage or the benefit of only one party.

EC-1.2(b) A paralegal shall not communicate, or cause another to communicate, with a party the paralegal knows to be represented by a lawyer in a pending matter without the prior consent of the lawyer representing such other party.

EC-1.2(c) A paralegal shall ensure that all timekeeping and billing records prepared by the paralegal are thorough, accurate, honest, and complete.

EC-1.2(d) A paralegal shall not knowingly engage in fraudulent billing practices. Such practices may include, but are not limited to: inflation of hours billed to a client or employer; misrepresentation of the nature of tasks performed; and/or submission of fraudulent expense and disbursement documentation.

EC-1.2(e) A paralegal shall be scrupulous, thorough and honest in the identification and maintenance of all funds, securities, and other assets of a client and shall provide accurate accounting as appropriate.

EC-1.2(f) A paralegal shall advise the proper authority of non-confidential knowledge of any dishonest or fraudulent acts by any person pertaining to the handling of the funds, securities or other assets of a client. The authority to whom the report is made shall depend on the nature and circumstances of the possible misconduct, (e.g., ethics committees of law firms, corporations and/or paralegal associations, local or state bar associations, local prosecutors, administrative agencies, etc.). Failure to report such knowledge is in itself misconduct and shall be treated as such under these rules.

1.3 A PARALEGAL SHALL MAINTAIN A HIGH STANDARD OF PROFESSIONAL CONDUCT

Ethical Considerations

EC-1.3(a) A paralegal shall refrain from engaging in any conduct that offends the dignity and decorum of proceedings before a court or other adjudicatory body and shall be respectful of all rules and procedures.

EC-1.3(b) A paralegal shall avoid impropriety and the appearance of impropriety and shall not engage in any conduct that would adversely affect his/her fitness to practice. Such conduct may include, but is not limited to: violence, dishonesty, interference with the administration of justice, and/or abuse of a professional position or public office.

EC-1.3(c) Should a paralegal's fitness to practice be compromised by physical or mental illness, causing that paralegal to commit an act that is in direct violation of the *Model Code/Model Rules* and/or the rules and/or laws governing the jurisdiction in which the paralegal practices, that paralegal may be protected from sanction upon review of the nature and circumstances of that illness.

EC-1.3(d) A paralegal shall advise the proper authority of non-confidential knowledge of any action of another legal professional that clearly demonstrates fraud, deceit, dishonesty, or misrepresentation. The authority to whom the report is made shall depend on the nature and circumstances of the possible misconduct, (e.g., ethics committees of law firms, corporations and/or paralegal associations, local or state bar associations, local prosecutors, administrative agencies, etc.). Failure to report such knowledge is in itself misconduct and shall be treated as such under these rules.

EC-1.3(e) A paralegal shall not knowingly assist any individual with the commission of an act that is in direct violation of the *Model Code/Model Rules* and/or the rules and/or laws governing the jurisdiction in which the paralegal practices.

EC-1.3(f) If a paralegal possesses knowledge of future criminal activity, that knowledge must be reported to the appropriate authority immediately.

1.4 A PARALEGAL SHALL SERVE THE PUBLIC INTEREST BY CONTRIBUTING TO THE IMPROVEMENT OF THE LEGAL SYSTEM AND DELIVERY OF QUALITY LEGAL SERVICES, INCLUDING PRO BONO PUBLICO SERVICES

Ethical Considerations

EC-1.4(a) A paralegal shall be sensitive to the legal needs of the public and shall promote the development and implementation of programs that address those needs.

EC-1.4(b) A paralegal shall support efforts to improve the legal system and access thereto and shall assist in making changes.

EC-1.4(c) A paralegal shall support and participate in the delivery of Pro Bono Publico services directed toward implementing and improving access to justice, the law, the legal system or the paralegal and legal professions.

EC-1.4(d) A paralegal should aspire annually to contribute twenty-four (24) hours of Pro Bono Publico services under the supervision of an attorney or as authorized by administrative, statutory or court authority to:

> persons of limited means; or charitable, religious, civic, community, governmental and educational organizations in matters that are designed primarily to address the legal needs of persons with limited means; or

> individuals, groups or organizations seeking to secure or protect civil rights, civil liberties or public rights.

The twenty-four (24) hours of Pro Bono Publico services contributed annually by a paralegal may consist of such services as detailed in this EC-1.4(d), and/or administrative matters designed to develop and implement the attainment of this aspiration as detailed above in EC-1.4(a) B (c), or any combination of the two.

1.5 A PARALEGAL SHALL PRESERVE ALL CONFIDENTIAL INFORMATION PROVIDED BY THE CLIENT OR ACQUIRED FROM OTHER SOURCES BEFORE, DURING, AND AFTER THE COURSE OF THE PROFESSIONAL RELATIONSHIP

Ethical Considerations

EC-1.5(a) A paralegal shall be aware of and abide by all legal authority governing confidential information in the jurisdiction in which the paralegal practices.

EC-1.5(b) A paralegal shall not use confidential information to the disadvantage of the client.

EC-1.5(c) A paralegal shall not use confidential information to the advantage of the paralegal or of a third person.

EC-1.5(d) A paralegal may reveal confidential information only after full disclosure and with the client's written consent; or, when required by law or court order; or, when necessary to prevent the client from committing an act that could result in death or serious bodily harm.

EC-1.5(e) A paralegal shall keep those individuals responsible for the legal representation of a client fully informed of any confidential information the paralegal may have pertaining to that client.

EC-1.5(f) A paralegal shall not engage in any indiscreet communications concerning clients.

1.6 A PARALEGAL SHALL AVOID CONFLICTS OF INTEREST AND SHALL DISCLOSE ANY POSSIBLE CONFLICT TO THE EMPLOYER OR CLIENT, AS WELL AS TO THE PROSPECTIVE EMPLOYERS OR CLIENTS

Ethical Considerations

EC-1.6(a) A paralegal shall act within the bounds of the law, solely for the benefit of the client, and shall be free of compromising influences and loyalties. Neither the paralegal's personal or business interest, nor those of other clients or third persons, should compromise the paralegal's professional judgment and loyalty to the client.

EC-1.6(b) A paralegal shall avoid conflicts of interest that may arise from previous assignments, whether for a present or past employer or client.

EC-1.6(c) A paralegal shall avoid conflicts of interest that may arise from family relationships and from personal and business interests.

EC-1.6(d) In order to be able to determine whether an actual or potential conflict of interest exists a paralegal shall create and maintain an effective record-keeping system that identifies clients, matters, and parties with which the paralegal has worked.

EC-1.6(e) A paralegal shall reveal sufficient non-confidential information about a client or former client to reasonably ascertain if an actual or potential conflict of interest exists.

EC-1.6(f) A paralegal shall not participate in or conduct work on any matter where a conflict of interest has been identified.

EC-1.6(g) In matters where a conflict of interest has been identified and the client consents to continued representation, a paralegal shall comply fully with the implementation and maintenance of an Ethical Wall.

1.7 A PARALEGAL'S TITLE SHALL BE FULLY DISCLOSED

Ethical Considerations

EC-1.7(a) A paralegal's title shall clearly indicate the individual's status and shall be disclosed in all business and professional communications to avoid misunderstandings and misconceptions about the paralegal's role and responsibilities.

EC-1.7(b) A paralegal's title shall be included if the paralegal's name appears on business cards, letterhead, brochures, directories, and advertisements.

EC-1.7(c) A paralegal shall not use letterhead, business cards or other promotional materials to create a fraudulent impression of his/her status or ability to practice in the jurisdiction in which the paralegal practices.

EC-1.7(d) A paralegal shall not practice under color of any record, diploma, or certificate that has been illegally or fraudulently obtained or issued or which is misrepresentative in any way.

EC-1.7(e) A paralegal shall not participate in the creation, issuance, or dissemination of fraudulent records, diplomas, or certificates.

1.8 A PARALEGAL SHALL NOT ENGAGE IN THE UNAUTHORIZED PRACTICE OF LAW

Ethical Considerations

EC-1.8(a) A paralegal shall comply with the applicable legal authority governing the unauthorized practice of law in the jurisdiction in which the paralegal practices.

ABA Informal Opinion 1384 (1997)

1. Unless a client consents, a lawyer should not destroy or discard items that clearly or probably belong to the client. Such items include those furnished to the lawyer by or on behalf of the client, the return of which could reasonably be expected by the client, and original documents (especially when not filed or recorded in the public records).

2. A lawyer should use care not to destroy or discard information that the lawyer knows or should know may still be necessary or useful in the assertion or defense of the client's position in a matter for which the applicable statutory limitations period has not expired.

3. A lawyer should use care not to destroy or discard information that the client may need, has not previously been given to the client, is not otherwise readily available to the client, and that the client may reasonably expect will be preserved by the lawyer.

4. In determining the length of time for retention or disposition of a file, a lawyer should exercise discretion. The nature and contents of some files may indicate a need for longer retention than do the nature and contents of other files, based upon their obvious relevance and materiality to matters that can be expected to arise.

5. A lawyer should take special care to preserve indefinitely accurate and complete records of the lawyer's receipt and disbursement of trust funds.

6. In disposing of a file, a lawyer should protect the confidentiality of the contents.

7. A lawyer should not destroy or dispose of a file without screening it in order to determine that consideration has been given to the aforementioned matters.

8. A lawyer should preserve, perhaps for an extended time, an index or identification of the files that the lawyer has destroyed or disposed of.

APPENDIX

E

···························

Selections from the ABA Model Rules of Professional Conduct

CLIENT-LAWYER RELATIONSHIP

Rule 1.1 Competence

A lawyer shall provide competent representation to a client. Competent representation requires the legal knowledge, skill, thoroughness and preparation reasonably necessary for the representation.

Rule 1.1 Competence - Comment

Legal Knowledge and Skill

[1] In determining whether a lawyer employs the requisite knowledge and skill in a particular matter, relevant factors include the relative complexity and specialized nature of the matter, the lawyer's general experience, the lawyer's training and experience in the field in question, the preparation and study the lawyer is able to give the matter and whether it is feasible to refer the matter to, or associate or consult with, a lawyer of established competence in the field in question. In many instances, the required proficiency is that of a general practitioner. Expertise in a particular field of law may be required in some circumstances.

[2] A lawyer need not necessarily have special training or prior experience to handle legal problems of a type with which the lawyer is unfamiliar. A newly admitted lawyer can be as competent as a practitioner with long experience. Some important legal skills, such as the analysis of precedent, the evaluation of evidence and legal drafting, are required in all legal problems. Perhaps the most fundamental legal skill consists of determining what kind of legal problems a situation may involve, a

*ABA *Model Rules of Professional Conduct,* 2006 Edition. © 2006 by the American Bar Association. Reprinted with permission.

skill that necessarily transcends any particular specialized knowledge. A lawyer can provide adequate representation in a wholly novel field through necessary study. Competent representation can also be provided through the association of a lawyer of established competence in the field in question.

[3] In an emergency a lawyer may give advice or assistance in a matter in which the lawyer does not have the skill ordinarily required where referral to or consultation or association with another lawyer would be impractical. Even in an emergency, however, assistance should be limited to that reasonably necessary in the circumstances, for ill-considered action under emergency conditions can jeopardize the client's interest.

[4] A lawyer may accept representation where the requisite level of competence can be achieved by reasonable preparation. This applies as well to a lawyer who is appointed as counsel for an unrepresented person. See also Rule 6.2.

Thoroughness and Preparation

[5] Competent handling of a particular matter includes inquiry into and analysis of the factual and legal elements of the problem, and use of methods and procedures meeting the standards of competent practitioners. It also includes adequate preparation. The required attention and preparation are determined in part by what is at stake; major litigation and complex transactions ordinarily require more extensive treatment than matters of lesser complexity and consequence. An agreement between the lawyer and the client regarding the scope of the representation may limit the matters for which the lawyer is responsible. See Rule 1.2(c).

Maintaining Competence

[6] To maintain the requisite knowledge and skill, a lawyer should keep abreast of changes in the law and its practice, engage in continuing study and education and comply with all continuing legal education requirements to which the lawyer is subject.

Rule 1.3 Diligence

A lawyer shall act with reasonable diligence and promptness in representing a client.

Rule 1.3 Diligence - Comment

[1] A lawyer should pursue a matter on behalf of a client despite opposition, obstruction or personal inconvenience to the lawyer, and take whatever lawful and ethical measures are required to vindicate a client's cause or endeavor. A lawyer must also act with commitment and dedication to the interests of the client and with zeal in advocacy upon the client's behalf. A lawyer is not bound, however, to press for every advantage that might be realized for a client. For example, a lawyer may have authority to exercise professional discretion in determining the means by which a matter should be pursued. See Rule 1.2. The lawyer's duty to act with reasonable diligence does not require the use of offensive tactics or preclude the treating of all persons involved in the legal process with courtesy and respect.

[2] A lawyer's work load must be controlled so that each matter can be handled competently.

[3] Perhaps no professional shortcoming is more widely resented than procrastination. A client's interests often can be adversely affected by the passage of time or the change of conditions; in extreme instances, as when a lawyer overlooks a statute of limitations, the client's legal position may be destroyed. Even when the client's interests are not affected in substance, however, unreasonable delay can cause a client needless anxiety and undermine confidence in the lawyer's trustworthiness. A lawyer's duty to act with reasonable promptness, however, does not preclude the lawyer from agreeing to a reasonable request for a postponement that will not prejudice the lawyer's client.

[4] Unless the relationship is terminated as provided in Rule 1.16, a lawyer should carry through to conclusion all matters undertaken for a client. If a lawyer's employment is limited to a specific matter, the relationship terminates when the matter has been resolved. If a lawyer has served a client over a substantial period in a variety of matters, the client sometimes may assume that the lawyer will continue to serve on a continuing basis unless the lawyer gives notice of withdrawal. Doubt about whether a client-lawyer relationship still exists should be clarified by the lawyer, preferably in writing, so that the client will not mistakenly suppose the lawyer is looking after the client's affairs when the lawyer has ceased to do so. For example, if a lawyer has handled a judicial or administrative proceeding that produced a result adverse to the client and the lawyer and the client have not agreed that the lawyer will handle the matter on appeal, the lawyer must consult with the client about the possibility of appeal before relinquishing responsibility for the matter. See Rule 1.4(a)(2). Whether the lawyer is obligated to prosecute the appeal for the client depends on the scope of the representation the lawyer has agreed to provide to the client. See Rule 1.2.

[5] To prevent neglect of client matters in the event of a sole practitioner's death or disability, the duty of diligence may require that each sole practitioner prepare a plan, in conformity with applicable rules, that designates another competent lawyer to review client files, notify each client of the lawyer's death or disability, and determine whether there is a need for immediate protective action. Cf. Rule 28 of the American Bar Association Model Rules for Lawyer Disciplinary Enforcement (providing for court appointment of a lawyer to inventory files and take other protective action in absence of a plan providing for another lawyer to protect the interests of the clients of a deceased or disabled lawyer).

Rule 1.5 Fees

a. A lawyer shall not make an agreement for, charge, or collect an unreasonable fee or an unreasonable amount for expenses. The factors to be considered in determining the reasonableness of a fee include the following:
   1. the time and labor required, the novelty and difficulty of the questions involved, and the skill requisite to perform the legal service properly;
   2. the likelihood, if apparent to the client, that the acceptance of the particular employment will preclude other employment by the lawyer;

3. the fee customarily charged in the locality for similar legal services;
4. the amount involved and the results obtained;
5. the time limitations imposed by the client or by the circumstances;
6. the nature and length of the professional relationship with the client;
7. the experience, reputation, and ability of the lawyer or lawyers performing the services; and
8. whether the fee is fixed or contingent.

b. The scope of the representation and the basis or rate of the fee and expenses for which the client will be responsible shall be communicated to the client, preferably in writing, before or within a reasonable time after commencing the representation, except when the lawyer will charge a regularly represented client on the same basis or rate. Any changes in the basis or rate of the fee or expenses shall also be communicated to the client.

c. A fee may be contingent on the outcome of the matter for which the service is rendered, except in a matter in which a contingent fee is prohibited by paragraph (d) or other law. A contingent fee agreement shall be in a writing signed by the client and shall state the method by which the fee is to be determined, including the percentage or percentages that shall accrue to the lawyer in the event of settlement, trial or appeal; litigation and other expenses to be deducted from the recovery; and whether such expenses are to be deducted before or after the contingent fee is calculated. The agreement must clearly notify the client of any expenses for which the client will be liable whether or not the client is the prevailing party. Upon conclusion of a contingent fee matter, the lawyer shall provide the client with a written statement stating the outcome of the matter and, if there is a recovery, showing the remittance to the client and the method of its determination.

d. A lawyer shall not enter into an arrangement for, charge, or collect:
1. any fee in a domestic relations matter, the payment or amount of which is contingent upon the securing of a divorce or upon the amount of alimony or support, or property settlement in lieu thereof; or
2. a contingent fee for representing a defendant in a criminal case.

e. A division of a fee between lawyers who are not in the same firm may be made only if:
1. the division is in proportion to the services performed by each lawyer or each lawyer assumes joint responsibility for the representation;
2. the client agrees to the arrangement, including the share each lawyer will receive, and the agreement is confirmed in writing; and
3. the total fee is reasonable.

Rule 1.5 Fees - Comment

Reasonableness of Fee and Expenses

[1] Paragraph (a) requires that lawyers charge fees that are reasonable under the circumstances. The factors specified in (1) through (8) are not exclusive. Nor will each

factor be relevant in each instance. Paragraph (a) also requires that expenses for which the client will be charged must be reasonable. A lawyer may seek reimbursement for the cost of services performed in-house, such as copying, or for other expenses incurred in-house, such as telephone charges, either by charging a reasonable amount to which the client has agreed in advance or by charging an amount that reasonably reflects the cost incurred by the lawyer.

Basis or Rate of Fee

[2] When the lawyer has regularly represented a client, they ordinarily will have evolved an understanding concerning the basis or rate of the fee and the expenses for which the client will be responsible. In a new client-lawyer relationship, however, an understanding as to fees and expenses must be promptly established. Generally, it is desirable to furnish the client with at least a simple memorandum or copy of the lawyer's customary fee arrangements that states the general nature of the legal services to be provided, the basis, rate or total amount of the fee and whether and to what extent the client will be responsible for any costs, expenses or disbursements in the course of the representation. A written statement concerning the terms of the engagement reduces the possibility of misunderstanding.

[3] Contingent fees, like any other fees, are subject to the reasonableness standard of paragraph (a) of this Rule. In determining whether a particular contingent fee is reasonable, or whether it is reasonable to charge any form of contingent fee, a lawyer must consider the factors that are relevant under the circumstances. Applicable law may impose limitations on contingent fees, such as a ceiling on the percentage allowable, or may require a lawyer to offer clients an alternative basis for the fee. Applicable law also may apply to situations other than a contingent fee, for example, government regulations regarding fees in certain tax matters.

Terms of Payment

[4] A lawyer may require advance payment of a fee, but is obliged to return any unearned portion. See Rule 1.16(d). A lawyer may accept property in payment for services, such as an ownership interest in an enterprise, providing this does not involve acquisition of a proprietary interest in the cause of action or subject matter of the litigation contrary to Rule 1.8 (i). However, a fee paid in property instead of money may be subject to the requirements of Rule 1.8(a) because such fees often have the essential qualities of a business transaction with the client.

[5] An agreement may not be made whose terms might induce the lawyer improperly to curtail services for the client or perform them in a way contrary to the client's interest. For example, a lawyer should not enter into an agreement whereby services are to be provided only up to a stated amount when it is foreseeable that more extensive services probably will be required, unless the situation is adequately explained to the client. Otherwise, the client might have to bargain for further assistance in the midst of a proceeding or transaction. However, it is proper to define the extent of services in light of the client's ability to pay. A lawyer should not exploit a fee arrangement based primarily on hourly charges by using wasteful procedures.

Prohibited Contingent Fees

[6] Paragraph (d) prohibits a lawyer from charging a contingent fee in a domestic relations matter when payment is contingent upon the securing of a divorce or upon the amount of alimony or support or property settlement to be obtained. This provision does not preclude a contract for a contingent fee for legal representation in connection with the recovery of post-judgment balances due under support, alimony or other financial orders because such contracts do not implicate the same policy concerns.

Division of Fee

[7] A division of fee is a single billing to a client covering the fee of two or more lawyers who are not in the same firm. A division of fee facilitates association of more than one lawyer in a matter in which neither alone could serve the client as well, and most often is used when the fee is contingent and the division is between a referring lawyer and a trial specialist. Paragraph (e) permits the lawyers to divide a fee either on the basis of the proportion of services they render or if each lawyer assumes responsibility for the representation as a whole. In addition, the client must agree to the arrangement, including the share that each lawyer is to receive, and the agreement must be confirmed in writing. Contingent fee agreements must be in a writing signed by the client and must otherwise comply with paragraph (c) of this Rule. Joint responsibility for the representation entails financial and ethical responsibility for the representation as if the lawyers were associated in a partnership. A lawyer should only refer a matter to a lawyer whom the referring lawyer reasonably believes is competent to handle the matter. See Rule 1.1.

[8] Paragraph (e) does not prohibit or regulate division of fees to be received in the future for work done when lawyers were previously associated in a law firm.

Disputes over Fees

[9] If a procedure has been established for resolution of fee disputes, such as an arbitration or mediation procedure established by the bar, the lawyer must comply with the procedure when it is mandatory, and, even when it is voluntary, the lawyer should conscientiously consider submitting to it. Law may prescribe a procedure for determining a lawyer's fee, for example, in representation of an executor or administrator, a class or a person entitled to a reasonable fee as part of the measure of damages. The lawyer entitled to such a fee and a lawyer representing another party concerned with the fee should comply with the prescribed procedure.

Rule 2.1 Advisor

In representing a client, a lawyer shall exercise independent professional judgment and render candid advice. In rendering advice, a lawyer may refer not only to law but to other considerations such as moral, economic, social and political factors, that may be relevant to the client's situation.

Rule 2.1 Advisor - Comment

Scope of Advice

[1] A client is entitled to straightforward advice expressing the lawyer's honest assessment. Legal advice often involves unpleasant facts and alternatives that a client may be disinclined to confront. In presenting advice, a lawyer endeavors to sustain the client's morale and may put advice in as acceptable a form as honesty permits. However, a lawyer should not be deterred from giving candid advice by the prospect that the advice will be unpalatable to the client.

[2] Advice couched in narrow legal terms may be of little value to a client, especially where practical considerations, such as cost or effects on other people, are predominant. Purely technical legal advice, therefore, can sometimes be inadequate. It is proper for a lawyer to refer to relevant moral and ethical considerations in giving advice. Although a lawyer is not a moral advisor as such, moral and ethical considerations impinge upon most legal questions and may decisively influence how the law will be applied.

[3] A client may expressly or impliedly ask the lawyer for purely technical advice. When such a request is made by a client experienced in legal matters, the lawyer may accept it at face value. When such a request is made by a client inexperienced in legal matters, however, the lawyer's responsibility as advisor may include indicating that more may be involved than strictly legal considerations.

[4] Matters that go beyond strictly legal questions may also be in the domain of another profession. Family matters can involve problems within the professional competence of psychiatry, clinical psychology or social work; business matters can involve problems within the competence of the accounting profession or of financial specialists. Where consultation with a professional in another field is itself something a competent lawyer would recommend, the lawyer should make such a recommendation. At the same time, a lawyer's advice at its best often consists of recommending a course of action in the face of conflicting recommendations of experts.

Offering Advice

[5] In general, a lawyer is not expected to give advice until asked by the client. However, when a lawyer knows that a client proposes a course of action that is likely to result in substantial adverse legal consequences to the client, the lawyer's duty to the client under Rule 1.4 may require that the lawyer offer advice if the client's course of action is related to the representation. Similarly, when a matter is likely to involve litigation, it may be necessary under Rule 1.4 to inform the client of forms of dispute resolution that might constitute reasonable alternatives to litigation. A lawyer ordinarily has no duty to initiate investigation of a client's affairs or to give advice that the client has indicated is unwanted, but a lawyer may initiate advice to a client when doing so appears to be in the client's interest.

Rule 3.5 Impartiality And Decorum Of The Tribunal

A lawyer shall not:

    a. seek to influence a judge, juror, prospective juror or other official by means prohibited by law;

    b. communicate ex parte with such a person during the proceeding unless authorized to do so by law or court order;

    c. communicate with a juror or prospective juror after discharge of the jury if:
        1. the communication is prohibited by law or court order;
        2. the juror has made known to the lawyer a desire not to communicate; or
        3. the communication involves misrepresentation, coercion, duress or harassment; or

    d. engage in conduct intended to disrupt a tribunal.

Rule 3.5 Impartiality And Decorum Of The Tribunal - Comment

[1] Many forms of improper influence upon a tribunal are proscribed by criminal law. Others are specified in the ABA Model Code of Judicial Conduct, with which an advocate should be familiar. A lawyer is required to avoid contributing to a violation of such provisions.

[2] During a proceeding a lawyer may not communicate ex parte with persons serving in an official capacity in the proceeding, such as judges, masters or jurors, unless authorized to do so by law or court order.

[3] A lawyer may on occasion want to communicate with a juror or prospective juror after the jury has been discharged. The lawyer may do so unless the communication is prohibited by law or a court order but must respect the desire of the juror not to talk with the lawyer. The lawyer may not engage in improper conduct during the communication.

[4] The advocate's function is to present evidence and argument so that the cause may be decided according to law. Refraining from abusive or obstreperous conduct is a corollary of the advocate's right to speak on behalf of litigants. A lawyer may stand firm against abuse by a judge but should avoid reciprocation; the judge's default is no justification for similar dereliction by an advocate. An advocate can present the cause, protect the record for subsequent review and preserve professional integrity by patient firmness no less effectively than by belligerence or theatrics.

[5] The duty to refrain from disruptive conduct applies to any proceeding of a tribunal, including a deposition. See Rule 1.0(m).

Rule 3.6 Trial Publicity

    a. A lawyer who is participating or has participated in the investigation or litigation of a matter shall not make an extrajudicial statement that the lawyer knows or reasonably should know will be disseminated by means of public communication and will have a substantial likelihood of materially prejudicing an adjudicative proceeding in the matter.

b. Notwithstanding paragraph (a), a lawyer may state:
1. the claim, offense or defense involved and, except when prohibited by law, the identity of the persons involved;
2. information contained in a public record;
3. that an investigation of a matter is in progress;
4. the scheduling or result of any step in litigation;
5. a request for assistance in obtaining evidence and information necessary thereto;
6. a warning of danger concerning the behavior of a person involved, when there is reason to believe that there exists the likelihood of substantial harm to an individual or to the public interest; and
7. in a criminal case, in addition to subparagraphs (1) through (6):
   i. the identity, residence, occupation and family status of the accused;
   ii. if the accused has not been apprehended, information necessary to aid in apprehension of that person;
   iii. the fact, time and place of arrest; and
   iv. the identity of investigating and arresting officers or agencies and the length of the investigation.

c. Notwithstanding paragraph (a), a lawyer may make a statement that a reasonable lawyer would believe is required to protect a client from the substantial undue prejudicial effect of recent publicity not initiated by the lawyer or the lawyer's client. A statement made pursuant to this paragraph shall be limited to such information as is necessary to mitigate the recent adverse publicity.

d. No lawyer associated in a firm or government agency with a lawyer subject to paragraph (a) shall make a statement prohibited by paragraph (a).

Rule 3.6 Trial Publicity - Comment

Comment

[1] It is difficult to strike a balance between protecting the right to a fair trial and safeguarding the right of free expression. Preserving the right to a fair trial necessarily entails some curtailment of the information that may be disseminated about a party prior to trial, particularly where trial by jury is involved. If there were no such limits, the result would be the practical nullification of the protective effect of the rules of forensic decorum and the exclusionary rules of evidence. On the other hand, there are vital social interests served by the free dissemination of information about events having legal consequences and about legal proceedings themselves. The public has a right to know about threats to its safety and measures aimed at assuring its security. It also has a legitimate interest in the conduct of judicial proceedings, particularly in matters of general public concern. Furthermore, the subject matter of legal proceedings is often of direct significance in debate and deliberation over questions of public policy.

[2] Special rules of confidentiality may validly govern proceedings in juvenile, domestic relations and mental disability proceedings, and perhaps other types of litigation. Rule 3.4(c) requires compliance with such rules.

[3] The Rule sets forth a basic general prohibition against a lawyer's making statements that the lawyer knows or should know will have a substantial likelihood of materially prejudicing an adjudicative proceeding. Recognizing that the public value of informed commentary is great and the likelihood of prejudice to a proceeding by the commentary of a lawyer who is not involved in the proceeding is small, the rule applies only to lawyers who are, or who have been involved in the investigation or litigation of a case, and their associates.

[4] Paragraph (b) identifies specific matters about which a lawyer's statements would not ordinarily be considered to present a substantial likelihood of material prejudice, and should not in any event be considered prohibited by the general prohibition of paragraph (a). Paragraph (b) is not intended to be an exhaustive listing of the subjects upon which a lawyer may make a statement, but statements on other matters may be subject to paragraph (a).

[5] There are, on the other hand, certain subjects that are more likely than not to have a material prejudicial effect on a proceeding, particularly when they refer to a civil matter triable to a jury, a criminal matter, or any other proceeding that could result in incarceration. These subjects relate to:

(1) the character, credibility, reputation or criminal record of a party, suspect in a criminal investigation or witness, or the identity of a witness, or the expected testimony of a party or witness;

(2) in a criminal case or proceeding that could result in incarceration, the possibility of a plea of guilty to the offense or the existence or contents of any confession, admission, or statement given by a defendant or suspect or that person's refusal or failure to make a statement;

(3) the performance or results of any examination or test or the refusal or failure of a person to submit to an examination or test, or the identity or nature of physical evidence expected to be presented;

(4) any opinion as to the guilt or innocence of a defendant or suspect in a criminal case or proceeding that could result in incarceration;

(5) information that the lawyer knows or reasonably should know is likely to be inadmissible as evidence in a trial and that would, if disclosed, create a substantial risk of prejudicing an impartial trial; or

(6) the fact that a defendant has been charged with a crime, unless there is included therein a statement explaining that the charge is merely an accusation and that the defendant is presumed innocent until and unless proven guilty.

[6] Another relevant factor in determining prejudice is the nature of the proceeding involved. Criminal jury trials will be most sensitive to extrajudicial speech. Civil trials may be less sensitive. Non-jury hearings and arbitration proceedings may be even less affected. The Rule will still place limitations on prejudicial comments in these cases, but the likelihood of prejudice may be different depending on the type of proceeding.

[7] Finally, extrajudicial statements that might otherwise raise a question under this Rule may be permissible when they are made in response to statements made publicly by another party, another party's lawyer, or third persons, where a reasonable lawyer would believe a public response is required in order to avoid prejudice to the lawyer's client. When prejudicial statements have been publicly made by others, responsive statements may have the salutary effect of lessening any

resulting adverse impact on the adjudicative proceeding. Such responsive statements should be limited to contain only such information as is necessary to mitigate undue prejudice created by the statements made by others.

[8] See Rule 3.8(f) for additional duties of prosecutors in connection with extrajudicial statements about criminal proceedings.

Rule 3.7 Lawyer As Witness

a. A lawyer shall not act as advocate at a trial in which the lawyer is likely to be a necessary witness unless:
  1. the testimony relates to an uncontested issue;
  2. the testimony relates to the nature and value of legal services rendered in the case; or
  3. disqualification of the lawyer would work substantial hardship on the client.

b. A lawyer may act as advocate in a trial in which another lawyer in the lawyer's firm is likely to be called as a witness unless precluded from doing so by Rule 1.7 or Rule 1.9.

Rule 3.7 Lawyer As Witness - Comment

[1] Combining the roles of advocate and witness can prejudice the tribunal and the opposing party and can also involve a conflict of interest between the lawyer and client.

Advocate-Witness Rule

[2] The tribunal has proper objection when the trier of fact may be confused or misled by a lawyer serving as both advocate and witness. The opposing party has proper objection where the combination of roles may prejudice that party's rights in the litigation. A witness is required to testify on the basis of personal knowledge, while an advocate is expected to explain and comment on evidence given by others. It may not be clear whether a statement by an advocate-witness should be taken as proof or as an analysis of the proof.

[3] To protect the tribunal, paragraph (a) prohibits a lawyer from simultaneously serving as advocate and necessary witness except in those circumstances specified in paragraphs (a)(1) through (a)(3). Paragraph (a)(1) recognizes that if the testimony will be uncontested, the ambiguities in the dual role are purely theoretical. Paragraph (a)(2) recognizes that where the testimony concerns the extent and value of legal services rendered in the action in which the testimony is offered, permitting the lawyers to testify avoids the need for a second trial with new counsel to resolve that issue. Moreover, in such a situation the judge has firsthand knowledge of the matter in issue; hence, there is less dependence on the adversary process to test the credibility of the testimony.

[4] Apart from these two exceptions, paragraph (a)(3) recognizes that a balancing is required between the interests of the client and those of the tribunal and

the opposing party. Whether the tribunal is likely to be misled or the opposing party is likely to suffer prejudice depends on the nature of the case, the importance and probable tenor of the lawyer's testimony, and the probability that the lawyer's testimony will conflict with that of other witnesses. Even if there is risk of such prejudice, in determining whether the lawyer should be disqualified, due regard must be given to the effect of disqualification on the lawyer's client. It is relevant that one or both parties could reasonably foresee that the lawyer would probably be a witness. The conflict of interest principles stated in Rules 1.7, 1.9 and 1.10 have no application to this aspect of the problem.

[5] Because the tribunal is not likely to be misled when a lawyer acts as advocate in a trial in which another lawyer in the lawyer's firm will testify as a necessary witness, paragraph (b) permits the lawyer to do so except in situations involving a conflict of interest.

Conflict of Interest

[6] In determining if it is permissible to act as advocate in a trial in which the lawyer will be a necessary witness, the lawyer must also consider that the dual role may give rise to a conflict of interest that will require compliance with Rules 1.7 or 1.9. For example, if there is likely to be substantial conflict between the testimony of the client and that of the lawyer the representation involves a conflict of interest that requires compliance with Rule 1.7. This would be true even though the lawyer might not be prohibited by paragraph (a) from simultaneously serving as advocate and witness because the lawyer's disqualification would work a substantial hardship on the client. Similarly, a lawyer who might be permitted to simultaneously serve as an advocate and a witness by paragraph (a)(3) might be precluded from doing so by Rule 1.9. The problem can arise whether the lawyer is called as a witness on behalf of the client or is called by the opposing party. Determining whether or not such a conflict exists is primarily the responsibility of the lawyer involved. If there is a conflict of interest, the lawyer must secure the client's informed consent, confirmed in writing. In some cases, the lawyer will be precluded from seeking the client's consent. See Rule 1.7. See Rule 1.0(b) for the definition of "confirmed in writing" and Rule 1.0(e) for the definition of "informed consent."

[7] Paragraph (b) provides that a lawyer is not disqualified from serving as an advocate because a lawyer with whom the lawyer is associated in a firm is precluded from doing so by paragraph (a). If, however, the testifying lawyer would also be disqualified by Rule 1.7 or Rule 1.9 from representing the client in the matter, other lawyers in the firm will be precluded from representing the client by Rule 1.10 unless the client gives informed consent under the conditions stated in Rule 1.7.

Rule 4.1 Truthfulness In Statements To Others

In the course of representing a client a lawyer shall not knowingly:

(a) make a false statement of material fact or law to a third person; or

(b) fail to disclose a material fact to a third person when disclosure is necessary to avoid assisting a criminal or fraudulent act by a client, unless disclosure is prohibited by Rule 1.6.

Rule 4.1 Truthfulness In Statements To Others - Comment

Misrepresentation

[1] A lawyer is required to be truthful when dealing with others on a client's behalf, but generally has no affirmative duty to inform an opposing party of relevant facts. A misrepresentation can occur if the lawyer incorporates or affirms a statement of another person that the lawyer knows is false. Misrepresentations can also occur by partially true but misleading statements or omissions that are the equivalent of affirmative false statements. For dishonest conduct that does not amount to a false statement or for misrepresentations by a lawyer other than in the course of representing a client, see Rule 8.4.

Statements of Fact

[2] This Rule refers to statements of fact. Whether a particular statement should be regarded as one of fact can depend on the circumstances. Under generally accepted conventions in negotiation, certain types of statements ordinarily are not taken as statements of material fact. Estimates of price or value placed on the subject of a transaction and a party's intentions as to an acceptable settlement of a claim are ordinarily in this category, and so is the existence of an undisclosed principal except where nondisclosure of the principal would constitute fraud. Lawyers should be mindful of their obligations under applicable law to avoid criminal and tortious misrepresentation.

Crime or Fraud by Client

[3] Under Rule 1.2(d), a lawyer is prohibited from counseling or assisting a client in conduct that the lawyer knows is criminal or fraudulent. Paragraph (b) states a specific application of the principle set forth in Rule 1.2(d) and addresses the situation where a client's crime or fraud takes the form of a lie or misrepresentation. Ordinarily, a lawyer can avoid assisting a client's crime or fraud by withdrawing from the representation. Sometimes it may be necessary for the lawyer to give notice of the fact of withdrawal and to disaffirm an opinion, document, affirmation or the like. In extreme cases, substantive law may require a lawyer to disclose information relating to the representation to avoid being deemed to have assisted the client's crime or fraud. If the lawyer can avoid assisting a client's crime or fraud only by disclosing this information, then under paragraph (b) the lawyer is required to do so, unless the disclosure is prohibited by Rule 1.6.

Rule 4.4 Respect For Rights Of Third Persons

(a) In representing a client, a lawyer shall not use means that have no substantial purpose other than to embarrass, delay, or burden a third person, or use methods of obtaining evidence that violate the legal rights of such a person.

(b) A lawyer who receives a document relating to the representation of the lawyer's client and knows or reasonably should know that the document was inadvertently sent shall promptly notify the sender.

Rule 4.4 Respect For Rights Of Third Persons - Comment

[1] Responsibility to a client requires a lawyer to subordinate the interests of others to those of the client, but that responsibility does not imply that a lawyer may disregard the rights of third persons. It is impractical to catalogue all such rights, but they include legal restrictions on methods of obtaining evidence from third persons and unwarranted intrusions into privileged relationships, such as the client-lawyer relationship.

[2] Paragraph (b) recognizes that lawyers sometimes receive documents that were mistakenly sent or produced by opposing parties or their lawyers. If a lawyer knows or reasonably should know that such a document was sent inadvertently, then this Rule requires the lawyer to promptly notify the sender in order to permit that person to take protective measures. Whether the lawyer is required to take additional steps, such as returning the original document, is a matter of law beyond the scope of these Rules, as is the question of whether the privileged status of a document has been waived. Similarly, this Rule does not address the legal duties of a lawyer who receives a document that the lawyer knows or reasonably should know may have been wrongfully obtained by the sending person. For purposes of this Rule, "document" includes e-mail or other electronic modes of transmission subject to being read or put into readable form.

[3] Some lawyers may choose to return a document unread, for example, when the lawyer learns before receiving the document that it was inadvertently sent to the wrong address. Where a lawyer is not required by applicable law to do so, the decision to voluntarily return such a document is a matter of professional judgment ordinarily reserved to the lawyer. See Rules 1.2 and 1.4.

Rule 5.1 Responsibilities Of Partners, Managers, And Supervisory Lawyers

a. A partner in a law firm, and a lawyer who individually or together with other lawyers possesses comparable managerial authority in a law firm, shall make reasonable efforts to ensure that the firm has in effect measures giving reasonable assurance that all lawyers in the firm conform to the Rules of Professional Conduct.

b. A lawyer having direct supervisory authority over another lawyer shall make reasonable efforts to ensure that the other lawyer conforms to the Rules of Professional Conduct.

c. A lawyer shall be responsible for another lawyer's violation of the Rules of Professional Conduct if:
   1. the lawyer orders or, with knowledge of the specific conduct, ratifies the conduct involved; or
   2. the lawyer is a partner or has comparable managerial authority in the law firm in which the other lawyer practices, or has direct supervisory authority over the other lawyer, and knows of the conduct at a time when its consequences can be avoided or mitigated but fails to take reasonable remedial action.

Rule 5.1 Responsibilities Of Partners, Managers, And Supervisory Lawyers - Comment

[1] Paragraph (a) applies to lawyers who have managerial authority over the professional work of a firm. See Rule 1.0(c). This includes members of a partnership, the shareholders in a law firm organized as a professional corporation, and members of other associations authorized to practice law; lawyers having comparable managerial authority in a legal services organization or a law department of an enterprise or government agency; and lawyers who have intermediate managerial responsibilities in a firm. Paragraph (b) applies to lawyers who have supervisory authority over the work of other lawyers in a firm.

[2] Paragraph (a) requires lawyers with managerial authority within a firm to make reasonable efforts to establish internal policies and procedures designed to provide reasonable assurance that all lawyers in the firm will conform to the Rules of Professional Conduct. Such policies and procedures include those designed to detect and resolve conflicts of interest, identify dates by which actions must be taken in pending matters, account for client funds and property and ensure that inexperienced lawyers are properly supervised.

[3] Other measures that may be required to fulfill the responsibility prescribed in paragraph (a) can depend on the firm's structure and the nature of its practice. In a small firm of experienced lawyers, informal supervision and periodic review of compliance with the required systems ordinarily will suffice. In a large firm, or in practice situations in which difficult ethical problems frequently arise, more elaborate measures may be necessary. Some firms, for example, have a procedure whereby junior lawyers can make confidential referral of ethical problems directly to a designated senior partner or special committee. See Rule 5.2. Firms, whether large or small, may also rely on continuing legal education in professional ethics. In any event, the ethical atmosphere of a firm can influence the conduct of all its members and the partners may not assume that all lawyers associated with the firm will inevitably conform to the Rules.

[4] Paragraph (c) expresses a general principle of personal responsibility for acts of another. See also Rule 8.4(a).

[5] Paragraph (c)(2) defines the duty of a partner or other lawyer having comparable managerial authority in a law firm, as well as a lawyer who has direct supervisory authority over performance of specific legal work by another lawyer. Whether a lawyer has supervisory authority in particular circumstances is a question of fact. Partners and lawyers with comparable authority have at least indirect responsibility for all work being done by the firm, while a partner or manager in charge of a particular matter ordinarily also has supervisory responsibility for the work of other firm lawyers engaged in the matter. Appropriate remedial action by a partner or managing lawyer would depend on the immediacy of that lawyer's involvement and the seriousness of the misconduct. A supervisor is required to intervene to prevent avoidable consequences of misconduct if the supervisor knows that the misconduct occurred. Thus, if a supervising lawyer knows that a subordinate misrepresented a matter to an opposing party in negotiation, the supervisor as well as the subordinate has a duty to correct the resulting misapprehension.

[6] Professional misconduct by a lawyer under supervision could reveal a violation of paragraph (b) on the part of the supervisory lawyer even though it does not entail a violation of paragraph (c) because there was no direction, ratification or knowledge of the violation.

[7] Apart from this Rule and Rule 8.4(a), a lawyer does not have disciplinary liability for the conduct of a partner, associate or subordinate. Whether a lawyer may be liable civilly or criminally for another lawyer's conduct is a question of law beyond the scope of these Rules.

[8] The duties imposed by this Rule on managing and supervising lawyers do not alter the personal duty of each lawyer in a firm to abide by the Rules of Professional Conduct. See Rule 5.2(a).

Rule 5.3 Responsibilities Regarding Nonlawyer Assistants

With respect to a nonlawyer employed or retained by or associated with a lawyer:

a. a partner, and a lawyer who individually or together with other lawyers possesses comparable managerial authority in a law firm shall make reasonable efforts to ensure that the firm has in effect measures giving reasonable assurance that the person's conduct is compatible with the professional obligations of the lawyer;

b. a lawyer having direct supervisory authority over the nonlawyer shall make reasonable efforts to ensure that the person's conduct is compatible with the professional obligations of the lawyer; and

c. a lawyer shall be responsible for conduct of such a person that would be a violation of the Rules of Professional Conduct if engaged in by a lawyer if:
   1. the lawyer orders or, with the knowledge of the specific conduct, ratifies the conduct involved; or
   2. the lawyer is a partner or has comparable managerial authority in the law firm in which the person is employed, or has direct supervisory authority over the person, and knows of the conduct at a time when its consequences can be avoided or mitigated but fails to take reasonable remedial action.

Rule 5.3 Responsibilities Regarding Nonlawyer Assistants - Comment

[1] Lawyers generally employ assistants in their practice, including secretaries, investigators, law student interns, and paraprofessionals. Such assistants, whether employees or independent contractors, act for the lawyer in rendition of the lawyer's professional services. A lawyer must give such assistants appropriate instruction and supervision concerning the ethical aspects of their employment, particularly regarding the obligation not to disclose information relating to representation of the client, and should be responsible for their work product. The measures employed in supervising nonlawyers should take account of the fact that they do not have legal training and are not subject to professional discipline.

[2] Paragraph (a) requires lawyers with managerial authority within a law firm to make reasonable efforts to establish internal policies and procedures designed to provide reasonable assurance that nonlawyers in the firm will act in a way compatible with the Rules of Professional Conduct. See Comment [1] to Rule 5.1. Paragraph (b) applies to lawyers who have supervisory authority over the work of a nonlawyer. Paragraph (c) specifies the circumstances in which a lawyer is responsible for conduct of a nonlawyer that would be a violation of the Rules of Professional Conduct if engaged in by a lawyer.

Rule 5.4 Professional Independence Of A Lawyer

a. A lawyer or law firm shall not share legal fees with a nonlawyer, except that:
   1. an agreement by a lawyer with the lawyer's firm, partner, or associate may provide for the payment of money, over a reasonable period of time after the lawyer's death, to the lawyer's estate or to one or more specified persons;
   2. a lawyer who purchases the practice of a deceased, disabled, or disappeared lawyer may, pursuant to the provisions of Rule 1.17, pay to the estate or other representative of that lawyer the agreed-upon purchase price;
   3. a lawyer or law firm may include nonlawyer employees in a compensation or retirement plan, even though the plan is based in whole or in part on a profit-sharing arrangement; and
   4. a lawyer may share court-awarded legal fees with a nonprofit organization that employed, retained or recommended employment of the lawyer in the matter.

b. A lawyer shall not form a partnership with a nonlawyer if any of the activities of the partnership consist of the practice of law.

c. A lawyer shall not permit a person who recommends, employs, or pays the lawyer to render legal services for another to direct or regulate the lawyer's professional judgment in rendering such legal services.

d. A lawyer shall not practice with or in the form of a professional corporation or association authorized to practice law for a profit, if:
   1. a nonlawyer owns any interest therein, except that a fiduciary representative of the estate of a lawyer may hold the stock or interest of the lawyer for a reasonable time during administration;
   2. a nonlawyer is a corporate director or officer thereof or occupies the position of similar responsibility in any form of association other than a corporation ; or
   3. a nonlawyer has the right to direct or control the professional judgment of a lawyer.

Rule 5.4 Professional Independence Of A Lawyer - Comment

[1] The provisions of this Rule express traditional limitations on sharing fees. These limitations are to protect the lawyer's professional independence of judgment.

Where someone other than the client pays the lawyer's fee or salary, or recommends employment of the lawyer, that arrangement does not modify the lawyer's obligation to the client. As stated in paragraph (c), such arrangements should not interfere with the lawyer's professional judgment.

[2] This Rule also expresses traditional limitations on permitting a third party to direct or regulate the lawyer's professional judgment in rendering legal services to another. See also Rule 1.8(f) (lawyer may accept compensation from a third party as long as there is no interference with the lawyer's independent professional judgment and the client gives informed consent).

Rule 6.2 Accepting Appointments

A lawyer shall not seek to avoid appointment by a tribunal to represent a person except for good cause, such as:

a. representing the client is likely to result in violation of the Rules of Professional Conduct or other law;

b. representing the client is likely to result in an unreasonable financial burden on the lawyer; or

c. the client or the cause is so repugnant to the lawyer as to be likely to impair the client-lawyer relationship or the lawyer's ability to represent the client.

Rule 6.2 Accepting Appointments - Comment

[1] A lawyer ordinarily is not obliged to accept a client whose character or cause the lawyer regards as repugnant. The lawyer's freedom to select clients is, however, qualified. All lawyers have a responsibility to assist in providing pro bono publico service. See Rule 6.1. An individual lawyer fulfills this responsibility by accepting a fair share of unpopular matters or indigent or unpopular clients. A lawyer may also be subject to appointment by a court to serve unpopular clients or persons unable to afford legal services.

Appointed Counsel

[2] For good cause a lawyer may seek to decline an appointment to represent a person who cannot afford to retain counsel or whose cause is unpopular. Good cause exists if the lawyer could not handle the matter competently, see Rule 1.1, or if undertaking the representation would result in an improper conflict of interest, for example, when the client or the cause is so repugnant to the lawyer as to be likely to impair the client-lawyer relationship or the lawyer's ability to represent the client. A lawyer may also seek to decline an appointment if acceptance would be unreasonably burdensome, for example, when it would impose a financial sacrifice so great as to be unjust.

[3] An appointed lawyer has the same obligations to the client as retained counsel, including the obligations of loyalty and confidentiality, and is subject to the same limitations on the client-lawyer relationship, such as the obligation to refrain from assisting the client in violation of the Rules.

Rule 6.3 Membership In Legal Services Organization

A lawyer may serve as a director, officer or member of a legal services organization, apart from the law firm in which the lawyer practices, notwithstanding that the organization serves persons having interests adverse to a client of the lawyer. The lawyer shall not knowingly participate in a decision or action of the organization:

a. if participating in the decision or action would be incompatible with the lawyer's obligations to a client under Rule 1.7; or

b. (b) where the decision or action could have a material adverse effect on the representation of a client of the organization whose interests are adverse to a client of the lawyer.

Rule 6.3 Membership In Legal Services Organization - Comment

[1] Lawyers should be encouraged to support and participate in legal service organizations. A lawyer who is an officer or a member of such an organization does not thereby have a client-lawyer relationship with persons served by the organization. However, there is potential conflict between the interests of such persons and the interests of the lawyer's clients. If the possibility of such conflict disqualified a lawyer from serving on the board of a legal services organization, the profession's involvement in such organizations would be severely curtailed.

[2] It may be necessary in appropriate cases to reassure a client of the organization that the representation will not be affected by conflicting loyalties of a member of the board. Established, written policies in this respect can enhance the credibility of such assurances.

Rule 6.4 Law Reform Activities Affecting Client Interests

A lawyer may serve as a director, officer or member of an organization involved in reform of the law or its administration notwithstanding that the reform may affect the interests of a client of the lawyer. When the lawyer knows that the interests of a client may be materially benefitted by a decision in which the lawyer participates, the lawyer shall disclose that fact but need not identify the client.

Rule 6.4 Law Reform Activities Affecting Client Interests - Comment

[1] Lawyers involved in organizations seeking law reform generally do not have a client-lawyer relationship with the organization. Otherwise, it might follow that a lawyer could not be involved in a bar association law reform program that might indirectly affect a client. See also Rule 1.2(b). For example, a lawyer specializing in antitrust litigation might be regarded as disqualified from participating in drafting revisions of rules governing that subject. In determining the nature and scope of participation in such activities, a lawyer should be mindful of obligations to clients under other Rules, particularly Rule 1.7. A lawyer is professionally obligated to protect

the integrity of the program by making an appropriate disclosure within the organization when the lawyer knows a private client might be materially benefitted.

Rule 7.2 Advertising

a. Subject to the requirements of Rules 7.1 and 7.3, a lawyer may advertise services through written, recorded or electronic communication, including public media.

b. A lawyer shall not give anything of value to a person for recommending the lawyer's services except that a lawyer may
   1. pay the reasonable costs of advertisements or communications permitted by this Rule;
   2. pay the usual charges of a legal service plan or a not-for-profit or qualified lawyer referral service. A qualified lawyer referral service is a lawyer referral service that has been approved by an appropriate regulatory authority;
   3. pay for a law practice in accordance with Rule 1.17; and
   4. refer clients to another lawyer or a nonlawyer professional pursuant to an agreement not otherwise prohibited under these Rules that provides for the other person to refer clients or customers to the lawyer, if
      i. the reciprocal referral agreement is not exclusive, and
      ii. the client is informed of the existence and nature of the agreement.

c. Any communication made pursuant to this rule shall include the name and office address of at least one lawyer or law firm responsible for its content.

Rule 7.2 Advertising - Comment

[1] To assist the public in obtaining legal services, lawyers should be allowed to make known their services not only through reputation but also through organized information campaigns in the form of advertising. Advertising involves an active quest for clients, contrary to the tradition that a lawyer should not seek clientele. However, the public's need to know about legal services can be fulfilled in part through advertising. This need is particularly acute in the case of persons of moderate means who have not made extensive use of legal services. The interest in expanding public information about legal services ought to prevail over considerations of tradition. Nevertheless, advertising by lawyers entails the risk of practices that are misleading or overreaching.

[2] This Rule permits public dissemination of information concerning a lawyer's name or firm name, address and telephone number; the kinds of services the lawyer will undertake; the basis on which the lawyer's fees are determined, including prices for specific services and payment and credit arrangements; a lawyer's foreign language ability; names of references and, with their consent, names of clients regularly represented; and other information that might invite the attention of those seeking legal assistance.

[3] Questions of effectiveness and taste in advertising are matters of speculation and subjective judgment. Some jurisdictions have had extensive prohibitions against television advertising, against advertising going beyond specified facts about a lawyer, or against "undignified" advertising. Television is now one of the most powerful media for getting information to the public, particularly persons of low and moderate income; prohibiting television advertising, therefore, would impede the flow of information about legal services to many sectors of the public. Limiting the information that may be advertised has a similar effect and assumes that the bar can accurately forecast the kind of information that the public would regard as relevant. Similarly, electronic media, such as the Internet, can be an important source of information about legal services, and lawful communication by electronic mail is permitted by this Rule. But see Rule 7.3(a) for the prohibition against the solicitation of a prospective client through a real-time electronic exchange that is not initiated by the prospective client.

[4] Neither this Rule nor Rule 7.3 prohibits communications authorized by law, such as notice to members of a class in class action litigation.

Paying Others to Recommend a Lawyer

[5] Lawyers are not permitted to pay others for channeling professional work. Paragraph (b)(1), however, allows a lawyer to pay for advertising and communications permitted by this Rule, including the costs of print directory listings, online directory listings, newspaper ads, television and radio airtime, domain-name registrations, sponsorship fees, banner ads, and group advertising. A lawyer may compensate employees, agents and vendors who are engaged to provide marketing or client-development services, such as publicists, public-relations personnel, business-development staff and website designers. See Rule 5.3 for the duties of lawyers and law firms with respect to the conduct of nonlawyers who prepare marketing materials for them.

[6] A lawyer may pay the usual charges of a legal service plan or a not-for-profit or qualified lawyer referral service. A legal service plan is a prepaid or group legal service plan or a similar delivery system that assists prospective clients to secure legal representation. A lawyer referral service, on the other hand, is any organization that holds itself out to the public as a lawyer referral service. Such referral services are understood by laypersons to be consumer-oriented organizations that provide unbiased referrals to lawyers with appropriate experience in the subject matter of the representation and afford other client protections, such as complaint procedures or malpractice insurance requirements. Consequently, this Rule only permits a lawyer to pay the usual charges of a not-for-profit or qualified lawyer referral service. A qualified lawyer referral service is one that is approved by an appropriate regulatory authority as affording adequate protections for prospective clients. See, e.g., the American Bar Association's Model Supreme Court Rules Governing Lawyer Referral Services and Model Lawyer Referral and Information Service Quality Assurance Act (requiring that organizations that are identified as lawyer referral services (i) permit the participation of all lawyers who are licensed and eligible to practice in the jurisdiction and who meet reasonable objective eligibility requirements as may be established by the referral service for the protection

of prospective clients; (ii) require each participating lawyer to carry reasonably adequate malpractice insurance; (iii) act reasonably to assess client satisfaction and address client complaints; and (iv) do not refer prospective clients to lawyers who own, operate or are employed by the referral service.)

[7] A lawyer who accepts assignments or referrals from a legal service plan or referrals from a lawyer referral service must act reasonably to assure that the activities of the plan or service are compatible with the lawyer's professional obligations. See Rule 5.3. Legal service plans and lawyer referral services may communicate with prospective clients, but such communication must be in conformity with these Rules. Thus, advertising must not be false or misleading, as would be the case if the communications of a group advertising program or a group legal services plan would mislead prospective clients to think that it was a lawyer referral service sponsored by a state agency or bar association. Nor could the lawyer allow in-person, telephonic, or real-time contacts that would violate Rule 7.3.

[8] A lawyer also may agree to refer clients to another lawyer or a nonlawyer professional, in return for the undertaking of that person to refer clients or customers to the lawyer. Such reciprocal referral arrangements must not interfere with the lawyer's professional judgment as to making referrals or as to providing substantive legal services. See Rules 2.1 and 5.4(c). Except as provided in Rule 1.5(e), a lawyer who receives referrals from a lawyer or nonlawyer professional must not pay anything solely for the referral, but the lawyer does not violate paragraph (b) of this Rule by agreeing to refer clients to the other lawyer or nonlawyer professional, so long as the reciprocal referral agreement is not exclusive and the client is informed of the referral agreement. Conflicts of interest created by such arrangements are governed by Rule 1.7. Reciprocal referral agreements should not be of indefinite duration and should be reviewed periodically to determine whether they comply with these Rules. This Rule does not restrict referrals or divisions of revenues or net income among lawyers within firms comprised of multiple entities.

Rule 7.3 Direct Contact With Prospective Clients

a. A lawyer shall not by in-person, live telephone or real-time electronic contact solicit professional employment from a prospective client when a significant motive for the lawyer's doing so is the lawyer's pecuniary gain, unless the person contacted:
   1. is a lawyer; or
   2. has a family, close personal, or prior professional relationship with the lawyer.
b. A lawyer shall not solicit professional employment from a prospective client by written, recorded or electronic communication or by in-person, telephone or real-time electronic contact even when not otherwise prohibited by paragraph (a), if:
   1. the prospective client has made known to the lawyer a desire not to be solicited by the lawyer; or
   2. the solicitation involves coercion, duress or harassment.

c. Every written, recorded or electronic communication from a lawyer soliciting professional employment from a prospective client known to be in need of legal services in a particular matter shall include the words "Advertising Material" on the outside envelope, if any, and at the beginning and ending of any recorded or electronic communication, unless the recipient of the communication is a person specified in paragraphs (a)(1) or (a)(2).

d. Notwithstanding the prohibitions in paragraph (a), a lawyer may participate with a prepaid or group legal service plan operated by an organization not owned or directed by the lawyer that uses in-person or telephone contact to solicit memberships or subscriptions for the plan from persons who are not known to need legal services in a particular matter covered by the plan.

Rule 7.3 Direct Contact With Prospective Clients - Comment

[1] There is a potential for abuse inherent in direct in-person, live telephone or real-time electronic contact by a lawyer with a prospective client known to need legal services. These forms of contact between a lawyer and a prospective client subject the layperson to the private importuning of the trained advocate in a direct interpersonal encounter. The prospective client, who may already feel overwhelmed by the circumstances giving rise to the need for legal services, may find it difficult fully to evaluate all available alternatives with reasoned judgment and appropriate self-interest in the face of the lawyer's presence and insistence upon being retained immediately. The situation is fraught with the possibility of undue influence, intimidation, and over-reaching.

[2] This potential for abuse inherent in direct in-person, live telephone or real-time electronic solicitation of prospective clients justifies its prohibition, particularly since lawyer advertising and written and recorded communication permitted under Rule 7.2 offer alternative means of conveying necessary information to those who may be in need of legal services. Advertising and written and recorded communications which may be mailed or autodialed make it possible for a prospective client to be informed about the need for legal services, and about the qualifications of available lawyers and law firms, without subjecting the prospective client to direct in-person, telephone or real-time electronic persuasion that may overwhelm the client's judgment.

[3] The use of general advertising and written, recorded or electronic communications to transmit information from lawyer to prospective client, rather than direct in-person, live telephone or real-time electronic contact, will help to assure that the information flows cleanly as well as freely. The contents of advertisements and communications permitted under Rule 7.2 can be permanently recorded so that they cannot be disputed and may be shared with others who know the lawyer. This potential for informal review is itself likely to help guard against statements and claims that might constitute false and misleading communications, in violation of Rule 7.1. The contents of direct in-person, live telephone or real-time electronic conversations between a lawyer and a prospective client can be disputed and may

not be subject to third-party scrutiny. Consequently, they are much more likely to approach (and occasionally cross) the dividing line between accurate representations and those that are false and misleading.

[4] There is far less likelihood that a lawyer would engage in abusive practices against an individual who is a former client, or with whom the lawyer has close personal or family relationship, or in situations in which the lawyer is motivated by considerations other than the lawyer's pecuniary gain. Nor is there a serious potential for abuse when the person contacted is a lawyer. Consequently, the general prohibition in Rule 7.3(a) and the requirements of Rule 7.3(c) are not applicable in those situations. Also, paragraph (a) is not intended to prohibit a lawyer from participating in constitutionally protected activities of public or charitable legal- service organizations or bona fide political, social, civic, fraternal, employee or trade organizations whose purposes include providing or recommending legal services to its members or beneficiaries.

[5] But even permitted forms of solicitation can be abused. Thus, any solicitation which contains information which is false or misleading within the meaning of Rule 7.1, which involves coercion, duress or harassment within the meaning of Rule 7.3(b)(2), or which involves contact with a prospective client who has made known to the lawyer a desire not to be solicited by the lawyer within the meaning of Rule 7.3(b)(1) is prohibited. Moreover, if after sending a letter or other communication to a client as permitted by Rule 7.2 the lawyer receives no response, any further effort to communicate with the prospective client may violate the provisions of Rule 7.3(b).

[6] This Rule is not intended to prohibit a lawyer from contacting representatives of organizations or groups that may be interested in establishing a group or prepaid legal plan for their members, insureds, beneficiaries or other third parties for the purpose of informing such entities of the availability of and details concerning the plan or arrangement which the lawyer or lawyer's firm is willing to offer. This form of communication is not directed to a prospective client. Rather, it is usually addressed to an individual acting in a fiduciary capacity seeking a supplier of legal services for others who may, if they choose, become prospective clients of the lawyer. Under these circumstances, the activity which the lawyer undertakes in communicating with such representatives and the type of information transmitted to the individual are functionally similar to and serve the same purpose as advertising permitted under Rule 7.2.

[7] The requirement in Rule 7.3(c) that certain communications be marked "Advertising Material" does not apply to communications sent in response to requests of potential clients or their spokespersons or sponsors. General announcements by lawyers, including changes in personnel or office location, do not constitute communications soliciting professional employment from a client known to be in need of legal services within the meaning of this Rule.

[8] Paragraph (d) of this Rule permits a lawyer to participate with an organization which uses personal contact to solicit members for its group or prepaid legal service plan, provided that the personal contact is not undertaken by any lawyer who would be a provider of legal services through the plan. The organization must not be owned by or directed (whether as manager or otherwise) by any lawyer or law firm that participates in the plan. For example, paragraph (d) would not permit

a lawyer to create an organization controlled directly or indirectly by the lawyer and use the organization for the in-person or telephone solicitation of legal employment of the lawyer through memberships in the plan or otherwise. The communication permitted by these organizations also must not be directed to a person known to need legal services in a particular matter, but is to be designed to inform potential plan members generally of another means of affordable legal services. Lawyers who participate in a legal service plan must reasonably assure that the plan sponsors are in compliance with Rules 7.1, 7.2 and 7.3(b). See 8.4(a).

Rule 8.2 Judicial And Legal Officials

a. A lawyer shall not make a statement that the lawyer knows to be false or with reckless disregard as to its truth or falsity concerning the qualifications or integrity of a judge, adjudicatory officer or public legal officer, or of a candidate for election or appointment to judicial or legal office.

b. A lawyer who is a candidate for judicial office shall comply with the applicable provisions of the Code of Judicial Conduct.

Rule 8.2 Judicial And Legal Officials - Comment

[1] Assessments by lawyers are relied on in evaluating the professional or personal fitness of persons being considered for election or appointment to judicial office and to public legal offices, such as attorney general, prosecuting attorney and public defender. Expressing honest and candid opinions on such matters contributes to improving the administration of justice. Conversely, false statements by a lawyer can unfairly undermine public confidence in the administration of justice.

[2] When a lawyer seeks judicial office, the lawyer should be bound by applicable limitations on political activity.

[3] To maintain the fair and independent administration of justice, lawyers are encouraged to continue traditional efforts to defend judges and courts unjustly criticized.

Rule 8.3 Reporting Professional Misconduct

a. A lawyer who knows that another lawyer has committed a violation of the Rules of Professional Conduct that raises a substantial question as to that lawyer's honesty, trustworthiness or fitness as a lawyer in other respects, shall inform the appropriate professional authority.

b. A lawyer who knows that a judge has committed a violation of applicable rules of judicial conduct that raises a substantial question as to the judge's fitness for office shall inform the appropriate authority.

c. This Rule does not require disclosure of information otherwise protected by Rule 1.6 or information gained by a lawyer or judge while participating in an approved lawyers assistance program.

Rule 8.3 Reporting Professional Misconduct - Comment

[1] Self-regulation of the legal profession requires that members of the profession initiate disciplinary investigation when they know of a violation of the Rules of Professional Conduct. Lawyers have a similar obligation with respect to judicial misconduct. An apparently isolated violation may indicate a pattern of misconduct that only a disciplinary investigation can uncover. Reporting a violation is especially important where the victim is unlikely to discover the offense.

[2] A report about misconduct is not required where it would involve violation of Rule 1.6. However, a lawyer should encourage a client to consent to disclosure where prosecution would not substantially prejudice the client's interests.

[3] If a lawyer were obliged to report every violation of the Rules, the failure to report any violation would itself be a professional offense. Such a requirement existed in many jurisdictions but proved to be unenforceable. This Rule limits the reporting obligation to those offenses that a self-regulating profession must vigorously endeavor to prevent. A measure of judgment is, therefore, required in complying with the provisions of this Rule. The term "substantial" refers to the seriousness of the possible offense and not the quantum of evidence of which the lawyer is aware. A report should be made to the bar disciplinary agency unless some other agency, such as a peer review agency, is more appropriate in the circumstances. Similar considerations apply to the reporting of judicial misconduct.

[4] The duty to report professional misconduct does not apply to a lawyer retained to represent a lawyer whose professional conduct is in question. Such a situation is governed by the Rules applicable to the client-lawyer relationship.

[5] Information about a lawyer's or judge's misconduct or fitness may be received by a lawyer in the course of that lawyer's participation in an approved lawyers or judges assistance program. In that circumstance, providing for an exception to the reporting requirements of paragraphs (a) and (b) of this Rule encourages lawyers and judges to seek treatment through such a program. Conversely, without such an exception, lawyers and judges may hesitate to seek assistance from these programs, which may then result in additional harm to their professional careers and additional injury to the welfare of clients and the public. These Rules do not otherwise address the confidentiality of information received by a lawyer or judge participating in an approved lawyers assistance program; such an obligation, however, may be imposed by the rules of the program or other law.

Rule 8.4 Misconduct

It is professional misconduct for a lawyer to:

a. violate or attempt to violate the Rules of Professional Conduct, knowingly assist or induce another to do so, or do so through the acts of another;

b. commit a criminal act that reflects adversely on the lawyer's honesty, trustworthiness or fitness as a lawyer in other respects;

c. engage in conduct involving dishonesty, fraud, deceit or misrepresentation;

d. engage in conduct that is prejudicial to the administration of justice;

e. state or imply an ability to influence improperly a government agency or official or to achieve results by means that violate the Rules of Professional Conduct or other law; or

f. knowingly assist a judge or judicial officer in conduct that is a violation of applicable rules of judicial conduct or other law.

Rule 8.4 Misconduct - Comment

[1] Lawyers are subject to discipline when they violate or attempt to violate the Rules of Professional Conduct, knowingly assist or induce another to do so or do so through the acts of another, as when they request or instruct an agent to do so on the lawyer's behalf. Paragraph (a), however, does not prohibit a lawyer from advising a client concerning action the client is legally entitled to take.

[2] Many kinds of illegal conduct reflect adversely on fitness to practice law, such as offenses involving fraud and the offense of willful failure to file an income tax return. However, some kinds of offenses carry no such implication. Traditionally, the distinction was drawn in terms of offenses involving "moral turpitude." That concept can be construed to include offenses concerning some matters of personal morality, such as adultery and comparable offenses, that have no specific connection to fitness for the practice of law. Although a lawyer is personally answerable to the entire criminal law, a lawyer should be professionally answerable only for offenses that indicate lack of those characteristics relevant to law practice. Offenses involving violence, dishonesty, breach of trust, or serious interference with the administration of justice are in that category. A pattern of repeated offenses, even ones of minor significance when considered separately, can indicate indifference to legal obligation.

[3] A lawyer who, in the course of representing a client, knowingly manifests by words or conduct, bias or prejudice based upon race, sex, religion, national origin, disability, age, sexual orientation or socioeconomic status, violates paragraph (d) when such actions are prejudicial to the administration of justice. Legitimate advocacy respecting the foregoing factors does not violate paragraph (d). A trial judge's finding that peremptory challenges were exercised on a discriminatory basis does not alone establish a violation of this rule.

[4] A lawyer may refuse to comply with an obligation imposed by law upon a good faith belief that no valid obligation exists. The provisions of Rule 1.2(d) concerning a good faith challenge to the validity, scope, meaning or application of the law apply to challenges of legal regulation of the practice of law.

[5] Lawyers holding public office assume legal responsibilities going beyond those of other citizens. A lawyer's abuse of public office can suggest an inability to fulfill the professional role of lawyers. The same is true of abuse of positions of private trust such as trustee, executor, administrator, guardian, agent and officer, director or manager of a corporation or other organization.

END NOTES

INTRODUCTION

[1]ESSAY CONCERNING HUMAN UNDERSTANDING 44 (A.C. Fraser ed., Dover 1959)

[2]CHARACTERISTICS OF MEN, MANNERS, OPINIONS, TIMES 17 (Grant Richards 1900)

CHAPTER 1

[1]353 U.S. 252 (1957)

[2]366 U.S. 36 (1960)

[3]Florida Board of Bar Examiners re M.C.A., 650 So.2d 34 (Fla.Sup.Ct. 1995)

[4]*In re Corrigan,* 546 N.E.2d 1315 (Ohio Sup.Ct. 1989)

[5]*In re Hamm,* Ariz., No. SB-04-0079-M Dec. 7, 2005, reported in ABA LMPC 21, 26. Hamm was a convicted murderer but the Arizona Supreme Court's decision to not admit him to the bar was based on Hamm's failure to disclose facts relating to an altercation with the police arising from a dispute with his second wife and his failure to make some child support payments to his first wife.

[6]Louisiana's court rule requiring every bar applicant to be a U.S. citizen or a resident alien is constitutional. *LeClerc v. Webb,* 5th Cir. No. 03-30752 Dec. 29, 2005

[7]An occupational tax is different from a licensing fee in that they are imposed for revenue only. *Royall v. Virginia,* 116 U.S. 572, 6 S.Ct. 510 (1886)

[8]*Nicholson v. Board of Commissions* (M.D. Ala. 1972) 338 F.Supp. 48

[9]*Keller v. California State Bar,* 496 U.S. 1 (U.S. Sup.Ct. 1990). Even though the Supreme Court has said that both mandatory bar membership and mandatory bar dues are constitutional, it is not constitutional for state bars to make lawyers pay money that goes to support the political causes of the bar association. To fund those causes, the bar may request a donation as part of bar dues.

[10]David Hoffman, *A Course of Legal Study,* 2d ed., (1836)

[11]Canon 37, added 1928

[12]Added to the ABA Canons in 1928

[13]*Astarte, Inc. v. Pac. Indus. Sys., Inc.,* 865 F.Supp. 693 (D. Colo. 1994)

[14]*Florida Bar v. Karahalis,* 780 So.2d 27 (2001). The Florida Supreme Court found that bribery is a particularly bad violation of the ethics rules that "strikes at the very heart of the attorney's responsibility to the public and profession."

[15]*In re Law Firm of Wilens and Baker,* N.Y. Sup.Ct. App.Div. 1st Dept. No. M-5132 May 20, 2004

[16]*In re Cohen,* D.C. No. 02-BG-863, Apr. 29, 2004, 20, at 259

[17]*See, e.g.,* Washington's WSBA Formal Opinion 184 (1996); but also see North Dakota Opinion 01-02 (May 24, 2001) (opining that a suspended lawyer can act as a paralegal but shouldn't do so in the office from which he was disbarred because the urge to practice law will be too great) and North Carolina State Bar 98 Formal Ethics Opinion 7 (1998)

[18]*In re Comish* (Dec. 13, 2004)

[19]25 C.F.R. 541

[20]*See, e.g., Richards v. Jain,* 168 F.Supp. 2d 1195 (W.D. Wash. 2001); *Daines v. Alcatel,* 194 F.R.D. 678 (E.D. Wash. 2000)

[21]*See also In re Estate of Myers,* Colo., No. 05SA231 Feb. 21, 2006

[22]491 U.S. 274 (1989)

[23]LOS ANGELES TIMES, Tuesday, January 16, 1990, at A3

CHAPTER 2

[1]Alan Morison, *Defining the Unauthorized Practice of Law,* 4 NOVA L.J. 363 (1980)

[2]For more information on this, see Documenting the Justice Gap in America, A report of the Legal Service Corporation, Sept. 2005. The Legal Service Corporation is a private, non-profit corporation established by Congress in 1974. Its mission is to ensure equal access to justice for all Americans.

[3]This famous quote is taken from *Jacob Ellis v. Ohio,* 378 U.S. 184 (1964) where, declining to attempt a comprehensive definition of pornography, said "But I know it when I see it."

[4]*State Bar of Arizona v. Arizona Land Title & Trust Co.,* 366 P.2d 1 (Ariz. 1961)

[5]*See id*

[6]*Baron v. City of Los Angeles,* 469 P.2d 353 (Cal. 1970)

[7]*New York Lawyers Association v. Dacey,* 234 N.E.2d 459 (N.Y. 1967)

[8]*Le Doux v. Credit Research Corp.,* 125 Cal.Rptr. 166 (1975)

[9]There is a good discussion of these conflicting interests in 11(2) LEGAL ASSISTANT TODAY, Nov. to Dec. 1993, at 40–46

[10]422 U.S. 806, 75 S.Ct. 2625 (1975)

[11]*People v. Perez,* 594 P.2d 1 (Cal. 1979)

[12]ABA Standing Committee on Lawyers' Responsibility for Client Protection and Center for Professional Responsibility, Results of the 1984 Non Lawyer Practice Before Federal Administrative Agencies (1985), cited in 5 ALEXANDRA ASHBROOK, UNAUTHORIZED PRACTICE IN IMMIGRATION 222 at FN 3 (1991)

[13]380 So.2d 412 (Fla. 1980)

[14]373 U.S. 379, 83 S.Ct. 1322 (1963)

[15]*See, e.g.,* the Indian Child Welfare Act of 1978, 25 U.S.C.A. § 1911(c), which allows for nonattorney representation. Since the Act is federal law, the state UPL laws are preempted. *See also* 9 JOUR. OF PARA. ED. & PRAC. 1, April (1993) for a comprehensive article on paralegal representation before the Social Security Administration.

[16]*State Bar of New Mexico v. Guardian Abstract and Title Co., Inc.,* 575 P.2d 943 (N.M. 1978)

[17]*Real estate broker: Conway-Bogue Realty Insurance Company v. Denver Bar Association,* 312 P.2d 998 (Colo. 1957); title company: *State Bar of New Mexico v. Guardian Abstract & Title Co., Inc.,* 575 P.2d 943 (1978).

[18]Note, *Unlawful Practice of Law by Trust Companies and Banks,* JEROME GLASER, 32 So.Cal.Rptr. 425 (1959)

[19]*Cohn v. Thompson,* 16 P.2d 364 (Cal.App.Supp. 1932)

[20]*Zelkin v. Caruso Discount Corp.,* 9 Cal.Rptr. 220 (1960)

[21]355 So.2d 1186 (Fla. 1978)

[22]*In re Calzadilla,* 151 B.R. 622 (Fla. 1993)

[23]*See Florida Bar v. Furman* at the end of Chapter 2.

[24]*Florida Bar v. We the People,* 883 So.2d 1280 (Fla 2004)

[25]*Statewide Grievance Committee v. Patton,* 683 A.2d 1359 (Conn. 1996)

[26]348 N.Y.S.2d 270 (1973)

[27]*Trust Mill Halted,* CAL. B. J. (1 December 1997)

[28]*In re NOLO Press,* 991 S.W.2d 768 (Tex, 1999)

[29]1999 WL 47235 (N.D. Tex. 1999)

[30]*Unauthorized Practice of Law Committee v. Parsons Technology, Inc.,* 179 F.3d 956 (Tex. 1999)

[31]*In Eckles v. Atlanta Technology Group, Inc.,* 485 S.E.2d 22 (Ga. 1997), the Georgia Supreme Court held that the corporation does not have the right of self-representation. However, a Georgia appellate court allowed a corporation to be represented by a nonlawyer

before the county board of equalization in Grand Partners Joint Venture I v. Realtax Resource, Inc., 1997 Ga. App. LEXIS 392 (1997)

[32]Vol. 21 at 473

[33]627 So.2d 485 (1993)

[34]202 N.E.2d 841 (Ill. App. 1964)

[35]149 B.R. 162 (1992)

[36]446 N.E.2d 236 (Ill. 1983)

[37]Office of Disciplinary Counsel v. Ball, 67 Ohio St.3d 401 (1993)

[38]In Matter of Martinez, 754 P.2d 842 (N.M. 1988)

[39]865 S.W.2d 533 (Tex. 1993)

[40]See Plumlee v. Paddock (832 S.W.2d 757 (Tex. 1992)) where the lawyer paid an ambulance company a set fee plus a percentage of attorneys' fees for personal injury case referrals. The court found that the contract was an illegal business relationship as to both parties and refused to enforce the agreement

[41]Several states specifically require that paralegals identify their nonlawyer status immediately to every person with whom they have professional contact. Georgia [Advisory Op. No. 21 (1977) Rev'd (1983)]; Illinois [GUIDELINES FOR THE USE OF ATTORNEY ASSISTANTS (1977)]; Iowa [CODE OF PROFESSIONAL RESPONSIBILITY EC3-6]; Missouri [State Bar Advisory Committee Op. (1981)]; Oklahoma [GUIDELINES FOR THE UTILIZATION OF LEGAL ASSISTANTS]. The N. Y. S. B. GUIDELINES ON LEGAL ASSISTANTS requires the lawyer to specify that the "contact" person he or she gives to a client or other person is a paralegal and to explain what a paralegal is if the client does not know

[42]320 P.2d 16 (Cal. 1958)

[43]137 F.Supp. 628 (N.C. 1956)

[44]25 Pa.D. & C.3d 191 (Pa 1980)

[45]Birbower, Montalbano, Condon & Frank, P.C., v. Superior Court, 17 Cal.4th 119 (1998)

CHAPTER 3

[1]Paragraph (b) has two exceptions to the rule on confidentiality. The first is to prevent the client from committing a criminal act that the lawyer believes will result in death or substantial bodily harm. The second is that the lawyer can reveal certain confidences in an action to collect the fee or defend against criminal or civil charges against the lawyer based on conduct in which the client was involved or to defend a malpractice or similar claim.

[2]296 F.2d 918 (2d Cir. 1961)

[3]WIGMORE ON EVIDENCE Section 2290 (3d ed. 1961)

[4]416 U.S. 396, 94 S.Ct. 1800 (1974)

[5]For an interesting article on confidentiality, see 8 J. PARALEGAL EDU. & PRAC. 1, Summer 1990, at 167

[6]United States v. BDO Seidman, 225 F.Supp.2d 918 (2002)

[7]Hickman v. Taylor, 329 U.S. 495, 67 S.Ct. 385 (1947)

[8]City of Reno v. Reno Police Protective Assn., 59 P.3d 1212 (Nev. 2002)

[9]In re Grand Jury Proceedings, 43 F.3d 966, 972 (5th Cir. 1994)

[10]Rickman v. Deere & Co., 154 F.R.D. 137, 138 (E.D. Va. 1993)

[11]Simmons Foods, Inc. v. Willis, 196 F.R.D. 610 (Kan. 2000)

[12]See, e.g., California's rule (CCP 2018(c)). Any writing that reflects an attorney's impressions, conclusions, opinions, or legal research or theories shall not be discoverable under any circumstances.

[13]Eddy v. Fields, 121 Cal.App.4th 1543 (2004)

[14]See California's CCP. § 2018: Duty to advise opposing counsel of receipt of work product document

[15](RESTATEMENT (THIRD) OF LAW GOVERNING LAWYERS § 46(1)9(1)

CHAPTER 4

[1]518 F.2d 751 (2d Cir. 1975)

[2]703 F.2d 252 (7th Cir. 1983)

[3]See also Contant v. Kawasaki Motors Corp., 826 F.Supp. 427 (M.D. Fla. 1993)

[4]621 F.2d 994 (9th Cir. 1980)

[5]People v. Lopez, 796 P.2d 957 (Colo. 1990)

[6]The executrix of an estate is a female executor.

[7]Eschwig v. State Bar, 459 P.2d 904 (Cal. 1969)

[8]Champerty and Maintenance, 14 AM. JUR. 2d, at 2

[9]Under the ABA Model Code, the lawyer could not pay expenses of litigation for a client, unlike the ABA Model Rule's position on that issue.

ABA MODEL CODE DR 5-103 (A) A lawyer shall not acquire a proprietary interest in the cause of action or subject matter of litigation he is conducting for a client, except that he may: (1) Acquire a lien granted by law to secure his fee or expenses. (2) Contract with a client for a reasonable contingent fee in a civil case. (B) While representing a client in connection with contemplated or pending litigation, a lawyer shall not advance or guarantee financial assistance to his client, except that a lawyer may advance or guarantee the expenses of litigation, including court costs, expenses of investigation, expenses of medical examination, and costs of obtaining and presenting evidence, provided the client remains ultimately liable for such expense.

[10] *Fletcher v. Davis,* 33 Cal.4th 61, 90 P.3d 1216 (2004)

[11] Formal Op. 92-364 (1992)

[12] Okla. Bar Assn., Legal Ethics Comm., Op. 308 (1994).

[13] For an interesting article on this subject, see IV GEO. J. LEGAL ETHICS 1, 169 (Summer 1990)

[14] The bulk of this rule is substantially similar to DR 3-102, 3-103, and 5-107

[15] *Miller v. Sears,* 636 P.2d 1183 (Alaska 1991)

[16] *In re Greenberg,* 121 A.2d 520 (N.J. 1956)

[17] 194 A.2d 236 (N.J. 1963)

[18] 322 A.2d 445 (N.J. 1974)

[19] *See, e.g., Gibbs v. Lappies,* 828 F.Supp. 6 (D.N.H. 1993)

[20] 162 Cal.App.3d 358 (1984). This case has been limited by CIVIL CODE section 2860 and Buss v. Superior Court, 16 Cal. 4th 35 (1997).

[21] *Columbia Bar Assn. v. Grelle* [237 N.E.2d 298 (Ohio 1968)

[22] 590 F.2d 168 (5th Cir. 1979)

[23] *In re Banks and Thompson,* 584 P.2d 284 (Or. 1978)

[24] 357 F.Supp. 905 (W.D. Pa. 1973)

[25] 545 F.Supp. 1124 (N.D. Ill. 1982)

[26] See earlier discussion in Chapter 2, regarding corporation's inability to request review of employment benefits through a corporate employee.

[27] 435 U.S. 475, 98 S.Ct. 1173 (1978)

[28] 209 P. 363 (Cal. 1922)

[29] *NAACP v. Button,* 371 U.S. 415, 83 S.Ct. 328 (1963)

[30] 377 U.S. 1 (1963), *reh'g den.* 377 U.S. 960, 84 S.Ct. 1625

[31] See *In re O'Neill,* 5 F.Supp. 465 (E.D.N.Y. 1933); *Ryan v. Penn.* R. Co., 268 Ill.App. 364 (1932); *Hulse v. Brotherhood of Railway Trainmen,* 340 S.W.2d 404 (Mo. 1960); State *ex rel Beck v. Lush,* 103 N.W.2d 136 (Neb. 1960); *Hildebrand v. State Bar,* 117 P.2d 860 and

Hildebrand v. State Bar, 225 P.2d 508 (Cal. 1950), in which the dissenting opinions of Justices Carter and Trayner are cited. *See also* the auto club cases; *Re Maclub of America, Inc.,* 3 N.E. 272 (Mass. 1936); *Rhode Island Bar Assn. v. Automobile Service Assn.,* 179 A. 139 (R.I. 1935) [prohibiting auto club intervention or lawyer referral] and *In re Thibodeau,* 3 N.E. 749 (Mass. 1936) [permitting].

[32] 86 Cal.Rptr. 367 (1970)

[33] ABA Opinion No.303. *See also Azzanello v. Legal Aid Society,* 185 N.E.2d 566 (Ohio 1962) and *Re Opinion of Justices,* 194 N.E. 313 (Mass. 1935), which discusses the propriety of a statute that permits lawyer referrals by legal aid societies

[34] *Cannon v. U.S. Acoustics Corp.* [398 F.Supp. 209 (N.D. Ill. 1975)] held that once a substantial relationship has been established, the new representation in and of itself violates the lawyer's ethical duty to former clients. The court ruled that it is not necessary to prove that confidences and secrets were told to the lawyers in the former representation: it will be presumed.

[35] *Brown v. Miller,* 286 F. 994 (D.C. Cir. 1923)

[36] 139 So.2d 712 (Fla. 1962)

[37] 470 F.Supp. 495 (N.D. Cal. 1979)

[38] *In re Corrugated Container Antitrust Litigation,* 659 F.2d 1341 (5th Cir. 1981)

[39] *See also* the student note in 42 HASTINGS L. J. 1667 (August 1991) suggesting a four-part test for disqualification of a firm as a result of nonlawyer staff members "switching sides."

[40] 555 F.2d 791 (Ct. Cl. 1977)

[41] 588 F.2d 221 (7th Cir. 1978)

[42] 534 F.2d 194 (9th Cir. 1976)

CHAPTER 5

[1] *Bates & O'Steen v. State Bar of Arizona,* 433 U.S. 350, 97 S.Ct. 2691 (1977)

[2] 105 S.Ct. 2265 (1985)

[3] Virginia Bar Association, VA Lawyer Register May 2006, Legal Ethics Opinion 1750

[4] 816 P.2d 335 (Idaho 1991)

[5] Taken from the ABA Model Rules Rule 5.3

[6] *See Ficker v. Curran,* 950 F.Supp. 123 (D. Md. 1996), striking down a statute banning written solicitation of persons charged with jailable traffic offenses for thirty

days and *Florida Bar v. Went For It, Inc.,* 515 U.S. 619 (1995), upholding a statute banning contact with victims and families of victims of mass disasters for thirty days

[7]San Diego Bar Assn. Ethics Op. 1976-9 (Advertisement of Paralegals) prohibits any advertisement that may imply that paralegals are authorized to provide legal services. California has a new law, however, that allows laypeople to help others fill out forms in "self-help" situations. See also State Bar of Georgia Advisory Op. 21 (1977); New Jersey Bar Assn. Op. 296 (1975); Minnesota Lawyers Professional Responsibility Board Amended Op. 8 (1980); Connecticut Inf. Op. 82-19 (1982); District of Columbia Op. 172 (1986).

[8]950 F.Supp. 123 (D. Md. 1996)

[9]515 U.S. 619 (1995)

CHAPTER 6

[1]*Goldfarb v. Virginia State Bar,* 421 U.S. 773 (1975)

[2]*Louisiana Bar v. Edwins,* 540 So.2d 294 (La. 1989)

[3]This is supposed to be a play on the expression GNP—Gross National Product. Perhaps it's not funny

[4]For an interesting case on this issue, *see* Ramirez v. Sturdevant [21 Cal.App.4th 904, 26 Cal.Rptr.2d 554 (1994)], where the California court discussed the problem of the conflict of interest that arises between the client and lawyer when the lawyer negotiates his own fees as part of the settlement of the client's case against the defendant

[5]LOS ANGELES DAILY JOURNAL, Wednesday, Jan. 7, 1998, at. 1

[6]Model Rule 1.5

[7]*See Rogers v. Webb,* 558 N.W.2d 155 (Iowa 1997), where the court said that any contract for a contingent fee in a domestic relations case was void.

[8]Virginia Bar Association, VA. LAWYER REGISTER, May 2006, Legal Ethics Opinion 1750

[9]*In re GOCO Realty Fund I,* 151 BR 241 (N.D. Cal 1993)

[10]*In re Cooperman,* 633 N.E.2d 1069 (N.Y. 1994)

[11]*See Brown v. Legal Foundation of Washington,* 538 U.S. 216 (2003)

[12]"Ours is a learned profession, not a mere money-getting trade. . . . Suits to collect fees should be avoided. Only where the circumstances imperatively require, should resort be had to a suit to compel payment." ABA Opinion No. 250 (1943).

[13]Comment to ABA MODEL RULES OF PROFESSIONAL CONDUCT, Rule 1.5

[14]*Kizer v. Davis,* 369 N.E.2d 439 (Ind. 1977)

[15]*Estate of Anderson v. Smith,* 316 N.E.2d 592 (Ind. 1974)

[16]In England (the English Rule), the prevailing party always gets fees from the other side

[17]29 U.S.C § 794 *et seq*

[18]Ibid.

[19]806 S.W.2d 560 (Tex. App. 1990)

[20]850 P.2d 1188 (Utah 1993)

[21]*Continental Townhouses v. Brockbank,* 733 P.2d 1120 (Ariz. App. 1986)

[22]As a side matter, it appears that Baldwin's lawyer assigned his right in the attorney's fee award to Richins, the independent paralegal. Richins then appeared before the Utah Supreme Court to argue in favor of upholding the trial court's award of attorneys' fees and paralegal costs. The court said that his appearance on his own behalf to represent his interest in the appeal was the unauthorized practice of law. See Chapter 2.

[23]*Hines v. Hines,* 129 Idaho 847, 853, 934 P.2d 20, 26 (1997)

[24]*Salovaara v. Eckert,* 94 Civ. 3430 (KMW 1999)

[25]*Yousuf v. UHS of De La Ronde, Inc.,* 110 F.Supp.2d 482 (1999)

[26]*Mason v. Oklahoma Turnpike Authority,* 1997 WL 311880 (U.S.C.A., 10th Cir. Okla. 1997)

[27]*Berchin v. General Dynamics Corp.,* 1996 WL 465752 (S.D.N.Y. 1996)

[28]Alaska Supreme Court Order No. 1200 (May 4, 1995) amending Rules 79 and 82

[29]*Smith v. Roher,* 1997 U.S. Dist. LEXIS 1411 (1997)

[30]*Shaffer v. Superior Court,* 33 Cal.App.4th 993, 39 Cal.Rptr.2d 506 (1995)

[31]*In re Healey,* 295 N.E.2d 594 (Ind. 1973)

[32]*Fitzgerald v. Wasson Coal Mining Corp.,* 138 Ind. App. 176, 212 N.E.2d 398 (1965)

[33]*In re The Colad Group, Inc.,* 336 B.R. 36, Banks. W.D.N.Y., 2005

[34]*In re Khan's Corp.,* 184 B.R. 398, Banks. S.D. Fla., 1995

[35]*See Rhodes v. Martinez,* 925 P.2d 1201 (N.M. App. 1996). For a case where the law firm was entitled to a charging lien, *see Kiernan v. Kiernan* [649 N.Y.S.2d 612 (1996)].

CHAPTER 7

[1]*Pearson v. Darrington,* 32 Ala. 227 (1858)

[2]*Christy v. Saliterman,* 179 N.W.2d 288 (Minn. 1970)

[3]*Gyler v. Mission Insurance Co.,* 514 P.2d 1219 (Cal. 1973)

[4]*Connaughton v. Gertz,* 418 N.E.2d 858 (Ill. App. 1981)

[5]For other cases on this issue, see Carey and *Emmings v. Ludowese,* 434 N.W.2d 483 (Minn.App. 1989) and *Stott v. Fox,* 805 P.2d 1305 (Mont. 1990)

[6]*George v. Caton,* 600 P.2d 822 (N.M. 1979), cert. quashed 98 P.2d 215

[7]*Stewart v. Sbarro,* 362 A.2d 581 (N.J. 1976), at 586, quoted from *McCullough v. Sullivan,* 132 A. 102 (N.J. 1925)

[8]*Medrano v. Miller,* 608 S.W.2d 81 (Tex. 1980)

[9]*In re Winston,* 528 N.Y.S2d 843 (1989)

[10]*Twohy v. State Bar,* 769 P.2d 976 (Cal 1989)

[11]*Lewis v. State Bar* 621, P.2d 258 (Cal. 1981)

[12]*Rodriguez v. Horton,* 622 P.2d 261 (N.M. 1980)

[13]*Wright v. Williams,* 47 Cal.App.3d 802, 121 Cal.Rptr. 194 (1975)

[14]575 P.2d 285 (Cal. 1978)

[15]*McCullough v. Sullivan,* 132 A. 102 (N.J. 1926)

[16]*Fowler v. American Federation of Tobacco Growers,* 80 S.E.2d 554 (Va. 1954)

[17]*Strangman v. Arc-Saws, Inc.,* 267 P.2d 395 (Cal. 1954)

[18]*Modica v. Crist,* 276 P.2d 614 (Cal. 1954)

[19]190 U.S. 1, 23 S.Ct. 718 (1903)

[20]*Millright v. Romer,* 322 N.W.2d 30 (Iowa 1982)

[21]California is an example. See *Neel v. Magana, Olney, Levy, Cathart & Gelfand,* 491 P.2d 421 (Cal. 1971)

[22]*Johnson v. Simonelli,* 231 Cal.App.3d 105, 282 Cal.Rptr. 205 (1991)

[23]*Bledstein v. Superior Court,* 62 Cal.App.3d 152, 208 Cal.Rptr. 428 (1984)

[24]*Weisblatt v. Chicago Bar Association,* No. 1-96-4461, Cook County, 1997, not reported; see also *Noris v. Silver,* 701 So.2d 1238 (Fla. 3rd DCA 1997)

[25]Reported in Sheree Swetin, 2 A.B.A DIALOGUE 3 (Summer 1998)

[26]*Allen v. Frawley,* 82 N.W. 593 (Wis. 1900)

[27]*Blackmon v. Hale,* 463 P.2d 418 (Cal. 1970)

[28]385 N.Y.S.2d 639 (1976)

[29]Just as the ABA provides *Model Rules of Professional Responsibility,* the National Conference of Commissioners on Uniform State Laws proposed the *Uniform Partnership Act* and added LLP laws to the Act in 1996. Most of the states have adopted this Act in some form.

[30]*Black v. State Bar,* 499 P.2d 968 (Cal. 1972)

[31]*Johnson v. Davidson,* 202 Cal.Rptr. 159 (1921)

[32]Business and Professionals Code § 6450

[33]310 P.2d 63 (Cal.App. 1957)

[34]*Matter of Laclas,* 410 N.Y.S.2d 307 (1978)

[35]*Leonard v. City of Brandenburg* Not Reported in S.W.3d, 2004 WL 2756229 (Ky.App., 2004); *The Florida Bar v. Dubbeld,* 748 So.2d 936 (Fla., 1999)

[36]*Goebel v. Lauderdale,* 214 Cal.App.3d 1502, 263 Cal.Rptr. 275 (1989); *Smith v. Lewis,* 530 P.2d 589 (Cal. 1975)

[37]291 N.W.2d 686 (Minn. 1980)

[38]772 S.W.2d 151 (Tex. 1989)

[39]415 S.W.2d 711 (Tex. 1967)

[40]*Rogers v. Robson, Masters, Ryan, Brumund & Belom,* 407 N.E.2d 47 (Ill. 1980)

[41]245 N.W.2d 869 (Minn. 1976)

[42]*Busch v. Flangas,* 837 P.2d 438 (Nev. 1992)

CHAPTER 8

[1]*Powell v. Alabama,* 287 U.S. 45, 53 S.Ct. 55 (1932)

[2]263 F.Supp. 360 (E.D.Va. 1967), aff'd 381 F2d. 713 (4th Cir. 1967)

[3]542 P.2d 631 (Cal. 1975)

[4]766 So.2d 1165 (Fla. 2000)

[5]*Reznick v. State Bar,* 460 P.2d 969 (Cal. 1969)

[6]*In re Wright,* 248 P.2d 1080 (Nev. 1952)

[7]*Vaughn v. State Bar,* 2 Cal.Rptr. 11 (1960)

[8]*Smith v. State,* 523 S.W.2d 1 (Tex.App. 1975)

[9]*In re Howard,* 372 N.E.2d 371 (Ill. 1976)

[10]*In re Ettinger,* 128 Ill.2d 351, 538 N.E.2d 1152 (Ill. 1989)

[11]*Committee on Professional Ethics v. Wenger,* 469 N.W.2d 678 (Iowa 1991)

[12]*Committee on Prof. Ethics and Conduct of the Iowa State Bar Assn. v. Crary,* 245 N.W.2d 298 (Iowa 1976)

[13]*In re Bishop,* 210 S.E.2d 235 (S.C. 1974)

[14]*In re Disciplinary Proceeding Against Poole,* 156 Wash.2d 196, 125 P.3d 954 (2006)

[15]Robert Traver (1958)

[16]For an interesting case on coaching a client, see *Geders v. United States,* 425 U.S. 80, 96 S.Ct. 1330 (1975)

[17]793 P.2d 544 (Ariz. 1990)

[18]660 P.2d 454 (Ariz. 1983)

[19]525 A.2d 493 (R.I. 1987)

[20]213 A.2d 411 (R.I. 1965)

[21]103 N.W.2d 325 (Neb. 1960)

[22]No. 02 Civ. 1243, 2003 WL 22410619 (S.D.N.Y. October 22, 2003)

[23]*Zubulake v. UBS Warburg LLC,* 217 F.R.D. 309 (S.D.N.Y. 2003)

[24]*In re Disciplinary Proceeding Against Robinson,* 282 Wis.2d 216, 700 N.W.2d 757 (2005)

[25]*In re Lowell,* 14 A.D.3d 41, 784 N.Y.S.2d 69 (2004)

[26]*In re Lawrence,* 884 So.2d 561

[27]*See* Rule 4.4, EC 7-30

[28]But *see State v. Bonner,* 587 P.2d 580 (Wash.App. 1978), in which the court held that a deputy prosecutor did not deliberately violate these rules when he commented on an active case to a reporter thinking he was speaking to the reporter off the record. The court admonished prosecutors and their assistants to "strictly adhere to the mandate of DR 7-107(b)(6) pertaining to extrajudicial statements."

[29]*Sheppard v. Maxwell,* 384 U.S. 333, 86 S.Ct. 1507 (1966), quoting from *Patterson v. State of Colorado,* 205 U.S. 454, 27 S.Ct. 556 (1907)

[30]992 F.2d 445 (2d Cir. 1993)

[31]116 A.D.2d 287 501 N.Y.S.2d 405 (1986)

[32]Rule 3.4(b) and EC 7-28

[33]Matter of Litman, 272 N.W.2d 264, 266 (Minn. 1978). In this case, the attorney and the judge had been friends of many years, and the judge was in serious financial difficulty. Litman loaned the judge money on several occasions. The court felt that, since Litman still practiced before that judge, he should have avoided even the appearance of an impropriety

[34]And the rule is substantially identical to DR 7-102(A)(3)

[35]*Principe v. Assay Partners,* 586 N.Y.S.2d 182 (1992)

[36]*Arrant v. State,* 537 So.2d 150 (Fla.App. 1989)

[37]*Laguna Auto Body v. Farmers Ins. Exchange,* 231 Cal.App.3d 481, 282 Cal.Rptr. 530 (1991)

[38]*Bates v. State Bar,* 51 Cal.3d 1056, 800 P.2d 859 (1990)

[39]*Id.*

[40]*Kohan v. Cohan,* 229 Cal.App.3d 967, 280 Cal.Rptr. 474 (1991)

[41]*In re Elam,* 211 S.W.2d 710, *cert. denied,* 335 U.S. 872, 69 S.Ct. 161 (1948)

[42]*Leimer v. Hulse,* 178 S.W.2d 336, *rein. denied,* 323 U.S. 744, 65 S.Ct. 60 (1944)

[43]*State v. Turner,* 538 P.2d 966 (Kan. 1975)

[44]*Snyder v. State Bar,* 555 P.2d 1104 (Cal. 1976)

[45]*In re Dinhofer,* 257 A.D.2d 326, 690 N.Y.S.2d 245 (1999)

[46]*McCann v. Municipal Court,* 221 Cal.App.3d 527, 270 Cal.Rptr. 640 (1990)

[47]*In re McKinney,* 447 P.2d 972 (Cal. 1968)

[48]*In re Cobb,* 445 Mass. 453, 838 N.E.2d 1197 (2005)

[49]514 P.2d 1201 (Cal. 1973)

[50]99 P.2d 555 (Cal.App. 1940)

[51]351 F.2d 91, *cert. denied,* 384 U.S. 1003, 86 S.Ct. 1914 (1965)

[52]182 F.2d 416 (2d Cir. 1950)

[53]422 P.2d 307 (Wash. 1966)

[54]370 F.Supp. 1166 (S.D.N.Y. 1973)

[55]404 U.S. 553, 92 S.Ct. 659 (1972)

[56]*See also In re McConnell,* 370 U.S. 230, 82 S.Ct. 1288 (1962), for lawyer's activities that were not sufficient to constitute an obstruction of justice.

[57]*See also* EC 7-4

[58]Some other definitions are "a ruling suggested by a court to be applied to a supposed statement of facts not involved in the case at bar" [*Union Pac. R. Co. v. Hanna,* 214 P. 550 (Colo. 1923)]; "a legal conclusion stated in the opinion but not applicable to the particular facts of the case" [*In re Schultz' Estate,* 172 A. 865 (Pa. 1934)]; "points arising outside of the case and not embodied in the determination made by the Court" [*Hayes v. City of Wilmington,* 91 S.E.2d 673 (N.C. 1956)]; "a particular discussion which is unnecessary to the decision in the case" [*U.S. v. Polan Industries, Inc.,* 196 F.Supp. 333 (D.C.W.Va. 1961)]

[59]*West Coast Devel. v. Read,* 2 Cal.App.4th 693, 3 Cal.Rptr.2d 796 (1992)

[60]Rules 1.2(d) and 3.1

[61]212 Cal.App.3d 96, 260 Cal.Rptr. 369 (1989)

[62]*See also* Reznick v. State Bar 1 Cal.3d 198, 460 P.2d 969 (Cal. 1969), where the California Supreme Court held that an attorney who had altered a check after it had been returned canceled and used a copy of the altered check as an exhibit filed with the court was in violation of the Rules of Professional Conduct. The court held that Reznik's intent was to deceive the court with the exhibit and, although he was representing himself in the transaction involving the check, it was improper to use an illegal scheme to further his interest

[63]248 So.2d 477 (Fla. 1971)

[64]86 Wash. 2d 655, 548 P.2d 297 (1976)

[65]Model Rule 3.8; People v. Zimmer, 414 N.E.2d 705 (N.Y. 1980)

[66]*EC* 7-13; People v. Ruthford, 14 Cal.3d 399, 534 P.2d 1341 (1975)

[67]Currie v. Superior Court, 230 Cal.App.3d 83, 281 Cal.Rptr. 250 (1991)

[68]California Rules of Professional Conduct, Rule 2-100

[69]Runsvold v. Idaho State Bar, 925 F.2d 1118 (Idaho 1996); Rule 4.2

[70]Cronin v. Eighth Judicial District Court, 105 Nev. 635, 781 P.2d 1150 (1989)

[71]Heavey v. State Bar, 17 Cal.3d 553, 551 P.2d 1238 (1976)

[72]Stern Bros., Inc. v. McClure, 160 W.Va. 567, 236 S.E.2d 222 (1977)

[73]Matter of J.B.K., 931 S.W.2d 581 (Tex.App. 1996)

CHAPTER 9

[1]SK Handtool Corp. v. Dresser Industries, 619 N.E.2d 1282 (Ill.App. 1993)

[2]Model Code EC 1-3

[3]Comment, *Procedural Due Process and Character Hearings for Bar Applicants,* 15 STAN.L.REV. 500 (1963)

[4]70 P.2d 402 (Colo. 1989)

[5]EC 1-4

[6]The Fink Rule is a descendant of ABA Canon 29 that advised that the lawyer should expose corrupt or dishonest conduct in the profession

[7]For a discussion of these privileges, see Chapter 4 on Preserving Confidences and Secrets

[8]502 N.E.2d 899 (Ind. 1987)

[9]582 A.2d 215 (Del.Supr. 1990)

[10]533 N.E.2d 790 (Ill. 1988)

[11]For further reading, see III GEO. J. LEGAL ETHICS 3, 643 (Winter 1990)

[12]*Cesena v. Du Page County,* 201 Ill.App.3d 96, 558 N.E.2d 1378 (1990)

[13]*Skolnick v. Altheimer & Gray,* 191 Ill.2d 214, 730 N.E.2d 4 (2000)

[14]See Chapter 4 for a discussion of what knowledge is privileged and therefore not subject to Rule 8.3 disclosure.

[15]First read *Skolnick v. Altheimer and Gray,* 303 Ill.App.3d 27 708, N.E.2d 1177 (1999); and then read *Skolnick v. Altheimer & Gray,* 191 Ill.2d 214, 730 N.E.2d 4 (2000).

[16]Attorney Registration and Disciplinary Commission

[17]977 S.W.2d 543 (Tex. 1998)

[18]512 A.2d 607 (Pa. 1986)

[19]NALA *Code of Ethics and Professional Responsibility,* Canon 8

[20]*See also* Ill. Op. 87-7 (1/29/88)

[21]*Brown v. Hammond,* 810F.Supp. 644 (E.D.Pa. 1993)

[22]*See also* EC 8-9

[23]441 P.2d 912 (Cal. 1968)

[24]*Attorney Grievance Com'n v. Alison,* 317 Md. 523, 565 A.2d 660 (1989)

[25]Matter of Westfall, 808 S.W.2d 829 (Mo. 1991) where the lawyer made televised statements alleging purposefully dishonest conduct by the Court of Appeals judge. The court found that attorney violated Rules 8.2(a) and 8.4(a) and (d).

[26]570 N.W.2d 262 (Mich. 1997)

[27]*Oklahoma Bar Association v. Patmon,* 939 P.2d 1155 (Okl. 1997)

[28]*Committee on Professional Ethics and Conduct of Iowa State Bar Assn. v. Horak,* 292 N.W.2d 129 (Iowa 1980).

[29]Matter of Redding, 672 N.E.2d 76 (Ind. 1996)

[30]*Perillo v. Advisory Comm. on Professional Ethics,* 416 A.2d 801 (N.J. 1980)

[31]566 N.E.2d 528 (Ind. 1991)

TABLE OF CASES

People ex. rel. Chicago Bar Assn. v. Edelson, 174
People ex. rel. Karlin v. Culkin, 286
People ex. rel. Kent v. Denious, 111
People v. Alexander, 50
People v. Hughes, 37
People v. Merchants Protective Corporation, 119
People v. Mitchell, 82
People v. Myers, 13, 36–37, 36–38
People v. Pierson, 36
People v. Rotenberg, 37
Phillips v. Washington Legal Foundation, 202, 206
Powell v. Alabama, 165, 166, 167
Prichec v. Tecon Corp., 121
Procunier v. Martinez, 82

Q

Quinones v. State, 251

R

Railroad Trainmen v. Virginia Bar, 172
Reich v. Page & Addison, 16, 28–32
Republic Ins. Co. v. Stoker, 239
Rice v. Forestier, 229
Richards v. Jain, 17, 18
Rico v. Mitsubishi Motors, 89
Rocca v. Southern Hills Counseling Center, 86
Rodriguez v. Montalvo, 97–101

S

Saenz v. Fidelity & Guar. Ins. Underwriters, 239
San Diego Federal Credit Union v. Cumis
    Insurance Society, 117, 143
San Francisco v. Superior Court, 104
Seabord Air Line Railroad v. Tampa Southern
    Railroad, 75
SEC v. Texas Gulf Sulphur Co., 171
Semler v. Oregon State Bd. of Dental
    Examiners, 173
Sheinkopf v. Stone, 100
Silver Chrysler Plymouth v. Chrysler Motor
    Corp., 208
Skolnick v. Kass, 288
Smith v. O'Grady, 166
South Carolina v. Despain, 61–63

Spencer v. Honorable Justices of the Supreme
    Court, 148
Spindell v. State Bar, 34
State v. Buyers Service Co., Inc., 62
State v. Caffrey, 263
State v. Hill, 243
State v. Hunt, 244
Sullins v. State Bar, 250
Swidler & Berlin v. United States, 83

T

Tank v. State Farm Fire & Cas. Co., 143
Taylor v. Chubb Group of Ins. Cos., 210
Tegman v. Accident & Medical Investigations,
    228, 241–247, 247
Tex. Bus. & Com. Code, 237, 238, 239
Touchton v. Touchton, 70

U

Union Sav. Assn. v. Home Owners Aid, Inc., 64
United States v. Kovel, 81
United States v. Salameh, 260
United Transportation Union v. Michigan
    Bar, 172
Universal Athletic Sales Co. v. American Gym,
    Recreational and Athletic Equipment
    Corp., 119
U.S. v. Schiffer, 263
U.S. v.Sacher, 263

V

Valley View Indus. Park v. City of Redmond, 243
Vaughn v. State Bar, 34
Virginia Pharmacy Board v. Virginia Citizens
    Consumer Council, 170

W

Walker v. City of Birmingham, 75
Wash. State Bar Ass'n v. Great W. Union Fed.
    Sav. & Loan Ass'n, 244
Washington Legal Foundation v. Legal
    Foundation of Washington, 205, 206

INDEX

Blended rate billing, 86
Bonus billing, 185
Boundary of the law, 249
Business and Professions Code, 23
Buying a claim today, 112–113

C

Canons of Professional Ethics, 1908, 9
Capper, 112
Cell phones, 90
Certificated legal assistant, 20
Champerty, 111–112, 156, 195
Charging lien, 196
CLA exam, 20
Classic retainer, 188
Client files, 91–92
Client trust accounts. *See* Trust accounts
Code of Ethics, 9
Common law retaining lien, 196
Competence
    measurement of, 218–220
    mental competence, 220–222
Computers, 90
Conduit theory, 46–47
Confidentiality
    cell phones, 90
    client files, 91–92
    computers, 90
    confidentiality *versus* attorney/client privilege,
        78, 80–84
    definition, 79–80
    divulging confidential information,
        85–86
    document protection, 91
    duty of confidentiality, 79, 80, 84–85
    e-mail, 89–90
    technology, role of, 88–89
    work product privilege, 86–88
Conflicts of interest
    adverse clients in unrelated actions, 118
    buying a claim today, 112–113
    champerty, 111–112
    corporations, representation of, 118–119
    creation of, 107–110
    disqualification, preventing, 122–123
    effects of, 121–122

ethical wall theory, 123
    financial interest in the case, 111–112
    firm's interest, protecting the, 114
    gifts, 113
    intimate relations with a client, 114–115
    joint representation of criminal
        defendants, 119
    lawyer referral services, 119–120
    multiple clients, representing, 116–117
    outside forces, conflicts as a result
        of, 115–116
    overreaching or fraud, 110–111
    pro bono law providers, 119–120
    publicity rights, 113–114
    resolving, 124–125
    transaction in good faith, 111
    waiver, 123–124
    witness, 111
Contingency fees, 181–183
Continuance, asking for a, 50
Corporate clients, 156
Corporations, 49–50, 118–119
Courtesy to the court, showing, 262–264

D

Dicta in court briefs, citing, 264
Direct mail, 152–153
Disciplinary actions, 12–14
Disciplinary Rules (DR), 10
Disclose, duty to, 261
Discovery, deceit in, 256–257
Disregard for the client, 224
Divulging confidential information, 85–86
Document protection, 91
Duty of confidentiality, 79, 80, 84–85
Duty of integrity. *See* Integrity, duty of

E

E-mail, 89–90
Encourage or aiding a client to commit a criminal
    act, 266–267
Errors and omissions (E & O) insurance, 231
Esquire, 8
Ethical Considerations (EC), 10
Ethical wall theory, 123

M

Materiality of the deceit, 256
Member of the bar, 6
Mental competence, 220–222
Misconduct, lawyer
  general misconduct, 293–295
  judicial reporting of, 286–287
  misconduct of others in firms, 288–289
  opposing council reporting of, 287–288
  paralegal reporting, 290–291
  proper authorities, 291–292
  self-reporting, 289
  threatening to report, 289–290
Model Code of Professional Responsibility, 9–10
Model Rules of Professional Conduct, 10–11
Moral character requirement, 7–8
Morality, 1
Morals
  definition of, 1
  dilemmas, 2
  theories of, 2
Moral turpitude, 13
Multidisciplinary practice, 54–55
Multiple clients, representing, 116–117

N

NALA certification, 20–21
National Association of Legal Assistants (NALA), 14–15
National Association of Legal Secretaries (NALS), 15
National Federation of Paralegal Associations (NFPA), 15
Negligence
  causes of action against negligent lawyers, 222
  disregard for the client, 224
  negligent preparation of documents, 224–225
  negligent referral, 226
  paralegal's negligence, 227–229
  responsibility for lawyer's negligence, 226
  specific acts or omissions as negligence, 229–230
  specific areas, in, 222–223
  statute of limitations in negligence actions, 225–226
  suing for professional negligence, 226

Negligent preparation of documents, 224–225
Negligent referral, 226
NFPA certification, 21
Nonrefundable retainer, 188
North Carolina Voluntary Paralegal Certification, 21

O

Ohio State Bar Certified Paralegal, 21
Outside forces, conflicts as a result of, 115–116
Overpaying expert witnesses, 260
Overreaching or fraud, 110–111

P

Paralegal Advanced Competency Exam (PACE), 21
Paralegal fees, 192–193
Paralegals
  ABA definition, 14
  advertising, 153–155
  American Association for Paralegal Education (AAfPE), 15–16
  Arizona Certification of Legal Document Preparers, 22
  certificated legal assistant, 20
  certification, 20–22
  CLA exam, 20
  definitions, 14
  Department of Labor, 16
  licensing, 19
  NALA certification, 20–21
  National Association of Legal Assistants (NALA), 14–15
  National Association of Legal Secretaries (NALS), 15
  National Federation of Paralegal Associations (NFPA), 15
  negligence, 227–229
  NFPA certification, 21
  North Carolina Voluntary Paralegal Certification, 21
  Ohio State Bar Certified Paralegal, 21
  Paralegal Advanced Competency Exam (PACE), 21
  registration, 22

V

Value billing, 185

W

Waiver, 123–124
Witness, 111
Work product privilege, 86–88

Z

Zealous representation
    accidentally deceitful, being, 255–256
    allowing a witness to lie, 252
    attitude toward opposing counsel, 261–262
    avoiding being told to be deceitful, 257–260
    boundary of the law, 249
    courtesy to the court, showing, 262–264
    definition of, 248
    dicta in court briefs, citing, 264
    disclose, duty to, 261
    discovery, deceit in, 256–257
    encourage or aiding a client to commit a
        criminal act, 266–267
    fabricating evidence, 251–253
    false affidavits, making, 252–253
    false documents, making, 253
    frivolous claims, 264–265
    inducing a witness to lie, 251
    judges, gifts to, 260–261
    jurors, investigating, 259
    loopholes, using, 264
    materiality of the deceit, 256
    overpaying expert witnesses, 260
    penalty for creating or preserving false
        evidence, 253–255
    press, talking to the, 259–260
    pretexting, 257
    spoliation of evidence, 255
    suppressing evidence, 249